MEET ME
in the
UNDERWORLD

FEMININE WISDOM IN ACTION

HYPATIA
HOUSE

Santa Barbara, California

How 77 Sacred Sites,
770 Cappuccinos,
and 26,000 Miles
Led Me to My Soul

MEET ME
in the
UNDERWORLD

Svetlana Meritt

Published by: Hypatia House, Santa Barbara, California
email: hypatiahouse@svetlanameritt.com
website: www.svetlanameritt.com

Library of Congress Control Number: 2014917685

Publisher's Cataloging-in-Publication (Provided by Quality Books, Inc.)

Meritt, Svetlana.
  Meet me in the underworld : how 77 sacred sites, 770 cappuccinos,
  and 26,000 miles led me to my soul /
  Svetlana Meritt.
  pages cm
  Includes bibliographical references.
  LCCN 2014917685
  ISBN 978-0-9908284-1-9
  ISBN 978-0-9908284-3-3

  1. Meritt, Svetlana--Travel. 2. Women travelers--Biography.
  3. Sacred space. 4. Spiritual biography.
  I. Title.

BL73.M47A3 2014   204.092
        QBI14-600170

First printing 2015
ISBN: 978-0-9908284-1-9

Cover Design: Barbara Cooper
Interior Design: Adina Cucicov, Flamingo Designs
Map Design: Steven Catizone
Logo Design and Graphic Consultation: Vesna Petrovic

To Dwight,
my beloved mentor and husband

Without you,
this book would not have existed,
the journey would not have been made,
and I would not have been the same.
Until we meet again...

CONTENTS

Journeys, like artists, are born and not made.
A thousand different circumstances contribute to them, few of them willed or determined by the will—whatever we may think. They flower spontaneously out of the demands of our natures—and the best of them lead us not only outwards in space, but inward as well.
Travel can be one of the most rewarding forms of introspection....

LAWRENCE DURRELL

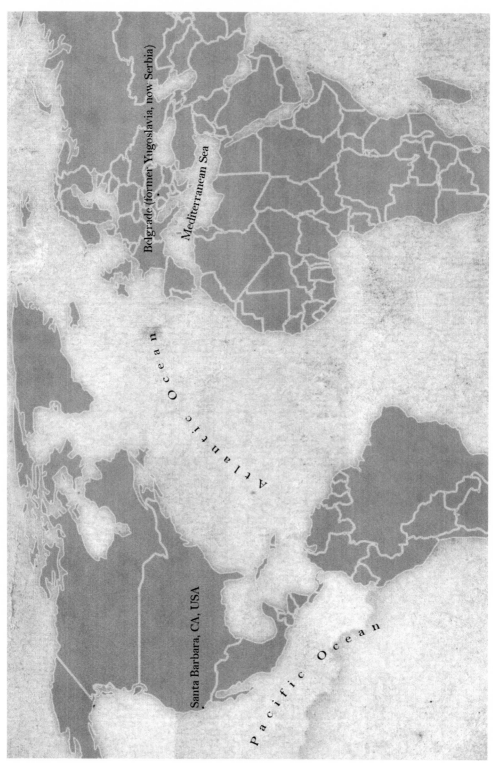

Belgrade (former Yugoslavia, now Serbia)

Mediterranean Sea

Atlantic Ocean

Pacific Ocean

Santa Barbara, CA, USA

Follow my journey through photos at: www.svetlanameritt.com

THE BEGINNINGS...

My spiritual journey started when I chose my future beloved, Dwight Johnson, over a high-profile interview with Antonio Banderas. It was as simple as that. And as complex.

By the time I reached thirty, the trajectory of my life had been an upward arc of worldly achievements. For over ten years I had been a successful journalist in Belgrade, the capital of my native country Serbia. My domain was a weekly column that took up the entire second page of one of Serbia's most popular magazines, *Illustrated Politics*. Foreign artists, musicians, actors—everyone who was anyone in the world of culture was featured in my column. At the same time, the French Cultural Center had appointed me as its exclusive reporter. Film premières, art receptions, and exhibition openings were part of my everyday life.

And journalism was not all I did. Trained as a classical ballerina in childhood, I had performed modern dance in large venues and on television. I was a summer tour guide for foreign VIP groups along the Adriatic Coast. I had lovers lined up, earned journalistic and academic awards, and crossed the globe to do graduate studies in far-off California. As a foreign correspondent, I covered the Academy Awards in Hollywood and rubbed shoulders with Yoko Ono, the Dalai Lama, and Giorgio Armani.

I defined myself by my successes.

Despite my reflective and introverted nature as a child, in my twenties I chose to live fast and fly high. The external world offered me so much and I took all I could get. As my mother used to warn me, "Svetlana, you are burning the candle at *three* ends!"

And so it was that I found myself on a desolate beach in Mexico, with a lover who turned out to be an alcoholic *and* a schizophrenic. From the seeming top of the world—I had just added a Master's degree in French Literature to my list of achievements—I had suddenly tumbled to the very bottom, lying in a tent under the drunken body of a man who threatened to kill me. As I lay helpless, my nostrils full of the stench of his vomit, scenes from my earlier life flashed before my eyes…

I saw my three-year-old self crawling under the side table in the bedroom—my first memory. I had just unwrapped myself from a tightly tucked blanket in my little bed and tumbled onto the floor. It was in the semi-darkness of the room, under that table, that I heard a voice in my head for the first time. It simply called, "Svetlana," as if to draw my attention to itself, as if to etch itself into the folds of my brain so I would not forget it.

I saw my five-year-old self, nose pressed against the kitchen window, dreading the punishment I'd get for breaking my mother's most precious vase. As I shivered with fear, that same voice whispered in my head, "This is not real." All of a sudden, I had found myself outside and above my body. I looked down at the souvenir plates hanging on the kitchen walls and my small, terrified self, staring through the window at the naked branches of the autumn trees. "This world is not real," I heard. "Even the girl called 'Svetlana' is not real." I watched and listened, strangely identifying with what I then began to call "the Voice."

That event foreshadowed what was to come later in my life: transmissions of higher frequencies I would periodically receive. For years I didn't know what I was receiving. Was it my intuition? Or was it a higher presence I'd later call my Guidance? Or my Soul?

The image of a hospital room flashed before my eyes. I saw my thirteen-year-old self stretched out on a belt, one rope tied around my chin and head, the other around my hips. I had been diagnosed with a fast-progressing spinal curvature and had to be put in a plaster cast to correct it. The nurses cranked the handles, pulling my vertebrae apart, one by one. Pain shot through my body as the cranking continued, and my vertebrae moved farther apart. The belt was suddenly released, and I remained suspended, tied to the two opposite poles. Then the layering of plaster-strips began; the cold, clammy, gooey strips swathing my torso and making me into a mummy.

I saw my sixteen-year-old self studying at a desk, finally cast-free. I had endured years of solitude and pain, been teased endlessly as "turtle girl" and shunned as an out*cast* at class parties and outings. My promising classical ballet career had been foiled; I was too old to resume the training. But I'd been reading avidly, and the books I'd devoured during those years of forced isolation made me reflect on the meaning and purpose of life, on the immensity of universe, and my role in the grand scheme. I was filled with urgent existential questions, but no one had been able to help me find the answers. When I glanced at the open window by my desk, the thoughts of both jumping and of continuing to live had the same appeal.

The image of my eighteen-year-old self flashed by ... standing on Le Pont des Arts in Paris and watching the waters of the Seine roll underneath the bridge. It was my first trip abroad by myself. I had just broken up with my first boyfriend, a man who had been my high school philosophy teacher. (It was a bit unconventional, I know, but I was desperate to find out the purpose of life and had approached my philosophy teacher with that question. I mean, what better person to know the answer than a philosopher? But to my dismay, he said only, "Love." So I decided to try it—with him!)

Disillusioned by love that summer in Paris, I was again in the throes of a powerful existential crisis. I had also just enrolled at the University of Belgrade and chosen World Literature as my major. Having published poems and articles in Serbia, I was seriously considering being a writer. As I looked down at the Seine, a wave of resignation washed over me. *What was the point of writing when all the great books had already been written? If I can't write something original, I'm not going to write at all.* As I formulated that decision, gazing at the ripples of the river below, a heaviness fell like a tombstone over my lower abdomen. I felt as if a lid had closed off the source of my creativity, filling me with an unshakable gloom.

A lid as heavy as the drunken body that lay on top of me on that desolate beach in Mexico, muttering incoherent threats. With all my force, I wriggled underneath the weight and pushed it away. In a drunken stupor, the body toppled over and splayed out in a pool of its vomit. And as it did, so splashed my entire life.

I whispered out loud, "What have I done with myself—to myself, to my *life*?"

Tears of terror and desperation rolled down my face. What had brought me here? Was it my pride? Had I assumed that just because I was "successful" I could get away with anything? Was it my excessive search for love, a love I still hadn't found? Or was it my *need* to be liked and accepted which I carried like a scar from the years I'd been scorned as the "turtle girl?"

Through the sobbing, a realization dawned: I had abandoned the search for the meaning of life I had pursued as a teenager. I had deserted the part of myself that wanted to know who I really was. Instead, I had gotten caught in the endless pursuit of rewards—illusory rewards—and distractions of the material world: success, beautiful clothes, lovers. In the confusion and clamor, I had lost track of the Voice. And it had completely vanished.

But behind my glamorous façade, deep inside my heart, there was a spot that always throbbed with a vague sense of something *missing*. That feeling became the backdrop of my life and pushed me to live with abandon as I tried to fill the void. Over the years, the feeling became a full-blown yearning that propelled me to leave my home country and come to the other side of the globe.

The reek of vomit in the tent had become suffocating. And so was my desperation. For the first time in my life, I—born and raised in an atheist, communist country—formed words of prayer and addressed them to … God.

Or at least what I conjured in my mind as God. Fervently, desperately, I called for help. Through my sobbing, the words formed in my head: "It is time to change."

Astonished, I recognized the long-lost Voice from my youth. I lay there in that tent, frozen, eyes wide open, staring at the faded canvas above my head. The Voice continued: "It is time to let go of the way you have lived your life. It is time to examine your values." The Voice felt like a forgotten friend who had not forgotten me.

I cried out silently: *I will change, I PROMISE I will! Just get me out of here, PLEASE! I'll do ANYTHING to get out of here!*

Of all the places and circumstances, Dwight's journey began with a mind-altering enlightenment experience that happened at a bar, while drinking beer with fellow students. What a place to have a mystical experience—*a bar*! While drinking! But see, this kind of situation was so much in line with Dwight's character. At the time, he was a dashing, unruly, arrogant young man of twenty-one. Seven years earlier, he'd taken off on his bicycle from the family home in Los Angeles, destination Mexico. His parents were worried sick, but he forged ahead, stopping at farms along the way to make money for his trip.

Dwight was the kind of young man who pushed limits, broke conventions, and challenged authority. Perhaps, that "bar-awakening" gave him the sense of invincibility that was so much a part of him, even a part of the mature, responsible Dwight I would come to know.

But, oh, I so much wish I had known the Dwight from years back! The Dwight who drove the Vincent Black Shadow (the classic English superbike) and was chased by the police for speeding, always managing to escape. The Dwight who worked as the first officer on a French ship that smuggled cigarettes from Tangiers to Italy. The Dwight who raced cars. And the radiant, magnetic, handsome Dwight who instigated discussions about so many of the new ideas surfacing during the Beatnik era such as: always question authority; marriage is a social convention, follow free love; there is more to life than the materialistic, middle-class existence, because we are ultimately spiritual beings.

Those ideas paved the road to the hippy movement of the '60s, an early part of which started at a house in Palo Alto where Dwight lived with a few roommates, all Stanford graduate students. Among them was Dwight's best friend Vic Lovell, who worked nights as a watchman in the local Veterans Hospital. One night Vic brought back a gallon of LSD, which he stole from the psychiatric ward of the hospital and shared with his adventurous roommates, including Dwight. But by the time the nightly LSD tripping exploded in that house, Dwight had left for France to race cars and study at the Sorbonne. A new roommate moved in to take his place by the name of Ken Kesey. The rest of the story became history, recorded in the iconic movie *One Flew Over the Cuckoo's Nest*.

Living on the edge was the kind of life Dwight always sought. Jerry Garcia of the Grateful Dead talked about "DJ" (as Dwight's students called him) as "a wild guy who was out there" in an interview in *Rolling Stone*. Garcia was a rebellious, undisciplined, bored-to-death seventh-grader in the Menlo Park middle school where Dwight taught. DJ recognized an exceptional artistic talent in Garcia and steered him in that direction. "He's partly responsible for me being here," Garcia said in the same interview.

I'm convinced that Dwight's mission in the first half of his life was to change lives. At the boarding school where he worked, he was a role model to many students. He introduced them to Eastern religions, esoteric teachings, and dream analysis, and brought spiritual teachers from India as guest speakers. He took his students on sailing trips around the Mediterranean to follow in the footsteps of Odysseus, as well as to retreat centers—sometimes in his race car.

It seemed that every life he touched, he changed in a positive, expansive way. He certainly changed mine when I met him soon after my terrifying ordeal on that beach in Mexico.

My desperate call for help to God (or the powers that be), backed-up by my firm promise to change, was answered the very next day. I was saved by a couple who heard my calls for help when they drove by the pick-up truck I'd locked myself in to escape my schizophrenic lover. Two months later, I was led to a prestigious boarding school located a few miles south of Santa Barbara, where I was interviewed for the position of French teacher. I kept my job as a foreign correspondent for the magazine, but the course of my life, so it seemed, was now unfolding along a new, different path.

At the beginning of September I found myself in the dining hall of the boarding school, seated next to a man whose name-card on the table read *Dwight Johnson*. He introduced himself to me as the head of the psychology and philosophy department. I scanned his distinguished and reserved appearance, guessed his age to be in the early fifties, and wondered what his eyes, hidden behind thick glasses, really looked like.

I immediately discovered that I shared a lot of common interests with this silver-haired man who taught exotic-sounding courses like History of Ideas, Spiritual Psychology, and Comparative Religions. He talked about Jung, dreams, philosophy, his life in France, and many other topics I found supremely interesting. We discovered that we had the same taste in classical music and art, and shared a love of travel. But most amazingly, he had great appreciation for classical ballet.

"You mean you really *love* ballet?" I asked incredulously.

"Oh, very much," he replied with a hint of excitement at now meeting a former ballerina. (Well, all right—a ballerina *manquée*.) "As a student in Paris," he went on, "I'd watch all the ballets at the Opera. After the show I'd wait at the back door to see the ballerinas come out."

I told him that I envied his students.

"How so?" he glanced at me with a slightly different expression.

"Because they can talk about all these exciting ideas with you and about all these books that make you think."

He fell silent for a moment, looking away from me, then said, "You can do that too. But you have to ask the right questions."

Ask the right questions? No kidding!

With that casual interaction my spiritual education had begun. For the next two years, Dwight and I met platonically, as teacher and student, to discuss the major spiritual teachings and the tenets of what I came to know as the Ageless Wisdom. I asked all the questions I've ever had and then some more. Finally, I'd met someone who could answer *all* my questions, a man I'd call—*wise*. I felt as though all my life I'd been in a pitch-dark room and someone had just turned the lights on.

Dwight. Destiny.
And I could finally see.

True to the promise I'd given to the Voice on that desolate beach in Mexico, I did change. I turned inward, studying new ideas, practicing meditation, trying to become a better person. I no longer took on new lovers and didn't miss any of my old life. The world of spiritual ideas that Dwight was opening up to me was infinitely more exciting than any of the worldly pleasures I had previously indulged in.

I was beginning to understand the yearning that had brought me to California: to go beyond my materialistic life and *know* myself as a spiritual being, an immortal Soul. But how to fulfill that longing? Reading and discussing was one thing, but *becoming*—well, that was something entirely different.

And then, Dwight offered me an adventure that was to change my life in the most far-reaching way possible.

Dwight had just retired after receiving a modest inheritance and was thinking of taking a new direction in his life—"A new field of service," as he called it. Chores, socializing, and domestic life were not his cup of tea. Then out of the blue came a letter from an old friend he hadn't seen in thirty years. The friend wrote to tell Dwight about a book, *The Magus of Strovolos* by Kyriacos Markides. In the fashion of Carlos Castaneda, Markides had recorded the work and teachings of a remarkable healer and spiritual teacher who lived in Cyprus, a man named Daskalos. The friend offered to put Dwight in contact with the author of the book.

After Dwight read *The Magus of Strovolos*, he became more inspired than I had ever seen him before. One evening he came over for dinner (by that time our study relationship had blossomed into love), beaming with excitement. "Let's go study with this teacher!" he exclaimed, as he swept me up in his arms. "We'll take a year off, spend a couple of months in India, go to Egypt and visit all the temples and pyramids, and study with Daskalos." As he put me down, he said emphatically, "Our life here has become too ... cushioned."

Which was a good word to describe the kind of life Dwight didn't care for. You know, a comfortable life—a good car, the latest model TV and other electronics, Sunday brunches in good restaurants, lucrative investments, everything around you safe and familiar and, well, *cushioned*. All the edge taken out of life.

I looked at Dwight, at first flabbergasted, then bewildered, and finally delighted, as enticing images succeeded one another before my eyes. An adventure! A chance to take a sabbatical from a humdrum teaching routine. A chance to see exotic places, meet new people, learn new ideas. An opportunity to go deep inside, to spend hours in meditation. I could hear an echo in my head. It wasn't the Voice which, by the way, I no longer heard since that fateful night in the tent. It was a compelling urge that swooped down and filled my body with a profound sense of I-can't-do-otherwise certainty.

"Yes," I said. "I'm with you."

Still, I had to raise a couple of practical questions, such as—how were we going to pay for a year of traveling? After all, Dwight's inheritance was not that lavish.

"Don't worry about that," Dwight replied with utter confidence. "If we are doing the right thing—from the higher point of view, that of the Soul, naturally—we'll be helped."

A few days later, a check arrived in the mail. It was a payment of interest accumulated over many years on an account Dwight had completely forgotten about—just the right amount for the plane tickets. My jaw dropped, but Dwight was unfazed. "What did I tell you?" he said, looking at the check. "Opportunities present themselves when we take chances, not when we play it safe."

And so I took my chance. How could I say no? Granted, the big interview with Antonio Banderas was looming and it was slated to be a cover piece, which would give me great exposure. But I had to ask myself … *to what end*? At that moment something snapped inside me, something like the automatic switching of railroad tracks, and the train of my life was re-routed to an entirely different destination. I dropped my journalist career. I chose to follow the spiritual path instead of the path of worldly success. I left my secure teaching job to go on a spiritual pilgrimage, and in that moment of choice, my journey began.

Of course, at the time, I had no idea that our original plan to spend a year traveling would extend into three years of living and studying in Cyprus, then another two years of exploring sacred sites in Greece, Italy, and France. All along, we had to reassess our motivation and goals, because every time we made a decision, it entailed some kind of sacrifice. It can't be otherwise: if you say *yes* to something, you have to say *no* to something else.

Years later, after we had traveled the world, married, and soared to the heights of love and soul commitment, I would find in Dwight's posthumous notes these words: "The impossible is possible with fearlessness, will, imagination, and metaphysical grounding."

As I read his notes, I thought back to the many situations filled with danger and hardship, inner turmoil and duels with fear I would have thought impossible to overcome before I started my journey. Now I know that every high point and every trial had a part to play in making me who I have become and bringing me where I am at this point in my life—at my desk writing this spiritual travelogue.

And it all started with a journey…

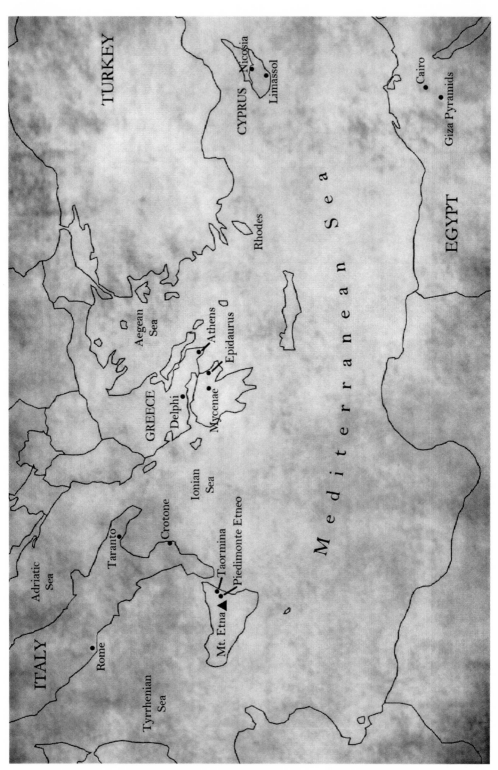

Follow my journey through photos at: www.svetlanameritt.com

PART 1

CYPRUS TO ITALY:

OPENING OF THE WAY

CHAPTER 1

CROSSING THE MEDITERRANEAN:
BLUE AND GOLDEN

n image of rocky, barren cliffs floats into my mind as I hold onto the railings of a ferry boat crossing the Mediterranean Sea. Cliffs baked golden by a fierce sun. Space filled with blueness, the hazy blue of a cloudless sky merging into the shimmering, deep blue of an unrestrained sea. Blue and golden, wherever the eye reaches.

In that blue and golden space that shimmers on the screen of my mind coalesces slowly a face: the long, white hair tied back into a ponytail; the dark, intensely piercing eyes, made formidable by thick glasses; a smile, warm, embracing, compassionate, that spills over into the eyes, softening them with a stroke of deep love; a nose prominent and willful. Truly, a face that might have belonged to a Yaqui Indian shaman, but actually belongs to Kostas, our teacher in Cyprus. He is gazing at me, steadily and powerfully, and I feel a lump form in my throat. But then he cracks a smile, the flicker of a smile, and makes a slight nod, as if to say, "Go. Don't worry. My protection is always with you."

Our ferry plows doggedly through the foaming waves. There is unrest in the swell of the sea, and the ship porpoises through the water. The wind scours my skin with salty mist. But I stay and stare at the waves, occasionally licking my dry, salty lips. Kostas' face now dissolves and turns into another face. I'm looking at Emily, our exuberant friend and a relentless fighter for peace and a unified Cyprus. It was the books of her husband Kyriacos that had brought us to Cyprus exactly four years ago, when we flew to that tiny island in the southeast part of the Mediterranean Sea to study with Daskalos. But when we arrived in Limassol, after months of planning and leaving everything behind, we learned to our dismay that Daskalos had died.

What bad luck! We had burnt our bridges behind us—and for what? Did I misunderstand that compelling urge which overtook me the day I made the decision? But Dwight took the twist of events with more dispassion than I did. Reasonably, he pointed out that we never know why things happen the way they do because we don't really know how the higher help works, and that we should explore other possibilities. So we decided to attend a lecture given by Kostas, Daskalos' closest disciple and assigned successor. And our journey took a new turn.

Of course, true journeys are never created beforehand. They constantly create and recreate themselves as we travel. What we had planned to see, do, and experience that first (and initially—only) year turned into something we could not have imagined. Our planned meditation retreat at the Ramana Maharshi Ashram in south India was cut short by late monsoon floods that turned everything into mold and caused Dwight a near-fatal illness. All his life he had asthma and a severe allergy to mold. We had to flee for his life to Madras where we found a dry refuge at the Krishnamurti Foundation. In Egypt, our tourist visit to the Great Pyramid at Giza turned into a solitary meditation inside the King's Chamber, as we sat alone, locked in the darkness-plunged pyramid hit by an unexpected power outage.

"It's not what we expected," Dwight said both times.

And the planned one year of travels extended into two, then three, and finally four years, as we stayed in Cyprus to study with Kostas.

Definitely not what we expected.

It was from Emily and Kyriacos' apartment in Limassol that we left yesterday, the second day of September, and put our car on a ferry to move to Italy. The beginning and the end, *alpha* and *omega*, the full circle. I feel the lump in my throat get scratchy.

Blue and golden, the colors of inner peace, of pure joy and absolute freedom. Like two notes they play over and over in my memory of the past four years. Blue was everywhere: in the sky above, lapping to our toes on the golden beaches of the western coast of Cyprus, dappling the white-washed houses with blue shutters, outlining the view from a villa that was our home for two years—a blue slice of luminous sea trembling beyond a valley framed by craggy hills, barren and baked golden.

The villa belonged to Jessica, whom we met through Eileen, whom we met through "crazy" George, whom we met.... That's how it was, that magical first year of our travels: one person led us to another, to a third—to a tenth. Doors opened everywhere and all the time. We were "in the flow." We were invited to coffee, lunches, parties, outings, meetings, lectures, and were even a part of an eco-village project that was just getting under way when we arrived. We met psychologists, engineers, lawyers, businessmen, customs officers, poets, psychics, healers, yoga teachers, artists, musicians, architects, diplomats … almost all of whom were, believe it or not, on a spiritual path of one kind or another. We were introduced to ten different spiritual groups, and this on an island—no, half an island, the Greek half—whose entire population is less than that of San Francisco.

Blue and golden. The colors of my favorite café by the sea where I spent many mornings sipping cappuccino and writing in my journal. As I sat at a table, filling in blank pages with words, I gazed at the vastness of the ever-changing shades of emerald-turquoise-azure blue. I inhaled the briny air tinged with orange blossoms in winter and rosemary and lavender in summer. In the simplicity of the unbroken blue space, in the purity of white-washed walls, in the golden intensity of the Mediterranean sun, I found freedom and archetypal timelessness.

Which, I now realize, I'm sad to leave.

The lump in my throat seems to double, and half of it slides down into my heart as another face emerges in the mist of fine spray—that of Stalo. My soul sister. We became friends because Dwight said to her, "smile!" and laughed. The only problem was that she was the customs officer checking our papers at the airport in Larnaca. She lifted her heavily made-up eyes and looked at Dwight incredulously. Under her severe, deep gaze Dwight broke into peals of laughter. The dark-lipsticked mouth of the officer trembled, then eased into a smile. And with that smile began our long-lasting friendship.

How much I'm going to miss that smile, the gleam of love in Stalo's magnificent eyes, and the summer nights we spent on the balcony of her family home in Nicosia, overlooking orange and lemon groves. The nights were sensuously warm and dry, suffused with the fragrance of Mediterranean vegetation and pierced by the incessant, rhythmic chirping of cicadas. In the distance loomed the Pentadactylos mountain range which, after the Turkish invasion of Cyprus in 1974, remained in the occupied half of the island. On the slope facing the capital city of Nicosia, the Turks have etched their flag, which at night shone brightly and defiantly, ever-present, inescapable. Stalo always sat on a chair that faced away from the mountains. Her hometown, Famagusta, had become a ghost city, invaded, pillaged, and left abandoned. Like many Greek Cypriots, her family had to flee before the invasion, leaving all their possessions behind.

And how I'm going to miss all our friends, lunches at the unspoiled beaches in Akamas or old village taverns in the mountains, dinners filled with laughter and music, sharing of our life experiences, exploring of metaphysical ideas, passionate discussions of the future of Cyprus, dreaming of a better world without wars.

The pang of sadness I felt that morning on the ferry as we were sailing away from Cyprus was only the beginning of what was to become a permanent feeling over the years ahead, as we moved to Italy to France to California to Belgrade to New Zealand, and finally to California again. I made friends and loved them, only to have to leave them behind. I saw visions of what we should do and followed them, only to have to replace them by others. I had realizations I thought were pinnacles, only to have to transcend them by ever higher realizations. My life continued to be one of constant movement and change, continuous building and breaking, planning and seeing those plans thwarted. It was a life of ceaseless trials, shattered beliefs and concepts, frequent clashes with the surrounding circumstances. It was the life of a seeker.

So if I say that I really didn't know what I was seeking when I first set off on the voyage with Dwight, it is true in many ways. I had reformulated the purpose of my journey many times over those years as I struggled with my obstinate personality flaws, as I diligently practiced meditation, as I studied and researched Truth with Kostas and his organization called Erevna ("Research of Truth"). Until a new purpose vaguely, timidly began to form itself at the end of the third year—much like a wispy cloud gathering ever more vapor from the air and becoming puffy and plump and distended with collected moisture until it's ready to burst with rain. By the end of the third year the tenuous purpose of the journey had swollen to saturate my whole body and fill my heart to the brim. I was bursting with the desire—to meet my Soul.

And not only meet, but stay together forever and ever. Truth be told, I've already had glimpses of that higher, better, and truer part of me, my essence, who I am at my core. In those rare moments I would soar upward, transcend the limitations of my body and psyche, and feel all-knowing, all-good, all-loving. Those moments were so rapturous that I wanted to feel that way at all times.

Now you may ask: How does one meet one's Soul at will?

That's exactly what I asked Dwight several times (well, to be honest, I'd been asking him every other day or so). Initially, he'd take the time to answer in great detail—about various meditation techniques, working on your character to become a better person, doing evening reviews of what you did well and didn't do well during the day, reading inspiring spiritual literature and things like that, all essential stepping stones on the road to your Soul. Which I did with a zeal and discipline because, after all, I have always been an "A" student. But apart from those occasional glimpses and fleeting transports, my Soul remained elusive, and Dwight got tired of repeating the same things.

Finally one day he replied to my tedious questioning in a somewhat exasperated tone: "Don't worry, your Soul will come to meet *you*." Then he added in a slightly different voice, "When you are ready."

In addition to looking for my Soul, I had also been pondering over the past year what my real life's work, my mission, should be. I knew I was done with being a journalist; chasing after celebrities to get an interview was no longer fulfilling. I was done with teaching French too. (I mean, how rewarding it is to teach the conjugation of French irregular verbs to a bunch of high school teen-agers who couldn't care less!) I had even stopped dancing altogether, having given the last public performance a year before we left on our journey. I knew what I no longer was, but I didn't know what I should be, what my role in life was as my Soul-self, rather than as my personality-self. I had entered an unknown territory, the shaky, uncomfortable zone in between the old and the new. Everything I was good at I'd left behind. With no regrets. But who and what I should become, I had no idea. And I wouldn't have for many more years.

Nevertheless, there were hints of something new emerging in that "no-mission" land I was stuck in. Inspired by our long visits to Egypt, time in the desert with the Bedouins, and strange experiences at the ancient temples and pyramids, I had an idea for a novel—a spiritual novel, as I called it—which I diligently applied myself to write. It took two years from the conception to the actual physical book in my hands, titled *Legacy of the Future*, which I self-published with a help of a friend. *And now what?*

In the moments of greatest self-confidence and inspiration (which, strangely, happened while I would be taking sage baths under candle lights), I'd ask myself: *Svetlana, what do you really want to do?* I floated weightless in the bathtub filled with foamy, fragrant water. My body was so light that it seemed as if the heavy lid in my womb had been lifted, and I could, perhaps, let out what lay pulped below it since that day on the bridge in Paris sixteen years before. Those evenings when I floated light in the bathtub, I believed that anything was possible. In the flickering shadows cast by flames, strange ideas hovered above me, such as ... spiritual literature. *I want to write spiritual literature,* I formulated, my heart aflutter.

Which is exactly *what?*—the voice of self-doubt immediately retorted, a tad scornfully.

Well, literature inspired by higher values rather than the lowest common denominator.

Oh, yeah? And how do you think to make that ... whatever-you-call-it literature, believable?

In the shadowy, sweet-smelling bathroom where I floated between two worlds, everything seemed easy. I promptly dismissed the voice of self-doubt which, since we made Cyprus our home, had gradually taken residence in my head. I felt something wafting in the steamy air, a reassuring and supporting presence that infused me with strength. A feeling of just-rightness, of poise and inner confidence filled my heart. *I can do anything I set my mind to!* Inspiration, creativity, ideas—everything seemed within my reach.

But during the bright, hot days, especially the days when I crawled around the house in utter exhaustion, self-doubt would reassert itself. *What was I dreaming of? I don't even have energy to make a meal, let alone write ... spiritual fiction, ha!*

How did I transform into this insecure, easy-to-defeat wimp from the strong, ambitious, and confident woman I used to be? Well, the truth is that after our first "magical year" when doors opened everywhere and all the time, all of a sudden they remained tightly shut—bolted, as it were. The promising, rosy path of spiritual growth transformed into a grim and thorny ravine of health struggles and deeply rooted psychological conditioning that had to be overcome, step by arduous step. During our first year as residents of Cyprus, Dwight had one health problem after another, each one requiring that I turn into a nurse. Then my mother fell seriously ill and I had to fly to Belgrade to help her. At the end of which period *my* health buckled and fell apart. For the next two years I struggled with a debilitating health condition called systemic Candida, which had occupied my body like an invisible invader. Fatigue was my constant companion. The grind of inner toils and struggles with the body were my daily chores. Slowly, gradually, I sank into the "ordinary" state of consciousness. Life became tedious and dull, devoid of any higher contacts, insights, inspiration. My self-confidence wore thinner and thinner, until it wore off. I no longer had any successes to define myself by. I no longer knew who I was.

And so it came as a total surprise when sometime during our fourth year on the journey, I had a vision of moving to Italy. It happened during my visit to Ostia Antica, a vast archaeological site outside of Rome, where I had stopped over en route to the United States (one of my yearly mandatory trips in order to keep my green card valid). I sat atop the theater overlooking a temple in ruins surrounded by a ring of parasol pines and suddenly felt an overwhelming impression swoop down into my heart. A compelling urge spread throughout my whole body and exploded in my head: *Move to Italy to write a book*. There was something in the air, a different frequency that filled me with inspiration, strength, utter certainty and confidence, much like the feeling I'd had during the sage baths. It was the same feeling that took me over on the day I said "yes" to Dwight and "no" to the interview with Antonio Banderas. I recognized it also as the propelling force the day I bolted alone through the pitch-dark of the Great Pyramid in Egypt and lay in the sarcophagus of the King's Chamber to conquer my claustrophobia. It was a feeling of an all-pervading certainty. A compelling urge. Invincibility.

It was then that I called this higher presence, this sense of inevitability—the Guidance.

So I promptly launched the question: *What would I write about?*

I looked at the sinewy trunks of parasol pines and saw myself sitting at a desk and writing. Ideas flashed through my mind until one felt right—I'd write about the Medici and art.

Fortunately, Dwight has complete confidence in my inner sensitivity and impressions. So when I told him about "the Guidance" and the vision I had in Ostia Antica, he fell silent for a moment, then began to nod. "Okay," he said calmly, "let's move to Italy."

Italy. The country where we are headed now. The next leg of our journey. The new chapter in our lives. But not just yet.

Between Cyprus, a tiny island near the coast of Turkey, and the peninsula of Italy, between the Adriatic and the Tyrrhenian Sea, lies the country from which the whole Western civilization sprouted, the country that is a must-see if you're working in the fields of art, philosophy, literature, architecture, religion, and of course, mythology, earth energies, and sacred sites. Greece. It is also the place to visit if you are seeking for answers about, let's say, your mission in life.

This is where we are going to disembark in just a few hours.

CHAPTER 2

EPIDAUROS:

THE GAZE OF ANUBIS

Pines. I first smell the scent of pines, pure and fresh, coming to greet me like an old friend. As far as my eyes reach, the earth is covered with a carpet of pine needles. They make a crunching sound, a sort of slithering *skweet skweet* as I walk. A soft silence surrounds me, as if the needles are muffling the noises of life, and I'm moving through a timeless, enchanted forest.

A pine forest.

I marvel at the tall trunks and cross-hatched branches that reach up towards the sky to form a canopy over my head. Pine trees were considered special in ancient Greece, believed to be cleansing to their surroundings and healing for the body. It's only fitting that there should be a pine forest here at Epidauros—the most famous healing center of the classical world and the burial place of Asclepios, the god of medicine and healing.

The site of the *ascleipeion,* or healing sanctuary, stretches like a long hand through a clearing dotted with ruins, the pine forest a winding bracelet around it. It's already late afternoon when Dwight and I arrive at Epidauros, only two hours before closing time. We face the vast remains of ancient temples, priests' quarters, sanatoria, hotels, baths, theaters, and a stadium. Across from the healing sanctuary is the most famous theater of the ancient world. It has perfect acoustics, unsurpassed even in our century, and is still in use for performances of classical Greek plays.

I saw the theater many years ago when, as a college freshman, I took a trip to Greece to see the places I'd been learning about in my classical drama class. Back then, I was impressed by the beauty and symmetry of the edifice, soaring uphill like an eagle with outstretched wings. But more so, I was in awe of its acoustics. I stood in the last of the fifty-five rows that offered a bird's-eye view of the stage, while my companions seemed like tiny puppets far below. One of them, standing in the center of the stage, whispered a line from *Antigone*. All the way up below the clouds, I heard every word with exquisite clarity, as if his lips were pressed against my ear.

That was then—as I explored ancient Greek history, literature, and philosophy, looking for knowledge to appease my adolescent restlessness and disquietude. But now, almost twenty years later, I'm back searching for something entirely different. Now my visit has a double purpose: I seek healing and a vision quest. Since we disembarked in the port of Piraeus a week ago, we've been driving around Greece, visiting some of the greatest sites of the ancient world: Delphi, Thebes, Corinth, Argos, Tiryns, Mycenae. Each site pulled a different string in my subconscious and a different note resonated in my body, revealing sensations, emotions, and longings I had no idea were stored deep down. That's what Greece does to a seeker: if you are really open and ready, it will bring to the surface depths and heights of your inner self; it will split asunder your carefully built façade and expose you where you are raw; it will crack your defenses and push you toward self-discovery. It might also work magic—as it did to me. The ancient myths are still embedded in the very soil of sacred sites and etched in the sky that vaults over the sere plains. And just as Theseus was led by Ariadne's thread out of the deadly labyrinth where he killed the Minotaur, I felt directed to come to Epidauros.

Now on this late afternoon in early September, a day before we head north to catch a ferry to Italy, I know exactly what I want to see at this sacred site.

First, the *tholos*. The mysterious round structure shaped as a labyrinth that stands at the heart of this sanctuary, in the sacred grove where—astonishingly—death was banned! Although *ascleipeion* was for the ancients what hospitals are for us today, no one was allowed to die while staying here, and by the same token, no woman was permitted to give birth. Without death and without birth there is only eternity, a conquest over human mortality, and men, in a way, can assume the power of gods.

"A labyrinth at the heart of a healing center," Dwight says reflectively, "now there is something to think about. A symbol of the journey through life, a sort of pilgrimage ... like ours has been."

In silence, we walk past the Temple of Asclepios, past the priests' quarters, and reach the far end of the sacred grove. In front of us lies the enclosure of the *tholos*, actually only the basement of it, which is all that is left of a circular building, at one time colonnaded and richly decorated. It's surprisingly small—and it's sealed off to the public.

Dwight carefully looks around for a guard, but at this late afternoon hour there are hardly any tourists, let alone guards. He gives me a "go" with his eyes, and I jump over the ropes.

I find myself within the confines of concentric walls about six feet high, built of stone blocks and without a roof. I go around in one direction, then around in the opposite direction, and around again until I reach where it ends at the center—a tiny, circular space capped by a wooden roof, and just big enough for one person. I gingerly step into the semi-darkness of the tiny enclosure, mind alert, senses like antennae, body taut like a bow.

I'm in the center of the labyrinth—and now what do I do? How do I seek to be healed from Candida? For the past two years I had tried a full arsenal of traditional and alternative cures, with only temporary and minor results. All this time I haven't put a trace of sugar in my mouth, following a strict—boring—diet. And my body is still weak, energy the most precious commodity in my life. So how on earth am I going to be cured *here*, in this teensy earthen cubbyhole?

Just as the skeptical part of me is waking up, a thought emerges in my mind and I know what I should do. A healing ritual. It is difficult to describe how this *knowing* comes about. Over the years I've learned to recognize it as my intuition—an instantaneous knowing that appears in my head without active thinking, as if deposited from above. So now, I just *know* that I should slowly turn around to face the four directions. The South to shed the old. Then East for a new birth. North to align myself with the magnetic field of the Earth, and finally West, to pay my respects to the forces of decay and death.

I begin by facing the South and ask fervently that my body be cleansed of all parasites, germs, and Candida. As I am visualizing streams of muck leaving my body, suddenly I feel tingling in the soles of my feet and a strong pull from below. It's as if a powerful vacuum cleaner is positioned beneath my feet and is sucking the crud down and out. As this happens, an intense wave of heat starts mounting up my legs and moves up my body. The sensations are so strong that only a few years ago I would have been too afraid to continue. But I've since gone through so many out-of-the-ordinary and sometimes dangerous experiences—shifts of consciousness in dark caves, long hours of meditation in ashrams, inexplicable déjà-vus in Egyptian temples, paralyzing fear in the pitch-black of the Great Pyramid—that by now I have become quite familiar with the happenings on the inner planes. As familiar, that is, as a person could be with such uncharted territory.

Which is why the heat I'm feeling right now spreading throughout my body and pulsing in my head doesn't frighten me. I know that the inner experience always manifests in the outer environment, however subtle—or strong—the sensations may be. I've learned that sooner or later on the spiritual path there must be a purging, a purification, to eliminate the old so the new can be born. I also know, because of my experience, that there are places on earth, ancient centers of worship, that still throb with a powerful energy that affects us, whether we are aware of that energy or not.

When I turn to face the East, I feel a surge of joy, a shimmering white, an unsullied transport which lifts me up above my body—the all-knowing, all-good observer, the true Me: my Soul. Oh, how ecstatic I feel! *This* is what I've been seeking in the ashrams in India during long hours of meditation. *This* is what I'd glimpsed on and off over the past years. The memory of its presence remained like a beacon on my path. I am infused now with the energy of a new beginning, something like a slate wiped clean, a new road opening in front of me, diamond-polished and glistening.

But then I feel a prod, more like a command to turn and face the North. As I do that, the shimmering white begins to fade and fizzle out. *Wait, don't go!* I cry out silently. *You're so beautiful, don't leave me! I want to be with you all the time!* I try desperately to seize that shimmering energy, but the more I try, the faster it fades. I want to turn back to recapture the presence of my Soul, but something is holding me rooted in the spot. I start to feel a busy, agitated energy all around me, making adjustments to my body like a crew of mechanics swarming over a race car at a pit stop. A thought appears that this is a necessary part of my healing from Candida, something that, after all, I had asked for and came to Epidauros to find. So I remain still and patient.

When the sensation subsides I know it's time to turn to the West and offer my gratitude. Gratitude, I've learned over and over, is the single most important state of being one can cultivate in life. Now I offer gratitude for all the times when I received help seemingly from nowhere (like at that deserted beach in Mexico). And especially for having met Dwight. *My Dwighty* ... my wise man, my guide, my perfect companion, my *twin flame*.

"Hey, what have you been doing here all this time?" A sudden whisper interrupts my ritual. Dwight's broad shoulders appear in the opening of my little cubbyhole and completely obscure the faint light. In darkness, I step toward him and whisper back, "I just did a healing ritual. Maybe you want to try it?"

Before he can answer, I fling my arms around his neck and kiss him. But there is no room for both of us in here, so I leave Dwight with my instructions, fervently hoping that the healing energy of the *tholos* might alleviate the severity of his heart condition. For the past two years he has been suffering from fitful spells of heart related issues—arrhythmias, fibrillation, tachycardia, you name it—which at times were so severe that he couldn't get out of bed for days.

I wait for him sitting atop the enclosure wall, alone, perfectly poised, feeling renewed, uplifted, strong. I had forgotten how good it is to feel strong! Every muscle of my body vibrates with energy; all my cells throb with power, a stream of power that flows through me like a mountain river. I inhale deeply, so deeply as if to rob the air of every scent.

The dusk is silently gliding into the grove, bringing violet shades and air redolent with herbs. I think I'm smelling sage, and certainly thyme. Herbs, especially those that helped to cleanse the body, were an important part of the healing protocol in the sanctuary, combined with dietary prescriptions, exercises, occasional simple surgery, and even the presence of sacred snakes and dogs (being licked by these animals was believed to heal wounds).

But the most important part of the ancient protocol for those seeking a cure was a stay at the *abaton*, or sleeping ward, set to the side of the *tholos*. After a period of cleansing and purification, the sick—who were also the seekers— entered the ward that contained narrow chambers. There, in those cocoon-like cavities, wrapped like larvae, the supplicants were left to wait for the appearance of Asclepios in their dreams. This process was known as incubation, and it could last from several hours to several days, depending on how long it took for the god to appear. Eventually, Asclepios would show up in one of his several guises, two of which were his sacred animals: a snake and a dog. If healing did not occur right away through the touch of Asclepios, then the god—or his guise—would provide some kind of instruction that pointed to a cure. In the case of a vision or a dream image, the priests would interpret it to prescribe a therapy.

The *abaton*—that's where I want to go next, as soon as Dwight emerges from the *tholos*. I want to ask for an image, a symbol—anything—about my life's mission, some sort of a signpost: *This is what you're supposed to do.* I had wanted to address my vision quest to the sun god Apollo, father of Asclepios, when we visited his temple at Delphi the day before. I mean, what better place to ask about my mission in life than at the most famous oracle of the ancient world? But the temple where Apollo's priestesses once prophesied was so heavily guarded that I found no place where I could commune with the spirit of the oracle. So this comes as the second best, staying within the family, so to speak.

My thoughts are interrupted by a thud and a rattling of stones. Dwight emerges from the labyrinth, a bit disheveled, blinking at the light and smiling serenely.

"That place is certainly a vortex of Earth energy," he exclaims, as he walks toward me. "Possibly the whole area as well, but you can feel it most in there." He sits down on the wall next to me, looking a bit dazed, then adds, "You know, the priests might very well have kept the sacred snakes in that center space where the labyrinth ends. After all, that was underground, the basement of the building. And to the ancients, serpents were a symbol of the underworld. In fact, didn't Asclepios have powers to bring souls back from the dead?"

"Yes, that's what the myth says," I reply. "But don't you think the *tholos* could have been an initiation chamber for the priests, you know, where they'd undergo a symbolic death and rebirth?" It suddenly occurs to me that what I had just experienced might have been related to rites once held in the central chamber. Rites of cleansing, of renewal, of endings and beginnings.

Dwight nods. "It could be," he says reflectively, then adds in his teacher's voice: "I think that both snakes and Asclepios are symbols for Earth energy, which the ancients were very familiar with and could sense directly. Here, they used it for healing. At Delphi, for divining the future—"

"True," I interrupt, glancing at my watch. "But we don't have much time left. Let's move on."

We walk away from the *tholos* towards the fragments of columns strewn about on the ground. According to our map, this must be the older wing of the sleeping ward, and we head for the remains of the wall, knee-level and flat. It is wide enough to actually lie on top and pretend to sleep, like the pilgrims of the past … and wait for a vision to come through.

Maybe I could actually take a nap, I muse, just to make sure Asclepios pays me a visit. As I'm lying on the hard surface, I conjure his image in my mind: a well-proportioned frame with a bearded, middle-aged face, his gaze lost in another world. His expression is enigmatic, a bit detached and impassive. Or perhaps it is wistful, showing his regret for having trespassed the regions of Hades to bring back the dead. This so enraged Zeus that he sent a thunderbolt from his throne atop Mt. Olympus to kill the upstart.

I'm waiting.

To pass the time, I recall what I read about the birth of Asclepios, whose coming into life was as violent as his departure. His mortal mother was impregnated by Apollo, who killed her after she had an affair with a mortal lover. While her corpse was lying on a funeral pyre, Apollo rescued his unborn son from her womb, hence the name Asclepios—"to cut open." The child was then given to Chiron, a wise centaur, who raised and instructed him in the healing arts.

I'm still waiting....

Asclepios is always represented with a snake, one of his sacred animals. Usually the snake is entwined around his staff, and this became not only his signature, but also the well-known symbol of medicine and the healing arts. In his temple here at Epidauros, there was a statue of Asclepios at one time, his one hand resting on the head of a giant serpent, the other holding a rod, and by his feet, a dog, his second most sacred animal.

Still waiting....

"Wow! Don't move...."

My ears perk up. No, it's not Asclepios talking to me, it's Dwight whispering from behind, the two of us lying on the wall head to foot. "Open your eyes," he goes on, "but don't get up. You're going to be *really* surprised."

I open my eyes wide, raise my head, and meet the gaze of another pair of eyes ... that belong to a dog. The dog is lying on the wall at my feet and staring intensely at me. I stare back for a long moment. We stare at each other, a dog and a woman, lying on the wall of this ancient sleeping ward.

There is something unusual about this dog. He reminds me of something ... his posture, so immobile like the Sphinx, front paws pointed straight out in front, rear legs tucked under, and tail hanging limp down the side of the low wall. He reminds me of something, no, not the Sphinx, a statue, an Egyptian statue ... a statue of, of ... Anubis! Yes, the Egyptian deity Anubis, the guide, would you believe it—to the Underworld! The dog before me is jet black and looks exactly like the sculpture of the jackal-dog from Tuthankhamun's tomb, the sculpture we saw in the Cairo Museum. Even the ears are long and perked high up to give him a wise but slightly sinister expression. The resemblance is utterly uncanny.

But why, I'm left to wonder, has Asclepios sent me this guide to the Underworld?

"*Oriste!* Welcome, welcome! Sit where you want." A short, stocky man greets us in both Greek and English, waving his arm over a room of empty tables. His dark eyes look at us with a glint of a smile, and his face radiates kindness.

We are a bit confused. Such a big restaurant, yet empty? And it was recommended at our hotel as the best in town. ("All the celebrities eat there," the receptionist assured us.)

"Well…" begins Dwight hesitantly, "we'd like to have dinner. What do you have on the menu tonight?"

"Anything you want," the man replies, beaming. "Have *koupepia, souvlaki, moussaka*…."

Dwight is not convinced. "But nothing is microwaved?" he asks, eyeing the Greek with obvious suspicion. Dwight, you should know, is a gourmet. He likes his food, and he likes to eat good food. Bad food—bad mood. He says it's because he lived in France for so many years.

"Ah, *endaxi,* very good." The Greek nods, smiling. "You come with me, I show you."

He takes us between the tables to the back of the room and through swinging doors right into the kitchen. "Now, we can make what you want." He points to a middle-aged woman, also short and stocky, and clad in the black garb of Mediterranean women in mourning. She gives us a motherly smile, then turns to the oven and takes out a large dish of freshly baked, softly bubbling, golden *moussaka*.

"That!" Dwight and I yelp at the same time. We love *moussaka*, rich and creamy like a cake. The layers of eggplant, potatoes, and minced meat melt in your mouth, and the béchamel sauce tops it off like a delicious frosting. We walk back into the empty room and choose a table in a corner. We can't help but wonder: *Where is everybody?* Granted, it's no longer peak tourist season, but it's only the beginning of September.

The owner brings several small plates and lovingly lines them up in front of us. "*Meze,*" he says, as we gaze at the array of appetizers. "On the house." His face breaks into a wide smile.

I love these little dishes, mouthfuls of delightful surprises. There are slices of Feta cheese and stuffed mushrooms and a couple of *dolmates* and *tahini* and *tzatziki* and, of course, olives. Small, shriveled, glistening-black, and, ah, divine. I've never tasted olives like these. They are not big and plump like the much vaunted Kalamatas; they are midgets, but what midgets! As I squash one between my teeth (carefully avoiding the pit), the flesh bursts in my mouth with all the flavors of the Mediterranean: dry herbs, goats, pine trees, briny sea air, and above all, the hot noon-day sun. Olives full of sun.

"You like it, eh?" The round face shows a smile of content.

"Do I like it? No. I *love* it!" I say ecstatically.

Maybe because he's bored, or maybe because he's friendly, or maybe because he enjoys our enjoyment, the owner keeps us company at the table. He sighs and says, "Today, slow. No people." Yes, we can see that. "No play, no people," he sighs again.

"No play...?" I ask.

"In theater, no play today," he attempts to explain, his arm sweeping across the empty room. "Everybody comes here to eat after play. Look…" Now both arms are in the air, pointing at walls that, I notice, are completely covered with framed photographs of people. I angle myself just enough to see the one above our table that shows a small group with a dignified-looking man in the middle resembling the former French president, François Mittérrand.

"Actors, politicians, singers, they all come here, to Leonidas," he says with an air of pride. "Come, I show you."

Intrigued, we get up and look closely at the photos on the other walls. Yes, that is Melina Mercouri with our host, and over there, Sir Peter Hall. And I think I recognize Maria Callas. All the photos are signed, with the signature under a greeting or an expression of appreciation.

"Famous people." I nod, quite impressed. "Like a Hall of Fame."

Leonidas seems quite pleased. "Good food, good food," he repeats, tapping his belly. "Ah, but you must eat." He interrupts the tour and points us back to our table, then walks jauntily off into to the kitchen. When he comes out, he's loaded with plates of *moussaka* and salads and bread.

After we've polished off half of our portions, Dwight throws out casually, "So … it seems you got your message."

"Ma-sha-ge?" I've just stuffed my mouth with a huge, creamy bite.

"Yes, the one you were asking for. The guidance at Epidauros."

"Ah, yes." I swallow my mouthful. I see again the persistent gaze of the Anubis-like dog. "Most puzzling, isn't it?"

"Uh-huh," Dwight nods, putting his fork down. "What do you make of it?"

"Good question." I hadn't really had a chance to think about it, we were so preoccupied with finding a hotel, unpacking, then rushing off to dinner.

"It surely was a message, there's no doubt about it," Dwight repeats. "I've never seen a dog behave that way—sit in such a still position, stare for so long and so intently, then disappear as it did after we got up. Not to mention that dogs were sacred to Asclepios."

"Come to think of it," I say excitedly, "it was like a dream the sick pilgrims would have!"

Dwight nods. "Now you must interpret it, just as the priests would do. You have to find out what the appearance of the dog represents symbolically for you."

I know that, and I'm trying to remember everything I've ever read about Anubis. Like all other deities in the Egyptian pantheon, Anubis had many names and many roles, one of which, I recall reading, was Upuat or "Opener of the Way."

"Well, maybe the dog symbolizes a new beginning. You know, as the Opener of the Way, the dog's appearance could point to a new path for me."

"A new path," Dwight repeats slowly. "Hmm. To where? Doesn't Anubis take the souls of the deceased on their journey into the Underworld?"

True, I have to admit, Anubis is better known to show people the end, not the beginning. I shake my head. "I really have no idea."

It always amazes me how the most obvious things escape us at the time we're searching for them. It would take me two years of seeking, stumbling, falling, facing my deep fears, battling my stormy emotions, overcoming dangerous situations, having a brush with death, before I finally found the answer—ending my journey in another underground chamber, far from Epidauros. But at that moment, in that empty restaurant, I had no idea.

"What do you suggest?" I ask Dwight, as I always do when I feel spiritually stranded.

"I think we have to first look at the question of what *is* the Underworld?"

"Well, in mythology, that's the world of the dead," I answer tentatively, not sure where he's going.

"Okay. But how about thinking symbolically? What is *under*—or *beyond*—the world?"

I shrug, puzzled.

Dwight clears his throat, and I know he's about to say something he considers important. "I think," he begins, "that the 'underworld' may not be a place physically below us, but rather a place we don't perceive with our senses. Our world, the manifest world, exists in a certain visible frequency range. But there are other worlds with different frequencies that are not visible to us. We could interpret those invisible or 'underground' worlds as *collective unconscious*, the realm Carl Jung says we all share but are not aware of through our ordinary senses. A world where much more is available than in this visible world." Dwight pauses, looking at me intently from behind his glasses, then says with emphasis, "And *there* lies the source of creativity."

"Wait, are you're saying that the appearance of the dog was a message about my creativity?" I stare at Dwight.

"It could be…. Didn't you say you wanted to write a book about the Medici?" He tilts his head, eyeing me. "Didn't you want to find a place in Italy where you could settle in and write?"

"Well, yes, but—"

"So there you are. You've now been given a guide to your creative processes," he concludes in a matter-is-settled tone of voice.

Before I have time to ponder Dwight's words, Leonidas appears, carrying a black plastic bag. "You still eating? This no good?" He asks with concern, eyeing our half-eaten meals.

"Oh, heavens no," Dwight hurries to reassure him. "It's delicious! We were just talking."

"Ah, *endaxi*. Enjoy. *Siga, siga*. Slowly, slowly." He sits obligingly next to Dwight and plants the bag on the table, its blackness in stark contrast with the white tablecloth. I wonder what's in it, the black plastic bag tied with a double knot. I stare at it and feel today's events, insights, and Dwight's words crowd in my head, clamoring, demanding my attention. If only I could pack this whole day, all the experiences, into a bag like this one and take them with me to digest later, bit by bit.

We finish our meal while Leonidas tells us anecdotes from his life. I ask if he has travelled much. "The world come to me, I no need go nowhere," he says shaking his head in reply. "Here, the most beautiful place in the world. Have everything—history, curing, sea, trees, tourists … and peace. Why go?" He shrugs, as if this should be obvious to everybody.

Really, why go? What is it that makes me want to keep moving, to explore, search, learn, understand, meet people, hear stories, take everything in. *Why go?* Why can't I just sit in one place, content like Leonidas with what I already have?

Even when I was a teenage girl in Belgrade, I felt something calling me from far away. I would often stand alone on the wall of an ancient fortress called Kalemegdan, the plaster cast clamping my body like armor from neck to hips. The fortress where I stood was first erected by the Celts on a hill which overlooked the confluence of two rivers, the mighty Danube and the tamer Sava. That was the beginning of Singidunum, the city-fort that had since been destroyed and rebuilt over forty times, eventually changing its name to Belgrade (The White City) when the Slavs took it over in the sixth century. The fort witnessed two millennia of continuous sieges, bloody battles, and fierce conquests by Romans, Goths, Huns, Byzantines, Slavs, Avars, Bulgarians, Serbs, Hungarians, Turks, Austrians, Serbs again, Germans, and finally Serbs. It had witnessed boiling oil poured down its walls, sabers slashing, spears piercing bodies, maces tearing flesh, cannon balls, gun fire, fleets of boats, cavalry attacks, air raids, shrill cries, blood-curdling cruelty, centuries of Ottoman occupation, fights for power, for domination, for independence, for beloved ones—for freedom.

All of that had transpired on the spot where I stood and gazed towards the other shore in the far distance and the trees that formed a sometimes hazy, sometimes beryl-green blanket that stretched all the way to the horizon. The gentle shimmering of far-away leaves echoed a stirring in my own heart. The stirring of a yearning, of a strange calling I couldn't understand, of a longing for something I couldn't quite formulate.

But always, a sense of inevitability.

"Before you go," Leonidas' voice brings me back, "I give you something." He carefully lifts the black bag with his robust, stocky hands and says, "Because you like so much."

"What is it?" I'm taken by surprise, looking at the tightly tied double knot.

"Olives. A kilo of olives for you." He smiles so warmly that I take the bag in my arms like a pet and smile back with gratitude.

Olives full of sun.

A treasure to take back with me and slowly digest, bite by tangy bite.

CHAPTER 3

SAILING TO ITALY:

RESEARCHING TRUTH

Did I plan this on purpose—to be sailing to Italy on my birthday? In my own personal calendar, you should know, the new year always begins in September. That's when all the major changes have occurred in my life, beginning, naturally, with my birth: becoming a journalist, leaving my birth country for graduate studies in California, then getting a job as a French teacher and meeting Dwight. It was also in September four years ago that we left everything behind to begin a pilgrimage to Cyprus, India, and Egypt. And it was a week ago, the second day of September, that we put our car on the ferry in Limassol and left Cyprus.

Always—September.

Because it's my birthday today—the beginning of my new year—and because we're on our way to Italy, and perhaps also because the weather is so gray and heavy, I feel introspective. The encounter with the Anubis-like dog looms in my mind, mysterious. The slaps of wind muss my hair and also my thoughts as I stand at the ship's railing. I retreat into the lounge on the deck, which is almost empty. I sit at a table by huge windows. Not much to see, only the gray sea and the cloudy sky, but still, it's a view. And a view of any kind helps me to overcome the confines of my thoughts; it pulls me high above them and I watch my life like a movie. "If you want to know the future, look into the past," I read somewhere.

The past.... What have I learned so far over the past eight years with Dwight?

I smile, remembering one distant Saturday afternoon when my spiritual education formally began. Dwight and I were sitting at a table in my living room, talking about our lives.

"So what did you basically want in life?" I asked, fascinated, as he finished telling me the abbreviated story of his beatnik days in Palo Alto.

Dwight thought for a moment. "I guess on the mundane level I wanted to experience the world," he said. "I wanted to be *vividly* alive. You could say I wanted challenge—no, adventure, with a capital 'A.'" He cracked a smile. "But on the spiritual level I always wanted freedom."

"With a capital 'F'?" I quipped.

Naturally this got me thinking about my own life. What did *I* really want?

When I met Dwight, I was deeply curious to understand my dreams and to get answers to my endless questions. You could say I wanted knowledge. But what kind of knowledge? As we started discussing books and ideas, I gradually realized I wanted to understand nothing less than how life and the universe functioned, the causes behind the effects, and why we are here and where we are going.

"In other words," Dwight said that Saturday, "you want to know the principles of the Ageless Wisdom."

"Ageless Wisdom? What's that?"

Dwight fidgeted in his chair and assumed his teaching position—back erect, right shoulder higher, hands pointed up as if holding a ball. "Ageless Wisdom," he began, shaking the invisible ball, "is a body of eternal knowledge that goes back to the beginning of the civilized world in India, to the *Vedas* and *Upanishads*. It's the source of all major religions and philosophies. All of them scooped out bigger or smaller chunks of this knowledge and absorbed it as their dogmas or doctrines. In the Sanskrit it's called *Gupta–vidya*, meaning 'hidden wisdom.' Aldous Huxley called it 'the perennial philosophy.' Huston Smith uses the term 'primordial tradition—'"

"Wait, you mean, that's all the same ... teaching?"

"Yes. The same basic principles and ideas about how the universe was created, how it functions, the goal of evolution, and so on."

"But every religion has different answers, every philosopher offers different views," I objected.

"That's because they distorted the fundamental principles according to their own level of understanding. But there has always been an underlying current of teachings that has preserved those principles in their original form. The teachings of the esoteric schools that survived."

"The esoteric schools," I repeated. "Like what?"

"Like Hermetic philosophy, Gnosticism, Kabbalah, Alchemy, Sufism,

Rosicrucianism. Basically all the major religions had an esoteric undercurrent. For example, Christianity had Gnosticism, Judaism had Kabbalah, Islam had Sufism, and so on. Throughout history there have always been *exoteric* religions and *esoteric* counterparts. You follow? Exoteric for the masses, and esoteric for the few. That's because in the past, you had to prove you were ready for the higher knowledge, ready to apply it without misusing it. Nowadays, this knowledge is widely available. Everyone is given a chance to know."

I took my own chance to know seriously and avidly. I read, reflected, questioned, and reflected again. I took the books with me and read in the mountains behind Santa Barbara, pondered the ideas while walking on the beach, discussed them with Dwight at our meetings. Those ideas soon consumed my life.

I've never been a devotee and never prayed in my life. My mother was so anti-religious that when I announced my intention to get baptized—in my own Orthodox Christian religion, mind you, at the tender age of twenty-six—her face turned from bright red to deep green as she furiously threatened to commit suicide if I dared to do that. (So I didn't....) Consequently, gurus, ashrams, praying, chanting, and such are not my path. But ideas and knowledge—*wisdom*, more precisely—is something else. Because I always want to understand.

Later on, our teacher in Cyprus confirmed my instinctive searching. "Accept nothing on blind faith," Kostas admonished us. "Always question. Question what I say too."

But there were certain ideas that I didn't question because they simply *felt* right. It was like recognition of something I'd known a long time ago, but had forgotten. So when Dwight told me that according to the Ageless Wisdom human beings are dual in nature, with a lower part or personality and a higher aspect or Soul, I said quietly, "Ah! Of course." I felt as if I'd always known that.

"The Soul is our true identity," Dwight added. "It never dies and is never born. That's why it's been called our immortal Essence." Yes, it felt so right: somewhere, on some level we never die—and I'd always known that.

Other ideas came as an awakening, especially the first principle of the Ageless Wisdom which states that everything in the universe—from a dust particle to a star—is energy at a different rate of vibration. The first time Dwight told me this, he knocked on the table top and boomed, "You think this is solid? Of course not, it's energy!"

I gasped, but he went on, "As quantum physics shows, nothing is solid, the trees, the houses, the rocks ... nothing! It's all energy."

I felt the crumbling of my beliefs in the recesses of my brain. "But, but...,"

I sputtered, "they look so *solid*!"

"That's because our bodies vibrate within the same frequency range as the objects we touch," he replied, amused by my shock.

"Those different rates of vibration are called *planes*," Dwight explained. "There are seven planes all together that range from the densest physical matter, through the emotional and mental planes, to higher planes that vibrate ever faster, to the most subtle one, which we can hardly conceive of. In fact, we can't. But we give different names to it, like the Absolute, the Prime Mover, the Ground of all Being, Brahman, the Tao, Buddha Nature … or just simply—God."

When Dwight announced that there was no empty space in the universe, I was bewildered. "How is it possible?" I asked. "There is so much space all around us." I waved my arms around my living room and the sky outside.

Dwight smiled. "That 'empty space' is the *etheric*," he replied.

Ether? I'd heard that word before. It's the substance used in the past to put patients to sleep before a surgery.

But Dwight corrected me. "The etheric is a more subtle plane of matter than the physical dense. Think of ether," he tried to create a vivid picture, "as an invisible sea that permeates everything. Physical objects, such as galaxies, planets, humans, are immersed in it. In this vast etheric ocean all objects are interconnected, every planet with every other planet, star, human being, plant, or rock, and they affect one another."

"Oh, now I understand the saying: 'When a butterfly flutters its wings on one side of the Earth, the ripples can cause a tornado on the other side.'" I beamed.

"Exactly. What's more, every physical object has an etheric counterpart that surrounds and interpenetrates it like a blueprint. This etheric energy grid has been photographed by Kirlian, a Russian scientist. In cutting-edge science, it is referred to as a 'bio-electric energy field.'"

"But," I had an afterthought, "how come we don't perceive the etheric?"

"Oh, very simple. Our visual apparatus can't register higher frequency vibrations, just as it can't register radio waves, or microwaves, or electricity, right? But there are exceptions. Some people can perceive etheric frequencies, and they describe them as golden filaments or tubes. In the future, the human race will develop etheric vision."

Still other ideas were more of a shock. Once when we were discussing Jung's *Memories, Dreams, Reflections*, I commented how strange it was that Jung was afraid of going to Rome.

"It's very easy to explain," Dwight said breezily with a wave of a hand. "Jung didn't want to face his past life memories. Obviously, he had an incarnation there before."

Now that came as a surprise to me—past lives?

Instead of answering my question, Dwight asked another question, "You want to know about reincarnation? Okay, what do you think is the goal of the Soul?"

Like I would know! I shrugged.

"Well, the Soul, too, is learning and growing. And how do you think it can grow if it doesn't have repeated opportunities?"

Good point. I'd never thought of that.

"We grow through experimenting, trying, making mistakes, and learning from them," Dwight went on. "So does the Soul. Every time the Soul goes through one cycle of life, it accumulates experiences, develops skills, expands understanding ... through the vehicle of an incarnated personality—you. The Soul learns and experiences the world through you," he pronounced the last words slowly, emphasizing each one, then just to make sure I got it, he rephrased.

"You are like a TV screen for the Soul—it lives vicariously through you. That's why we all go through a multitude of lives so that we—and our Souls through us—can know what it means to be a soldier, a miner, a king, a beggar, a nun, a prostitute, a thief, an artist ... you get the point?" Dwight paused, fixing his gaze upon me.

I was thinking feverishly. Somewhere deep down what he was saying rang true. But my mind, my rational conditioning was fighting furiously. An inner battle was raging. I asked, "But how can you know this? Nobody ever came back from the other side to tell us."

"Not true," Dwight brushed me off. "Read all the accounts of near-death experiences. Those people were dead clinically, then came back to life." Then he added in another tone of voice, "Jesus, too, taught reincarnation."

"Jesus? I've never heard *that*!"

"Of course not. It was condemned as anathema by Justinian, at the Second Council at Constantinople in the sixth century. From then on reincarnation fell out of public teaching and got lost to the Western world. But it has always been taught in every Eastern religion. And it remained in the teachings of Gnosticism, the esoteric counterpart of Christianity."

"Wait a second ... are you saying that reincarnation was part of mainstream Christianity until as late as sixth century?"

"Very much so." He shook his head vigorously. "One of the early church fathers, Origen, codified it into a doctrine in the third century."

Dwight should know this, I was thinking; his Ph.D. was in Medieval History. "But why was it condemned then?"

"Because of the fight for power and control, obviously. By condemning the teaching of rebirth, the Church secured its supremacy. Think about it: if we had *only* one life, then our salvation would depend entirely on the intermediary of the Church. But if we indeed do reincarnate repeatedly—as the Ageless Wisdom says, as all the Eastern religions teach, as Jesus proclaimed—then the responsibility for our salvation would be our own, and would depend on our efforts alone, not on the church, right?"

I fell silent. It made sense. But this was such a big change in my beliefs that I was reeling from all the implications. I had to rethink my whole life!

I suddenly remembered two dreams I'd had one after another when I was about fifteen. *I was on stage, dancing, but I in the dream didn't look like me in real life. I was pirouetting on my toes in the pool of light. Then I heard a voice, a male voice that said: "In your previous life you were a ballerina, a prima-ballerina."* It was so weird that I dismissed the dream. My previous life? What previous life? But the following night, the dream was repeated. *Again, a male voice without a face said: "And in the life before you were a ballerina also."*

Dwight mistook my silence for disagreement so he went on, "Really, when you look at it without preconceptions, reincarnation is not such an outrageous concept. All it means is that manifestation is cyclical. Nothing else. And we don't have to look farther than nature for the examples of cycles in life. Take trees: they lose their leaves and become dormant during winter, then return to life in spring, and bigger than before. Likewise, we, as Souls, spend our winters out of manifestation then return to this world in the spring of another incarnation. In and out, birth and death, ebb and flow… life is cyclical, from the smallest scale of cells in our bodies, to the largest scale of galaxies in the universe. Cycles. Periodicity. Rebirth. Reincarnation."

Once I came to terms with this Law of Reincarnation, as the Ageless Wisdom refers to it, it was only one small step to accepting the next law—the Law of Karma. Over the months of our studying, Dwight repeated many times his favorite metaphor of Earth being a school. "We are here, in this Earth-school," he'd say over and over, "so that we learn how to develop more of our higher nature and gain better control over our lower nature. Earth is like an obstacle course, where we build our spiritual muscles through hardship, mistakes, and suffering. The way this is done is through karma," he pronounced.

In the past, I'd wince at this word. It sounded so heavy, like a judge's gavel after the death sentence. *Karma*, something inexorable, like a massive slab of stone that seals the opening of a pyramid (and I'm inside). So Dwight would often tell me, "Don't get hung up on words. They don't matter. Think of concepts." And the concept behind this Sanskrit word which means, simply, "action" is that every action has its reaction, or a consequence.

"We don't need to use a Sanskrit word," Dwight would add. "We have our Western equivalent, the good old Newton's Law of Cause and Effect: For every action there is an equal and opposite reaction." Then he asked me to give some examples of it. My mind stalled and I couldn't think of anything.

"C'mon," he nudged me, "you don't have to write a dissertation, just think of everyday situations."

"Everyday situations? Like, say, if I dial the number of my friend, her phone will ring?"

"Uh-huh. It's that simple."

"Or if I buy an expensive pair of shoes, my bank account will be reduced?"

Dwight laughed. "A very *Svetlanesque* example. Or try a little more pertinent example. If you are depressed and brooding over your break-up with a boyfriend, you'll dump low frequency energy that will affect people around you."

I made little embarrassed coughs. How many times have I done that in the past! All my passionate relationships and even more passionate break-ups. All the tears and dark, dark thoughts.

"Or on the other hand, if you cultivate joy and gratitude, you will radiate energy of much higher frequency that will color the atmosphere around you," Dwight concluded.

Several years later, our teacher Kostas would repeat these words in a somewhat different way. He called karma the Law of Balance. "Actions, emotions, and thoughts may not get balanced right away," he'd say in his full, booming voice, "but, in the final analysis, they will be. As you sow, so shall you reap—through lifetime after lifetime."

I'm gazing through the window at the gray sea and the pallid sky that begins to flush pink on the horizon. It won't be long before we reach Italy. The trip takes about ten hours and we've been sailing the whole day, the whole gray, cloudy day. The curtain of clouds finally lifts on the western horizon, just enough to let the drowsy sun shine through before retiring. The sea is bathed in a golden glow. A shaft of golden light floods the lounge through the far left window.

What have I learned from the past three years with Kostas? I ask myself. I see our teacher's face, powerful and daunting, yet compassionate. We stare at each other, a long, deep gaze, deep as this inky shade of blue that has painted the sea.

"Always you have to remember," his words materialize in my head, "theoretical knowledge is all fine and necessary, but if it is not put into practice, it is not assimilated. In the final analysis, it is not through what we *say* but through what we *are* that we make a difference in our environment. It is our example that matters, not our words."

That's exactly why my heart leaped when I met Kostas—because beneath the severe and tough façade, the loud voice, and commanding behavior, there was a depth of love and an uncompromising integrity. He never took one penny for the spiritual or healing services he generously provided to many Cypriots and foreigners. All lectures, consultations, and healing treatments were always free. "How can I charge for healing?" he'd say with a shrug. "It is not me who is doing it. I am just a conduit for higher power." So he made a living as owner of an auto repair shop.

At this point, I open my journal and make a new entry:

My 38th birthday on the ferry from Greece to Italy.

I'm deeply grateful to Kostas for teaching me how to walk my talk. I will call those lessons:

MY THREE FUNDAMENTALS:

1. Practice harmlessness. Or, as Kostas repeated a zillion times, "Do not offend." It goes without saying that I shouldn't offend, not only with words and deeds, but also with my emotions and thoughts.

2. Examine your motives. Always ask yourself, "Why do I do this?" and "Who wants it, the personality or the Soul?" Because the lower self, or ego, or present personality (as Kostas called it) is a most devious and cunning fellow; it will try to trick you on every step of the path.

3. Express goodwill. Cultivate simple altruism or, as Kostas said, "be helpful and kind to your fellow human beings."

That's it. Simple and succinct. Harmlessness. Motives. Goodwill. Now I have to live those Three Fundamentals: Ha-Mo-Go. Live them daily, hourly, by the minute—"

At this moment a mother and a son enter the lounge and sit at the table next to me. In the usual Greek way, they speak loudly. The boy is restless and keeps asking for something, while the mother keeps shaking her head, "*Oxi, oxi!* No, no!" Then the boy jumps up and bolts to the door. The mother launches after him, gives him a spanking, and the boy bursts into tears and screams.

Darn it! I dart irritated eyefuls at them, but the mother is completely oblivious. She brings the boy back to the table and now they continue in a duet: she yells at him and he hollers with tears streaming down his face. *I can't stand it!* My goodwill is shattered, my motives are highly personal, and I shoot hostile angry thoughts at them. I slam my notebook theatrically and in an indignant way rise to my feet, push back the chair with a screech, then bang it down on the floor. No effect. The mother pinches the boy's arm and his screams rise to a shrieking pitch. *Oh, this is unbearable.* I pack up my things and leave the lounge.

Defeated, I stand by the railing, watching the waves foam against the boat. I'm trying to calm my irritation. *Why is it so difficult to walk your talk? Why is it so darn difficult…?* In my mind's eye, I see Kostas' smiling face.

"You do not want to fight your negative tendencies," he said once, "because when you fight something, you energize it, you give it fuel through thinking about it. Instead, you want to direct your attention to its opposite and cultivate the positive aspect. Do not fight fear, cultivate courage; do not fight depression, cultivate joy." He looked through his large glasses at all of us in the room, and I could swear his eyes stopped on me.

"But that's so difficult," I piped up despite myself and immediately felt embarrassed.

"Of course it is," he smiled with compassion, his voice turning just a tiny bit mellow. "The most difficult thing in the world."

He kept his gaze upon me for one long moment, his eyes radiating love of the kind that a mother feels when watching her toddler wobble unsteadily. Then he said slowly, "Even masters can't be perfect or infallible as long as they live within a dense-physical body. Do not idealize them. Teachers and gurus are also human beings prone to ordinary human weaknesses."

That's why he never allowed us to address him as a master or even a teacher. "I'm your brother. I'm no different from you," he'd say over and over, a wide grin on his daunting face. "When you finally perfect yourself, you will not need the body any longer," he joked. "But you know what … let us not go into that. It is so, so far ahead that, rather than speculate about it, we had better direct our attention and efforts to the problems at hand, such as our meditation exercise.…"

The ship begins to heave on the slow-rolling waves: a long, slow, dizzy dip, and a fainting swoon upwards; the long, slow lift and the long, slow slide forward; the long, slow, rhythmic rise and fall—quite gentle, but dizzying, this gallop of the sea.

It won't be long before we reach Italy.

CHAPTER 4

SICILY:

UNDER THE VOLCANO

If you look at the map of Italy, you'll see how much this country literally resembles a boot, a very tall, above-the-knee boot, stepping between two seas: the Adriatic on the right, and the Tyrrhenian on the left. This perfectly-shaped riding boot even sports a spur (Gargano Promontory). So it's only natural, I think, that Italians became such skilled shoemakers and that Italian shoes are so famous all over the world. And of course, being a shoe-lover, I'm drawn to this country.

How exciting, I'm going to be living in a shoe!

We've spent our first night in Taranto, a major port on the inner side of the Italian heel. So now we are driving along the arch of the sole toward the toe, where we'll catch a ferry to Sicily. This is the southernmost part of Italy, the part that, in the shoe analogy, walks the roads and touches the ground; the part of Italy that has endured centuries of foreign occupation, decline and poverty—a backward, fatalistic region baked by fierce sun. At least that's what you see in the old Italian movies. And what we are seeing now are muddy roads, torn trees, and huge water pockets everywhere. It must have been raining buckets before we arrived!

What I don't understand is this feeling that has overcome me, the feeling of anxiety that is rising like a river after heavy storms and has turned into naked fear. Is this a premonition of another car accident? The one we had in Delphi, a week ago, left our Honda Prelude without the front bumper and blind in one eye. And it happened because we switched to driving on the right side of the road after three years of driving on the left (a British legacy to Cyprus).

After a couple of hours, we come to an area of devastation: torn trees are lying like dead soldiers by the road, houses are squatting in water, and our Honda is plowing through a thick layer of mud. "There is your explanation," motions Dwight with his head. "You've been picking up on the panic of people. Looks like they had serious flash floods here." Dwight was right. Later we found out that people were caught by torrents gushing through the canyons. There were many casualties, some of whom were camping in the dry riverbed when the rainstorm hit. It was the day after the flooding that we drove through the inundated area.

When we arrive at Crotone my fear begins to fade away and I start to relax. I'm actually quite curious because this is *the* famous ancient Croton, the home of the Pythagoras Academy. Besides being the brilliant mathematician who left us the Pythagorean Theorem and the Tetractys (the perfect triangle), Pythagoras was the first in the Western world to call himself a philosopher, meaning "lover of wisdom" (from Greek *philo,* "love" and *sophia,* "wisdom"). His legacy was so fundamental in the development of the Western mind that some modern philosophers consider Pythagoras the most influential of all the Western philosophers. The Academy of Pythagoras was the first western esoteric school to teach the principles of the Ageless Wisdom: formulated in the remote sixth century BC, Pythagoras' teaching of the transmigration of the soul (in other words—reincarnation) would influence Plato's philosophy, as well as the later development of esoteric thought in Europe.

Crotone is the very south of the South. We are driving along the very sole of the boot, and on the other side of the street is the end of Italy and the Ionian Sea. Which, as we slowly edge through the Sunday afternoon traffic, is getting wilder and wilder, waves crashing into and spilling over the stone barrier, while dark-gray clouds are piling up in heavy heaps on the horizon.

My initial plans to explore the hills above Crotone and search for the site of Pythagoras' Academy are dashed. The sky is so menacing that it would be sheer foolishness to wade through the already muddy hill slopes. We don't even want to follow the road along the sole, but decide to take a shortcut, a "strap" as it were, to the toe of the boot. So we drive through a sea of fog to Reggio di Calabria, where we catch a ferry to Sicily.

The small town of Piedimonte Etneo is located underneath the volcano of Etna and it's about as typical a Sicilian town as can be found. The reason we've come here is to meet with a friend from Cyprus who is actually Sicilian and had moved back to the island only a few months ago with his new Swedish girlfriend, a tall, blonde, willowy former model. We were close friends with

Lorenzo in Cyprus, having had much in common: dedication to spiritual values, love of art, a tendency to look at the bigger picture. Lorenzo is one of the most creative persons I've known in my life. I love his poetry and absolutely adore his paintings: colors bursting with light and brush strokes exuding wonder and freedom.

When I first met Lorenzo, I was struck by his mesmerizing, lustrous sea-green eyes that dominated the landscape of his face. Imagine my surprise when I saw similar green eyes walking the streets of Catania, Taormina, and other Sicilian towns. I don't know from which conqueror Sicilians got those emerald-green eyes. Sicily was invaded enough times to have collected a bit of every ethnicity: Phoenician, Greek, Roman, Byzantine, Saracen, Norman, Spanish.

But those eyes … there was something else about them. When I overcame their immediate magnetism I started noticing another quality. Somewhere deep down, past the surface ripples of sensuality and warmth, there was the coldness of ocean depths. Deep down at their core, those eyes were beautiful like marble.

My first days in Sicily passed in a strange state of detachment. I was expecting to feel ecstatic, exuberant, buoyant. After all, it's so beautiful here, nature so lavishly green, the landscape so picturesque. After all, we are staying in a place that offers spectacular views: down the verdant hills to the unending sweep of lapis-blue sea, and behind the house up the cone of Etna to a scoop of white clouds atop the crater. After all, this *is* the beginning of our life in Italy. So what's the matter with me?

Dwight would like to know that too. He says I'm just not myself. I tend to agree—I feel frazzled, unhappy, and above all, nostalgic. I catch myself thinking of our travels in Greece, remembering the sharp heights of Delphi, the massive antiquity of Mycenae, the luminous quality of light on Rhodes, the sense of freedom, expansion, and lightness I felt under the Grecian sky. Here wherever I look, there are abandoned houses, sometimes even whole towns—like Castiglione—empty, forlorn, ghostly in their emptiness. There is a strange feeling of lifelessness as we walk the streets of Giardini, Linguaglossa, Piedimonte. Surprisingly few shops, a trickle of people in the streets, no stalls selling goods on the pavement, no hangout *piazzas*, and worst of all—no cafés with outdoor seating. *Am I really in Italy?* Everything and everyone seems to be locked inside. Life is taking place indoors, behind heavy doors, shuttered windows, stone walls, in the dim shadows of palm trees, in the silence of unuttered words, unsung songs, unscreamed cries of children.

This is a strange place, Sicily.

"Not strange," disagrees Lorenzo when I tell him of my impressions. "Only poor and afraid." But afraid of what? "Of death, of soldiers, of invasions, of hunger, of Mafia," he says in his slow and soft voice, with expressive lifting of eyebrows used as punctuation marks. Then he tells a story that etches in my memory.

His grandmother used to coo to the children, saying, "*Te mazzo.* (I'll kill you.)" Because that's what her mother used to tell her, and her mother's mother before her, all the way back into the past, throughout the centuries of being invaded, occupied, killed, pillaged, and raped by foreign armies. Families would hide in the bushes on the hillsides hoping that soldiers wouldn't discover them. But a baby's cry, a child's scream would give them away and everybody would be slaughtered. So mothers would threaten children that they'd kill them if they cried. The habit remained even after foreign armies were long gone, but changed its connotation and became "baby talk."

Like the rest of southern Italy, Sicily suffered badly under the occupying forces, whether the royal houses of Aragon, Anjou, or Bourbon. Sicily's fertile soil was exploited, its forests cleared, its people used, and the island was prevented from developing. "Sicily was treated like a fertile cow, milked but never fed," Lorenzo adds, "and so it became impoverished." When in 1870 Garibaldi's revolution finally united all the separate bits of the Italian continent—the forlorn South, the stodgy Papal states, the independence-loving hill-towns of middle Italy, the industrious North—Sicilians faced a grim future. There was no work, and no food. Akin in some ways to the Irish potato famine, the hopelessness of Sicily's struggle for survival impelled half of the population to immigrate to America, in particular to New York. That was the beginning of Little Italy.

Around the time of Garibaldi's revolution, amid poverty and general lawlessness, the Mafia was born. Ruled by a strict code of conduct, the Mafia was a secretive society that operated mostly in the western part of the island, with its seat in Palermo. The sociological phenomenon of this organization is, of course, much more complicated, but it is a reflection of the dire situation in Sicily at that time. (The older cousin of the Mafia, the Camorra, sprang up in Naples a couple of centuries earlier under similar social conditions—occupying forces were unable to maintain social order, while at the same time inflicting poverty on the population. By contrast, no such criminal organizations appeared in the affluent and independent North.)

Everything I've so far said about Sicily—this underlying dismal energy, the vague sense of oppression, the sadness of abandoned houses—all this disappeared, as if magically erased, when we started to ascend the road to Taormina. Ascent is a good word to describe the steep precipice one must climb to reach this "most beautiful town in the world," according to the famous Indian teacher Krishnamurti. (His second choice was Ojai, near Santa Barbara, where my romance with Dwight began.) The list of Taormina's famous residents is really impressive: Alexandre Dumas, Anatole France, André Gide, Paul Klee, Oscar Wilde, Friedrich Nietzsche, Richard Wagner.... In the early twentieth century, the town was a colony of expatriate artists, writers, and intellectuals, my favorite being D.H. Lawrence. (The villa where he had stayed on and off for two years, later became home to Truman Capote.)

I can't agree more with the choice of all these artists. Taormina is so beautiful that it almost hurts. You feel like pinching yourself just to make sure it's not an illusion. This is really how I imagine my dream place: the vibrant explosion of Mediterranean vegetation cascading down the steep slopes, lemon and orange groves, fragrant bushes of mimosa and jasmine, ripe vines shading terraces that overlook a craggy coastline, cypresses needling silence around them, majestic palms swaying in the breeze, and my favorite—the fireworks of oleanders and bougainvillea shooting pinks and reds and whites wherever you look. Elegant villas painted in Roman terracotta dot the hillside. And from every point on the road, from every curve—there is The View. The breathtaking, sweeping, majestic view of the deep blue sea. Ionian Sea. And on it, as if on some huge canvas, the brush-like wakes of sailboats and yachts paint white streaks on the shimmering surface.

I must have been gushing insufferably about the beauty of Taormina because Lorenzo coolly said that he never came here during the summer season. I flinched. "It's so crowded you can't drive around ... or even walk through the streets." He shrugged and flung out his arms to emphasize the hopelessness of summer in Taormina.

I understood why Lorenzo didn't come here in summer when, all of a sudden, an onslaught of people flooded the street. The main Corso Umberto, where we were strolling leisurely, was invaded by an army of tourists—the human cargo of a monstrous cruise boat. Thousands of people were dumped in the narrow streets of, really, quite a small town. We dodged them by escaping to the Greek theater, one of the most celebrated ruins on the island. Perched high up on a hill-terrace, it resembles an abode of gods: it contemplates not only the sea, but also the whole coastline to the south, presided over by the dignified, secretive Etna.

Dwight immediately fell in love with the volcano. He was so fascinated by the imposing cone of the "wicked witch" (as D.H. Lawrence called Etna), that he wasn't the least bit interested in the theater. He sat on the stone steps and steadily gazed at Etna. I wasn't sure what fascinated him so about volcanoes. They seem scary to me; like grumpy old men they puff smoke, sometimes grumble and tremble and cough, and occasionally erupt in violent fits of rage.

But leave it up to me to find *the* beautiful setting for enjoying the view. Like a homing pigeon I was drawn to an elegant hotel and landed on a large terrace with cast-iron tables, cushioned chairs, and open umbrellas—everything provided just for the purpose of enjoying the view. The cappuccino was served in elegant cups with silver spoons, an assortment of biscotti placed like an open fan on the table. Dwight looked at me amused and said, "This is the style you'd like to get accustomed to, isn't it?" But in the next moment, he approvingly dipped an almond biscotto into his cappuccino and smiled blissfully.

Today, on the day of the Full Moon, we ionized Etna.

I know this must sound like a strange thing to say, but this event would later play such a key part in Dwight's own quest, as well as our journey, that I have to give it proper attention.

It all began in Cyprus when our acupuncturist friend Yuri first demonstrated to us the use of a pendulum. The pendulum is only one of the tools that can be used for the purpose of dowsing. Other tools are angle-rods, y-rods (forked twigs), bobbers, or your good old metal coat hanger (cut in two and cropped to make two pistol-shaped wires), Dwight's tool of choice.

Although dowsing has often been ridiculed and dismissed in the past, it has sloughed off its quackish reputation since proving to be an invaluable tool in finding underground sources of water. England is far ahead of America in accepting dowsing as an art and a science in its own right, which is useful in finding not only water, but also minerals and hidden or lost objects.

But dowsing has another, if more tenuous and esoteric, application: registering currents of Earth energy. This energy has been known by various names, from the Druidic *Wouivre* or "serpent current," to the Australian Aborigines' "Earth spirit," to the more modern "terrestrial energy" and "telluric force." All these names have been used to denote and describe the animating but invisible power of the Earth, the vital Life Force on which everything depends.

Today many dowsers regard this energy as electro-magnetic in essence. Others compare these currents that flow over the surface of the Earth to acupuncture meridians, and the places where they intersect to meridian points. There are so many currents—weaker, stronger, wider, narrower—which cross and crisscross each other that a comparison with the human nervous or circulatory system might offer a more vivid analogy.

Even though modern civilization is mostly out of touch with this energy, examples of its interaction with living beings are numerous. Birds, for example, follow Earth currents in their migrations. And so did people of the past. Ancient pilgrim routes frequently coincided with these currents, while Australian Aborigines walked the paths of Earth energy in their "dream time." Ancient shrines, sanctuaries, and oracles, as well as Christian churches before the Reformation, were invariably situated on these pathways. Civilized humanity has forgotten what people of the past knew very well: that Earth energy has a definite effect on every living thing, from its more subtle effects on human consciousness, to its more tangible effects in healing the body.

According to Yuri, everyone has the potential to dowse. Some of us develop it into a reliable technique (or even a medical diagnostic tool, as he did), while the rest of us toy with it (as I do), "penduluming" foods for pesticides, vitamins for their quality in processing, and occasionally maps and hotels to choose where to stay. Yuri compared the human body to a highly sensitive instrument that can register subtle frequencies in the environment. But this instrument needs "meter needles" to show those frequencies. That's the role of dowsing rods (or pendulums). As quantum biologist and former Stanford Research Fellow Bruce Lipton demonstrated, our subconscious can register twenty million stimuli per second, but our conscious mind can process *only* forty. And so, where do the other 19,999,960 stimuli go? They remain stored in our subconscious, without our ever becoming aware of their presence in our database. That's why we use dowsing rods—to help us transfer subconscious stimuli into the conscious part of our mind.

"Dowsing is a strange skill," Yuri told us at the beginning of our apprenticeship. "You have to train your mind to focus only on what you are looking for."

As Dwight later put it, the trick is to tune your mind like a radio station, to receive *only* the signals you intend to find.

The second prerequisite for dowsing is to relax your body and your thoughts. This means that before you begin, you have to empty your mind of other contents that can interfere with the reception. (And this is where I stumble, even before I start!) Many times Dwight has tried to coach me in achieving this state of "intense relaxation."

"*Relax* completely your body and your thoughts," he would repeat, "but keep your intention in mind and totally *concentrate* on the goal."

Yeah, good luck!

The third rule in dowsing is that questions must be phrased with perfect clarity and precision; dowsing rods do *not* respond to any judgment questions or to a vague wanting to know. As you phrase your question in yes-or-no form, your dowsing tool responds by moving into its designated way for "yes" or "no" answers.

And that's the fourth thing you need to learn in dowsing: what are the yes-no movements of your dowsing tool. Usually, rods cross to make an "X" when you hit the water source; the forked twig or bobbers start to yo-yo. But the pendulum might have several different movements—clockwise and counter-clockwise, back-and-forth, or left-right. Obviously, you have to learn the "language" of your tool before it can communicate with you.

Dwight was way ahead of me in dowsing. Actually he was quite a "natural." He practiced diligently, first indoors, finding the harmful radiation of household appliances (about which I'll say more later). Then he moved outdoors, dowsing for water and Earth currents. Finally, he started experimenting with rocks and discovered that different kinds of rock—sedimentary, igneous, or metamorphic—have different energy. And then, like a catalyst, came an unexpected prod of fate: an Ayurvedic doctor friend gave Dwight a stone (quite an ordinary pebble, in my opinion) which he claimed would raise the energy level of igneous rock. He called this shift in energy—ionization.

"Ionization," Dwight replied to Lorenzo's question about the actual mechanism at work, "is raising the vibratory level of a rock. This is achieved by tightening, in other words, reducing the spin radius of its electrons."

Like the good teacher that he is, Dwight then used the analogy of the solar system to clarify his explanation. The solar system, when you think about it, is really like a big atom: the Sun as its nucleus, the planets orbiting like electrons. "Reducing the spin radius of electrons is like moving planets into orbits closer to the Sun. Now, what would happen if the planets were to orbit closer to the Sun?" Dwight asked a rhetorical question, then replied, "On Earth, the year would shorten, time would speed up, or perhaps, we would perceive it differently altogether. Also, we would have more kinetic energy. But most importantly, the atoms in our bodies would spin faster and make us more aware, so that we become able to tune into higher levels of consciousness."

For some reason, neither Lorenzo nor his girlfriend Brigit found this explanation far-out. They both thought for a while, then Lorenzo said, "Why don't we ionize Etna?"

That's how all four of us found ourselves on a lava road that runs down the crater of Etna somewhere around Nikolosi, the village closest to the crater. When you look at the volcano from, say, Taormina, it's difficult to tell exactly where it begins. The mountain trails up in a long craggy line from the sea's edge to the blunt cone, and there isn't really a clear demarcation line. And on the slopes, like a colorful pleated skirt, villages with their lemon and blood-orange groves, fruit orchards, grape vines, and pecan trees surround the cone. In the past, Etna had destroyed these villages many times, and occasionally its lava had flowed all the way down to the sea, obliterating Catania on the western coast in the late seventeenth century, and wiping out Messina in the north at the turn of the past century. Unlike its cousin Vesuvius above Naples, Etna is *always* active. It smokes, rumbles, shakes, periodically spews out lava and spits out pumice, and the ashes frequently flake over trees, cars, and laundry drying on the lines. Because of volcanic debris, the soil under Etna is unusually fertile. The fruit and vegetables grown here taste better than anywhere else in Sicily, and the yields are abundant. This is the reward that the volcano bestows upon its residents, to make up for the anxiety she causes and the destruction she inflicts. Fair enough.

The day was clear and warm, and a sense of expectant silence hung all around us as we stood on the lava flow facing the smoking cone. Despite my initial discomfort caused by the proximity of the volcano, I now looked in awe at the sight of the plume of white smoke trailing up into the sky. It was as though Etna were smoking a pipe—a peace pipe, quipped Lorenzo. Dwight checked the lava with his coat hangers-turned-dowsing rods; they remained still, like two cocked pistols, in his *intensely relaxed* hands.

Everything was ready for the ceremony. I looked at my companions, and they all seemed to be perfectly at ease, alert with anticipation. I felt a bit out of place, uncomfortable and insecure. *What exactly was I doing here? Ionizing a volcano??* The skeptical part of my mind began to reel with questioning and disbelief. *A consecration ceremony? Geez....*

From my mental niche I watched the three of them say a little invocation and place the already-ionized pumice from Lorenzo's garden in the three cardinal directions. When my turn came, I stiffly placed another pumice rock in the remaining direction and mumbled something about the expansion of consciousness. When Dwight checked the lava flow his rods jumped and spun, as if the volcano was indeed telling him something. The same reaction happened further down past the asphalt road, then on the other side of the slope, and finally by Lorenzo's house. The ionization had spread in all directions, as far as the edge of lava flow. I decided to rethink my initial reaction to the ionization feat.

Later that afternoon, in a gem shop in Linguaglossa, I saw a necklace made of blue lace agate stones, my favorite shade of blue. This necklace became my belated birthday present—to always remind me of this baffling, yet fascinating exploration of consciousness.

When I woke up the next morning, our last morning in Sicily, I stepped out onto the side terrace where we had the view of Etna. In the unusual crispness of the morning air, the cone of Etna stood out, beautifully chiseled. Two columns of smoke—dark-gray and pearl-white—rose from the crater and braided up into the sky, intertwining gently. There was something numinous about this sight, as if the whole volcano had been purified.

When we came to Lorenzo's for a farewell visit, he said that he'd never seen Etna puffing two columns of smoke of distinctly different colors. "There was a change," he marveled, "I can feel it in the air." All of us did. We gathered behind his house, at the farthest end of his orange grove, to look together at the volcano one last time. And we watched her at length, quietly, admiringly, in silent communion.

This is how we bade farewell to Sicily.

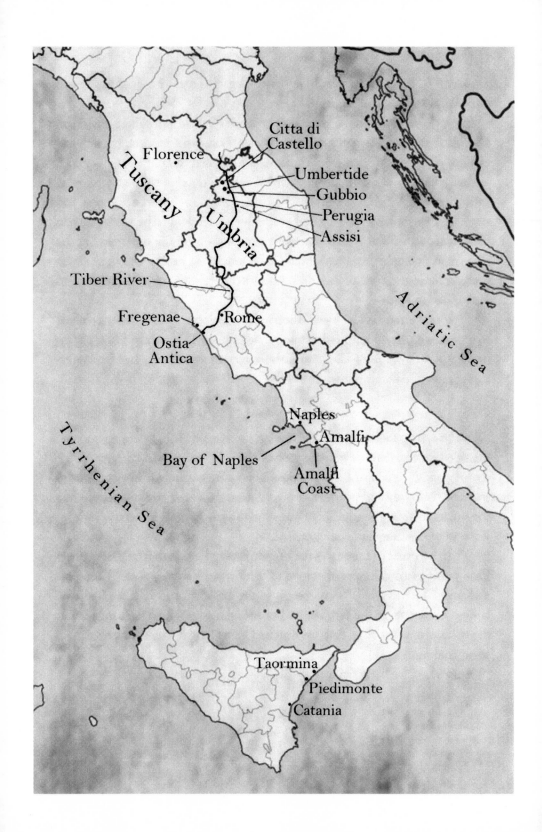

PART 2

CRISSCROSSING ITALY:
WHERE IS MY GUIDANCE?

CHAPTER 5

OSTIA ANTICA AND UMBRIA:
A VISION VEILED

Our drive up the boot, toward Rome, passed in sweet expectation. I drove, heart aflutter, as if going on a first date. At last we were headed toward Ostia Antica, a little town just outside of Rome, where the Tiber River flows into the Tyrrhenian Sea—a town where I'd had a vision of moving to Italy almost a year ago.

In the distant past, Ostia had been a vital port of the Roman Empire, where cargos of grain were unloaded daily to feed the exploding population of neighboring Rome. But nowadays Ostia Antica is seemingly an insignificant town—a town-museum, if you will—whose only attraction is the extensive and well-preserved ruins of ancient Ostia. And it was there, sitting atop the amphitheater and gazing at the parasol pines that I had felt infused with a compelling urge to move to Italy, the urge I then called my Guidance.

In hindsight, I realize that I had also fallen in love with the sinewy pines, the *pinetas*. I gazed at their wide crowns that spread out like open umbrellas and felt my heart unlock. Had I been talking about a person instead of a tree, I would have called it love. I felt a peculiar sense of familiarity, as if I belonged where they grew, as if we were a family.

In the past, *pinetas* used to flank all the roads leading to Rome, as well as many avenues on the outskirts of the eternal city. They were the darlings of the Romans. I had first heard of them in an orchestral work when I was in my early teens. My mother had come home with a record she bought for me—Ottorino Respighi's *The Pines of Rome*. I listened and imagined myself in another world, in another period. I saw Roman legions march between rows of *pinetas*, victoriously returning home from conquests; I saw packs of Visigoths ferociously run by them to sack Rome; I saw the Renaissance *gentiles* trot by them on their way to their country estates; and peasants, seeking shade and rest under their crowns; and lovers, sitting underneath them in passionate moonlit embraces. When my mother and I made a trip to Rome a couple of years later, I saw the *pinetas* for the first time. They looked so beautiful to me, delicate and strong at the same time, just as Respighi's composition is both lyrical and powerful. Then I understood his inspiration to compose such magnificent music for, well, trees.

But the beauty of nature, even when revered in music, even when adored by people, even when protected by law, cannot withstand human greed. After World War II the *pinetas* got in the way of construction development and profit-hungry real estate companies. In the 1960s a wave of mysterious dying off, like an epidemic, spread through the *pineta* population and decimated it. Rumor has it that the developers had hired "tree hit men" who surreptitiously, under the cover of night, injected hot water into the trees. After the *pinetas* slowly died off, the land was available for developing.

I'm glad I didn't know this at the time of my first visit to Ostia Antica. It would have spoiled the idealistic image of Romans I had formed on my previous trips to Italy. And I'm also glad I didn't know that the very people who were supposed to protect the *pinetas* had set them on fire just a week before we arrived. (A clique in the Government Organization for the Protection of the Natural Environment had a strong disagreement with the new appointments within the organization, so they decided to express their disagreement mafia style.)

Now as we drive along the ancient Roman Apia Antica that connects Rome to Ostia, we stare, stunned and aghast, at the sight of a charred forest. The blackened trunks protrude from the blackened earth like corpses; the charred branches stick out as if frozen in terror. The air is thick with heavy energy, so heavy that even the traffic slows down. My throat fills with swallowed tears and chokes me.

Luckily, Ostia Antica is nearby, so I have to turn my attention to finding the address of our American contact here, a former secretary of my Congressman friend from Illinois. Marie lives in the medieval part of Ostia Antica. When I first called her from Cyprus to arrange our meeting, I'd launched eagerly, "Well, how amazing that you live in Ostia where we want to—"

"No, no, no," she cut me off. "I don't live in Ostia. I live in Ostia *Antica*. It's a *huge* difference. Ostia is just a modern, plain beach town. But Ostia Antica has a soul."

We have arrived in front of the massive walls of the fifteenth-century castle. Dwight triumphantly turns off the engine after parking our accident-battered Honda. With a sigh of relief he says, "There! I got us here almost intact!" Then he turns to me and declares, as if passing the ball, "Now it's up to you and your Guidance to get us to where we need to be."

With enthusiasm and confidence, I get out of the car and follow the directions to Marie's home, situated inside the medieval *borgo*, a strictly pedestrian area. When we find the house, the door is wide open and Marie is watering the plants.

"Where did you park?" she asks as soon as we exchange greetings.

When she hears that we left the car on the main street, she clicks her tongue in disapproval. "No, no, no," she says quickly, vigorously shaking her head, "that's not a good place. Thieves break into cars and steal everything." So she instructs us to park the car behind her home, in the no-parking, no-traffic zone of the *borgo*—the only place where it's safe.

Our Honda is now tucked in right behind Marie's laundry drying in the middle of the street. "What a weird place to dry clothes!" I blurt out.

"Oh, but there is nowhere else to dry them," she hurries to explain, as she shows us her peculiar living arrangement—her bedroom and bathroom are *across* the street. (Truth be told, medieval streets are very narrow; you can cross them in a few steps.) But come to think of it, where *did* they actually dry their clothes in the Middle Ages?

We go back to Marie's living room (on the other side of the street), where five cats are perched on various pieces of furniture, and plunk down on the soft armchairs. Everything in the room seems plush and tucked in: piles of cushions on the floor, two overstuffed sofas with clusters of pillows, several throws hugging the chairs, heavy curtains pulled aside to reveal vibrant geraniums in window planters, huge ferns filling up the corners. Only the heavy, dark beams above our heads had managed to escape the "softening" and seem to glower down with hardness and indignation.

Marie busies herself with refreshments. Bubbly and cheerful, she moves about like a hummingbird, preparing tea cups and cookies and fruit and telling us the history of Ostia Antica and how she *so* loves it here in the medieval *borgo* that she declined an offer to live in Rome.

"Modern housing complexes are *sooo* ugly, with no charm, don't you think so?" she chirps as she arranges cookies on a plate. "Here everything has character. Every cobblestone street has a story to tell you. It's *sooo* exciting to live in a fifteenth century house, don't you think so?"

"What about something a bit, er, newer?" Dwight asks as he watches Marie struggle to fit a kettle under the faucet in a medieval-looking sink.

But Marie doesn't seem to hear Dwight's question. She opens a cupboard and buries her head inside, trying to extricate an enormous serving tray, very antique-looking. "Soooo different from young and sterile and uniform America, don't you think so?" she continues after she re-emerges from the cupboard. "Here, the history is part of the present. Ahh, I so looove the *scavi!*"

"Me too!" I exclaim, then tell her of my last year's visit to the *scavi* (ruins) of Roman Ostia, and how it has brought us to Italy. Marie now actually stops her kitchen activities and listens to me with full attention. She doesn't comment, but she looks at me in a different way now. Then she nods, pensively, and tells us that she takes walks in the *scavi* almost every day.

"It's like therapy," she says slowly, in a different tone of voice. "The silence of the ruins, of ancient streets, temples, baths, it's so … melancholic. Reminds you how ephemeral life is…"

Her voice trails off. After a whole day of traveling in the September heat, I feel dazed. It's a strange feeling to arrive at a long-yearned-for destination after so many months of planning, preparation, and anticipation. I feel surprisingly detached, almost numb.

So we are here, finally. Really here. And now what?

All of a sudden the immensity of our decision dawns on me, and the reality of finding a place to live sinks in as Marie warns us about the slim rental prospects in Ostia Antica.

"Now it's up to you and your Guidance…." Dwight's words echo in my mind and a sense of responsibility suddenly weighs on me. I feel like I have to deliver now—I or my Guidance. *We* brought us here, so *we* better show up. Just then I feel the first squeeze of uncertainty in my heart. A worm of self-doubt wriggles a bit, as if waking up. But I squash it immediately, confident in the Guidance and my impressions through which it manifests.

So we get up to follow our host to the bed-and-breakfast accommodation that her friend runs as a side job. After we rest for a couple of days and organize ourselves, we'll tackle the housing prospects, I say to myself.

Well, ten days later we are still in Ostia Antica and we haven't found a single rental possibility. What we have found out, however, is that Ostia Antica (outside the *borgo*) is dreary, depressing, windy, humid, and full of mosquitoes.

Three kinds of mosquitoes, at that! The worst bunch being the tiger mosquitoes, a new breed imported from Asia on one of many boats that arrive daily at the modern port of Ostia.

I didn't want to admit it, but I was starting to question my overwhelming certainty about moving here. Every night before going to sleep I replayed my experience at the ancient theater: higher presence in the air, exaltation, ideas for the book, the compelling urge to move, the swooping of this-is-where-I-have-to-be certainty. Everywhere reigned peace and serenity; the peace of an ancient mausoleum, a serenity of wisdom that comes with the passing of time.

Was that all my imagination?... No, it couldn't be! ... Then what was it all about?

"It just means that we shouldn't live in Ostia Antica," Dwight said reassuringly one morning at breakfast after I had run through my monologue of surprise, disbelief, doubt, and discouragement for the umpteenth time. "The Guidance appeared to you in the amphitheater because that's where you happened to be. But that doesn't mean we should live in this place. It's that simple." He shrugged. "So we'd better stop wasting our time here and start looking somewhere else," he concluded in a matter-is-settled tone of voice.

"Yes, but where?"

"I don't know," he shrugged again. "Let's see where synchronicity takes us. We'll just follow the leads."

Dwight's version of Guidance is synchronicity. He had told me years ago, when we were just beginning to study together, that synchronicity is one of the ways through which our Higher Self (that's how he sometimes refers to the Soul) can manifest and guide us. Ever since we made the decision to undertake a spiritual journey five years ago, we've been following the leads that came through synchronistically. It seemed the way to go, the way in which we were directed to where we needed to be.

So this time the lead came through Gianfranco, in whose house we were renting a room. After we had mentioned that we should probably look for a place to stay in another part of Italy, he remembered a friend of a friend who ran an agro-tourism accommodation in Umbria.

"Umbria is a beautiful part of the country," said Gianfranco. "We call it 'the green heart' of Italy. There are many restored farmhouses and the prices are cheaper than in Rome."

Umbria does lie like a heart, as Gianfranco said, right in the middle of the Italian peninsula, both horizontally and vertically. On the left, it's flanked by its more popular and fashionable sister, Toscana; on the right, by the little-known Marche. Between Umbria and Toscana flows the River Tiber, in ancient times a natural borderline between two tribes: the Etruscans on the west side of the river in what is now Toscana, and the Umbri east of the Tiber, in present-day Umbria.

During the Middle Ages, Umbria was plagued by rivalries between fortified, independent hill-towns that fought endlessly with each other. Eventually, almost all of them fell into the clutches of the Papal States, marking the beginning of economic and cultural stagnation in Umbria, a situation that continued until the very recent past. That's why Umbria has also been referred to as the "backwater" of Italy. This can be to our advantage, we figure, because it means that this region has not yet been discovered by the northern invaders hunting for old farmhouses to restore and the sweet life as extolled in Frances Mayes' bestseller *Bella Tuscany*.

We are heading for Umbertide, a small industrial town in the Upper Tiber Valley, about 150 miles north of Rome. Somewhere in the rolling hills above the town is Maridiana, the alpaca farm and *agro-tourismo* run by Gianni, a friend of Gianfranco's friend. "Alpaca farm, how interesting," I chatter in the car while Dwight is driving. I've never seen any alpacas. And I've never been to an *agro-tourismo* either, a very popular type of holiday accommodation: restored old farmhouses with modern amenities, situated in the beautiful Italian countryside.

But as soon as we arrive at Maridiana, our car battery dies. And tomorrow is Sunday, a non-working day. *Is this a sign that we should live here,* I wonder. Then I look around and sigh—*yes*! Wherever I turn unrolls a bird's eye view of spectacularly rolling hills. Like a huge quilt, green patches of woods weave into golden meadows, sewn together with white hems of undulating roads and speckled with gray dots of stone farmhouses. A luminous haze hovers over the horizon, and a sense of unrestrained freedom fills the air. Definitely, this is a place where the Soul can soar. In fact, it's so gorgeous that I have a crush on the landscape—for a short two hours. Then the clouds curdle over the sky and fog swallows the view.

Gianni informs us that he has several promising accommodations lined up for us to see, "very picturesque and desirable." So we set off with him as our guide. I've never had any experience with restored farmhouses. Otherwise I would have known that they are dark and gloomy, with massive stone walls, crudely finished interiors, dark beams pressing heavily from the ceilings, and worst of all, tiny openings in the walls that could hardly be called windows—air holes, perhaps? I've realized that in the Middle Ages large windows were a liability. People had to protect themselves from the cold of winters and attacks by roving marauders. A view? I don't think they even had that concept; it simply wasn't a part of their life experience.

So much for my romantic idea of country living! Gianni will probably think that I'm a spoiled *cittadina* (which sounds so much nicer than the plain English "city girl"), but that doesn't really explain why I experience these farmhouses as oppressive. For me, living in such a house is like wearing a turtleneck in the middle of summer. A view, on the other hand, brings a sense of expansion and stillness of mind. Open space is like a field of endless possibilities where my imagination can roam free and create, pluck inspiration hidden in the heaps of clouds and entangled in the crowns of trees.

Really, all I'm asking for is an attractive, bright, nicely-finished house with a view. I take it back: just one room with a view—my study. And ... I'm even willing to bargain about an attractive interior!

We are disappointed, no question about that. Perhaps sensing our disappointment and wanting to cheer us up, Gianni takes us to see his alpaca farm. He shows us the animals imported from South America, over fifty gentle, big-eyed, silky-haired alpacas, close relatives of llamas. They have something adorable about them like little kittens, and something gentle that you find in cows, and something snuggly like teddy bears. Their hair grows to be very long, soft, and silky (dirty too!), and is then sheared, spun, and woven into exquisite sweaters, cardigans, shawls, and coats.

"Alpaca's wool is much softer than sheep's wool," Gianni explains while I'm admiring one cardigan, *molto carino*, very cute. "It compares to cashmere in its silky feel."

And its price, I find out as I look at the tag.

So this is what Gianni does, I finally understand: a complete production line from alpacas to apparel.

While Gianni is explaining the special dying process they've developed, I look at him with attention really for the first time. And I am amazed to see how much he reminds me of alpacas. Not only because of his whitish, longish hair, but there is also something about his gentle energy that is so alpaca-like. He moves with deliberation, sort of gliding through the air with a little sway (just as alpacas move); his large dark eyes gaze at us, penetrating, yet gentle (just like alpacas' eyes). And when he turns to me, I feel as if he is gazing deep into my heart, past my eyes, and seeing me as a Soul, who I really am—a truly beautiful feeling.

Gianni's life story is quite unusual, we find out while having a morning cappuccino the following day. He escaped the "chaos of Rome" where he was a senior economist in the Ministry for Agriculture and moved to Umbria to start a private enterprise. Since his alpaca farm and the fiber production program are unique in Italy, the European Economic Community has designated Maridiana a demonstration breeding farm and is co-financing the project.

"And why not alpacas?" shrugs Gianni when I ask why he has chosen those animals. "If we can raise sheep, we can raise alpacas too. No?"

We are sitting in an outdoor café on the main *piazza* in Umbertide, a perfect little square framed by medieval *palazzi* and the thirteenth-century church of St. Francis. All around us are locals, not a single tourist in sight. Life goes on, crisscrossing the *piazza*: matrons on their daily errands between a bakery and a grocery and a butcher shop, youngsters self-consciously parading their sunglasses and stopping by the café for a quick espresso at the counter, noisy pensioners hanging around in groups and discussing politics and football. It's so perfectly Italian, the past and present blended harmoniously into one whole.

"Gianni, *eccoti qua! Ho bisogno di te.* (There you are, Gianni. I need you.)"

A straw-blond, middle-aged woman approaches our table and I recognize Noemi, Gianni's assistant, accountant, alpaca-feeder—in brief, a woman with many hats in Maridiana. She has an unexpected problem to discuss with Gianni, but first things first: she orders a cappuccino and we have a friendly chat about her daughters, the apartment in Rome she'd left behind to follow her boss from the Ministry, and her new life in Umbria. Noemi, too, is very warm and unhurried. And she talks with us as if she'd known us for a long time.

"Ah, you know," she says in English with that charming accentuating of final syllables, so typically Italian, "if you don't find anything else and my daughter is not coming to Rome, you can stay in my apartment there. *Bene?*"

I nod politely, but don't say what I'm really thinking—I'd prefer to live in the quiet of nature where I can have a beautiful view and write, not in the noise and bustle of Rome. (Little did I know then what was in store for us, for *me!*)

"But where would you suggest we look for a house?" Dwight asks.

"*Ah, bene,* maybe in Città di Castello," Noemi replies after a moment. "I know a real estate agent there. Maybe he has something nice. You tell 'im you're my friends."

So we pack, and with a new battery in our Honda, we say goodbye to Maridiana and Umbertide. Dwight is sorry to leave this town. He likes its unpretentious atmosphere, flagstone streets, the unspoiled historic center surrounded by medieval walls and a deep moat.

"No great wealth, no flashy churches, no art glory to attract tourists … just simply … Italian," Dwight says wistfully as we drive north.

We stayed in Città di Castello for the next several days, several perfectly uneventful days. None of the houses that Noemi's agent friend showed us were suitable, so we drove around aimlessly, exploring the nearby villages and towns in search of a place to settle down. Then we went to Gubbio, a small medieval town, founded some 2,500 years ago in the far northeastern part of Umbria. It's our last lead here that we got from Bruno, an Italian acquaintance we met at Mycenae, during our trip through Greece. "You'll find some of the best views in Umbria there," the young man assured us.

True. The view that Gubbio offers from its narrow, steep, twisting streets is breathtaking. The medieval houses are neatly lined up, beautifully preserved, and the gothic features of the main palaces are outstanding. All in all, Gubbio is the coffee-table-book model of a medieval Italian town. But from the moment we started climbing the steep streets I sensed a mounting feeling of discomfort. I glanced at Dwight who was clambering slowly, turning right and left, like a hunting dog. He shook his head and said, "Something doesn't feel right here." My feeling exactly.

We've learned to pay attention to those feelings thanks to Nicos, a lawyer friend in Cyprus who had an exceptional gift for dream interpretation. "When you visit a place," he once told us, "don't just rely on your five senses. Tune into your, let's call them, subtle senses so you can feel the energy field of your surroundings." These fields are subtle, he explained, a combination of Earth energies and human emanations. The exterior may seem appealing, but energetically, there may be residues of fear, greed, or hatred.

We were painfully aware of that as we climbed to the fourteenth-century Piazza Grande. From the terrace that hovered over a steep drop exploded a stunning view of cascading terracotta-tiled roofs and the valley. But the buildings around us, though remarkably beautiful, exuded an invisible cloud of heart-smothering energy.

There is an interesting local legend about this hill-town, which says that Rome had for centuries exported its lunatics to Gubbio (then called Iguvium). Maybe this wasn't just a story after all, because even today, the town celebrates the Day of the Mad, with a contest that takes place around the Fountain of the Mad. The winner receives the honorary title of Gubbio's Madman. What a custom! I've never heard of a place in the world where being nuts is an honor.

Now, this may have nothing to do with our experience, but nevertheless we left as fast as we could, back to Castello and our hotel. And back to no leads and no housing prospects.

At this point my certainty about my Guidance had become dangerously shaken. I felt no clear urges; no doors opened. This is not how I expected our Italian journey to be. I am supposed to be led to where I need to be, as our psychic friend Liana from Colorado assured us over the phone before we left Cyprus. *Why am I not helped? And what am I supposed to do?*

But most importantly, WHERE should we go now?

But no answer came through, not a peep. No Guidance.

In the evening, crestfallen, we are having another mediocre dinner at our mediocre hotel. There is an awkward, heavy silence. The whole evening Dwight has been gazing strangely into space, without saying a word. (*Has the energy of Gubbio gotten to him?*) So now, still looking to my right and with the same vacant expression in his eyes, he starts to nod and make tight little coughs. (*Oh, dear, it must be Gubbio.*)

Finally, he clears his throat and begins, "Well, I was thinking ... seems like your Guidance isn't working, so we may as well go where we would like to go."

"And just where would that be?" I raise my brow.

"How about Perugia?"

"PERUGIA?! Why Perugia?"

"And why not?" Dwight looks at me surprised. "It's the capital of Umbria, it has really beautiful art and architecture, plus one of the oldest Universities in Italy. And it's a short distance from here."

Really, why not Perugia?

We like *everything* about the capital of Umbria from the moment we step out of the car: our charming hotel with a gorgeous view of the valley, the small irregular *piazzas* with lovely cafés full of students, the vaulted passages between narrow streets, the magnificent buildings on the main *piazza*, even the tall flight of stairs we have to climb to get from our high-altitude hotel to the even higher-altitude city center. There is something fresh and dynamic that percolates amid the somber stone facades. The body of Perugia is old, but its spirit is fresh, upbeat, lively.

"What good energy, can you feel it?" asks Dwight as we come to yet another *piazzetta*, with yet another outdoor café full of students. Of course I can. Actually, I'm convinced that a city whose main industry is the production of chocolate *has* to have good energy. And especially if that chocolate is called *Baci*, Kisses. Its shiny-blue wrappers are famous all over Europe, its only rival being the golden-wrapped Ferrero Rocher. Chocolate aside, Perugia's second most important industry is shoe-making for ladies! Isn't that just about a perfect combination—shoes and chocolate (and in that order)?

But before I have a chance to enjoy those spectacular views from our balcony, gray clouds cloak the sky, the temperature drops, and by the next morning it begins to drizzle. We are shivering in our summer clothes while having our breakfast on the main *piazza*. We have no warm clothes and no shoes for the rain either. We didn't expect it would take so long to find a place to live. Our shipment of household goods has arrived in Milan but we have no address to have it shipped to. Dispiritedly, we flip through rental ads in local newspapers. We find a couple of possibilities and manage to get an appointment for later in the day.

Despite the gloomy weather, Perugia still feels vibrant to us as we drive through meandering streets, following the rental agent. The apartment he wants to show us is near our hotel, well, by an arrow's flight; but by car it's quite a long drive, as we have to circumnavigate the whole center. We leave the Honda on the street and go upstairs to the apartment that is ... AH! OH! WOW! ... a dream apartment: huge living and dining rooms, beautiful hardwood floors, a modern kitchen that's been recently renovated and is fully equipped. But best of all—a big, big terrace overlooking, well, now the fog, but normally, the agent says, *tutta la valle.*

I'm in ecstasy. Finally, here is *the* place, the promised abode we never found in Ostia Antica. And we stumbled upon it just by accident, no leads or anything! I'm willing to swallow the high price and to overlook the fact that the apartment is not furnished and that it would cost us a small fortune and gobs of time to buy furniture.

Then we go to see the bedrooms—and something changes. My heart shrinks and heaviness settles on my shoulders, as if some invisible weight is pressing down on me. Dwight walks around, puzzled by the decrepit look of the whole back half of the apartment. Peeled walls, cracked tiles in the bathroom, bad, bad energy. "What's going on here?" he mutters.

The agent notices our confusion and assures us that the remodeling will be finished in a month. We believe him, that's not the problem; he gives us the impression of an open, honest, straightforward young man. But we don't understand why we have this feeling of something dark and foreboding. And that, we cannot explain to him. I steal one last look at the terrace and the veiled view. Who knows, on a sunny day, with a magnificent view in front of me, I might have dismissed that feeling of foreboding … and our life in Italy would have taken a completely different turn.

That night in bed my head is reeling with dark thoughts, as dark as the starless sky outside. We have no home, we have no idea where to look for one, and what I thought were synchronistic leads turned out to be to dead ends. I'm no longer in touch with my Guidance. To make matters worse, I have to go back to the United States to keep my green card valid and I don't know where to fly from. And where is Dwight going to stay in the meantime? And when are we going to get our Italian resident permits? And how are we going to get hold of our things, still locked up at the customs in Milan?

With no hope of falling asleep and to get my mind off depressing thoughts, I start to read about the history of Perugia. Which turns out to be equally as dark and turbulent as my thoughts. Perhaps this is not the best choice for bedtime reading, but I'm curious and I go on. And I learn that Perugia had a feisty reputation throughout medieval times. Its inhabitants were so belligerent that their main activity was subjugating their neighbors, and in their spare time, fighting among themselves. In the Middle Ages, every town had an annual festival to prove the valor of its youth: horse races in Siena, archery in Cortona, jousting in Florence. But Perugia had the "Battle of Stones." Its inhabitants thrilled at throwing stones at each other, which caused many casualties. So wild and unruly was the populace that even the Popes couldn't control this city, which in principle belonged to the Holy See. While attempting to tame this shrew of a city, no fewer than three Popes were poisoned during their visits to Perugia (one of them by a nun!).

So it's probably befitting the Perugian character and thirst for blood that the most bloody religious cult in the history of Christianity commenced right here—the gruesome Flagellants. The then bishop of Perugia liked so much the idea proposed to him by a local hermit that he ordered a two-week city-wide flagellation! From Perugia this mass psychosis of penitence by whipping one's bare back until it is dripping blood spread throughout Italy and Europe like a wildfire.

I read page after bloody page of fighting, betrayal, torture, and beheading that form the history of this city. Until one of the Popes finally had enough of the troublemaking Perugians, gathered a mighty army, and crushed Perugia for good. To top it off, rather than destroying the city—as was customary in those times—he spared it, but instead built his fortress and a whole new city *over* the conquered one. In that way, he sent an unmistakable message to Perugians: I have subjugated you.

At this point in the history of Perugia I finally fall asleep and have the following dream.

I'm riding on a bus and I get off two stops before the place where I have to go, which is a well-lit, safe, and orderly piazza. Instead, I walk through dangerous neighborhoods, populated by prostitutes, pimps, and criminals, to collect the material for a story I'm writing for my magazine.

When I wake up I have an unmistakable feeling that the dream was trying to tell me something … something about my journey, my destination, my purpose. But I'm not sure what.

Today is our last day in Perugia. There is no point in staying here; we have explored all rental possibilities, and the weather is still foggy, cold, and drizzling. With our expectations sandwiched between the gray skies and foggy landscape, and no promising leads ahead, our spirits have sunk so low that they have vanished somewhere in the fog.

We're too cold to even go sightseeing. So we do the only sensible and practical thing we can do right now and right here—go shopping. Dwight wants to get a warm jacket and I desperately need shoes for rain (in fact, I have no shoes period, only sandals and thongs). Perugia makes its living from ladies' shoes, right? No better place, then, to get the kind of shoes I need, right?

Wrong. All I see are elegant, delicate, dainty, beautiful, sensual, sexy, soft-leathered, finely-made—I could go on with adjectives, but I'll refrain—shoes that I would *love* to have at any other time but now. I have to confess (if you haven't gathered already) that shoes are one of my two vices. The shoe fetish, I had to explain to Dwight at the beginning of our relationship, is in my genes; in fact, it's one of the national traits of my country. So he would just have to put up with it. Case closed.

Ironically, I end up buying shoes in the street market (very humiliating for a shoe-devotee), because they were the only suitable ones for rain I could find. And even more ironically, I have to buy shoes that are a half-size too small—the only pair left. I'm crushed.

I'm actually upset by my Guidance. Worse, I'm at the point of seriously questioning its existence, my impressions. What if ... what if it was all illusion? I shudder.

Dwight, on the other hand, landed in a fancy boutique for gentlemen on the main *corso*. The prices are exorbitant. But the clothes are, oh, *so* beautiful. No, they don't have warm jackets for winter yet ... well, the summer was here until three days ago ... but they do have overcoats, *perfetto* for this kind of weather. And Dwight smugly walks out with a smashingly elegant, impeccably made, outrageously expensive, *light-weight* overcoat. I'm not sure how warm the coat will be, but it certainly looks fabulous on him. Which, as I look down at my street market, half-size-too-small shoes, makes me feel even worse.

CHAPTER 6

ASSISSI:

BAD NEWS, GOOD NEWS ...
AND BAD NEWS AGAIN

And that's why we have come to Assisi, a town in the close neighborhood of Perugia, a mere thirteen miles to the east toward the Adriatic Sea. Dwight has concluded that we (*I* in particular) were getting seriously compromised—spiritually, of course—and in need of reinforcement. I'm a bit ashamed to admit that he is right. I had already started thinking about giving up on our journey, disregarding the search for my Soul and going back to the States to find an ordinary job and live a perfectly normal and ordinary existence, thank you very much.

Why do I get discouraged so easily?

I so much wish I were stronger, taking adversities and obstacles stoically, calmly, without whimpering. From all the books I've ever read, the hero I chose for a role model was the figure of a wise, calm, powerful Mage—like Gandalf in *The Lord of the Rings*, or Dumbledore in the Harry Potter books, or Ged in Ursula Le Guin's *Earthsea Trilogy*. This is what I want to become. This is how I want to be—strong, serene, poised, unflappable. Which is almost the opposite of how I'm acting right now! And that's why, as I said earlier, we are in Assisi: because Assisi is the home town of Dwight's spiritual hero and inspiration—Saint Francis.

In Italy, every region is famous for something. Tuscany, for the beauty of nature and Chianti wines. Emilia-Romagna for Parmesan cheese and prosciutto. Rome for being the cradle of Christianity and the seat of the Vatican. And Umbria is famous for its saints and religious fervor, earning her nicknames such as The Land of Saints and Mystical Umbria.

Two of the most important saints who reformed Christianity were born in this region: St. Benedict, who fathered monastic life in the sixth century, and St. Francis, who spiritually renewed Christianity in the thirteenth century. (Of course, Dwight's hero would be a spiritual reformer). The effect St. Francis had on the religious life not only of his time, but of the centuries to come, was so great that many regard him as one of the most remarkable men to have ever lived, second in influence only to Christ himself. This influence continues even to this day—he is the patron-saint of all of Italy, and in 1980 was adopted as the official patron-saint of ecology. This is indeed an amazing achievement for someone who rebelled against authority, who was against organized religious institutions, and who was *never* actually ordained as a priest.

Francesco Bernardone was born into wealth. Like Gautama (the Buddha) before him, he knew no deprivation, poverty, or hardship while young. Unlike Gautama, however, he was an unruly, boisterous, womanizing young man, getting into fights and trouble all the time. At age twenty-two, he fought in a military campaign against the neighboring city of Perugia, was captured, and spent a year in a jail. At this point in the life story of St. Francis, Dwight would say, "Bad news, good news." For it was thanks to this miserable, painful, and illness-ridden year of imprisonment that Francesco began his transformation into a person who would subsequently serve as an ideal for the whole of Christendom.

His revolutionary teaching comprised three radical concepts: rejection of material possessions, the sanctity of nature, and a personal approach to faith without the intermediary of the Church. Francis preached and lived absolute poverty; and "absolute" meant exactly that—begging for food and living on alms. He didn't even own a habit, but wore whatever he was given. In fact, he described himself as "in love with Lady Poverty."

Many times I've tried imagining life without owning *anything*. I go as far as *no car* (okay, I didn't have a car when I came to Santa Barbara as a grad student); *no home* (no problem, I still don't own a house); *no furniture* (fine, I'm getting used to living with other people's stuff); *no food* (well, I guess I can beg as so many Buddhist monks still do). But when I get to *no books* I start having trouble. At *no clothes* I get seriously disturbed. At *no shoes* I give up. I could never be a nun, that much I know for sure.

The second concept—mystical communion with nature—strikes me as so modern, so well before its time that it makes St. Francis a true visionary. In an era when Church dogma considered nature a mere stepping stone toward the

Kingdom of Heaven (attainable only through the intermediary of the Church, of course), Francis preached the oneness of all Creation. He revived the idea of the sacredness of nature, common to all the mystery religions of the ancient world. For him, nature was alive, and all its creatures, including the elements, were his brothers and sisters. (Once when a physician attempted to cure Francis' approaching blindness by searing his face with a red-hot iron, Francis even thanked "Brother Fire.")

Now we come to the most controversial part of St. Francis' life—his death. At this point when talking about his spiritual hero, the usually calm Dwight begins to bristle, because the Church blatantly violated Francis' death wish by doing precisely the opposite of what he wanted. It established a "doctrinally correct" Franciscan order and used it to solicit generous donations. In fact, the then cardinal had the nerve to reject St. Francis' testament altogether.

But the Church also did something much worse: it burned at the stake all the followers of St. Francis who adhered to his original teachings and refused to renounce their vow of poverty.

With bitterness in his voice, Dwight relates this history to me as we stand in front of the imposing Basilica of St. Francis. The Basilica consists of the Lower Church, where the remains of St. Francis are kept, and the Upper Church, decorated with beautiful frescoes by Giotto.

"Here is a perfect example of how apostolic poverty gave way to church opulence," Dwight says, jutting his chin contemptuously toward the basilicas.

At this moment, two dozen buses filled with pilgrims are circulating around the vast parking area. "But if the churches were not built," I say, "where would all these people be making their pilgrimage? And look at all the magnificent art in the churches! So, maybe bad news turned into good news after all," I remind Dwight of his favorite saying.

Dwight makes a faint nod and grunts a little "humph," something between "yes" and "no." He is still appalled by the size and bulk of the churches, which take up the whole western hill of Assisi, as well as by the enormous convent behind them, visible for miles around. I remind him that he himself made regular pilgrimages to Assisi when he was teaching in Switzerland. That was at the time when Dwight was young and searching for his path. St. Francis was such a magnet to him that he felt compelled to spend every free weekend in Assisi: he would drive all Friday night, spend two days here, then drive back Sunday night to resume teaching on Monday.

"Yes, but I don't need any edifice to revere his spirit," Dwight protests.

"*You* don't, but other people do. They need material reminders—like big churches and relics. Anyhow, time to look for a hotel," I add, inspecting the brightening sky. At this moment, I'm becoming hopeful that we might yet catch a view of the valley.

"Don't worry about the hotel," Dwight says in a perky voice. "I know a charming little *albergo* off the main *piazza*. We'll go there."

I make a little coughing noise. "It looks like we might get some sun," I try to bargain. "How about that hotel we drove by? It had a lovely terrace overlooking the valley."

"Wait a minute—that's all the way on the other side of town! Actually, it's *outside* the town!" Dwight doesn't seem to like my suggestion. "You *do* realize how much walking we'd have to do?" No, he definitely doesn't like it.

"Yes, but, we would be able to enjoy the view...." I say in my sweetest voice (Dwight calls it a "manipulating" voice).

"Heavens, we are not here for the view, but for Assisi and the spiritual uplift."

"Yes, but ... I'd get more uplifted if I could lose myself in the view instead of being cooped up in narrow streets." Then I say smugly, "Besides, the car and our luggage will be safer there. We can park on the gated hotel grounds."

Checkmate! Dwight grudgingly agrees and we drive off to the other side of Assisi.

The next morning I wake up early, while outside it's still dark and cold. Last night I firmly decided to get to St. Francis' church as it opens, before the crowds of pilgrims descend on it. I need solitude, quiet, inspiration, insights. Most of all, I desperately need to get in touch with my Guidance! So I push my exhausted body out of a warm, comfortable bed and out the door into a cold, foggy dawn, and start on a long, long walk from one end of this steep, hilly town to the other. As I'm walking down one of many steep streets, I'm regretting we didn't go to the hotel Dwight had suggested. My whole body is aching with fatigue, my shoes are pinching me, and I'm shivering from the cold.

But on the other hand, I comfort myself, I get to experience Assisi as it's waking up, at this special moment when nature just begins to stir, when the dawning sky casts a surreal light on the stone streets below, and when the air is full of the tension of a new birth. Truly, Assisi feels magical at this moment. I walk through empty streets in perfect silence. Only the rhythmic *click-clack* of my new shoes echoes in the cobbled streets. I look in awe at the gothic stone facades, so beautifully preserved. (Later that day, I read in my guidebook that Assisi was severely damaged by an earthquake in 1997. And thanks to that calamity, the whole town received a complete facelift. *Bad news, good news,* I smiled to myself.) As I walk, I feel infused with the energy of Assisi, the energy of spiritual fervor and aspiration. The usual chatter in my mind has died down; I've become poised and serene, my Soul breathing in my heartbeats. My body feels light like a feather, and I even forget about my half-size-too-small shoes.

When I get to the Lower Church, where the remains of St. Francis are kept in the crypt, I discover to my unpleasant surprise that the church is still closed. The priest whom I'd asked the day before about the opening hours had misinformed me. *Oh, well, never mind,* I shrug serenely. But when the church does open half an hour later, there are already tour groups waiting to enter. And what's worse, when I get down to the crypt, I find a TV crew interviewing a priest in front of a flock ready for the morning mass! Here, my newly regained equanimity is shattered like Assisi in the earthquake. I can't believe my bad luck! Now, had this been only one occurrence, I would have just shrugged it off—you know, these things happen. But it hadn't. This is so typical of what we've been going through since we left Ostia Antica: if something could go wrong, it did. The whole trip has so far been strewn with misleading synchronicities.

As I'm climbing back up to the nave of the church, I'm really annoyed—worse, I'm disgusted. I'm actually shooting arrows of anger at anyone who gets in my way, like these two matrons in front of me negotiating the stairs at tortoise pace.

I'm off to a bad start, I realize. I've completely failed my Three Fundamentals. In the morning semi-darkness, the nave throbs with intense quiet. This church is so charged that even as frazzled as I'm now, I feel slight shivers. I choose the darkest corner where I seat myself in a pew, take ten deep breaths, and utter silently: *"Okay, Guidance, could you help me, please, to regain my balance? Could you help me understand <u>why</u> this is all happening? And <u>where</u> we should live?*

I sit, motionless, and wait. All of a sudden, I remember two dreams I had last night.

In the first one, I was looking for a place to stay. I found one right away: it was a large house, divided into two parts. The left and right side of the house were identical, but somehow, I knew that I was supposed to live in the left side of the house; the right side was already occupied.

In the second dream I was in my old room in my parents' apartment in Belgrade, where I'd spent my whole life before coming to the States. My mother was there also, and she was insisting that I do a major clean-up of my room the day before my big trip. I obey, and I have to move every single object, dust every book, clean every corner the very day when I have to pack. I'm freaking out. At least, I don't have to do it alone—my mother is helping me.

I slouch down in my pew, cock my head, and stare at the low, blue-painted ceiling speckled with golden stars. The partitioned house in my first dream ... the symbolism seems quite obvious. The left and right sides stand for the two brain hemispheres: the right lobe which has to do with feelings, intuition, creativity, mystical experiences; and the left lobe which represents the rational mind, analytical and linear thinking, planning and organizing.

The second dream is clear too. I have to brush up my old skills, symbolized by the objects left in my room to gather dust—like reasoning, resourcefulness, self-reliance, taking action. And the cleaning is supervised by my mother, who is the symbol par excellence of a left-lobe person, always *in control.*

I stare at the golden stars on the ceiling. Dwight and I were wrong to think that synchronicity would lead us where we needed to go. We came here relying completely on the Guidance, but instead found ourselves alone. I, in particular, assumed a passive attitude, waiting for things to happen through synchronicity rather than taking initiative.

Granted, I had a very good reason to do that. For the past five years we've been showered with incredible synchronicity. Effortlessly, what we needed was provided: Dwight's friend introduced us to Kyriacos who gave us a long list of contacts in Cyprus, one of whom invited us to stay at his beach house in the most beautiful part of the island. We found lodging in Madras in India when it seemed impossible. We were led to a non-touristy pension in Cairo where we met many Egyptologists and learned unpublished information. We were given time *alone* in the Great Pyramid. An elegant villa on top of a hill became our home in Cyprus. Later, just when we needed temporary housing, we were asked to house-sit in a gorgeous beach villa. We were introduced to John Anthony West (the foremost esoteric Egyptologist), who invited us to join his group on a tour in Egypt, and we spent another night in the Great Pyramid with his group. Finally, we even met the cultural attaché of Italy, who helped us get visas.... I mean, really! Wasn't it only *natural* to rely on the Guidance, to expect synchronicity, to ... ahem, become dependent on it?

So why has it deserted us ever since we got to Ostia Antica?

Why were we left spiritual orphans?

I have no idea. I just know that my dream seems to be telling me not to rely on the Guidance but instead to take action, to search *actively* rather than passively. This, I have to say, came as a great surprise. I thought following the spiritual path meant surrendering your will to the higher Will. Did I get something wrong?

At that moment the bells begin to toll. It's a lovely sound, round and full, and almost hypnotizing if you let the resonance carry you with it...

DAAANG ... DOOONG...

DAAAAANG, one side ... DOOOOONG, other side...

DAAAAANG, left ... DOOOOONG, right...

DAAAAANG, left lobe ... DOOOOOONG, right lobe...

DAAAAANG, call to prayer ... DOOOOOONG...

DOOOOOONG...

...and another insight came...

...that the two lobes would also point to the two paths one can take toward self-realization, the two paths contained within the Ageless Wisdom: the heart and the head path. The right lobe stands for union with the Divine through prayer and devotion—the mystical path. It is based on a passive attitude of renunciation and merging with God's consciousness. In contrast, the left lobe represents the path of active knowledge, of self-inquiry and studying the laws that govern the Universe, understanding the causes behind the phenomena. In the West there is another term for the head path, which, unfortunately, has been abused and distorted in the past—occult philosophy.

Disregarding all the hodgepodge claims of channeling and all the hype about initiations, what occultism is really about is the study of the "why" and "how" of phenomenal existence, the *science* of how it works. To find the answers one must go beyond the visible world, as our teacher Kostas said. Hence the name occultism—"hidden, or concealed from view" (from the Latin *occultere,* "to hide"). Kostas would begin every meeting of our group by reminding us that our task is to start living consciously. "This involves," he'd say solemnly, "close analysis of events and circumstances to discover their governing laws."

Isn't this what I always wanted to know: why things happen the way they do? Isn't this what I wanted to understand even when I was a teenager? Isn't this why—when Dwight asked me before we began our study together, "What is for you the single most important thing without which life is meaningless?"— I answered unequivocally and unwaveringly: WISDOM.

Because that's what the occult path ultimately leads to: not some kind of bookish knowledge, but deeply understood, personally experienced and applied esoteric teaching. Wisdom is knowledge in action; it's the understanding of invisible laws; it's a highly developed blend of intellect and intuition that one reaches *only* through experience, through failing and learning from mistakes, through suffering and rising above it, through fearing the unknown and fearlessly facing it.

Let's put my "plight" into perspective. Why exactly am I balking now? Why do I want to go back to the States? Just because I don't know where I'm supposed to live and can't find a house? And the weather is foggy and rainy? Is this it?

I clear my throat in embarrassment.

Let's practice my Second Fundamental here, "Mo"—for motives: Who doesn't like fog and rain? Who wants to enjoy the view? I *the personality*, or I *the Soul*?

Er ... the personality, I have to admit to myself very reluctantly.

At this point in my inner monologue something pops in my head, just like that—*pop*. You know, like when you are driving down from a higher altitude and your ears are plugged up and all of a sudden—*pop!*—they clear. So, in the same way, the fog in my head clears and I decide, *rationally*, what we should do....

Thank you, San Francesco, for all these insights!

When I emerge from the shadows of the church, I'm amazed that the fog outside has cleared as well. I can actually see the countryside. If this isn't symbolic, I don't know what is!

Symbolic ... what did Kostas say about symbols? That our Soul sends us symbols through dreams, or meditation, or sometimes through life events. They veil deeper meanings so that we can't understand them until we are ready, that is, until we develop intuition (which is how our Soul communicates with us). And that's why it's crucial to work with symbols—they are our tickets to higher worlds. "Always ask yourself," Kostas urged us, "'what is the symbolism of what's happening in my life?'" And he would explain how the twelve labors of Hercules were symbolic of different stages on the spiritual path.

Oh, I feel so much better now. I always do when I understand what's going on. Then, I can wade through heaps of refuse; I can drive through fog; I can walk in tight shoes—because I know where I'm going and can see light at the end of the tunnel. Limping but radiant, I walk through the gate of our hotel. Dwight is waiting for me on a bench outside, a broad grin on his face. "Guess what? I've reserved us a table for breakfast at the terrace," he says triumphantly.

Oh, wow! I can't believe my good luck. The table is at the far end of the garden-terrace, right beside The View. After all these days of fog and cold, we can finally enjoy breakfast in the sun! I'm delighted. No, I'm ecstatic. Is this my reward for learning a new insight?

I indulge.

Life is beautiful, the moment special; my Soul is within me, Dwight across from me. I kick off my shoes and feel the coolness of the grass, the life force that flows through it, the vibrancy of the soil. And through my feet the life force flows into my body. I feel so acutely, vibrantly alive. Life is beautiful!

At that moment my cell phone rings.

It's an acquaintance from Ostia Antica who had promised to keep an ear out for houses for rent. She has heard of a woman in Fregene who wants to rent her house. The house is near the beach, and it's new and big. And furnished. And Rome is not too far either, only one hour by bus. Are we interested? Yes? Then we can meet the day after tomorrow. *Ecco*, our problems are solved, *la casa e bellissima. Ciao.*

Dwight and I look at each other, confused, not knowing what to think or say, but knowing how we feel—we don't want to leave Assisi. But the magic of the moment is dispelled. The grass feels cold and damp, and I put my tight shoes back on.

"I'm telling you, it's not set in stone! We don't *have* to see that house," Dwight repeats while we're walking to the Basilica of Ste. Clare.

"I know we don't, but what if this is the right one?" I say in a small voice.

"What if, what if...." Dwight waves his arm is if to chase away a pesky fly. "You're not following your new insights from this morning—use your left lobe to make a decision."

I cough in embarrassment. "I know, but this phone call ... maybe—"

"Just forget about it for a while, will you?"

The best way to make a decision, Dwight believes, is to get away from it for some time. That's why we're heading to the Basilica of Ste. Clare, or Santa Chiara, Francis' spiritual partner who headed the female side of the Franciscan Order—the Poor Clares.

St. Francis' love for Clare is another fascinating aspect of the life of this spiritual reformer. At the age when Judeo-Christian dogma had degraded women to second-rate creatures (at best—remember, Eve tempted Adam, so it's all *her* fault!), Francis showed the world that true religion was not a male prerogative, but a harmony between the male and the female. His belief that the female principle in nature is equally important represented a departure from the dogma that didn't (and seven centuries later, still doesn't!) allow women to officiate as priests.

The life of Clare is also an example of total dedication, sacrifice, and service. She renounced her wealthy family and ran away from her husband to join Francis and establish the Order of the Poor Clares. Not only was she living the vow of absolute poverty, she didn't even beg for food—and, together with a handful of her followers, she nearly starved.

As I'm looking at the pink-and-white striped church with lovely rose windows and huge flying buttresses, I begin to register the feeling of a sweet, gentle energy that permeates this place. Dwight is off, wandering around with his dowsing rods, checking the energy flow. I'm sitting on a low wall that over-looks the valley below, listening to the gurgling of the fountain and the soft rustling of trees that flank the *piazzetta* in front of the church.

It's so soothing here, I could stay forever floating in this daze, this reverie, semi-absent from the real world. My worries seem so unreal now, something I have created and made real, like a holodeck program in Star Trek. Really, what *is* real?

"You know, this is amazing!" Dwight's voice startles me. He has sneaked up behind me and is now beaming in that just-about-to-burst-with-ideas way of his. "Do you realize," he booms as he straddles the wall, "this place has yin energy, as opposed to the yang energy of St. Francis' church! I should have thought of it, the two churches are built at the opposite ends of town as yin-yang complements. And even this setting—look, the round *piazza*, the fountain in the middle, the trees around—is so very yin."

"In contrast to the rectangular courtyards with no trees of St. Francis' church," I exclaim.

"Yep, obvious, isn't it?"

Then I remember my dream with a partitioned house. "I'm still confused," I say, "is my dream telling me that I have to abandon developing intuition and meditating? Go back to my old journalist ways of I'm-the-doer attitude?

"Not necessarily." Dwight shakes his head. "You just have to use both equally."

"But why should I inhabit only the left side of the house, then?"

"Well, isn't the right side of the house in your dream already inhabited?"

I avert my gaze. *Duh.*

"You've been doing all of that," Dwight continues. "You've been recording your dreams, meditating, developing intuition. In fact, you've switched completely into your right lobe—haven't you changed your attitude from one of active inquiry to one of passive reliance on Guidance?" Dwight makes a pause here as if waiting for my reply, but he actually isn't. "Well, I have news for you … the spiritual path is not only about love and bliss and faith—"

"Wait, what about St. Francis? His was the heart path—prayer, devotion, mystical communion with nature. That's a perfect example of the religion of love."

"Divine Love," Dwight corrects me.

"Okay, Divine Love, but still love. Where is the left lobe in his teachings?"

"There is none."

"So…?"

"So, what? That was the spirit of his time—heart approach, devotion, blind faith. That was right for these past two millennia, the Age of Pisces. But now the times are changing, we live in a different world, so we need a different approach. And that's the combination of heart and head. That's what Kostas is teaching. Remember what he said—what was right in the past may be wrong today. It's no longer enough to believe blindly, we need to understand the science of how things work, to see the causes behind the effects. That's the modern Western path."

We both remain silent for a while, watching the soft shimmering of air over the horizon, wisps of feathery clouds, cars slithering far down in the valley, a few swallows swooping through the air. Peaceful. Everywhere peaceful. Then Dwight turns to me. "And don't forget," he says as an after-thought, "being on the spiritual path doesn't mean giving up your will."

"Wait, what about 'not my will, but Thine?'" I ask, perplexed.

"Well, that doesn't mean you should give up your will. You need to develop the will to move on the path, very much so. It just means you have to *align* your will with the higher Will.

"Remember your dream in Perugia?" Dwight adds after a while.

"What about it?"

"You got off the bus two stops before your destination, right? The well-lit, safe square which would stand for…?"

"Um, it's … it's where I'm going."

"And where *are* you going?"

"I'm going …am going…." *I don't know where I'm going!*

"It's the ultimate goal of your life journey," Dwight is trying to help me. "What is it?"

"Oh, that, well ... Soul integration." I pipe up.

"Of course. In mystical terminology—enlightenment. That's your well-lit square. And what do you have to go through?"

"Dangerous and dark areas, suspicious-looking thugs and hookers...."

"In other words, the underground. A perfect symbol for the uncertainty of our journey, for obstacles, problems we have to overcome, possible dangers."

"But what about the story I have to write? I need to gather the material there."

"That I can't help you with. You have to figure it out for yourself. It's the task that your Soul has given you."

"You mean, it's my life mission?! What I was asking for at Epidauros?"

"Can't know," he says tersely and looks away from me.

Oh, I'm so confused. What story does my Soul want me to write? About the Medici? I'm not so sure anymore. But if not that, what then? I guess I can think about it later, when we find a house.... A house.... What if this lead is the right one? This morning, during the cascade of insights at the church, everything looked so perfectly clear. I rationally made a plan for what we should do—go back to Sicily and get our residence papers, then I'd fly to the States to keep my green card valid while Dwight stays in Sicily and looks for a house to rent. A perfect plan. A *logical* plan. But now, after this morning's phone call, I'm back to uncertainty, again juggling questions and options: do I follow one more lead, or do I use my reasoning to make decisions? Do I act upon my new insights, or do I continue in the old way? What if this house is where we're supposed to be? How to know?

The following day we arrived in Fregene in the late afternoon, tired, headachy, and edgy, having driven through Umbria in the thickest of fogs yet.

CHAPTER 7

FREGENE:

BREAKFAST AT FELLINI'S

"Wouldn't you know it!" snaps Dwight, then repeats slowly and forcefully, as if to hammer each word into my head: "W O U L D N' T Y O U K N O W I T!"

Dwight is angry. After all these years together, I've learned to recognize how he expresses his anger. He turns icy cold and prickly, so that being around him feels like touching a metal fence with bare hands in the middle of winter. So now, in addition to our dismal situation, I'm faced with Dwight's long-lasting anger.

Okay, he has a good reason to be angry, I don't deny it. I did revert to my old ways of following the leads, despite the new insights I had in the church. I took Dwight out of Assisi when he was most enjoying it, drove through the cheese-thick fog of Umbria to Fregene, only to find out that the woman who was renting her house had changed her mind just before we arrived. "For no apparent reason and with no explanation," our acquaintance told us apologetically. And, as if that wasn't enough, I chose a motel so dilapidated that it could rival the seediest skid row motel in downtown Los Angeles.

"Honestly, why didn't you follow through?" I'm hit by Dwight's icy snowball. "You get insights you ask for and then you don't act upon them! Wasn't this enough of a sign for you that you should change your ways?" He pulls back a curtain and a cloud of dust hits his face.

Oh, that's not good—now he'll begin to sneeze and get all allergic and asthmatic. I feel so guilty that I can't even utter an apology or an answer or soothing words … anything, something, just to begin melting the ice.

To redeem myself, I go to the front desk and explain in my pigeon Italian that the room is *molto sporco e brutto* (which means "dirty" and "ugly"—really easy to remember, like "sport" and "brute"), and that we definitely don't like it, and if they could please recommend another *albergo*? To my surprise, it worked! The receptionist, who could have been Middle-Eastern or Spanish, or any other dark-haired, swarthy nationality, nods in understanding and replies in broken English that he has something "very interested." He makes a short phone call, still nodding, then turns to me and says with an air of self-impor-tance that we can stay in Fellini's villa. Which, at first, I disregard as an absurd language error on his part and I ask him to repeat in Italian. But his answer is the same—yes, the Fellini villa is a part of the motel—well, sort of. It's used for special occasions and special guests, but it happens to be free right now, so we can stay there.

I'm still incredulous. Does he mean *the* Fellini—*Federico* Fellini, one of the greatest movie directors of all time? The nodding becomes more vigorous, accompanied by a wide grin, so I finally take it for real. *OH-MY-GOD! I'm going to be staying in the house that belonged to the famous Fellini!* I can't believe my luck. Fellini was one of my favorite European film directors when I was a student. In those undergraduate years, I spent almost every evening in a movie theater, a sort of film library that showed classical European movies. I saw all the Viscontis and Bertoluccis and Antonionis and Fassbinders and Bergmans and Tarkovskis and, of course, the French directors of the *Nouvelle Vague* period: the Chabrols and Truffauts and Godards. In fact, this became such an obsession that my father used to tease me that I was majoring in film, not literature.

So I bring the good news to Dwight but do not detect any sign of him mellowing. We load the car again, or more precisely, *I* load the car, because Dwight is so asthmatic he can barely breathe. The receptionist has given me directions to the villa, and I follow them with ease through this small seaside resort, a get-away for well-off Romans. We drive through grid-like, empty streets lined by two-story houses with gardens. An occasional café with empty tables gapes like a yawning mouth at the corner of two streets. There is nothing of interest here, *no soul*, as Marie from Ostia Antica would have said.

But when we arrive at the open gates of the Fellini estate, I sense the outer edges of the glacier next to me begin to melt. We drive through beautiful grounds, something between a garden and a park, with a dozen *pinetas* and palm trees, carpets of flowers and green grass.

At the end of the driveway is the villa—a large, two-story house with a huge terrace facing the garden. In front of the house stands a lanky man, vigor-ously motioning to us where to park. This could very well be an opening scene to a Fellini movie, I say to myself: a surly caretaker standing suspiciously and protectively in front of his domain, a house that immediately strikes the visitor as having a unique personality that will soon reveal itself. The villa is old and hasn't been repainted in a long time. Perhaps because of closed shutters with cobwebs, or perhaps because of the brooding, sharp-eyed caretaker dressed in something that could pass for hunting gear, I have the feeling of stepping into one of those dream worlds Fellini used to paint in his movies.

The scene is so unexpected and so out of the ordinary that when Dwight comes out of the car, the ice around him is completely melted! Instead of prickly aloofness, I sense a child-like curiosity and a desire to explore. *Now that's much better.*

"Bad news, good news," I casually toss out, as I walk toward the caretaker.

As soon as I greet him, I'm hit by a tornado of words, the last thing I expected from what I thought was a cranky, gruff geezer. I'm so surprised that I can't understand a single word, as if he were speaking another language, not Italian. (Well, I was right to a certain extent; I later found out that he was using a southern dialect, just for the fun of it, to enjoy my confusion.) Actually, the caretaker is so fast in his movements as well as in his speech that I have a hard time keeping up with him as he shows me around the house. We move rapidly through a huge living room downstairs with furniture mostly from the 1960s, a kitchen equally spacious and surprisingly cluttered with containers of all sizes, up the staircase to the master bedroom—our bedroom—that opens onto an impressive terrace overlooking the garden. "Happy, yes? Good. Breakfast tomorrow. Need anything—find in the kitchen." And, like Speedy Gonzales, he turns on his heels and glissades down the stairs past a bemused Dwight.

Whew, what a spin! I take a deep breath, look around, and decide to open all the windows to air out the stuffy room. I step out onto the terrace, inhaling the scents of dusk. The garden, peaceful and mysterious, rests in the darkening light of the early evening. The birds have already quieted down for the night, with only an occasional cry piercing the silence. The stars are beginning to shimmer in a cloudless sky, and the air is soft, carrying the salty smell of a sea breeze. Romantic? You bet. My senses are completely awake. My mind is barred from intruding, and I'm floating in a mellow, dreamy, sensual energy, my skin eager to be caressed … when Dwight barges in and shouts urgently, as if we're being attacked: "Damn it! What on earth are you doing? Close those windows right now! Do you want to feed the whole mosquito population with our blood?"

Oops, I've totally forgotten about the vicious tiger mosquitoes. Together, we close everything as fast as we can and look around apprehensively. The room is huge, the ceiling high, and there is a dim light coming from two lonely lamps—a perfect hideaway for ravenous mosquitoes. Forget about caresses under the stars and a romantic night at Fellini's! As a conciliatory gesture, I offer to go down and ask the caretaker for mosquito *pellets*, the only protection I can think of. "Anything!" snarls Dwight from the bathroom as he prepares weapons—wet hand towels to hurl at the buzzing enemy.

Down in the kitchen, Speedy Gonzales is watching the TV news and talking back to the anchor on the screen, a stubby glass of something red in his hand. For a moment I see his profile, revealing a strong but crooked nose, a hairy nostril, a bush of dark hair, a prominent cheek. He is not that old after all, just gives that impression. Noticing my presence, he jumps up quickly and faces me with a sharp look, then offers me a glass of Campari and a bowl of olives, reports the news he has just heard, and asks if we have everything we need—all of this at the same time. He talks so fast, as if there were five of him in his head, each carrying on a different line of conversation (he has now switched to Italian proper, so I can understand … partially). It's not only how fast he talks, but also what he says that bears a resemblance to a Fellini character. His comments about changing times, the corruption, the lost values—all spoken in a fragmented, a bit macabre, *non-sequitur* way—are so Fellini-esque.

I ask him if he'd acted in any of Fellini's movies. He cracks a smile and waves his arm evasively, then asks me if I like Fellini. "Gosh, yes!" I say emphatically. Then he tells me, with a slight clicking of his tongue and in a voice turned mellow, as if offering me a special dessert, that *Julia of the Spirits* and *8 ½* were filmed in this very villa. My eyes must have opened so widely and my face showed such awe that he takes me under the arm and leads me into the living room to show me the photographs—Fellini shooting *Julia* in the garden; Fellini giving directions to Marcello Mastroianni, Fellini looking through a camera, Fellini at the beach.

I only wish my Italian were better. No matter how many times I ask him to speak *piano, piano*, he is just not capable of slowing down. And I am not able to understand most of what he's saying—sadly. Sadly, because I miss all the delicacies from Fellini's life; I miss the intrigues and juicy details (I do much better at understanding abstract ideas, politics, and philosophy than gossip). All I get are first names—Giulietta (Messina, Fellini's wife who played the lead role in *Julia of the Spirits*), Claudia (Cardinale, who starred in *8 ½*), and Marcello

(Mastroianni, Fellini's favorite actor)—and bits of sentences that I can't string together in any meaningful combination.

Feeling as though I just got off a merry-go-round, I head for the bedroom, but then quickly retrace my steps—I forgot the *pelettes*! I enter the kitchen again and mimic what I need. "*A, zanzara!*" laughs Speedy Gonzales. *Zanzara*—what a good name for mosquitoes, sounds just like their buzzing, *zzzzzzan-zzzza-ra*. He opens one drawer after another, rummaging through piles of little notes and Band-Aids and old photographs and pencils and mouse traps and stamps and buttons and laces and razors. Finally, triumphantly, he unearths a packet and hands it to me. Now we can sleep calmly.

I walk up the wide, shadowy stairs. Around the house the darkness has settled over the dusty furniture and in unlit corners. I feel uneasy, as if I'm not alone. The upstairs hallway leading to our room creaks under my footsteps and the doors to other rooms gape open into realms of ominous darkness. In fact, I feel positively uncomfortable and rush into the bedroom. Dwight is taking a shower, and I drop onto the bed, suddenly feeling exhausted. No, I don't feel comfortable in the bedroom either; it looks so faded, pictures hanging on walls once white but now a dull shade of gray. It feels so sad and abandoned, like an old, old lady who is living off her memories. Every piece of furniture is from Fellini's time; nothing is new, nothing has been replaced (except, maybe, hopefully, the mattress). I wonder how many thoughts, how many passions, images, visions, ideas, script-lines must have been born in this space! Fellini was an unusually intuitive director with an unbridled imagination. His movies paint dreamscapes full of visions and fantastic imagery from his own dreams and subconscious.

I know what Dwight is going to say—the house is full of *thought-forms*, which is a term that describes the result of our thinking process. At the very beginning of our study meetings, Dwight had explained to me that thoughts are actually packets of energy—electro-magnetic impulses—our brain generates when we think. "Make no mistake," he'd said, "your emotions and thoughts are things too. They are composed of energy in just the same way as your computer, for example, or a house. And they remain around you, floating in the air."

"No way!"

"Oh, yes," he nodded vigorously.

I shuddered. All my minutest thoughts? All my yucky emotions? … When I'm furious with my mother, that too? And when I'm irritated and fuming at a poky driver in front of me? And when I'm cursing a neighbor's barking dog?

And when I think what a jerk my supervisor at school is? *Oh-my-gosh*, I shuddered even more, dismayed.

"Yep, it's all vibration, everything that exists," Dwight waved his arm, looking intensely at me. "What's more ... (there is more? I quivered ...) all your emotions and thoughts affect other people around you and even those far away."

I couldn't even look Dwight in the eye at this point. I riveted my eyes to my fingernails and tried hard not to think any thought, not to feel any emotion.

Some thought-forms are stronger and some weaker, Dwight explained, depending on how much energy is put into the thinking. Thoughts that are repeated over a longer period of time and with a strong emotional charge— desire, fear, hatred, or jealousy, for example—acquire an independent existence and remain lingering in the atmosphere. "You can imagine what happens," he gave an example, "when strong, collective thoughts, such as fear of terrorism or hatred of a neighboring nation, hover over large areas. They are like clouds, invisible clouds that affect all beneath them, just as physical clouds block the rays of the sun. This explains, by the way, those hunches and gut feelings you have when you go somewhere and the place gives you 'the creeps,' or you feel 'good vibes,'" he concluded.

As I'm looking around this glum bedroom with a huge bed in the center, I wonder what went on within its four walls. What inspirations did Fellini receive in this place? What ideas came to him? Did he conceive the storyline for *Julia* in this house? But I feel so tired that I can no longer wait for Dwight, let alone take a shower. Half undressed, I curl up under the covers, and the next moment I am in dreamland.

When I wake up the following morning, Dwight is already up and sitting out on the terrace. He is alert and enraptured, and impatiently waiting for me to collect myself so he can bombard me with his most recent insights. The trees, he says, have inspired him; they are like his friends, and these *pinetas* have particularly strong energy.

"Wait!" I interrupt him just as he is about to fire more ideas at me. "Let me first get us some coffee and breakfast."

I rush downstairs, glancing around curiously. In the morning light, with shafts of sun piercing through half-open shutters, the house exudes a cheerful mood. I head for the kitchen. It's empty. I look for Speedy Gonzales and see him in the back garden tending to the rose bushes. He seems so concentrated on trimming withered roses that I don't want to disturb him. Besides, the espresso maker is already on the stove, ready to go. I return to our room balancing a tray loaded with cups, the heavy coffee maker, and *cornettos* left for us on the counter.

Gingerly, I open the door with my elbow and step into the bedroom that is now bathed in the morning sunlight. Through the open door of the terrace, I see Dwight's back. He is sitting at a table towards the very end of the terrace, set against the green foliage and crowned by the parasol branches of *pinetas*. He is so immobile, rooted like a tree in his chair, that he seems embedded in the canopy like a Green Man. In moments like this, when time stops rushing, when a sense of harmony pervades nature, when the beauty strikes me with gentleness, I'm suddenly dropped into a state of poise, of deep gratitude and ardent spiritual aspiration. In those moments, I feel my Soul very close. I feel my whole body stirred, reaching up toward that missing part. In those moments, fervently, I renew my pledge to meet my Soul.

"Okay," begins Dwight business-like when I join him. "I've been thinking about our trip in Italy so far, and here is what came to me. We've been too caught up in house-hunting rather than learning from our experiences and enjoying the adventure. We had fixed ideas about what should happen according to what we assumed was the higher plan, instead of letting the future unfold on its own. And when all the possibilities failed, we became depressed. So what has been the main problem? Where did we go wrong?" Dwight looks at me, expecting an answer.

"Relying too much on the Guidance?" I offer.

"That too. But the main problem was—our expectations.

"Expectations," he repeats in a different key, tapping his knuckles on the table. "We were *expecting* to find a compatible place to settle down. I was *expecting* that everything would go smoothly, and that we would be taken care of. You were *expecting* to enjoy gorgeous views, right? And when we fell short of all this, we got caught in the web of our disappointment."

I fidget in my chair. I'm very good at creating expectations; actually, I have quite a talent for that. "So, then," I take Dwight's analysis a step further, "according to our expectations of how things should be, we interpret events and circumstances as either good or bad, fortunate or unfortunate. And when the reality doesn't correspond to our expectations, we label it a failure."

"That's right."

"So," I continue, "we can look at what is happening to us here in Italy as a string of obstacles and failures *or* we can see the same events as opportunities to learn, to experience different energies and meet interesting people."

"Exactly," Dwight nods. "And the wise person makes the choice to see everything as a learning experience—as a gain, rather than a loss."

Yes, perfectly clear and, frankly, quite obvious. How come it is so difficult to remember this simple truth in situations that bring hardship and challenges? … like the one that was to follow soon after our departure from Fregene.

CHAPTER 8

AMALFI:

A DAY IN PARADISE

My first sight of the Amalfi coast as we took the exit at Vietri sul Mare left me speechless. The view that burst in front of us—the deep blue shimmering with myriads of tiny crystals, the snake-like coast slithering lazily up toward the Bay of Naples twenty-something miles northwest, the steep ragged cliffs plummeting into the sea, the white houses perched one above the other like Lego cubes and hugged by rings of pine and cypress trees—was as close to my imagination of paradise as I've ever seen.

We'd left Fregene this morning determined to follow my previous—*logical*—decision to go back to Sicily and settle there, the decision I had made while having a breakthrough in St. Francis' church.

According to that plan, I had booked a flight to the States from Sicily, and Dwight had reserved an *agro-tourismo* accommodation just outside Piedimonte, near Lorenzo's house—a perfectly sensible and rational plan, a plan made with the *left* lobe of my brain. I'm determined to turn a new page now. Obviously, the Guidance had failed me. I can't rely on my impressions, urges, or synchronicities; now I have to rely on my own resources. I have to be in control.

As we start descending to the Costiera Amalfitana, it's almost noon: the time of the day when the air is throbbing with light, and the sun is spilling diamonds atop the sea and splashing colors with the zeal and force of a Jackson Pollock. Magic of light! I always wonder how many people actually observe the light quality (except artists and photographers, of course). Because if you really make an attempt to be aware of light, you'll see how landscapes can change with different light. Sensual, spectacular, exotic, dramatic, mysterious, plain, gloomy, desolate, ominous, apocalyptic—all these impressions can be evoked from a landscape by different qualities of light.

Which, at this moment, makes the Costiera Amalfitana look dazzling.

When we get to the coastal highway, however, I realize that the road to paradise is always dangerous and strewn with obstacles; in this case, big tour buses careening on the hairpin curves. We can't drive faster than thirty mph; the road is that narrow and twisting. Frequently we have to dodge the monster-buses and scuttle to the side of the road, watching the giant fender loom bigger in front of our eyes, then brushing our license plate. We are so squeezed that I can almost feel our Honda inhaling deeply and plastering itself against the rock, just to avoid the snap of the brightly-colored jaw.

But it's well worth it. After all the convolutions on this "road of 1,001 bends" (as it is known among seasoned bus drivers), arriving in Amalfi feels like a special prize. From the distance, this old coastal town rises steep and jewel-like, piled up a deep ravine, and beautifully irregular like an unpolished diamond. The houses wear pastel hues and bright-colored tiles, as the art of majolica is the specialty of the Amalfi coast. (I make a mental note to stop at Vietri on our way back and browse the shops.) The tall bell tower of the cathedral glistens yellow and sky-blue and indigo-purple and peacock-green, the tiles shining in the sun like a painting of Matisse.

The hotel where we've booked a room looks modest with its white-washed walls, but the interior is adorned with exquisite tiles which I now get to inspect color by magnificent color, pattern by intricate pattern. Our room, on the top floor and in the far corner, is the best in the hotel. The large terrace, tiled in light green, overlooks a small harbor below, the big blue sea all around, and the town of Amalfi to the left. Bright. Joyful. Uplifting. My heart sings these words as I hop around the room and out onto the terrace, inhale, take in, expand, back to the window, inhale, take in, rejoice. I dig out my pretty summer clothes from the bottom of the suitcase, unwrap my nicest jewelry to celebrate the coming into paradise, and hop in the shower, humming, singing, quivering in anticipation of a beautiful walk around Amalfi. Oh, I'm sooohaaapyyyy....

When I come out of the shower, the room looks gloomy. At first, I thought that Dwight had closed the shutters. But no. The shutters are open, but outside all the colors have faded, as if painted over by one and the same shade of gray. The sky and the sea have merged into a metallic sheet. From the horizon, menacing dark clouds scud toward the coast, swell quickly and sink down to the sea, then in a matter of minutes, burst with sheets of rain. I drop onto the bed, atop my carefully laid out silk skirt, and stare in disbelief. Then in disgust.

Then in anger, indignation, fury, rage. While the rain, the torrents of rain, are sloshing down the windowpanes.

I'm fuming with thoughts as nasty as the clouds that have ruined my paradise. While all along, Dwight is watching me, sort of amused. Rain doesn't seem to bother him. Sure, he would have preferred sun and warmth and a nice walk but, he shrugs his shoulders, just as well. *JUST AS WELL?!* I don't understand how he can be so calm and unperturbed, and so, so … unflappable. This is the fourth time that the weather has changed on us like this. It's *really* too much! Still, Dwight remains philosophical and only nods at my outburst of righteous indignation. "So what can you do?" he asks and looks at me seriously, probably trying to estimate how low I have fallen in my outburst of temper. All of a sudden it hits me that, really, there is *nothing* I can do. "So may as well take a nap," he adds in a perfectly good mood.

When we wake up an hour or so later, the sky is still metallic gray but it's not raining; and I feel completely refreshed and restored, my anger washed away like a sand castle by a wave. I realize that I have some serious thinking to do. I mean, just a couple of days ago I understood perfectly well that I should accept the whole of experience, including the fog and the rain. So why did I have this fit, *yet again*, when the weather changed? There is a pattern here; similar events have happened several times in a row. There must be a lesson for me to learn. And if I don't learn it, the same circumstances will happen again and again, only in a more drastic way, until I finally learn the lesson.

As I am sitting propped up in bed, I absent-mindedly watch Dwight unpack his suitcase. He takes out a pocket-size book titled *Light on the Path*, and puts it on his bedside table. The words I read in that book just the other day loom in my head, and I realize that they hold my lesson: *remain unperturbed by external circumstances.*

Yes, that's it: no matter what happens around me, I should not let myself be influenced by the circumstances; instead, I should turn within, align with my Soul, and remain calm. Unperturbed. Unruffled. Unfazed. I mean, how much more obvious could it get? Perhaps only to see it written in white on this dark gray sky:

LOOK FOR JOY AND INSPIRATION WITHIN.

DO NOT DEPEND ON EXTERNAL CIRCUMSTANCES.

And I finally let go of my grudge. I decide to accept our situation just as it is. I accept the clouds, and the cold, and the rain. I even accept the foggy outlines of the spectacular coast. As we set off on our walk around Amalfi, I can't recognize myself; I'm actually brimming with joy. I thrust my arms wide open to embrace everything around me—and scream with joy. I scream so hard, with all my lung-power, that Dwight jumps, startled. "What on—?" But before he could finish, I plant a kiss on his lips, on his cheek, on his eyes; I shower him with kisses and squeeze him in an embrace so tight as if to inhale him into myself.

"I accept ... everything!" I whisper.

Now, I don't attribute this achievement all to myself. I think that the happy energy of Amalfi had much to do with such a feeling of elation. But no matter how many guidebooks I leafed through, I couldn't find anything in particular that could account for such good vibes, such an undercurrent of joy that permeates this place. Sure, Amalfi had a glorious past. It was the most important naval power and maritime republic between the ninth and the thirteenth centuries, while Venice was still in its toddler stage. It was in Amalfi that the first maritime legal code was formulated—the famous *Tavole Amalfitane* (Amalfi Tables). And while most of Europe worked in a barter economy, Amalfi was minting its own gold and silver coins. It was one of the richest city-republics of the medieval world.

Trade aside, Amalfitans were the force behind the creation of two influential medieval orders: they founded a hospital in Jerusalem (which would later give rise to the Order of Knights Hospitallers) and the Order of Knights of Malta (hence the Amalfi cross became the Maltese cross). Small as it was, the Duchy of Amalfi always fought fiercely for independence, regardless of the strength and size of the enemy. And it wasn't the occupation by the Normans or the sacking by the Pisans that did Amalfi in. It was the fourteenth century seaquake during which most of the old city (and its population) slid into the sea, swallowed by a tsunami, after which Amalfi never recovered its political and economic importance.

Today, Amalfi certainly has tourist importance. At the beginning of the past century it was a favorite sea resort of British aristocracy (just as Taormina was a haven for artists), although other towns in the Gulf of Salerno offered competition, such as romantic Positano, or breathtaking Ravello, or the fashionable island of Capri.

After many stops at majolica shops that line the coastal promenade, we reach the heart of Amalfi—the Piazza Duomo, lined with cafés. Out of the colorful sea of umbrellas rises a steep flight of stairs that leads to the Duomo Sant'Andrea. (St. Andrew, brother of St. Peter and one of the first apostles, is the patron saint of Amalfi. His relics now lie in the crypt, having been stolen from Constantinople during the Fourth Crusade—the Sacking of *Christian* Constantinople by Other *Christians*.)

The thirteenth-century cathedral towers over the *piazza*, imposing, majestic, unavoidable like the cliffs on which Amalfi is built. There is something about this cathedral, perhaps the Moorish-Byzantine influence in its architecture, that makes me look at it in wonder: the tall, pointed arches with lace-like arabesques, the shimmering bits of mosaics interspersed in geometrical patterns on the façade, the golden mosaics that cover the gable and, on top, the magnificent, glistening dome. This is a happy church, I feel strongly. This is how churches should feel—celebrating life, not death. I could never understand why Christianity had to found its faith on guilt, on fear, on sins and expiation. Why do so many churches exude an atmosphere of grim, macabre gloom? I want to be inspired when I go to a church; I want to feel more than I am, not less, like an unworthy worm writhing in muck. I want to be reminded of what I can become, of what is God-like in me, not to be accused of sins I have never committed. I want to transcend my limitations and soar! Soar like an eagle, wings outstretched, gliding on the wind.

Amalfi makes me feel like that: free and unbound. Which is a sheer irony given its crouched position at the bottom of the gorge. As we stroll the covered passages and the souk-like streets behind the *piazza,* we soak up the joy that seems to be floating in the air. "Where does this joy come from?" wonders Dwight. For once, I don't care to know. It is. And I take it as it is. No vivisection, no analyzing. It just is, and I just am.

The next morning, we wake up to the smell of baking pastry wafting in from underneath the door. The day is staring at us, gorgeous, through the windows. The atmosphere is clear like glass, the sky is the palest shade of blue, and the sea drenched with light. The blue-and-white fishing boats bob on the calm waters of the little harbor below. We order breakfast in our room and plant ourselves on the terrace, our gaze swimming in different shades of blue. Everything is just ... perfect.

"We finally have our little paradise!" I enthuse, perfectly happy, perfectly idle and content, soaking up the pleasantly warm autumn sun. Dwight eyes me periodically, makes little "hum" noises, then finally says, "What about your insight from yesterday? What did you say about your 'penchant for beautiful settings?'"

"Oh, that ... yes. I have to overcome it, I know, but not just now. Next time, I promise."

And so I continue to enjoy, ahem, indulge in our paradise. I lazily remember the inscription I saw on the plaque under the gate of Porta Marina:

"The judgment day, when Amalfitans go to heaven, will be a day like any other."

Mmm, yes, a step from one paradise into another ... all the same. How does it feel, I wonder, to know only paradise? How do you know you're in paradise if you don't experience hell?

CHAPTER 9

SICILY:

A POISONOUS MUSHROOM

"Step aside, Miss, and follow me!" Two cold, impassive eyes slide over my stunned face, and the gray uniform rises in all its authority from inside the immigration booth. With my heart pounding in my ears, throat, and entrails, I scurry behind the peremptory figure of the customs officer. I feel a burning heat at the back of my neck, as if the eyes of hundreds of passengers patiently waiting in line to clear immigration at Los Angeles airport are riveted at that one spot at the back of my neck, all looking at me suspiciously.

And I remember that same heat, the heat and clammy fear I felt in the police headquarters in Belgrade when, at age twenty-two, I was summoned and interrogated: how long was I with my boyfriend? ("Former," I piped up.) Had he been calling me from Paris? ("We broke up," I quavered.) Did I read the articles he'd written against the communist system? Who were his friends? Where did they meet? What did they talk about? I was grilled for hours; every detail of my personal life was examined, every secret exposed.

I was interrogated because my former boyfriend, the philosophy teacher, was arrested at the border upon his return from a two-year sojourn in Paris. He was well known to the Yugoslav police for the anti-communist articles he'd published in France. He was detained for possession of seditious books. And they've also found love letters I wrote to him (I blushed from the roots of my hair to the tips of my fingers), as well as his notes to me, very tender—we must have been very much in love. (*Geez, do I have to explain to the police why I broke up with a boyfriend?*) The sternly polite interrogation ended with a request to report anything suspicious I hear or see.

"Take a seat here and someone will be with you shortly." The gray uniform turns around and without a further word leaves me in a side office of LAX, small, empty, and barren. Oh, I'm so miserable. I can't understand why they are not letting me into the country; I was away for a little over eleven months, which is allowed for permanent residents. I did not break any rules. Am I detained because of my Yugoslav passport, because I'm of Serbian origin?

I sit down and try to calm myself. I invoke Dwight's face in my mind's eye; he looks at me reassuringly and smiles gently. I know what he would say—this is just another test. Sure, like the one in Sicily, as soon as we left Amalfi.... I sigh, remembering the ordeal and feeling sorry for myself.

It was just as Dwight had said: our brief admittance to paradise was immediately followed by a plunge into hell. We'd crossed the river Styx while driving down to Sicily on a freeway under reconstruction, hemmed in between trucks in a miles-long line. Cars, trailers, and trucks wallowed through detour towns like monstrous tidal waves, and we were carried along. We arrived late in Piedimonte, frazzled and exhausted, and the next morning awoke early to present ourselves at the *Questura* in Catania (that's the Italian immigration office, otherwise known as the Fourth Ring of Hell, in my approximation). For several long hours we were wedged in the welter of bodies—north African, Indian, Asian, you name it—all anxiously waiting, their eyes riveted upon immigration officers who ambled to and fro behind the glass window.

Finally, after much shuffling of papers, disappearances, and endless questions (Where your home? Why you in Sicily? What income? Married?—what "c'mon law" marriage?), leafing through my passport for the umpteenth time and nodding gravely, we got our *Permessi di Soggiorno*. But contrary to our expectations, only for three months.

I look around the gray cubicle at LAX, sterile walls and empty counter, and wonder how long is "shortly" going to be—fifteen minutes, an hour, or several hours? What if I don't make it for the last airbus to Santa Barbara? I'll have to spend the night at the airport, I shudder. Wait, what if I don't make it at all? If they don't let me in, I'll lose my green card! I feel anxiety mounting and definitely lodging in my heart. My mouth is dry but I've run out of water. I make a desperate attempt to control my jittery leg. I close my eyes and inhale deeply. I try to visualize golden-white light spreading through my body, relieving tension....

"Miss," a shrill voice catches me by surprise. I jump to my feet, all relaxation gone to pieces, and stand with trepidation in front of an officer. I face another pair of cold, almost de-humanized eyes, a stone face without a smile, and I feel positively miserable. No, I feel guilty! As if I've done something wrong.

"Why were you absent for so long?" a stiff voice demands. And so begins another investigation into my life, comings and goings, reasons and financial means. In the end I'm reprimanded and warned that next time I stay away this long I need a re-entry permit or I will lose my green card. "If you don't want to live in this country, give your green card to someone who does!" the voice hisses angrily.

Okay, that was hellish, I think surprisingly calmly that night in bed. Immigration has always been my bogeyman; understandably so, traveling as I have been on a communist passport. By now, I've become conditioned to expect suspicious looks at the border, long waits, double-checking, phone calls, detailed searching of my luggage. I immediately lose my sense of dignity even when I'm with Dwight. I step back, leaving him to do the talking, and I assume the "shadow" position, like those swathed Muslim women. In fact, if I could, I'd cloak myself to become invisible to the authorities.

But right now, I have to resolve my situation, so I outline a plan of action (find an immigration lawyer), and the following day present myself at a law office recommended by a friend.

"Of course I'm positive," the smooth-talking, impeccably dressed lawyer says with a glint of annoyance in his eyes. I'd asked him for the third time if he was absolutely certain that I could stay out of the country for eleven months. "As long as it is less than a year," he repeats with authority.

"But … the officer said—" I pipe up.

"He didn't know what he was talking about," the lawyer cuts me off with a dismissive wave of his Rolex-clad wrist. "The law is quite clear: you have the right to be out of the country for up to a year, but not a day more."

So what was that intimidation at the airport all about? A mistake out of ignorance? Malice? Intentional harassment? Just to be on the safe side and to appease my anxiety, I ask the lawyer to procure for me a re-entry permit, valid for one year.

"Good morning and welcome back, my love," Dwight says brightly as I stagger into the kitchen the morning after my return to Sicily. He doesn't turn to kiss me, he is so concentrated on cooking something on the stove.

"What are you doing?" I inquire, slightly alarmed at the sight of Dwight by the stove (a highly unusual behavior—and dangerous).

"Oh, I'm cooking a miso-onion soup for breakfast."

"A *what?* ... What are you cooking?"

"Onion soup, with miso," he beams. "Lorenzo prescribed it for me and taught me how to make it." (Lorenzo has been working with Dwight on resolving Dwight's childhood traumas—a near-suffocation from two severe illnesses: whooping cough when Dwight was a six-month old baby and diphtheria at the age of four. As a consequence, Dwight has had respiratory problems—asthma and allergies—almost all his life.)

I slosh down the yellow-brownish contents of my bowl, concentrating on Dwight's report on sessions with Lorenzo. At one moment Dwight announces with a ring of importance in his voice: "I learned how to communicate with my organs."

I almost gag on my soup. I knew that Dwight had been disconnected from his body, so to speak, most of his life. The body was his servant, "a brother ass," who should always perform according to the master's bidding—just as St. Francis spoke of his body. So the thought of Dwight communicating with his organs seemed ... odd, at best.

"I go within," he explains with animation unusual for him, "and become this tiny dot of consciousness that travels through the veins and arteries. I look around to see which organs are in distress. Then I draw what I see. Lorenzo will work with you too," he adds, "so you get to the source of your candida and get over your fatigue."

Ah, fatigue. My constant companion over the past two years. There were times when I couldn't move, lying weak in bed with neither desire nor will power to do anything. So the prospect of working with Lorenzo seemed quite desirable. Just that ... since we came back to Sicily, I was sensing a change in our friend, which I couldn't pin down.

Dwight dismisses my misgivings. "Lorenzo's just stressed out because of the house." After they moved to Sicily, Lorenzo and Brigit had bought one of those abandoned farm houses that was practically in ruins—but dirt cheap—and started to restore it. When we arrived, the house was still unfinished.

"By the way," Dwight adds casually while I'm clearing up the dishes, "if you want to have coffee, we have an invitation from Ettore to join him."

While I was away, Dwight had made friends with Ettore, our landlord and a gardenia grower who, in his own words, has exchanged the highly-competitive world of fashion in Milan for the peaceful world of gardenias in Sicily. Ettore—which is Italian for Hector—does look the part of a fashionista. Handsome, hunky, with streaks of silver in his dark hair and lines around his deep-blue eyes, he exudes a certain restraint and aloof confidence (I didn't say haughtiness), which characterize a Northerner.

"Il profumo … è magnifico!" Ettore exclaims while we're sipping home espresso at the long wooden table on his veranda. In front of us, hanging between two portly columns like a crescent moon is a hammock, inviting in its loose, slumping curve, the curve of a relaxing body.

"The fragrance fills this place with joy," I turn to Ettore and say with the passion of a gardenia aficionado.

The handsome Milanese nods gravely, with a glint in his eyes. *"Eh, certo,* you understand. You love life when you grow gardenias," he says calmly, his hands resting on the table, fingers interlaced. I'm not used to seeing an Italian who doesn't use his hands as gestural punctuation marks while speaking. Is this another Northern Italian trait?

"You know," begins Ettore hesitantly after a pause, "I want to redo the small cottage below, and, er, I like you to, how you call it … *dose* it." He looks at Dwight expectantly.

I glance at Dwight, taken aback by this request. I knew what Ettore meant: if Dwight would *dowse* the old cottage for him. Dwight had already told me that while I was away, he'd dowsed our landlord's house. Ettore's wife had died of cancer, which had developed and claimed her life since they moved into this house, and now Ettore himself has been unwell. So Dwight insisted on checking the house for harmful energy, also known as "geopathic stress."

Geopathic stress is a term used to describe different types of invisible energy detrimental to human health. The most common one originates from underground water, especially at places where two underground streams cross. The negative radiation of water lines that run below a house can affect residents if they spend a large part of the day or night right over those streams, called by professional dowsers "black streams." The harmful radiation is not noticeable right away but has a cumulative effect. Over the years, people might develop arthritis or rheumatism in those parts of the extremities where the radiation of a black stream crosses the body. Or they might develop arteriosclerosis. Or cancer.

It wasn't exactly easy to explain this concept to a no-nonsense, cool and rational Milanese. In order to prove his point about invisible energies that fill our environment, Dwight suggested muscle-testing our landlord by pressing down on his raised arm. Now, Ettore is a sturdy, hale, hulk of a man. Dwight himself is not small or effete, but press with all his might on Ettore's wrist, he couldn't budge his steel-strong arm. Then Dwight asked him to put his free hand on top of a microwave oven. (Electrical devices, such as TV's, computers, microwaves, or cell phones, generate low frequency electromagnetic fields that are also harmful for human bodies.) And, lo, the steel beam of Ettore's arm went down with no resistance, like a knife through soft butter.

Ettore was dumbstruck.

Having made his point, Dwight then checked the bedroom. The spot where Ettore's deceased wife had slept for years was above a black stream. Now, having remarried, Ettore has been sleeping on that side of the bed. "If you don't change the position of your bed, my friend, you're heading for cancer!" Dwight said with urgency.

Ettore took it seriously. "You know, I moved my bed and my armchair. Now no more headaches," says the hulky Milanese, looking gratefully at Dwight. "So before I build other house, we go there together. You take your *pistolas* and find bad places." (Ettore had nicknamed Dwight's coat-hangers-turned-dowsing-rods *pistolas*.)

That's how Dwight earned our landlord's respect and a rent reduction. We had arranged to stay in the cottage next to the main house until we found something suitable to rent. The cottage was not dolled up as were the other *agro-tourismo* rentals, but it had everything we needed, and for a bargain price.

And so began the second installment of our Italian house-hunting. I called about one ad after another, always asking the same questions about the view, the heating, the utilities, the noise, the neighborhood. We covered a stretch of sixty miles on the east coast of Sicily, from Gardini all the way down to Siracuse. We saw various kinds of rentals from socialist-type apartment buildings with twin babies next door and the view of hanging laundry to charming villas on a remote beach, but found nothing suitable.

Not having an internet connection turned out to be a great hassle. I had brought a new computer from the States, but had to negotiate the internet-usage schedule with Ettore's French wife, always feeling as if I were importuning. Settling down in a foreign country is such an undertaking. I found myself always inquiring about how things are done: how do you apply for a telephone line, how do you get an internet connection, which provider is best for a cell phone, how do you pay the bills, where do you shop for vitamins?... I've been without a home before; I don't understand why I feel so helpless and insecure now. What did Dwight say the other day, that I seemed *fretful*? I didn't even know what that word meant. "Irritable," he clarified. Ah, with good reason! I've changed my inner attitude, taken matters in hand, but we're stuck again. We still have no home.

So, when after weeks of discouraging search we stumble upon a house in the remote village of Milo—a big, fully-furnished house with a balcony all along the second floor—we both light up. The house sits on a steep street, in a steep village, and feels friendly just like the middle-aged couple who greet us. The *signora* takes us upstairs to show us the bedrooms. No windows. But there is a big French door opening onto the terrace that offers a 300-degree view of—now darkening fog, but on a clear day—hills tumbling all the way down to the coast, and to the side, the bewitching cone of Etna. Had we not gotten lost on our way we would have made it here an hour earlier, enough to see everything in the daylight. So we arrange with the owners to come back the following day, assuring them that we're definitely prospective tenants, *molto serioso*.

We arrive at Lorenzo's in good spirits. Today is the Full Moon and our friend has invited us for a meditation and dinner afterwards. A friend of Brigit is visiting from Sweden, so the dinner will be special. I'm happy that we finally have some good news to report, after so many disappointments and my why-can't-something-work-out-in-Sicily complaints.

As I walk into the kitchen, gregarious and overflowing with enthusiasm, I feel as if I've bumped into something. The mood in the house is solemn. Well, maybe only serene, and certainly still. I have a difficult time calming down—after all, we've just found *the* house! I try hard not to fidget on the meditation cushion, but it's almost impossible to quiet my mind, which, at this moment, feels like a combination of effervescent water and champagne, fizzing and bubbling and spurting up.

After what seems like a long hour, a resonant *dooong* of the Tibetan bowl fills the room. Whew, it's finally over.

"Ah, we can laugh now," I say blithely as I stretch my legs. I'm also eyeing the pots on the stove, trying to guess what Lorenzo has cooked for dinner (he is such a good cook!). I'm so happy I feel like sharing my happiness with everybody.

"Argh," comes a growl from Lorenzo, "you come to our house to disturb the peace."

"W-what?" I sputter. For a moment I'm in disbelief of what I heard. Maybe I didn't understand what he meant.

Lorenzo glowers at me with his beautiful green eyes that now look hostile.

"You come here with your small talk and fake laughter and constant questions and you disturb the quiet of our home," he says in an unconvincingly casual voice.

"Well, maybe we disturb your peace," I reply back, my good mood shattered to smithereens, "but you don't see how *you* have changed since Cyprus."

Then without thinking, I add, "Your heart is closed."

"Oh, you think my heart is closed?" His voice is openly angry now. "Well, let me tell you something, my heart is fine and wide open and full of compassion, and I don't need *you* to tell me anything about *my* heart!"

"So you want us to leave?" I bristle now myself, while the feeling of hurt begins to grate in my heart. Dwight and Brigit are watching this scene without a word, glued to the floor, while Brigit's friend instinctively takes a few steps back.

"Yes, I want you to leave!" Lorenzo shouts, his lustrous green eyes turned opaque, as if glazed by a crust of ice. "I'm fed up with your empty chatter and blabber."

Dwight now clears his throat. "Are you fed up with me also, Lorenzo?" he asks in a calm, friendly voice.

"Yes, I am." Lorenzo snaps at Dwight. "You and your fake laughter!"

"So you don't want to work with me anymore?"

"No way." He stares at Dwight coldly.

Brigit now looks positively alarmed. "Lorenzo, are you sure?" she says in her always poised voice. "Shouldn't you—"

"Of course I am. I don't want them in my house!"

"Well, too bad for all this lovely food that's going to waste," I blurt out, with this particular knack of mine of rubbing people the wrong way.

I definitely should not have said that. Because Lorenzo becomes really furious now. I'm so hurt, so humiliated in front of that nice Swedish man, that my throat chokes and my eyes well up with tears. I dash out before anyone can see that I'm crying.

For a couple of days, Dwight has been silent. It's not just an ordinary silence, it's a silence impregnated with intense mental focus and bursting with unexpressed thoughts. I've been silent too, but only because I've been so profoundly shaken up that I feel disoriented. I walk out of the cottage and for a moment don't know which way to turn to go to the vista point where we do our morning

Qigong exercises; or I drive down the winding lanes to Piedimonte and forget where to turn. Every time I come back to our cottage, I step into Stygian gloom. Am I depressed? Or only discouraged? Defeated? Or just disheartened? (Why do so many words that describe dark emotional states start with a "d"? What is it about the letter "d" that's so dreary, devastating, desolate, desperate, despondent, destitute, deprived, or plain destructive, even—demonic?)

Finally, just before going to bed the second day after the falling-out, I can't stand the silence any longer. Gripped by anxiety, I grab Dwight's hands and stare into his eyes. "What are we going to do *now*?" I ask.

Surprisingly, he answers promptly and without hesitation, "Obviously, it's out of the question to stay here."

"It is?"

"Of course, Lorenzo was our main reason for settling down here. Now that this has happened, it's obvious that we're not supposed to live in Sicily. Your Guidance has used Lorenzo as an agent to deliver that message. Nothing is keeping us here anymore." Dwight pauses, looking away from me.

"So…?"

"So we'll go back to Rome and rent Noemi's apartment."

Now that the decision has been made, both Dwight and I switch into action-mode. I call Noemi and—hallelujah!—the apartment is free and she is happy to rent it to us. We apologize to those nice people whose house we thought of renting, and we set our departure date. Everything we do feels right. Living in Rome feels right now. Even the falling-out with Lorenzo no longer feels devastating. I'm ready for a new start.

The weather has gifted us with gorgeous, clear days. We want to say farewell to our last friend in Sicily—the volcano—from Taormina, from that elegant hotel with the superb view of Etna. We are the only guests on the sun-bathed terrace. Above us a cerulean sky (Dwight's word), a deep, almost ink-blue sea stretches all the way to the horizon, and to the right Etna pufs contentedly.

"So, what have you learned from this?" Dwight asks his usual question as soon as we seat ourselves.

I've been thinking about it for days, before going to sleep, upon waking, in the shower, trying to figure out what *I* have done to cause the event. "Well, for one thing," I begin, "I think I alienated both of them by complaining."

Dwight nods right away. (Why does he have to nod so readily? After all I am a Virgo, and everyone knows—should know—that's what Virgos are good at: criticizing. That should be taken as my mitigating circumstance.)

"You sure did complain a lot," he laughs heartily.

"But—that's, that's because I felt so insecure, see? When I have a place I call home, I feel safe and confident and grounded. Then I don't complain."

"Complaining is your defense mechanism, are you aware of that?" Dwight asks, eyeing me.

"How so?"

"When you feel threatened by the circumstances, by the unknown—which gives rise to insecurity—you start complaining. Remember how long you complained about those shoes in Perugia, *and* the weather, *and* our bad luck?" Dwight looks at me in that intense way of his.

"Well, because they didn't have my size and—" I make a feeble attempt to justify my reactions, but Dwight cuts me off. "It's a transference and projection on a basic psychological level, you follow?"

I nod non-committedly.

"Okay, let me put it this way," he is Dwight-the-teacher now, "when we feel inadequate and not up to the situation, we avoid seeing our shortcomings by finding something to criticize outside of ourselves. That's transference. Take the example of, say, religious bigots, who fight crusades against vices that they themselves secretly have."

"I follow now. So when I feel threatened by circumstances, I try to get even by criticizing them, and I see all sorts of faults. In fact, I focus on the faults."

"Exactly!" Dwight nods approvingly. "You got it."

"But…" I add after a pause, "I still don't understand Lorenzo's outburst. It was so irrational."

"Sure it was. Lorenzo is not a rational person. He's an artist at his core. He acts upon his emotions. Which," Dwight now looks at me with importance, "is something you have to outgrow."

Oh, that, I fidget.

"Most people behave irrationally, puppets of their emotions, even when those emotions are self-destructive. But you," he pauses significantly, "you're on the path. And when you are on the path, you don't let emotions control you."

Ahhh, will I ever, EVER, manage that?

"Remember Plato's allegory about the black and white horses?"

How can I not remember it? Dwight had told it so many times during our study meetings: "The black horse, that's your emotions; the white horse is your thoughts. But you, you are neither. You're the charioteer behind them, and you steer them where *you* want to go, not where *they* want to go."

"One day, I'll learn how to drive the chariot," I laugh, half-jokingly and half-seriously.

When we get home it's already dusk. The heady fragrance of gardenia infuses the air. In the crack between the door and the doorframe, a piece of paper is sticking. I unfold it. It's a message from Ettore: "Lorenzo called. Please call back."

Dwight and I look at each other.

"I certainly am *not* going to call," I declare. "You'll have to do it." (I know how much Dwight hates telephoning, but I am not willing to negotiate.)

Dwight huffs and coughs and bites his lower lip with small, unconscious bites, then finally asks me to dial the number. All ears, I sit next to him, but can't hear a word. And Dwight doesn't say much. Only "uh-huh," and "okay," and "mm-hmm," and "right." When he hangs up, he says, "Lorenzo has invited me to come over. He has a lot to tell me. He is apologizing for what he did. But … he didn't invite you."

I blink. He didn't? "Oh, well, suits me fine," I fumble. "I wouldn't go anyway."

When Dwight returns later in the evening, I'm all antsy. What did Lorenzo have to say about his behavior? Dwight is unusually affectionate. He sweeps me into his arms and holds me for a long time, pouring into me the energy of well-being (it's the closest I can come to describing that mixture of encouragement and protection and sweet love.)

"You helped Lorenzo," he finally utters. "He went through a deep reflection over the past week. And he realized that he'd been deceiving himself that his heart was open. He admitted you were right. You helped him see that." Dwight looks at me warmly, almost proudly.

"Oh, and the explanation of his fit is so bizarre that it's got to be true," Dwight adds, shaking his head. "The afternoon before the meditation he'd been contemplating the beauty of a very poisonous mushroom. He was so mesmerized that he felt like eating it. It was this mushroom, he says, and the dark, deadly energy contained in it that penetrated his sensitive aura and caused that outburst of rage."

On our last day in Sicily, as we are buying provisions for the trip, I notice a dog tied up outside the supermarket. It's lithe, lean, and long-skulled with an elongated muzzle, and his unusually long ears are pointed up. I recognize a Cirneco, the dog unique to Sicily and found mostly in the Etna region. Cirneco is a very ancient breed, over 2,000 years old and unadulterated to this day, Lorenzo had told us earlier. The dog was brought to Sicily from Egypt, and is a direct descendant of—Anubis!

I tug at Dwight's sleeve and motion with my head toward the recumbent dog. The dog is staring at me with his almond-shaped eyes set far back on the head, his front legs outstretched, while his tail is resting neatly against his hocks.

"Ah, your friend Anubis," smiles Dwight. "He's seeing you on your way."

Ancient
Etruria

Tiber River

Orvieto

Bagnoregio

Lago di Bolsena

Bagnaia

Tuscania

Tarquinia

Santa Marinella

Rome

Frascati

Tyrrhenian Sea

Naples

Paestum

PART 3

ROME:

I LOVE YOU, I HATE YOU!

CHAPTER 10

ROME:

HOME, FINALLY!

We left Sicily and headed for Rome on a beautiful, glittering morning. Snow-covered Etna rose sharply, painted dramatically clear by the winter sun. Before we left, I picked a gardenia flower from the nursery. A little *memento* of Sicily, of Etna, of Ettore, of our learning here. Only one white gardenia that infused the whole car with its sweet, dense fragrance of love.

Once on the boot of Italy, I notice that the landscape now looks different from the last time we drove this same road. The winter light casts intense hues upon the land, and everything around us glows with more intensity.

"You realize," Dwight says in a reflective tone, as if talking to himself, "this is our second drive to Rome from Sicily."

I smile. It was only three months ago, but so much has happened! "We were so full of anticipation then," I say. "Now, I don't feel that same enthusiasm. I'm calm and happy, but also jaded by everything we went through."

"That's only normal. You lost the freshness of doing something for the first time but you gained more wisdom, right?" Dwight shoots a quick glance at me, then says, as if probing, "So that you can take events more calmly, with more, shall we say ... detachment?"

"Wish I could!" I sigh. "I guess what I should do is make a conscious decision not to have *any* expectations about Noemi's apartment. Wherever it is, however it looks, it's fine."

"That's the right attitude!" Dwight says, patting me on the knee. "But not only that. You should also practice being neutral, neither disappointed nor elated. Because any kind of reaction will be followed by its opposite: negative—positive, happy—disappointed.... Opposites always define each other."

"Right." My mind is made up. I'm determined to stop bouncing on the seesaw of my emotional reactions. I'm going to be *neutral*.

We pass the road to Paestum—originally Poseidonia—some sixty miles southeast of Naples. Paestum was one of the major early Greek colonies in Italy and it still offers a taste of Greece thanks to its astonishingly well-preserved temples. We spent the whole day there on our previous trip to Rome. I remember with fondness the feeling of peace that permeated the site and the sense of expansion in my heart as we strolled alone in and out of the temples. The oldest one, the Temple of Hera, is the most beautiful Archaic Doric temple in existence, better preserved than any early Doric temple in Greece itself. I marveled at the ingenuity of those early architects who designed deliberate imperfections in the proportions of columns so that from a distance the columns would create an illusion of perfection.

Neutral, stay neutral, I remind myself as we approach the ring road of Rome at rush hour and edge our way into a traffic jam that dwarfs the freeway traffic in Los Angeles. *Stay neutral*, I keep repeating while we snail to the exit for northern Rome, then toward the Pineta Saccheti area where Noemi's apartment is located.

At the sound of those words I pronounce silently—*Pineta Saccheti*—I feel the first, tiny flutter of happiness in my heart. *What a good omen to live in the area named after "my" trees!* But when we effortlessly find our way through a maze of one-way streets to Noemi's building, when I find the keys to the apartment just as Noemi had explained, and finally when I park our Honda right in front of the building, I forget all about my intention to be neutral and feel positively elated. I simply love this neighborhood, the sumptuous vegetation, the geraniums dripping from every balcony.

Planting a bird-like kiss on Dwight's cheek, I hop out of the car to scout the new territory. Elated, I walk into a foyer with marble floors, etchings of old Rome on the walls, wrought-iron railings, and an old-fashioned elevator with double doors made of wood. Second … third … fourth floor. The elevator stops with a rattle and a slight tremor, like an old man who has just dropped heavy grocery bags. I gingerly open first the inner then the outer door, step out, and look at the three tall entrance doors, all made of highly-polished, warm-colored wood. The door to the left with a gleaming brass plaque that reads "Puntel" is the one I open with surprising ease (I normally have trouble with keys and locks). I step into the darkness that feels friendly, like somebody's dog that comes to greet a stranger, wagging its tail. I hurry to turn on all the lights, so when the elevator brings Dwight with the suitcases, he walks into the already lit, welcoming apartment. Together, we step out onto the spacious balcony overlooking the streets and other buildings in the distance below. Noemi's neighborhood, we realize, takes up a hill-top.

Dwight gently places his arm on my shoulder and brings me close to him, and I curl my arm around his waist. Without a word, in a tight embrace, we gaze at the street lights, car lights, apartment lights, billboard lights, all sparkling down there at a safe distance, a distance that transforms them into colorful decorations, while a starry sky spreads unobstructed before and above us. Our lips meet naturally, softly, and I stare into Dwight's eyes that glint with the sheen of all the reflected lights around us—the whole world in Dwight's eyes.

We were in Rome.

Was it the magic I felt during our drive, was it the lights of Rome, was it Dwight's eyes that caused this shift in my perception? For days now I've been in this strange state of consciousness. It started the moment we stepped back into the living room from the balcony. I experienced a slight blur, a very, very slight tremor of time, as if the same moment had been repeated twice.

At first I thought I was having a déjà vu experience, an instantaneous and momentary recognition of the situation. I was quite familiar with this phenomenon, as I'd experienced it many times in the past. But this wasn't such a solitary moment of recognition, a fleeting feeling of "having seen it" before; rather it continued, a moment stitched to a moment, until it became a permanent state of vague familiarity—as if I had already been through it all.

Because I felt as if I'd already lived all these moments, I coined a term—*déjà vécu*, "already lived" (as opposed to déjà vu, "already seen"). It's very much like being aware on two levels—as an observer and as a doer. I'm both doing and observing, except that the observing happens first, and that's the weird part of it. A fraction of a moment before a situation occurs I have a glimpse of it. I have a glimpse that I'm going to find the bedroom armoire full of clothes that belong to Noemi and her two daughters; I have a glimpse that the bathroom is sparkling white, with enormous mirrors; I have a glimpse that golden-haired Giordanna, Noemi's younger daughter, is going to ring the bell and ask if she could do a load of laundry. (She is staying with her *nonna*, the grandmother, who lives in the apartment next door, but there is no washer in her apartment.) All this has already happened before! Or has it?

Four years ago when I experienced this state for the first time, I felt uncomfortable. It started in the shower of the hotel room in Limassol where we were staying upon our arrival in Cyprus. Then I called this state, "double perception." It was unsettling and somewhat alarming because it was so weird. Was I suffering some mental dislocation, or was it a sign that I was doing the right thing? Was it a symptom of a nervous condition, or an indication of a heightened state of consciousness?

Unfortunately, even my wise man couldn't help me. "I've never had that kind of experience." Dwight shook his head, perplexed. "And I haven't come across it in any literature. Sorry I can't help you."

Gradually, I got used to this new state of perception and even grew to like it. In a way, it gave an unusual richness even to ordinary actions, like brushing my teeth or making breakfast. Everything that was happening had more relief, like a drop shadow effect in graphic design, and I was fully aware of the most minute action I performed.

Then I lost it. And when I lost it, I realized how beautiful it had been. I was having an argument over the phone with a new Cypriot friend with whom we were planning to buy a used car to share. When I hung up, I was so angry that something snapped in my head and I found myself looking at Dwight, propped up in bed next to me, and seeing him "flat." Then I looked around the room and the room looked "flat." No drop shadow world, no double perception. Everything looked just plain ordinary.

This is why I now cherish this state. I interpret it as a sign that I'm on the right track. I even consider that this might be how the Guidance is now showing itself to me. I also notice that this state makes me feel stronger and more poised, and, come to think of it, makes me feel closer to embodying my role model of a wise Mage. So, finally, I'm behaving as Dwight had been patiently waiting to see me behave—without complaining. Not that there is much to complain about. Overall, the apartment has more or less everything we need to establish a normal life, including a large desk by the windows with a grand view of the neighborhood on the hill below. This is what I like most about the apartment: the vast swath of sky I can always lose myself in. I don't particularly care for the sight of other buildings, not very appealing to be sure, but Dwight likes it. He likes it very much, actually. He says the view reminds him of a cubist painting.

"Look at the roofs, the shapes, the colors!" He takes me by the arm and plants me in front of the window. "Don't you see the geometrical patterns?

Don't you see the angles, intersections of lines, patches of different colors joined in the corners? Very cubist."

I look, but see windows with blinds pulled down and balconies with hanging laundry and a swing on the terrace of a penthouse and a woman shaking blankets and another woman washing windows and a peeling façade here and there. Are we looking at the same view?

Dwight laughs. "You see too much," he says. "You clutter your vision with too many details. Try looking with your eyes half-closed. That will flatten what you see, so it looks two-dimensional."

I tried. It took me some time not to register the details and to see just the outlines, the shapes, and the abstract patterns. It was much more beautiful, I had to admit.

Our first walk in the neighborhood took us by surprise. We did not expect to see so many pine trees, palms, willows, bushes of plumbago, bougainvillea, oleander, potted plants on balconies, long green hedges. We did not expect to find so many inviting gardens, so many unexpected angles at which our street turned. Harmonious. Charming. Delightful, in fact. "Everything built to the measure of man," Dwight says with appreciation.

Small stores line the last block of our street before it flows into a *piazza*. A produce store, a bakery, a butcher, a florist, a general store, a hardware store, a newspaper stand ... a café! We've come to our destination, our favorite destination, always. The café is completely unpretentious and the cappuccino is one-fourth of what it costs in town. Over the months ahead, we'd get to know all the "regulars:" we'd nod to them in a greeting and participate indirectly in their lively conversations. We'd also get to know the waiters, and they'd get to know what to bring us even before we order.

"*Due cappucci, sì?*" The young, dark-haired, quick-moving waiter would shout as he would see us approaching the patio. (I love that colloquialism *cappucci*, short for *cappuccini*.)

"*E un cornetto, oggi* (And one croissant today)," I'd shout back, my Italian improving daily.

We love sitting on the café patio because it faces the charming Piazza Pio IX that has such good energy. The square used to be called Il Pinetto, after *my* trees, but since they'd been cleared, the square was renamed after a Pope. All the neighborhood streets flow into it, forming an eight-pointed star. In the middle is a little fountain, surrounded by parked scooters, as well as groups of young men thst change size as the individual members move from group to group. On the left a tall building presides over the square. In the niche atop stands a lovely sculpture of the Madonna with a raised arm, as if giving benediction to the people going about their business.

On Friday mornings, a small farmers' market takes place in one of the eight streets. I've gotten some great recipes from a vendor who always has the freshest greens. I've also gotten a few personal stories about his wife and how she left him for another man, taking their daughter with her, and how difficult it is to be alone. But for everything that befell this middle-aged, quick-eyed *venditore,* I've never seen him morose or grumpy. He always greets me cheerfully, choosing the good bunches for me (what does he do with the "bad" ones?), throwing in the bag a stray tomato or a sprig of parsley for seasoning.

Once when I was feeling particularly tired, I asked the *venditore* how he managed to be so cheerful all the time. He stopped rearranging piles of fennel and looked at me, squinting, as if not completely understanding my question. Then he said in Italian, "There is always something to be happy about," and he started motioning with both hands, "the sun, the smell of fennel, the espresso, the smile of a pretty girl, the sound of water, a song, always...."

These first several weeks *at home* would have been perfectly peaceful, lazy, and uneventful, had it not been for meeting Aldo.

Aldo....

Several months ago in Cyprus, when I looked at his name on the list of graduates from the Barbara Brennan School of Energy Healing, I very much liked the sound of the long "Aaaa" curling up into the "lllll" then suddenly dropping to "do"—like a bird soaring up, gliding over the sea, then plummeting down to scoop up a fish. We decided to take healing sessions from him, Dwight for his heart, and I for my fatigue.

That's why we are now in front of Sette Spigghe, which translates as "Seven Wheat Stalks," Aldo's health food store in the vicinity of the Vatican. When we step inside, at first we don't see anyone, the space is so small and bursting with bags of beans, rice, pasta, flour, dried mushrooms, nut butters, cookies, crackers, all wheat-free and sugar-free. Bottles of vitamins, chemical-free hair products and hygiene staples fill shelf after shelf in the back of the room. The door, when we open it, shakes a loudly-ringing bell attached to it, creating a commotion behind a huge glass case in the far end of the store. Out from behind it steps a man of slight build and average height. He moves toward us softly like a cat.

I'm first aware of a sense of power he exudes, his large, intense eyes fixing on us like cat's eyes (and I mean a wild cat, like a leopard or puma). Then he speaks in a soft, soft voice, *"Buon giorno, sono Alll-* (voice goes up)-*do* (then down)," and his eyes break into a smile and shower us with warm, loving energy. His handshake is strong and firm, as if he could easily break my delicate hand bones, but his hand is elegant with long, soft fingers. I look at the shaved head, small, thin lips, the oval face with firmly set features, the decisive expression, but can't tell his age. He must be in his late forties, but he is so trim and fit, not an ounce of fat on his slim body, that he could pass for being in his late thirties. When he turns to take us upstairs, I have a glimpse of his profile. An aquiline nose, added to the shaved head and thin lips, makes him look like a figure from a Renaissance painting, a figure one sees in a Masaccio or a Raphael.

When we climb up to the gallery, I realize that the downstairs is actually spacious by comparison. We promptly bump into a massage table that takes up all the empty space and have to move crab-like to the two chairs next to a huge desk. All around us are shelves stuffed with products and more products. The ceiling is so low that when Dwight tries to seat himself on the massage table, he hits his head against a light bulb shining from a socket without a shade. To complete the ambiance of this healing space is the background rumble: we can hardly hear Aldo speak, his voice is drowned out by the noise of downstairs refrigerators that sound more like industrial turbines up here.

We saw Aldo three times over the course of several weeks: three powerful healing experiences. Every time Aldo switched into a healing mode—as he aligned himself with *la volontà divina* (divine will), his invisible helpers, and our Souls—I felt the atmosphere in this cubicle distinctly change. It became charged. I no longer registered the groaning, rumbling noise from downstairs, no longer felt claustrophobic, and no longer smelled the vague, combined odor of past-the-pull-date foods which Aldo kept here until he dispensed with them. As a matter of fact, I felt as if I were plugged into an electrical socket. Aldo attributes his power to a macrobiotic diet—no wheat, no sweets, no dairy products (is he really Italian?)—and his meditation exercises.

After the sessions, I'd ask Aldo for a report. We figured out a pretty successful way of communicating: I speak in English, and Aldo understands me; then he speaks in Italian, and I understand him. Occasionally we'd both venture into the linguistic territory of the other, but when matters get complicated, we'd quickly return to the safety of our own languages.

It was during the second session that Aldo worked on deeper causes behind Dwight's arrhythmia.

"Lot of crystalized energy around the heart," he said in Italian, making circular motions at the level of Dwight's heart. "Much trauma. Much, much trauma," he repeated in his soft yet penetrating voice. "The trauma caused the energy to crystalize and create the blockages in the heart chakra. This is now causing problems in the physical heart."

I translated to Dwight, knowing full well what this trauma was about. When he was four years old, Dwight had a friend, a little girl of his age, with whom he shared every day, every game, every exploration. There was no separation between them; he was she and she was he. One day the little girl did not come to play. The boy-Dwight waited, and waited, then went back home sad. The next day he waited, the third day he waited, until he finally went to her home. A grown-up came to the door. "Is Becky at home?" asked the little Dwight. The grown-up looked down at him for a long moment, then said, "You want to see Becky? Come." He took him inside, through one room full of people, through another room full of people, to the next room where in the middle lay Becky asleep. "Here is your friend," the grown-up said, "go and kiss her." The boy-Dwight did, and screamed in shock. Becky was cold and did not move.

For days he sat on the kitchen doorstep and stared at his shoes. His mother tried to cheer him up, invent games, buy new toys, but to no avail. "I want Becky," he repeated dolefully. Then, in the final attempt to help her son, she bought a girl-size doll. His eyes lit up at the sight of the doll and he reached for it. But the next day, the mother found the doll on the ground, abandoned. "It's not Becky," the boy-Dwight wept.

Dwight could not remember what happened after that. The memory seemed to have slipped into some recess of his brain and remained locked there for the duration of his adult life, until he recovered parts of it just a year before we left on our journey. What he remembered was the long, severe illness that followed—he came down with the diphtheria that had killed his little friend. For the second time in his short life, Dwight was fighting for air, gasping, suffocating, every breath a struggle. He survived due to mere luck: just at that time the family doctor obtained a new vaccine that he used on his young patient.

"You have to work on opening your heart," Aldo said in English, staring at Dwight. Then he turned to me and added in Italian, "His arrhythmia is a wake-up call. It's bringing his attention to the trauma that needs to be cleared."

Dwight was well aware of that. He'd been trying; he'd been working on that in Cyprus very intensely; he'd worked on that with Lorenzo, but so far, without much success. When Dwight and I began our study meetings, I'd noticed how elusive and neutral his eyes were, never returning my gaze, never showing any emotion. Only after we fell in love did the expression of those sky-blue eyes become softer and gradually warmer.

"Grief, still lot of grief!" Aldo exclaimed. "*Molto dolore!*" His face contorted as if he is the one who was feeling grief. "Inside—tears, congealed in the lungs. Outside—asthma." He stared at Dwight so intently, as if boring into his heart, into his lungs, trying to melt the frozen tears that had encased Dwight's heart in grief with the burning intensity of his gaze.

Then came Aldo's decree: new diet to reduce the mucus that is plugging up Dwight's sinuses and bronchia and causing a "yin condition" (as Chinese medicine refers to excessive dampness and cold in the body).

"No wheat, no cheese, no sugar," Aldo pronounced the verdict.

But, but—what about pasta and pizza?? We are in Italy, for heaven's sake!

But Aldo was not done yet. Then he turned to me and said gravely, "Your stomach is all flabby, strong yin condition. You must not have milk and cheese. Oh, and no cappuccino."

No cappuccino?!?!

…

No way!

CHAPTER 11

THE ETERNAL CITY:
ALL DREAMS LEAD TO ROME

Early this morning, the phone rang. Well, relatively early, shortly after eight. We have gotten into a new rhythm here, just as we do in every new place where we live: we wake up when the upstairs neighbor starts getting ready for work. Around 7:15 her high-heeled shoes begin a loud, clicking march above our bedroom, *click-clack*, back-and-forth, *click-clack*, in-and-out. I don't mind it; 7:15 is a good time to wake up.

Dwight would prefer to sleep in, but he too, has gotten used to the new rhythm. He gets up, turns the heat on, and prepares hot lemonade, which we sip propped up in bed looking out at the sky. As we wait for the apartment to warm up, we talk about our dreams, our plans for the day, or the new, strict dietary regimen that Aldo has prescribed for both of us. We've stocked up on brown rice and adzuki beans, spelt pasta, dried shitake mushrooms and miso, and for "dessert," pickled plums or *umeboshi*, a macrobiotic condiment that is especially good for Dwight. To be sure, we're not thrilled. We so much looked forward to indulging in pizza, ravioli, seafood pasta, buffalo mozzarella. With *gelati* and tiramisu already eliminated for health reasons, we craved some yummy treats. So this macrobiotic diet (or almost) came as quite a blow. I mean, really, how mouth-watering is a pickled plum?

That's when the phone rang. I hear Noemi's cheerful *Buon giorno, com'è stai?* (Good morning, how are you?), then she switches to English. We chat about this and that, our walks around Rome, and the tricky way of adjusting the hot water thermostat. Then Noemi changes the subject.

"I called to tell you that I got confirmation from my guests," she says breezily. "The apartment will be rented the following weekend and for the New Year.

And for Christmas, we'll come to stay for a few days...."

As her voice trails off, my knees buckle, but there is no chair around. Yes, Noemi told us about the reservations her regular guests had made almost a year ago, but nothing was certain. We knew that renting her apartment in Rome was a source of additional income for her. With two daughters at the university, the rent money is a big help in paying tuition bills. But somehow we forgot about all that—or maybe we *wanted* to forget and cling to the illusion of having found "our home."

We eat our miso-onion soup for breakfast (now we're adding some brown rice—how exciting!) and glumly discuss our options. "So we thought our home saga was over!" grunts Dwight, clearly perturbed.

I don't feel like moving again either; I'm so tired of it. All I want is to walk around Rome, visit museums and churches, sip cappuccino in cafés, and watch life. You know, just to catch my breath.

But Dwight is having second thoughts. "Maybe we'd better find another place right away, somewhere we don't have to move out of because other guests are coming. Something not *so* temporary."

Reluctantly, I set up a temporary office on the kitchen table, and a third round of calling about apartment ads begins. Except that this time, we have to drive through the wild traffic of Rome, combing the residential outskirts far away from where we live.

We saw so many dark, dingy, ugly cubby-holes that after a while, we became edgy and disheartened again. We were also getting weary of modern suburbs of Rome—expedient, desolate, cement deserts, sprawling in their ugliness like weeds in an unattended garden. I had no idea Rome had this "dark side." I had no idea such de-humanized, residential areas existed in Rome. How easy it is to idealize a city, to create an illusion, a glamour! I was beginning to develop a love-hate relationship with the Eternal City.

Then we searched an area known as Castelli Romani in an attempt to remain near the city, but away from traffic and pollution. Castelli is a collection of seventeen vine-producing towns and villages scattered over the wooded slopes of the Alban hills, about a half-hour southeast of Rome. Ancient Roman emperors, then medieval barons and Renaissance princes, as well as the Popes chose to build their summer residencies at Castelli. They must have known what they were doing!

We spent two days driving around Grottaferrata, Genzano, Nemi, Albano, Monte Porzio, Castel Gandolfo, and Rocca Priora, only to find out to our disappointment that the entire area has the same traffic plight as Rome: noisy, crowded, and polluted. But one town seduced me—Frascati. I could see myself living there, somewhere beneath the imposing palace of the once-powerful Aldobrandini family, which dominates the bustling center of the town. Frascati had the energy of Rome, the "bright side" of Rome, the Rome I was in love with. But by the time we got there, Dwight had had enough of the Castelli. He nodded at my enthusiasm, agreed with everything I said, enjoyed a light dinner in one of the town's elegant cafés, but then said, "Let's go back home."

"But—shouldn't we look at the ads here?"

He shook his head *no*. "I want to live in Rome."

"I thought you were fed up with noise and pollution?"

"I am," he replied, "but I've realized something. Rome is unique in the world. We are here for a year probably, and I want to immerse myself in its art and architecture. I want to feel the pulse of Rome." He looked away from me, playing absent-mindedly with a napkin, then continued in a different tone, "I also remembered something else. When I was young I had three wishes, three dreams. The first one was to have a ballerina girlfriend—"

"Ah, that's why you were hanging around the back door of the Opera in Paris!"

Dwight turned to me, smiling awkwardly.

"So, in a way, your dream came true," I added, having a sudden realization.

"Yes," he said, with a spark in his eyes. "When I first saw you dance in your apartment, I immediately recognized the ballerina in you." He took my hand in his and squeezed it gently. "It was like light shining forth. That's why I called you a 'creature of joy and beauty.' That's who you really are. You bring light around you."

Dwight is not someone who easily shows affection. He never actually called me by any nicknames, never used sweet endearments. The only affectionate thing he ever said was that—"creature of joy and beauty." Oddly, he'd said it before he knew what my given name, Svetlana, meant in my native tongue: "the one who comes from the light," "the shining one."

"What was your second dream?" I asked.

"To live in Rome."

Ah!

The image of a sixteen-year old girl came to my mind. I was in Rome for the first time, with my mother. We walked endlessly, shopped, walked more, shopped more. Then we climbed to Il Pincio, the little hill rising above the

Piazza di Poppoli. The terrace was famous for magnificent views of the sunset, but also as a romantic spot for couples in love. I stood next to my mother (not exactly romantic company), the sun bathing the domes of Rome in a golden glow, the needle-like Egyptian obelisk from Heliopolis rising from the *piazza* below, while all around us couples were smooching and watching the sunset entangled in passionate embraces. I felt lonely and sad, and wished from the bottom of my little heart to return there someday with the man of my dreams.

"What about the third dream?" I then asked.

"To spend a year in the sun in Provence."

Our dinner finished, we left the café and headed back to Rome.

We've stopped looking for apartments!

I've resigned from my part-time job as house-hunter and dismantled my temporary office because we received a phone call from our diplomat friend who helped us get our visas. Rafaelle told us last night that a good friend of his, an architect, wanted to rent his two-bedroom apartment—custom-designed and elegant, and in the very center of Rome. The only snag is that Massimo is not free to show us the apartment until Wednesday, just two days before we have to move out.

That's why we made an impromptu decision this morning to spend the day *nel centro* and enjoy the art and beauty of Rome. The weather is unusually warm for early December. There is something in the air, a balmy, fresh scent that reminds me of spring and new adventures. We walk along the commercial Via del Corso (I'm forbidden from entering stores today) to the fashionable Via Frattina where we start the day with a cappuccino in one of our favorite cafés. It's the best spot for watching the dressed-to-kill Roman *donne* (I love that word—it sounds so much more elegant and enticing than the amorphous "women") out on shopping safaris. Dwight is so amused at the sight of young Roman men, or *uomini*, who strut in such a self-conscious way—armed with sunglasses, their thick, black hair slathered with gel—that he calls them Roman Roosters.

Leisurely, we cross Via del Corso to the Palazzo Ruspoli, where the exhibit on Cleopatra is on display. Anything that has to do with Egypt is like a magnet to me. When I first laid my eyes on the Egyptian desert from the Temple of Dendera four years ago, I felt like I had come home at long last. The clusters of date palms, the patches of arable fields, the water buffalos lumbering on their way to nearby ponds, the flatness of the land, the thick and voluptuous light wrapping the far-away mountains in a reddish glow ... all that was so, so familiar. I loved every speck of sand, every throb of life, every shimmer of light. Only the figures of Arab men in long, drab-colored *galabiyas* seemed odd in this scene.

Dwight draws my attention to a panel describing impressions of Cleopatra's contemporaries, including her officials, as well as Roman dignitaries. According to these newly-found documents, Cleopatra was a clever, skilled diplomat, although rather ordinary-looking in terms of physical beauty (so much for the myth of her stunning beauty!). Her charm stemmed instead from inner qualities and her personality.

Musing about my own ordinary looks which I have to enhance with tedious make-overs, I sigh. "How long will it take to become detached from my appearance and not care about my looks?" I say, not really expecting an answer.

But Dwight gazes at me seriously and says, "You've got it wrong. It's not that you want to stop caring, oh no. You should care, you should make yourself beautiful, harmonize your colors and jewelry, be like a work of art—but don't *identify* with all of that. There's a big difference in caring about your looks and being identified with your looks. Remember the old saying, Be *in* this world, but not *of* it?"

I don't know how many times I've read that maxim in various books. Every time I read it, I put it into a different context, but I never thought of applying it to my physical appearance. *Should I make it my Fourth Fundamental?* I wonder.

When we walk out of the palace it's still early for lunch, so we decide to see another exhibit of the Russian-born abstract artist Wassily Kandinsky. Dwight had told me long ago that Kandinsky was influenced by the Theosophical teachings of H. P. Blavatsky, an early exponent of the Ageless Wisdom. As a result, the painter's theories reflect esoteric tenets, while his paintings strive to embody them in form and color. The most spiritual of modern artists, Kandinsky has been credited as the "father of abstract art."

As I'm now looking at his early works from what is called the Moscow period—the transition phase from figurative representation to abstract forms—I can hardly believe they were produced by the same painter I'd been admiring since high school. I'm surprised to see how jumbled the compositions are, without that fine balance of lines and surfaces that graces Kandinsky's later canvases.

"You see, no need to despair," muses Dwight, referring to my own aspirations. "Every artist has to go through a long period of growth before reaching excellence. What do you expect? To be a good writer from the start? Not possible." He shakes his head sympathetically.

"What a laborious path art is!" I sigh, thinking of all the years of relentless practice I went through before I could write in English, my third language.

"Not just art," Dwight corrects me, "every endeavor—if you're striving for excellence."

"Remember what Kostas said about art?" I ask Dwight, leaning forward to examine the brushstrokes on a canvas.

"Not sure what you're referring to."

"What makes us like or dislike a painting is the energy behind it, the vibrations of the artist at the time of creating the work," I remind Dwight. "If we are compatible with the frequency of energy that the artist has projected into a painting, we say that it *speaks* to us, that we are *moved* by it."

Kostas' own teacher, Daskalos, in addition to being an amazing healer was also an artist, although he didn't consider himself as one. Daskalos would say, "Out of a hundred artists, only two or three are *real* artists. The rest are just painters." I think the same could be said for literature: out of a hundred literary writers, only two or three are real artists, the rest are just writers. I'd like to be a real artist, but my fear is that I'm still just a writer.

After lunch we take a walk to Scalinata di Spagna (the Spanish Steps)—all 138 of them!), the widest staircase in Europe, climbing from the butterfly-shaped Piazza di Spagna up to the church of Trinita dei Monti. From the top of the steps, we take in the famous view of the Boat Fountain in the middle of the square and the elegant Via dei Condotti, lined up with the most famous designer boutiques: Armani, Valentino, Versace, Prada, Dolce e Gabbana.

To me, this very spot—Scalinata di Spagna and the Piazza di Spagna—is the quintessential Rome. To be sure, the city has so many faces, so many personalities that it's difficult to say which one is the true Rome. This is what makes the Eternal City unique in the world. There is the Rome of the ancient Empire present in the Fori Romani, the Coliseum, and the Pantheon. There is the early Christian Rome hidden in the catacombs, then the medieval Rome, the Renaissance Rome, and the Baroque Rome, all commingling in the meandering, narrow streets and unexpected little *piazzas*, charming fountains and magnificent churches. There's the Catholic Rome of the Vatican, and the *dolce vita* Rome of Via Venetto.

Finally, there is the Rome of the Romantic period, when the aristocratic youth of Europe, as well as artists and writers, considered Rome a must-see hub of Western civilization, an invaluable source of inspiration. And the Spanish Steps represent that Rome, the Rome of cultural and artistic aspirations, of searching, of yearning—the spot where all their dreams led. Just down the steps, in a house on the left, No. 26, the poet John Keats died; in the house next to it, Giorgio de Chirico lived. Shelley wrote his *Prometheus Unbound* while living a few blocks away from the *piazza*; Hans Christian Andersen lived on the upper floor of the Antico Caffè Greco on Via Condotti; Goethe spent many hours here inhaling the air of history; and Lord Byron lived briefly at No. 66 before heading to Greece to fight and die for liberty.

Never mind that nowadays this area is besieged mostly by tourists, it is still a pilgrimage spot, although it's rather a mixed pilgrimage, catering to art as well as shopping, lofty dreams as well as fashionable aspirations. Dwight and I dutifully follow the rules of the pilgrimage (of whatever kind) and sit on the steps and dream. Basking in this mild December sun, we dream of our life in Rome, in that lovely apartment from where we can walk to every church and *palazzo,* where I'm going to write my book, from where we are going to travel and explore Italy. I've regained confidence in my Guidance. I feel so inspired, so vibrantly alive. I dream big about meeting my Soul, about finally finding my creative mission, my service. Rome instills that in visitors—a desire to transcend, to dream something bigger. To dare.

Taking the last step of our pilgrimage and to finish this beautiful, inspiring day, we treat ourselves to *the* Antico Caffè Greco, one of the most famous cafés in Italy, the haunt of all artists and writers who once lived or passed through Rome. The first famous guest of the café was Casanova, who mentions it in his *Memoirs.* Then followed Stendhal, Dickens, Liszt, Hawthorne, Ibsen, who all came to sip coffee and meet friends here. The keenest minds of the turn of the century, *i glitterati* (the intellectuals) met here for political discussions over espresso. At that time, coffee was proclaimed the beverage of intellectuals— I'm all for that!

As we step into the gleaming interior of the mid-eighteenth century café, I'm awed. I look at the antique mirrors, the romantic paintings, the marble-topped tables and the crimson velvet-upholstered chairs against the backdrop of walls covered in red and gold damask. I feel as though the past is still alive. The famous, brilliant men of former centuries have left their invisible mark, and I feel an urge to bow to those giants.

The café is noisy, with tourists in the corners, the clatter of glasses and cups at the wooden bar, the hissing of the espresso machine, but I feel like whispering.

I feel like paying my respects to the memory of the noblest human endeavors ever envisaged, to the heights of artistic creation achieved—to Genius.

"Why can't every day be like this?" I softly ask my Guidance, but don't really expect an answer. I know well I'm not on a tourist trip, even though today it seemed so. I know even better that a spiritual journey is about obstacles and overcoming them, about challenges and difficulties and growing from them, triumphing over them.

And so, in line with that purpose of our journey, Dwight and I were forced to awake from our dream the moment we stepped into Massimo's apartment the following day. Not that the apartment wasn't beautiful; it was straight out of an interior decoration magazine. But … it was also on the ground floor, on the corner of two busy streets where the fierce Roman traffic stops and starts at a traffic light. Raffaelle didn't tell us that when you open the windows, the cars and buses fart exhaust fumes into the living room, not to mention the horrendous noise. And on the other side, the windows looked onto a grim, peeling light-well.

"A designer's dungeon," muttered Dwight while Massimo went to answer a phone call. When he returned, we thanked him and left promptly.

So here we are, a day before we have to leave Noemi's apartment, in a cul-de-sac.

Dwight has given himself over to depression while I, amazingly, have taken on his role and am reminding him that there is a reason for all these "failures." Didn't we decide in Fregene that we aren't going to allow ourselves to get caught in the house-search mania and forget the larger perspective of learning and growing? Dwight is nodding but still brooding. He doesn't complain as I do when faced with disappointment; instead he withdraws like a turtle into his shell and remains silent.

I wish my words had the same effect on Dwight as his have on me. But they don't. He always has to find a way to lift himself up by his own bootstraps, so to speak. Since I can't do anything for him, and I can't stand to be around that Dementor's gloom, I go out.

I walk to the nearby park which I haven't had a chance to explore yet. The common starts on the other side of the Via Pineta Saccheti, a street that used to be lined thickly with *my* trees, the umbrella pines, but now looks like an old man's jaw with half of the teeth missing. I'm walking across the vast, undulating green field, bordered by modern parts of Rome squatting on the neighboring hills, while still farther toward the horizon a long chain of mountains hems in the view. In the forefront to the right, I see the most significant dome of the Christian world—St. Peter's Basilica. I didn't realize we were so close to the Vatican.

I try hard to ignore the ugliness of the modern residential complexes, but it's not easy. How can these human barns exist in the country that has produced Berninis and Brunelleschis, Bramantes and Palladios? Wasn't any of their former glory passed on to later generations? At first I feel like pressing the delete button over some particularly ugly construction and banishing it to oblivion. But slowly, I begin to flatten my vision as Dwight taught me and defocus my sight from ugliness to abstraction. At the same time, I start to tune into a feeling in the air, comforting and gentle, yet strong. I can't "see" the energy, but I'm definitely sensing something hovering over the roofs of Rome. It's like a dome of protective energy, as if a vast umbrella has been erected above the city. I feel infused with a deep sense of well-being.

Slowly I become aware of another frequency in the air. My body becomes electrified, as if a current of much stronger energy is flowing down into me. With it is bestowed a feeling of just-rightness, of poise and inner confidence, of this-is-how-things-should-be certainty. My Guidance is back! Beyond a shadow of doubt I feel that nothing that has happened so far was an accident. I know that I am where I should be. This Italian odyssey, it dawns on me suddenly, is not about settling down in a quiet and inspiring place and writing (regardless of what the Anubis-dog symbolized), but about discovering and learning. The emphasis is on searching, not on finding. On the journey, not on the destination.

Everything is so clear now.

I walk as if in a dream, clarity in my head, certainty in my heart. *I now welcome everything!* I launch these words up to my Guidance. I feel poised and centered, and strangely strong. *I am prepared for whatever needs to happen. I can handle ANYTHING!* I cry out within, exultantly.

Good thing we're not given the ability to see the future. Good thing I had no idea about what was to happen in the time ahead. Otherwise, I don't know how strong and prepared I would have felt. And I'm not sure I would have made such a complete surrender, determined to face up to any hardship, any test…. *Good thing*, I say.

Back home, I find the clouds around Dwight almost dispelled, and the gloom lightened. "That's a nice surprise," I chirp. "How did you do it so quickly?"

"I figured out what we're going to do," Dwight says in a voice that has a ring of importance. "We'll go to Naples tomorrow!"

"Naples! What a great idea!" I say, delighted. "We wanted to see Naples anyway, so we may as well do it now when we have to clear out for the holidays."

Immediately, I get on the phone to reserve a hotel. I call one *albergo*, but everything is booked. I call another, but it's full. A third, a fourth, a fifth, always to hear the same answer, "*Niente, signora, mi dispiace. (Nothing, Ma'm, I'm sorry.)*" Finally, I call the last one on our list. In perfect English, the receptionist answers with a hint of disbelief (as if to say, "Are you kidding me?"), "A room for tomorrow? You're not going to find any in Naples. Don't you know? It's the Feast of Immaculate Conception tomorrow. The whole of Italy gets up and travels."

I hang up and stare at Dwight. He stares back at me. We stare at each other for a good long while before Dwight croaks, "Well, if we can't go south, let's try north."

"And more precisely...?"

"Let's head into Etruscan country."

CHAPTER 12

ETRUSCAN COUNTRY:
GIFTS AND OMENS

There are certain words that strike a chord in my innermost being for no particular reason, at least not that I'm aware of. "Etruscan" is one of those words. When I whisper it to myself: *e-trus-can*, the sound of its syllables carries a ring of mystery for me. Perhaps because the origin of the Etruscans *is* mysterious. We don't really know where this people, who inhabited central Italy from the eighth century BC, originally came from. But we do know that they had very different customs from all their neighbors. On top of that, we can't understand their language either, which is non-Indo-European and unrelated to any other known language groups. We can read the inscriptions, yes, but we don't understand the meaning of the words (except for a few hundred that have been translated). This is quite ironic if you consider that in the time of Caesar, Etruscan was the everyday language of the majority of people in central-west Italy.

There is really no deep understanding of the essence of Italian life without considering the Etruscan influence. From Pisa in the west to Perugia in the east, from Bologna in the north to Campania in the south, a layer of Etruscan heritage underlies the edifice of Roman culture. As D.H. Lawrence noticed, Italy today is far more Etruscan in its pulse than Roman.

For one thing, the Romans learned the art of writing from the Etruscans. (In fact, the alphabet we use today has come down to us through the Etruscans, who adapted the Greek letters. The Etruscan alphabet even crossed the Alps and gave birth to the runic characters of the Germanic people.) For another thing, they were excellent technicians and architects whose engineering skills provided much of Italy with roads, canals, and even sewers (and we thought it was all Roman invention!). And finally, Etruscans founded Rome, and the earliest government of Rome was Etruscan. The paraphernalia adorning the subsequent Roman rulers were of Etruscan origin: the golden crown, scepter, toga, even the throne on which they sat, and above all, the symbol of state power, *fasces* (a bundle of twelve rods surrounding a double-bladed axe)—all Etruscan!

But most importantly, their influence extended into religious matters. Etruscan leaders, *Lucumones*, were at the same time religious seers *and* princes: thier rule was based on a combination of divination and written civil codes. The Romans referred to the handbooks on divination as *disciplina Etrusca* and translated them into Latin. Roman aristocrats sent their youth to the Etruscan "Academy" to complete their religious education. The generals of Roman armies, too, were required to specialize in the subject of reading omens; it was an indispensable part of their training. Etruscan augurs were summoned to Rome to help emperors make important decisions.

Of everything I read about the origin of the Etruscans, what made the most sense to me was the hypothesis that their civilization was the last offshoot from the pre-historic Mediterranean world, and their language the last relic of an ancient family of languages common to the whole Mediterranean region (with other possible languages being Lemnian and Minoan). What they left us of art and what little we know of their government, customs, and beliefs, indicate the existence of a world view that saw everything as alive. Every tree and lake, every rock and mountain was animate; everything was endowed with consciousness. And the gods, really, were still only the expression of these elemental powers in nature, rather than the anthropomorphic gods of the Greeks and Romans. Moreover, for the Etruscans, life on earth was a reflection of the celestial realm, and for a society to be happy and prosperous it was essential to maintain a balanced order in harmony with the heavenly order.

The Etruscans organized themselves into twelve tribes ruled by twelve kings, later replaced by twelve city-states as a reflection of the twelve signs of the zodiac in the sky and the twelve months of the year. From archaeological records we know that they founded their cities along two axes (north-south and east-west), which divided the area of each city into quadrants corresponding to the four elements. The boundaries of the cities were considered sacred because they were the projection of cosmic order. In fact, before founding a new city the priests would draw a sacred circle around the precincts for protection from enemies. Breaking the circle by jumping over it would break the magical spell and bring ill fate to the new city. (This is why Romulus killed his brother Remus;

the latter had jumped over the circle that surrounded the newly-founded city of Rome, and had to be killed in order for the spell to be preserved.)

The Etruscan science of divination completely eludes the Western rational mind. What to us appear as arbitrary or superstitious beliefs—such as reading omens from the formations of flying birds or the shape of the liver of a sacrificial animal—were actually principles derived from their cosmology. To the Etruscans, who lived by the cosmic order and its reflection on earth, the living birds flew through the living universe in much the same way as hunches and impressions flutter through our hearts, or as thoughts flash through our minds.

Based on this cosmic order—as above, so below—the Etruscans believed that each nation had been assigned a life cycle, a certain number of years it would last. They even predicted their own demise in 44 BC, reading the omens in the sky. (They were very close.)

So where does one go to visit Etruscan country, as Dwight announced on the eve of our evacuation of the apartment in Rome? There was no Etruscan country as such; instead there was a loose confederation of twelve city-states. Historical records show three such confederations or leagues: Etruria proper (roughly present-day Tuscany down to Rome), Campania in the south (from Rome to the Amalfi coast), and the Po Valley city states in the north.

We've decided to visit the Etruscan territory immediately north of Rome; there are many Etruscan sites in that area, and the then chief city of the confederation, Tarquinia, is famous for its extensive necropolis where many fine frescoes, pieces of jewelry, and stone tombs were uncovered. We were lucky, very lucky, to find a room in an *albergo* in a little town called Bagnaia, conveniently located in the vicinity of all the sites we wanted to visit.

Through the window of our cozy room in the Albergo Biscetti I look at a blanket of haze wrapping the trees in the distance. All is gray. I'm about to voice a complaint about this darn fog that follows us everywhere, but I stop myself. Instead I say, "What are we going to do in this weather? The visibility is so poor." I can't help it, I *do* feel disappointed. I was so much looking forward to this trip!

"We'll just have to make the best of it," Dwight says judiciously.

So we decide to start with Orvieto, one of the twelve city-states of the Etruscan league, believed to be ancient Velzna. I'm surprised that despite the grim weather, despite the haze settled over the countryside like other-worldly vapors, the drive is actually beautiful. Mysterious, as Dwight says. We're alone on the road, driving through a forest that looks untouched.

On an impulse, I pull over and stop the car. There is a path leading into the forest, and we follow it. Silence falls upon us as soon as we step among the trees, the still silence of a winter forest. No wind rustling the leaves, no birds chirping in the crowns of trees, no insects crunching twigs. Only the trees rise, solemn, their contours looming mysteriously through the fog. Pristine and primeval. The path leads to a meadow which opens before us. The mist is rolling over the trees in the distance, shrouding the countryside. I didn't know there could be so many shades of gray: from silvery to chrome to ashen to leaden to taupe to charcoal, the whole gamut of shades is displayed on the palette of this winter landscape. Both Dwight and I are silent; there is no room for words in this silence-filled space. *The fog can actually be beautiful! I would have never thought that.*

The nicest moments in life happen spontaneously, without planning; so are the most attractive places found by accident. Perhaps it's the surprise that intensifies our reaction. When we're not *expecting* to have fun or to see something beautiful, our surprise bypasses all conditioned responses and we react freshly—like children. Those moments are a real gift.

Maybe because I feel a bit spaced out from our walk in the forest, or maybe because I just don't have a natural sense of direction, I make a wrong turn and miss the road to Orvieto. So now I'm driving along the road that would still get us there, but from another side. We're passing through a town called Bagnoregio. There again, I make another mistake and we end up on the wrong side of the town, at a parking area that seems like a dead-end. But there are signs pointing to a park, so we conclude that something must be out there after all. We walk through the wooden gate, then through the winter-barren park until we come to the vista point.

And there, wrapped up in the mist, is our surprise: perched atop a solitary pinnacle rising in the midst of a valley is the medieval, wall-girdled Cività di Bagnoregio. Snaking to it through the vapors of the mist is a narrow footbridge. Like an umbilical cord, the footbridge connects the modern Bagnoregio with the otherwise inaccessible medieval Cività.

We stand speechless before this dream-like sight. As before, mist and haze are mixing different shades of gray over a landscape that we must intuit more than we can see. There is something poignant about this sight, which calls yet hides; something that invokes restlessness, a desire to seek: a ribbon of a path trailing through the mist, a bouquet of houses tied together by a wall, all shrouded in the gauzy wrapper of fog like a gift.

"I want to come back here when the weather warms up," I whisper, mesmerized. "I want to walk the pathway." It's an archetypal image: walking a narrow pathway that meanders high above a valley, leading to something that is hard to reach, yet precious.

Dwight is silent, gazing meditatively into the distance. "It's so narrow, the footbridge, like a razor's edge," he finally utters.

I imagine that the road ascending to Orvieto would have been equally spectacular—if only we were able to see it. Orvieto has the same topography as Bagnoregio, only on a larger scale; it's nestled high on a large summit of volcanic tuff cliffs that rise almost vertically from the valley below. This whole area between the Tyrrhenian Sea and the Tiber valley is actually a low plateau (about 1,000 feet high), the edge of which is marked by deep ravines. These ravines separate long and narrow hills of tuff rock, very often having a flat top. The Etruscans chose these locations for their towns because they were easily defensible as well as a healthy environment. (The land near the Tiber was often marshy and exposed to floods—and mosquitoes.)

I have to make a confession here: I was beginning to entertain a thought (yet again) of how it would be to live here, in this land of dramatic cliffs and breathtaking views from hill-top towns. I guess my Guidance, which is watching over my little life and my stumbling through this country, is making sure I don't make such a decision just because I get enchanted by the view. So whenever I have a thought of moving to a place because of the view, I'm prevented from seeing it. Perhaps the gorgeous view is my Siren song; and fog and haze are like the ropes that bound Odysseus lest he fall under the Siren spell.

Orvieto charms us instantly. It's a rather small, neat, well-preserved medieval town with good, good energy and beautiful artwork. Ceramic shops alternate with jewelry shops, with leatherwork, woodcarving and lace shops. We delight in discovering pottery shops that display ceramics with intricate patterns of foliage. "It's always a good sign to find true art in a town," says Dwight, as we walk out of a small shop where we watched a young woman paint a bowl.

Orvieto certainly has a long tradition of ceramic work. In the thirteenth century it became one of the first Italian majolica centers, well before nowadays famous Deruta or Faenza (which developed three centuries later). Orvieto ceramics were so prized that even the Arabs, who had actually invented the majolica technique, were buying them.

We stroll around the busy streets and watch the crowd. Women are displaying *le belle figure* ("looking their best"), sporting fur coats and elegant shoes, walking arm-in-arm with their dignified-looking husbands clad in cashmere overcoats and hats. But the weather is getting colder and we take refuge in a patisserie on the main street. The spacious room is teeming with people, a murmur of voices merging into an indistinct buzz. We seat ourselves at a table from where I can watch people coming and going, families having *panettone* and hot choco-late, couples billing and cooing over tea, friends meeting at the counter for a shot of espresso, a flow of human faces, smiles, glances, laughter, handshakes, embraces, taps on shoulders, words thrown across the room, cups of espresso pulled forward, emptied, then pushed back, replaced by more cups and ever-new faces.

The dance of life in a small Italian town on a holiday afternoon.

While I'm watching people, Dwight is reading the *Herald Tribune*, our favorite activities at a café when we're not talking ideas. He shows me an article on Naples in the travel section. "We should save this for later, when we go there." I glance at the pages that describe new trends and changes in this southern city, the photos of the famous bay and narrow streets and a formidable fortress; then my eye is caught by the practical information section at the bottom of the page. There are several bed-and-breakfast accommodations listed, and for some reason I pause at the one with the address of Via Nicotera. I like that word, the sound of it. I tear the corner of the page and put it in my wallet.

The tuff butte on which Orvieto stands is honeycombed with caves and underground tunnels, galleries, cisterns, quarries, and cellars, both Etruscan and medieval. But at my mere mention of this Dwight gets alarmed. "You can't be serious," he retorts. "It's already so cold *above* the ground, I don't have the slightest intention of going *under* the ground."

"No…?"

"No!"

So we set off back to our hotel, now taking the road we missed this morning. Dwight is unusually silent but in an alert way, and his eyes are riveted on the brush-covered cliff that rises above the road. As soon as he spots a barren and accessible rock rising up above the road, he asks me to pull over. "What for?" I ask.

But he only says, "Wait for me," and steps out.

I watch him as he approaches the rock, takes the pendulum out of his pocket and checks the rock. Ah, the ionization! He repeats it several times at different outcrops, enters a brief meditation, then comes back to the car.

"So, what happened?"

"It's all volcanic," he says in a voice that sounds excited. "Volcanic tuff takes the charge, unlike sandstone. Different frequencies. You realize, by ionizing the bedrock of the town, the frequency of this whole area is going to be raised!" Then he explains, seeing my blank stare:

"You see, raising the frequency of the stone—by making its atoms spin faster—will make this whole area vibrate on a higher level. This, in turn, will attract more evolved souls to incarnate here, and those souls would then lift the whole society. Just as happened during Renaissance times when all those highly developed artists, like Leonardo and Michelangelo and Raphael and so many others, incarnated at the same time to create a revolution in the arts.

"In fact," he adds, "we'll do the ionization wherever we go in Etruscan country, wherever we find the tuff rock." Dwight now turns to look at Orvieto, which we've left behind, and the valley below. From the distance the town looks like a large animal poised in ambush. The spires of the Duomo protrude like huge ears pricked up in anticipation. Down below, we can just make out the view through the thinning mist—the valley, corrugated like elephant skin, the nubby hills, scattered like rabbits, the horizon mysterious and inviting. There is something subtle in this dramatic landscape, something unexpressed yet hinted, something hopeful like a promise.

Definitely, I could live here.

Time is a strange thing. That day as we were leaving Orvieto, we couldn't have known that several years later archaeologists would discover remains of the most sacred place of the Etruscan league right at the foot of Orvieto. Otherwise, we would have stopped the car and explored the ruins of the shrine of Voltumna, the supreme god of the Etruscans. Originally worshipped as the goddess of the Underworld, she was later transformed into a hermaphrodite deity, a deity of vegetation, abundance, and fecundity.

In Etruscan culture, a shrine was not a man-made temple but a sacred area in the countryside, a sacred grove, believed to be an *omphalos* or navel of the world. This site on a plain at the foot of Orvieto was, and still is, at a natural crossroads where major connecting roads intersected. So this was *the* geographical and spiritual center of the whole Etruscan league. Every year in spring, the Etruscans gathered here for a national festival and a trading fair, while the twelve *Lucumones* held a council on political, economic, and religious matters. Every year, one of the twelve was elected as the chief *Lucumo* of the League.

So we drove by the remains of a temple wall surrounding the remains of the sacred area. We drove by, oblivious that only a few years later a round fountain complex—the sacred spring—would be excavated on a rise above the temples; and sacred altars would be rediscovered, and roads.... The shrine was huge.

But that day, we drove by.

Time is a strange thing.

The next morning I'm staring in disbelief through the window of our room, looking at the same patch of greenery that yesterday appeared drab, but now is brilliantly verdant in the crisp winter sun. Today's good weather makes me feel positively elated, I can't help it. No matter how determined I was in Amalfi to remain neutral toward external circumstances, all I can do is to reduce the amplitude of my negative reactions. But my positive reactions remain unchecked. So I keep bouncing up and down on my emotional seesaw.

Dwight says it's a good start. No victories are won overnight.

"Remember," he repeats patiently, "the white and black horses of your personality have to be re-trained, and that's a process. Don't expect shortcuts." He smiles at me gently and lovingly, and all of a sudden I'm so glad I have him. I can't imagine what I would do without his support and wisdom, without his unconditional love. I'm awash with deep gratitude. I turn toward him, embrace him tightly, and bury my face in the spot between his neck and his shoulder. I love the breadth of his chest, wide, spacious, comforting; his shoulders, widening after a slight dip in the middle, just the size of my face—a perfect fit.

"My, you're affectionate this morning," he says, planting a gentle kiss on my hair.

"Ain't I always?" I joke.

"Uh-huh, always, when the weather is nice," Dwight replies, laughing. "So, where do you want to go today?"

"I don't really know, I haven't read the guidebook. I guess I want more surprise gifts." I smile, thinking of Bagnoregio.

So I take us first to Tuscania, an old Etruscan town, half-way between Tarquinia and Lago di Bolsena (Bolsena Lake). I don't know why I want to go there. On this trip, I've given up planning what to see; I act on an inner whim—a younger cousin, so to speak, of the compelling urge through which my Guidance manifests. Dwight happens to have confidence in my whims; he believes that I intuitively feel where we should go, even when it looks like I've made a mistake. He has his own agenda, of course, places where he feels he has work to do, but in between he leaves everything up to me—and my Guidance.

It seems that the whole of the Etruscan country is a gift for me. As soon as I step out of the car and look around at the medieval houses and cobblestone streets of Tuscania, I feel happy. Simply happy. Tucked comfortably into itself, the town has an air of antiquity, but a well-preserved antiquity. Everywhere I look, it's clean! No garbage lying around, no peeling façades, no abandoned houses. The town is pulsing with life, quiet, peaceful, content. You can feel its breathing, deep and steady, as though it has discovered the secret of time and is observing its passing with the wisdom of a sage.

Manicured lawns stretch along the ancient city walls, recently restored. I want to walk along the walls and gaze at this valley, soft and swooping, that Etruscans gazed at for so many centuries. I want to see it with their eyes and look for birds and observe them fly. I want to understand the omens that lie hidden in the patterns of nature, the omens that speak of order and chaos in the world, the omens that Etruscan *Lucumones* knew how to interpret … oh, I want so much! But above all, I want to lie in the sun, feel its warmth on my face, inhale the freshness of grass, touch its soft luxuriance with my hands—at least for a moment. I want to receive the gift of beautiful weather after so many cold, gray days.

But Dwight is gazing at the opposite hill, where the ruins of some medieval churches stand like desolate, lightning-struck trees. "That's the Città," he says, consulting the guidebook, "the former seat of a group of Etruscan villages."

"What?" I jump right up and join him at the parapet.

"Well, those are Romanesque churches, what you see, but they are built on the Etruscan site, an important city from the eighth century BC, although not one of the major twelve."

The hill is close by, a mere mile or so, and it does look like a sister-hill of the medieval Tuscania, as if the two settlements were connected. "Well, shall we…?" Dwight eyes me.

I glance once more at the lush grass, encompass the expanse of the valley, and for a moment teeter as my senses soak in the silence and the sun. Then I say, "Let's go."

There is something special about Etruscan places. For me, they have an aura of magic, just as they did for D.H. Lawrence. As I stand facing the site of the ancient Città—the remains of an Etruscan arch, two medieval bell towers, and the Romanesque façade of St. Peter's Basilica—I can feel that aura of magic. Something is still palpitating in this churchyard. But what? Even the guidebook (which I later read) talks about the "magic of the place!" Had the Etruscans really done something, had they enchanted the landscape, as John Michell postulates in his book *Twelve-Tribe Nations and the Science of Enchanting the Landscape*? Does the enchantment still survive because the site has not been built upon in modern times? According to Michell, the priesthood of the ancient times had skills to locate the naturally powerful centers of spiritual energy so the temples were built on the most auspicious places in a landscape, places where the powers of heaven and earth met.

I wonder if this skill of "enchanting the landscape" had anything to do with the Etruscan reputation for having had extraordinarily fertile land. The fertility of their soil was so famous that when the Roman army conquered an Etruscan city, many Romans would move to the new territory because the land bore such abundant fruit.

We walk through the wooden door into the interior of the church. Silently I greet the spirit of the sanctuary that feels more pagan than Christian. I've always had a special affinity with Romanesque churches. They speak to me, perhaps because they were built to the measure of man. Their size, proportions, and shapes seem to be in service of one goal: to facilitate the union with God—not in fear, but in joy. The Romanesque churches seem to sing praise to the glory of man: "Rejoice, for ye are the creation of God!"

Those were the times that still carried the traces of the Mother Goddess worship. The times before the scholastic, fear-of-damnation dogmas of later Christianity cut off the connection with nature and the feminine aspect of life. The times before the religious terror began, before the Inquisition started burning "witches" at the stake. The times before male supremacy and arrogance started to exploit and destroy nature.

The times before life became devoid of magic.

"This is quite amazing," whispers Dwight.

"What?"

"Well, all this … non-Christian imagery." He waves his arm at the area of the altar. "Look at all these Etruscan carvings … all purloined, then fitted into the Christian framework."

The carved decorations on the altar abound in organic motifs, common to all

Mother Goddess cultures: spirals, snakes, water motifs, flower-of-life patterns, grape and vine-leaf borders—everything so female, so beautifully yin. As I look around the interior, I distinctly feel the connection with Life, with nature.

Then we descend to the eleventh-century crypt and we gape, enchanted. Rows of columns—each capped by a different capital—support the arches to create a vaulted forest. I find myself enthralled by the magic of the crypt, its hidden pulse, its life currents still throbbing in the stone, in the vaulting, in the pavement, in the shafts of light dispersing through cracks. But it's cold, oh, so cold, in here. I feel the clammy chill mounting up my legs from the stone floor, seeping into my body from the frosty air. Dwight has asked me three times so far to leave; he's freezing. But I'm captivated by the crypt. I can't make myself go. "This chill," he repeats while raising the collar of his jacket, "it penetrates to the bones."

Finally, I tear myself away, and up we go into the sun. From the back of the churchyard we look at Tuscania on the opposite hill, at the waves of hills rippling all the way to the horizon. A sense of peace and harmony pervades the whole area. There is a feeling of just-rightness, the balance being struck between nature and men, the harmony of elements, an invisible order being maintained, perhaps by accident, perhaps by special design.

A flock of birds flies over, but I don't even know in which direction they are moving, let alone what kind of birds they are. I feel ridiculously disconnected from Life around me, like a foreigner who hears people talking but doesn't understand what they are saying. I see trees and birds and animals around me, but I don't know what they are, what they symbolize. Definitely a distinct language is being spoken around me, but I don't understand a single word.

Tarquinia was once a metropolis, the chief city of the great Etruscan league of twelve. We're heading for its necropolis, one of the biggest archaeological sites of the Etruscan culture. This time Dwight insisted I buy additional books about Tarquinia and read them in the car. He wants me to select the tombs I feel *drawn* to visit, just as I selected places I felt drawn to visit in Epidauros. "You should prepare yourself for this," he says somewhat mysteriously.

"But why?"

He darts a quick glance sideways, then asks, "Don't you feel anything?"

"Like what?" Now I'm really puzzled.

"Those birds did mean something...."

"Probably, but I don't know what—and neither do you."

"Doesn't matter. I can feel there is something in the air, something imminent waiting to happen."

When we arrive at the site of the necropolis, the afternoon light has already turned golden. We approach the ticket office with the map of the site in hand. I have marked the tombs that stirred something in me. But to my great surprise, the ticket seller informs me that some tombs are closed to the public, and it so happens that half of those I've selected are in that group. I stand in front of the booth, looking at his disinterested face through the glass and don't know what to say, what to ask. I feel crestfallen, in a way betrayed. I turn to Dwight, but he's not saying anything, just biting his lower lip.

"Well, we'll do the best we can in unexpected circumstances," he finally says.

So we go to the open tombs, descend into the holes, into the dimness of the underworld, look at the frescoes of dancing men and women, banqueting couples, scenes from everyday life, animals and birds, some preserved better than others. Death for the Etruscans was just a natural continuation of life. In the early tombs there is neither blissful heaven nor dreadful hell awaiting the dead; the underworld is a cheerful place, just as life is full of wonder and vitality, and ease.

We check the energy, ionize the doorways, then climb up into the golden winter sun; then down again into the darkness, then up again into the light ... many times. After a while, my sense of reality begins to shift; the alternation of up and down, darkness and light, the world of the dead and the world of the living, the life scenes captured on stone walls and the life moving in the fields around us, the cold and dim surroundings of the tomb chambers and the vibrant green surroundings of nature, finally begin to erode my sense of time and place. As if some trick is being played on my mind, I carry with me a patch of sunny hills into the dark tombs and bring back a slice of dimly-outlined, dancing silhouettes into the open fields.

Soon, the two worlds begin to overlap. I begin to see "my" world in the tombs, and the scenes from the underworld up above on the surrounding hills. I "see" a figure of an augur with a crooked staff standing erect on a hilltop and watching the birds, reading portents from the way they fly. I "see" a procession moving along the earthen road, men playing the double flute, women with their arms thrown up in the air, one foot in front of the other, bodies twisted in a wild dance. I "see" a couple: a woman leaning against the chest of her husband, who is embracing her and pointing at something in front of them, both high-cheeked, slant-eyed, long-headed, with that lovely, innocent, archaic smile, so typical of early Etruscan art. I "see" a room in a house, full of people; men and women, reclining together on couches, eating and listening to music, while slaves, bright-eyed and quick, bring forth dish after dish. Unlike more "civilized" Greek and Roman cultures, where women were not allowed at the banquets and reclining was considered inappropriate for virtuous women, Etruscans considered women equal—another indication of the "old religion," the worship of the Mother Goddess.

I finally had enough of tombs. There is nothing threatening in them, I'd simply had enough of dimness and small chambers with faded and partially destroyed frescoes. My inner world has become more alive and I want to immerse myself in it; I want to walk the fields around the necropolis. But Dwight is calling me to yet another tomb, this one recently discovered. As I walk down the steps into the darkness, I suddenly sense something foreboding which makes me recoil. There is a presence here, both Dwight and I agree, and that presence is not benevolent. In fact, it reminds me of what I felt in many Egyptian tombs—a negative elemental being placed at the doorway as a guardian. Dwight promptly takes out his pendulum, which begins to swing wildly. The place is definitely charged with some kind of energy, and as far as I can feel, it's not good.

"Leave it alone," I say to Dwight.

But he doesn't listen; his sense of duty tells him to do his work, to cleanse the place of negative energy.

"What if *it* didn't want you to do that?" I frown. "You don't know what it was, why it was there. It must have been conjured up for a purpose. You don't know anything about the magic of the ancients."

"No, I certainly don't," Dwight agrees. "But it's too late now."

Dwight looks around for a bench to rest and warm up, while I decide to walk the fields that surround the necropolis. This land calls me, stretching lazily like a woman waking up from sleep. Hill after hill I walk, a patch of brown, plowed field after a patch of wild green field, all unrestrained and free like hair tossed in the air, shining in the golden light of this winter afternoon. I feel a strange connection with this land. The Etruscan country speaks to me; I feel its pulse in my body.

On this hill, the guidebook says, archaeologists assume old Tarquinia stood. They have excavated remains of city walls and the foundation of a temple, so it must have been the sacred center of the city, the acropolis or *arx*, as it was called in Etruscan—the highest place. The rest of the commercial and residential districts spread on the lower, surrounding hills. It was at these walls here, called the Queen's Altar, that the famous terracotta winged horses were uncovered. We saw them as we made a quick stop at the Tarquinia Museum—those two proud, dignified horses with their wings flaring up and a look of poised self-confidence, as if they knew they were more than horses. But so the effigies of dead men, carved on the lids of sarcophagi, have that look: dignified, meaningful, a look that reflects a mindset shared by a whole society—of a life lived purposefully, of a world impregnated with meaning.

As I stand on this hill, as I face this land, these fields of wheat, I cannot but feel the same. Everything is breathing with life, every blade of grass, every block of stone that has survived from the Etruscan times, every lump of earth I step on. Alive. As I walk the plowed fields back to meet Dwight, I soak up the energy of the land through my soles and inhale deeply into my lungs the golden air. The land and the air meet in my heart, the above and the below, the powers of heaven and earth, and I feel deeply alive, just as this land is alive.

And I carry this gift of life with me.

I will need it to get me through what is to come.

When we reach the Tyrrhenian Sea and Santa Marinella—one of the three ports the Etruscans used for their sea trade—it's already dusk. We'll spend the night in an elegant hotel right on the beach. The room I've reserved has a spectacular view of the sea. Yet something doesn't feel right, both Dwight and I agree as we walk in. The energy, he says, feels sad and desolate. But he promptly jumps in the shower to warm up from the bone-deep chill that has settled in his body since our visit to the crypt.

I seat myself on the balcony and watch the changing shades of dusk. I inhale the air that carries no fragrance. Definitely, something doesn't feel right. Then I start thinking about everything that has happened today and can't help being amazed at how events *never* turn out the way we expect. Or maybe I should marvel at how the Guidance always pulls a trick on us whenever we have expectations and presents us with events that are opposite from what we thought they'd be. So Dwight wanted me to "prepare" myself for the visit to the tombs as I did in Epidauros, and sure enough, the plan was thwarted. And I thought I'd have some remarkable experience in the tombs, something revelatory *underground*, and instead it was *above* ground that I experienced the most beautiful moments, the deep aliveness, the unity with Life.

If only I could take things less seriously, I would actually be laughing.

The following morning I rise early to take a walk down on the beach. I bundle up and walk down the steps just as the day is breaking. At this virgin hour everything is deserted. I look at the wan sea, steely and flat, the sky, gray and shapeless, then around the pebbly beach, and I shudder. Everywhere—garbage. Plastic bags, soda cans, old shoes, broken chairs, amorphous piles of decomposing junk spilling over the rocks like vomit of an over-bloated, turgid civilization retching from indigestion. Trashed, desecrated, uncared for. Are we really more civilized than the "primitive" Etruscans who respected nature, who lived in harmony with her?

It hurts me to see nature so violated. I have a sensation of "shrinking," as if my energy field is actually recoiling. I turn my head away from the beach and fix my eyes upon the water, pallid and leaden at this hour before the sunrise, but at least clean on the surface. Still, the dismal energy of garbage is getting to me. The rocks, too, are getting bigger and harder to walk on, uglier, the color of turds, so I capitulate. *I'm going back!* But before I turn, I take a little pumice rock from Etna that lived in the pocket of my jacket and gently place it down on a rock.

I place it as an offering for a happier nature.

Nature more cared for.

Nature more loved.

CHAPTER 13
CHRISTMAS IN ROME:
BLACK SATIN

I finally lost it. My beautiful, serene state of *déjà vécu*—it's gone! That state of simultaneity of present and future, of having already *lived* the future, which started upon our arrival in Rome when I stepped into Noemi's apartment, I've lost it.

I don't really know how it happened … or maybe I do. It started when Dwight came down with a cold a few days after we returned to Rome from Etruscan country. Was it the stress from all the worry about having to leave the apartment for the holidays? Was it remembering all of Dwight's other illnesses I've been through on this journey? I'm not sure. I just know that now everything appears flat, in the normal three-dimensional way. Which means that life has resumed its ordinary, drab quality.

Let me correct myself: my perception of life has become drab, without the inner glow that comes from what I call a "fourth dimension," a depth of future time. But our life has, in fact, turned dramatic, rather than drab. Dwight says it's the usual alternation of the opposites—highs are always followed by lows. It's only to be expected that after our inspiring trip there would be a dip, a swing of the pendulum in the opposite direction.

As I said, it started with Dwight's cold. "It's the revenge of the tomb," I said to him half-jokingly, half-seriously, as he lay bundled and propped up in bed.

"Maybe," he replied, doubtfully shaking his head. "But more likely, it's that darn crypt in the church. It was freezing in there, and I stayed too long. I told you we should have left sooner. No, *I* should have left sooner, rather than waiting for you."

"Still," I insist, "whatever spirits you disturbed in that tomb by cleansing the energy may have intensified the effect of that chill in the crypt."

Now, you may wonder why I'm making such a big fuss over a simple cold. I have good reason, because what is a minor discomfort for most people is a serious illness for Dwight, due to his asthma and weak heart. Colds invariably spread into his bronchia, threaten to turn into pneumonia, endanger his heart by triggering arrhythmia through fits of coughing, and then his illness takes a long time to heal. For the past couple of days I've been watching with dread the same progression of symptoms I remember from previous years ... from Cyprus ... from the ashram in southern India....

In Tiruvannamalai, where we stayed just outside Ramana Maharshi's ashram, the monsoon rains had descended so hard, dropping torrents of water for days on end, that the streets were flooded and the electricity was cut off. Everything was damp in our room, pillows and mattresses turned moldy, and the air was heavy with humidity. With no electricity, we couldn't turn on the heater, couldn't dry our clothes. In just a few days, Dwight had completely lost his voice and was shivering with fever. He wheezed and rasped as he struggled for air, unable to get up, unable to eat, with no dry clothes, sheets, or pillows to bring relief—only rain, wetness, and mold.

That's when I saved his life, as he'd later tell all our friends.

That day holds a prominent place in the collection of the most miserable days of my life. The whole morning I'd been walking back and forth between the ashram and the telephone booth (both located on the main road where buses and trucks trundled endlessly), fighting sheets of rain blown by the wind, trying to organize our "escape" to drier Madras, to electricity and heat. Every bus, every truck that rumbled by, drenched me in muddy water, all of them blowing their horns as if to announce my splashing. The telephone lines worked only sporadically because of the wind, disrupting the connection suddenly and leaving the conversation and my very important question hanging in the air: "Do you have a free room for—?" So I had to come back again, and again. My clothes were filthy, sweaty, and wet, and so was my body, unwashed for six days, because I too, had a cold.

The climax came in the evening. I lunged forth into the curtain of rain yet again, this time to pick up an Ayurvedic medicine especially prepared for Dwight by the ashram doctor. The streets were plunged into darkness from a power outage, and I had to wade through ankle-deep water in which animals and people had relieved themselves at their convenience. Passing cars shed ghostly lights on what seemed like figures from hell, beggars wrapped in rags and writhing in their efforts to stay upright by the road.

And no rickshaws in sight! I stood in the rain, in the ghostly dark, shivering from cold and fever, waiting…. When finally one came, I quickly got in, but the churlish driver promptly took the road opposite from the direction in which I told him to go. I yelled from behind, he kept on driving; I kept screaming, he kept on driving. The rickety vehicle leaned dangerously from side to side; water rivulets licked my shoes. I was gripped by terror of toppling over into the vermin-filled water.

Oh, India! I don't know what was worse: being abducted by this rickshaw driver who didn't understand me, not getting Dwight's medicine, or keeling over into a waiting cesspool. I had reached such a point of "desperror" (that's a mix of desperation and terror), that the only thing I could do in my highly stressed state was—to laugh. Had I had more detachment from my emotions at that moment, I would have pondered such an interesting phenomenon: how emotions, when pushed to extremes, turn into their opposite expression.

But I didn't. Clinging to my seat, I rocked back and forth, laughing like a crazed woman and occasionally shouting to my driver to turn around. Finally, the words "ashram clinic" somehow penetrated his mind, and he turned the rickshaw around. When we got to the clinic (really only a shabby cottage), it was locked, and no doctor was around. Despair flooded my mind and body, and I stood there, sodden in the rain, unable to move, staring at the little effigy of the Hindu deity Shiva that hung above the door.

Shiva! Lord of Destruction and Transformation … this is his land, who else could help me but he? I decided to pray to Shiva. We have never been on great terms, Shiva and I, and I certainly was not his devotee, unable to resonate with the fiery and fierce energy he embodies. But what other deity to invoke here? So I started to pray. But pray for what? That the doctor will somehow appear at the door in this rain, at this late hour? That Dwight will be saved, just by miraculously recovering on his own?

It has been a pattern in my life that whenever I find myself in critical situations, a part of me is mobilized that is usually dormant, and I tap into a pool of strength I didn't know existed in me. At that moment of despair as I prayed in front of Shiva's effigy something snapped in me, and all of a sudden I felt strong and fearless. I stopped praying and slogged back to the ashram to ask for help in the office. The house coordinator, a calm and pleasant Indian man, told me to wait, while he disappeared. I waited. One person after another left the office and the ashram, while I waited. Finally, the house coordinator returned with another man. "He will help you find doctor's house," he said, and gave the man a little piece of paper.

Back in the flooded street, we hired a rickshaw, now anchored in the middle of a newly formed lake where the road used to be. And again, off into the darkness and water, mud and potholes, careening dangerously as we plowed through the thick mass of mud, trash, and water. But, oh, I was so grateful I was not alone this time! When we got to the doctor's house, the woman who opened the door spoke in a rapid, machine-gun manner and left us to wait on the veranda, amid squadrons of predatory mosquitoes. There were so many of them that in the dim light coming from the house, it looked as though the veranda were enveloped in thick smoke.

"Don't stand like that," my companion told me in a worried voice. "Move, like I do." He flung his arms back and forth, lifted his legs as if stomping out a fire, all along twisting his head left and right. I watched him and did the same. So we continued to dance this anti-mosquito ritual until the doctor came out with the bottle of medicine.

That bottle saved Dwight's life, from my point of view. Shortly after taking a spoonful of the brownish syrup, he was able to inhale more air. By the morning he could whisper and get out of bed. Shiva must have been with us after all, because we got word that the Krishnamurti Foundation in Madras, where we had been on a waiting list, could accommodate us immediately (someone had just cancelled a room). Then some other good things happened: I effortlessly hired a taxi to take us to Madras; the landlord, to our astonishment, returned the rent we had paid in advance; and it even stopped raining! The clouds parted like the Red Sea, the sun shone on the flooded road, and we made our escape. The following day the monsoon returned with a vengeance, the road had to be closed, and for the entire next week the traffic was cut off. But by then we were already in the safety of a dry and heated cottage in Madras.

Then there were Dwight's yearly illnesses during our stay in Cyprus, after leaving India. The most critical of these was exactly a year before our current Roman trial, when I had to put him in a hospital to be given oxygen and intravenous injections because he could neither breathe nor swallow food. Then, as now, we had to vacate the apartment we were renting from friends who were coming for the holidays. I couldn't think of anything else but Dwight's illness. It was as though something had taken me over—emotions old like time, the pain of centuries—and I walked around, locked up in my own personal prison.

After many days, the oxygen and antibiotics finally helped, and I took Dwight to Stalo's house where he finally recovered.

But where to take him now? Where to go in this cold weather, in a city where we have no friends, with him so ill?

Fortunately, I remembered, we have Aldo. When I called him, he said in his calm, husky voice, as if chanting, "Don't worry. Worry makes things worse. It carries energy that prevents healing. I'll order special herbs for Dwight and come over tonight after work."

The lozenges, the syrups, the compresses that Aldo brought smelled horrible. I never knew herbs could have such a repulsive odor. When I opened the brown bottle to pour out a spoonful of the gunk, the stink oozed out like a genie from a bottle, spreading throughout the whole house. I was almost expecting *nonna* from next door to knock and ask if we could, please, turn down the stink. But these arcane preparations of Aldo's stopped Dwight's symptoms from progressing. For the first time in his life, he was recovering without antibiotics.

There is a streak in Dwight's character that is very strong and so deeply ingrained that it's pretty much non-erasable: a fearlessness bordering on reck-lessness. I can easily see Dwight as an officer in the French cavalry, leading an attack on the enemy, dauntlessly charging with his sabre to lead his soldiers. Or as a Knight Templar, pledged to serve the cross and defending the besieged fortress with no thought of himself, only of service and duty. Invincible, that's how Dwight feels about himself deep down. The physical body doesn't matter—it's only here to serve him, and not the other way around.

Consequently, as soon as he felt better, Dwight decided to go out to the city center for a walk, completely against all my admonishments. He has already recovered, so he dismissed my warnings. It's reckless, I repeated, but he shrugged me off—he'd be fine. So we spent a lovely day sauntering around the Pantheon, paying a visit to Tazza d'Oro, a Mecca for coffee worshipers, and making plans where to spend the coming ten days of forced "vacation."

We actually have to move out in three days, it suddenly dawns on me. As soon as we get home, I promptly pick up the telephone to make another assault on the hotels in Naples and am defeated once again; there are no available rooms. The next morning I try Florence—another defeat. All the hotels that we can afford are booked solid.

What's going on in this country? How much in advance do you need to make reservations? What about spontaneity in life? I'm fuming in the hallway, leafing through our guidebook for the umpteenth time. After a while, I notice that Dwight is unusually quiet. I peek into the bedroom and see him lying in bed again. "Strange time to take a nap," I comment, but he doesn't answer. All of a sudden, I feel a pang in my heart.

"You're not feeling well?" I ask, walking in and seating myself gingerly on the bed. Dwight slowly opens his eyes, gives me a wan smile, and shakes his head.

At this moment, I feel a knock of destiny on the door of my life. It's an inexorable knock, like the opening notes of Beethoven's Fifth: *Tan-tan-tan-taaa.*

By the evening, Dwight is coughing continuously, and his chest has become tight, like dried cement.

There are mornings in my life when I don't want to wake up. I mean, I *do* wake up, but I want to go right back where I was. I don't want to face life.

This morning is one of them.

For most of the night I was wide awake, Dwight coughing fitfully next to me. His cough was harsh and pained, pleading for air. I lay helpless, having given him all the concoctions that Aldo had prescribed. Dismal thoughts of worry about our pending move swirled in my head, spinning like a merry-go-round.

As I now listen to the *click-clack* of our upstairs neighbor's high-heeled shoes, I suddenly envy her. I envy all the people who have a home, even a tiny room, a shelter! I feel darkness all around me, heavy darkness waiting to attack me as soon as I open my eyes, so I keep them tightly shut. *I so much want to be out of here! Out of this life!* My heart is full of dread, weighing like lead in my chest.

Dwight starts coughing, and I immediately open my eyes. "What can I get you, love?" I ask with concern. But he can't stop coughing. His face is all red, little beads of sweat popping up on his forehead, and the cough sounds cruel, as if ripping his chest apart.

"Go … look for an apartment," he whispers after a while.

"But—"

"We need to move."

Reluctantly, I go to the newspaper stand, get the day's paper, and start looking at the rental ads. One catches my attention; it's a refurbished apartment in the very heart of Rome, just off the famous Via Veneto, available for short-term rent. The agent can show it to me this morning, so I leave Dwight with supplies of water, tea, and Aldo's herbs, and head to the center.

The building is a sixteenth-century villa tucked away in a narrow street just below the wall that used to circumscribe Rome in Renaissance times. Really, it couldn't be a better location—Piazza di Spagna is just a few blocks away. I open the heavy, squeaking entrance door and climb the cold and dank staircase that is carved in stone. It must be the original staircase, the surface is quite uneven, the stairs polished by use.

When I get to the fourth floor, the rental agent greets me at the door. Everything has been refurbished, he tells me in a pleasant voice. I look around the living room, spacious and tastefully decorated in honey-ocher-sienna tones. It's actually quite pleasant here, even cozy with that nice sofa and plump cushions and a palm tree in the corner. I'm already seeing myself nursing Dwight here, when the agent calls me to see the bedroom. I sweep another contented glance around this charming room, then hop-skip to the bedroom—and freeze in the doorway.

Before me looms black: black satin shrouding a large bed, black satin ensconcing the pillows, black satin encasing two headrests that hang ominously above the bed like a pair of raven's wings.

The bedroom looks like the inside of a coffin!

"What—what's this...?" I stammer, then wave my arm around the room, unable to find words in Italian. (I probably would not have been able to remember English words for funeral accoutrements either had I tried; perhaps, maybe, Serbian.)

The agent shrugs his shoulders apologetically, spreading his arms in a helpless motion. "I know, it's a bit morbid, *un po' pazzo*. But the owner likes black."

I feel the ground under my feet begin to tremble, my heart lurches in a panic, and I feel, I *know*, that if I bring Dwight here, I'll be bringing him to his death bed.

It's Friday evening, only two days left before our move. Dwight has been watching me strangely all evening, without saying a word. I realize that he hasn't actually commented on the apartment, on what I told him about the bedroom.

"What are you thinking?" I finally ask.

He coughs a little, but it's not the bronchitis cough. It's his signature cough, announcing that he is about to say something important. "I was thinking that you should prepare yourself."

"Prepare myself for what?"

"Well, you know ... the possibility that I may go."

I stare at him mute, while through my veins I feel cold blood surging.

"You should remain joyful," he continues calmly, almost serenely, "because I will only be making a transition. Death doesn't really exist. What we call death is liberation. Liberation of our spirit from the prison of matter, this decaying body. I'm getting tired of struggling...." He points at his chest and starts coughing, this time the bronchitis cough.

I don't want to hear this. I don't want to admit that objectively this could happen. After all, Dwight is already seventy, almost twice my age—although he looks much, much younger. I don't want to face it, not yet. But somewhere in the background of my conscious thoughts, Doubt stirs, my own inner enemy that always sabotages me.

"You have chosen this," Doubt whispers maliciously. "It's the price you have to pay when your beloved is so much older than you."

But he doesn't look old, he has the looks and spirit and courage of a much younger man!

But Doubt, which has now assumed a vague face, just puckers its mouth. "Those are subjective things; the fact remains that flesh decays, and nothing can change that. This is what you signed up for six years ago when you fell in love."

Wait, that's not fair. Who thinks of death when in love?

"Ah, but what do you expect—that your love will change the laws of nature?" Doubt cackles.

But what should I have done? I had finally found someone perfect for me, not only my beloved but also a teacher and a best friend. It's such, such ... so rare. Such a gift!

"It is. That's why the price is high." And the face grins, a wicked little grin.

I feel so miserable.

Dwight struggles to speak, gasping for air. "You should remain full of light," he says in between coughs, "because that's who you truly are, a creature of light. There is nothing to be sad about. We take these bodies like garments. One wears out, we discard it, then get a new one."

I feel soooo miserable, but I try hard to smile.

"Remember what Kazantzakis wrote?" he asks. "That 'death is the work of God, but bodily deterioration is the treacherous work of the devil.'" Dwight takes my hand in his and presses a kiss upon it. "I don't mind dying. I'm not afraid of dying. But I don't want to linger and vegetate when the body is worn out." He smiles gently, so gently, and looks at me with so much love that I can't suppress the tears.

I don't want him to go! Please, Universe, don't let him go! I'm not ready.
I feel like a mountain climber clinging onto a ledge above a huge abyss.

We both had another sleepless night; Dwight because of constant coughing, and I because, well, because … I was consumed by a horrible fear I didn't know existed in me: *the fear of losing my beloved.* By the morning, this fear has taken over my heart and my mind, and is now looming in front of me, dire and foreboding.

I drag myself to the telephone and dial Aldo's number. I tell him what happened and beg him to come, although I know he's alone in the shop, his assistant having taken some days off; and it's the busiest shopping period of the year. Aldo's voice comes soothing through the receiver, almost hypnotizing. He will reorganize his obligations and come in the evening to give Dwight a healing.

Then I call Noemi. I plead that she allow us to stay in the apartment because Dwight is so ill. I don't know how my voice is sounding, because she says right away, "*Ah, certo.* Don't worry about moving. We will all stay at *nonna's* when we arrive this week. But the guests are coming next week. I can't cancel them."

Oh, but that's one whole week ahead, and one week is such a long, long time. The whole world can change in a week! My life, on the other hand, has slowed to a snail's pace, slipping by minute by minute, hour by hour.

A tremendous burden has been lifted off my shoulders. I hang up the phone and drop down, squatting by the cabinet, and stare at a spot on the wall. Nothing there, really, just one speck on the white wall. My heart begins to flutter like a little bird. *I love that speck on the wall!*

Aldo arrives at 10:30 in the evening with herbs, compresses, ointments—a full arsenal. By now, I'm so tired from lack of sleep and caring for Dwight that I'm shaking from fatigue. Aldo greets me and then puts his hands on my shoulders, his eyes boring into mine. Although he's not saying anything, I know he's giving me a transmission of energy. Then he walks into the bedroom and sits on the chair next to the bed. They are not speaking, these two men, just watching each other and faintly smiling. Aldo begins to nod and periodically closes his eyes. What is he doing, I wonder? Sitting on a chair by the door, I begin to feel more awake, even alert. The energy in the room has changed too; it feels thicker, charged. Aldo begins the healing, and I slip into a meditation.

An image flashes on the screen of my mind: a servant couple, thrown out by their masters into cold and snow with no place to go and no money—and he is gravely ill. The man and the woman have been together their whole life; they are like one being, one heart, one mind. She is he. And he is sick and out in the snow. She watches him suffer, devoured by fever in a delirium of pain, and it's her body that shakes in agony. No shelter, no heat, no dry clothes, only some old bread she begs from nearby houses.

He dies in her arms. Her heart is wrenched out; only a bleeding hole remains.

All of this I see within seconds. Those same emotions well up from the unknown depths of my being and are choking me now. Fear is washing my every cell, pain infusing my every thought. I start to cry silently. *O please, Universe, let him live! Don't ask me to renounce my beloved! I renounce everything else ... home ... my things ... even shoes!—take them all ... BUT NOT HIM!*

At that moment of anguish, something snaps in me. An insight suddenly appears and I *know* that this suffering is my prison from the past. With full clarity I see the chains of deeply rooted emotions that are binding me. I know that I have to break the chains to set myself *free*!

I stop sobbing and open my eyes to the dim light of the bedroom. It feels as if I've come from another world. Aldo is bent over Dwight lying in bed; all is peaceful but charged.

I HAVE TO FREE MYSELF FROM THE EMOTIONAL PRISON OF THIS FEAR!

These words surge through me like a powerful roar to dissolve the chains. It's an exhilarating feeling, the feeling of getting control of my emotions. *I want to be my own master, and not be enslaved by the past, by the fears from my subconscious!*

"Dwight," I hear Aldo's soft voice, "life and death are fighting in you. What do you wish, to die or to live?"

I bolt straight up in my chair and prick up my ears.

"I don't know," comes Dwight's muffled answer. "I'd like to live for Svetlana, but I'm tired of struggling with the body ... I'd like to go home."

I sit in my chair like a statue.

Aldo continues, "You have to make a choice. Have you finished everything here?"

Dwight is now thinking. "I'm not sure. There is my work with the Earth's energies I'd like to continue ... and I'd like to help Svetlana reach her goal." He darts a quick glance in my direction.

Aldo seats himself on the bed, takes Dwight's hand in his, and says softly but firmly, "You will recover *only* if you choose to live."

"Hmm," mutters Dwight.

"Do you want to live?" Aldo is now boring into Dwight's eyes with such intensity that I can feel it all the way where I'm sitting.

"Yeaaah…" I hear a little rasp. "For Svetlana."

"No!" snaps Aldo. "Not for Svetlana. For yourself!"

Aldo suddenly stands up, still holding Dwight's hand, and bellows, "I want to live now and here!" He starts jumping by the bed, like a shaman in a trance, shouting, "*Qui, Qui, Qui…*"

My eyes want to pop out, I'm so stunned by what I'm seeing.

"Here, here, here!" hoots Aldo now in English, jumping in the rhythm of the words and shaking Dwight's hand. "Now, Now, Now!"

Dwight, in sheer astonishment, begins to nod, at first slowly, then he croaks, "*Qui* … yes," while Aldo is still jumping, pouring the will-to-live into his patient.

In my chair by the door, I'm watching this scene as if in a movie theater, except that the movie is my life. And in that movie, the man I love beyond words was about to disappear from my life. I watch Aldo jump relentlessly, as if by jumping he's altering destiny itself, transmuting its lethal knock from *tan-tan-tan-taaa* to *here-now-here-now*. Grateful tears are rolling down my cheeks, as the whole room—the movie—turns into a blurry vision.

I only hope the neighbors downstairs are still watching TV….

CHAPTER 14

NEW YEAR IN ROME:

DUEL AT MIDNIGHT

Tonight is the beginning of the next thousand years in human history. I drive to the center of Rome to wait for the tick of the clock right there, in the heart of Western civilization. It's symbolic, to be in Rome at the turn of the millennium. I have much to be grateful for, much to congratulate myself about (although I'm not very good at patting myself on the back; I always feel I should do better). But really, I did well, and as Dwight said, I should acknowledge that. At the very last moment, after many phone calls and juggling options, I managed to do a switch: I rented the black satin apartment for Noemi's guests, who accepted going there with absolute delight. Of course, we paid for the difference in price (which was the equivalent of our month's rent), but it was well worth it—we stayed safely in Noemi's apartment.

Dwight, too, has been recovering. For a couple of days after Aldo's healing and the memorable jumping, Dwight was still teetering between life and death. It was the day after Christmas when he finally said "yes" to life and decided to continue living not only because of me, but because of himself, because of what he owed to his Soul—to heal a broken heart. This illness had brought to the surface the issue of grief that was buried throughout his entire life. He now recognized the pattern in the events of his early life, in the repeated situations of tragically losing that which he loved; the pattern which, he felt, went much deeper, into the remote past of other incarnations. It had created an emotional knot of grief and, as a result, Dwight had frozen his emotions and closed his heart in order to avoid further pain. "Now I have to live what I've taught all my life," he said reflectively one morning after his

151

meditation. "That if you cut out suffering and loss by closing your heart, you lose the opposite—happiness and gain. Because opposites are part of the same whole; you can't eliminate one without losing the other."

"But ... weren't you happy with me all these years?" I asked, a bit perplexed, a bit hurt.

"Of course I was!" Dwight nodded reassuringly. "But I now realize that I was living only on the surface of emotions. A closed heart prevented me from having deep and intense experiences. You see, to be fully alive it's not enough to climb the heights—you have to plumb the depths also," he said and fell silent.

I wish I had such a clear understanding of my own issues. I thought I came to grips with my fear, but now, as I'm walking toward the Cavour Bridge to cross the Tiber, my heart is twanging again with strange sadness. Gosh, inner work is so much like archaeological digging: you discover layer after layer, and there is no end to it. As I walk over the river, my mind is enveloped in a glum cloud. The weather is bitingly cold. Rome looks somber with only a few decorations. Groups of people are out, a few solitary walkers like me, the freezing wind is blowing, and I just don't feel a festive atmosphere in the air or in myself. *Maybe I should have stayed home with Dwight.*

I change my mind, turn around, and start walking toward St. Peter's. Maybe there, at the heart of Christianity, I'll feel something special, something inspiring, a new note for the new millennium. The walk feels interminably long in the freezing wind that sweeps along the Tiber.

I couldn't have made a worse choice. At the Piazza di San Pietro a terribly long queue is snaking toward the cathedral, curbed by railings, with police cars forming the outer circle. There is no chance I would make it inside before midnight. What to do?

I change my mind again. I decide to go back to my favorite place—the Spanish Steps. I walk along the Tiber again, the wind now blowing in my face. I feel so sad without Dwight. *Maybe I didn't do the right thing. Maybe I should have stayed home with him...*

As I am crossing the Ponte San Angelo, the New Year strikes. It has caught me by surprise. I stop to watch the groups of people on the bridge, opening bottles of champagne and toasting: men, boisterous, slapping each other on the back; *donne,* elegant-looking in their fur coats, glittery stockings (in this cold?!), and high-heeled shoes, laughing and sipping the champagne. Fireworks are exploding everywhere, from balconies, windows, bridges. This is a good place to watch these constellations of fire-red and phosphorescent-green and electric-blue and silvery-white and iridescent-gold, all pinwheeling above the domes of Rome.

The Eternal City is festively ablaze, finally.

But I still feel alone; worse, I feel lonely. *I should have stayed home!*

I continue my walk to the Spanish Steps. Only a few shopping streets are well-lit and the stores decorated; the rest of the streets look somber and gloomy. I pass young men with a bottle in one hand and a *telefonino* in the other, couples cuddling against one another blank-faced, groups of tourists strolling with forced smiles, packs of youngsters striding indifferently somewhere....

The icy wind is biting my forehead. The temperature must be below zero. An insidious feeling of desperation creeps into my body. I'd had enough. I want to be with Dwight. How foolish of me to separate on this night. Before I even reach the Spanish Steps I turn around and head back for the car.

I take a street that is wide and well-lit, and feels friendly because I know it so well; our favorite bakery is on the opposite sidewalk. As I lift my head to look in that direction, I catch a glimpse of a lump in a shadowy doorway: a woman sitting huddled against the door of a building. *She must be homeless,* flashes through my mind. She is wrapped in tatters, bedraggled and squalid, clenching her knees and bobbing her head, perhaps hungry, perhaps mad. Oh, the stab I feel in my heart at the sight of her! *Homeless in the cold ... HOMELESS!*

A sheer dread spreads through me and I quicken my steps. I almost start running, as if by running from her I could escape these dire emotions.

But no. They stay with me, the dread, the desperation, the hopelessness.

My car is far away.

With every stride, I sink deeper into misery. There is no avoiding it, no running away from it. I stop in my tracks.

Let's face it: *I HAVE A FEAR OF HOMELESSNESS.*

For a long moment I stand in the middle of the sidewalk, staring with unseeing eyes, feeling the fear take over my body, gripping my heart. The vision I had a few days days earlier—of the servant couple expelled from the master's mansion—invades my mind.

Then thoughts start pouring. Over the past two years and especially since we came to Italy, the pattern of difficulties in finding a place to stay has persisted: living with other people's things so I'm constantly reminded that I don't have a home; crisscrossing the Italian boot looking for somewhere to live; time after time being obliged to leave our temporary home when Dwight was gravely ill, with nowhere to go. What is this? Enactment of the past life I "saw" while Aldo was healing Dwight? A set-up for me to learn a lesson? Some kind of "house karma?" Rationally I recognize that we're not "homeless;" we have enough money for lodging. But rational or irrational, the fear pervading me is real.

I see now: this feeling of homelessness has been gradually intensifying through different circumstances so that, finally, I have no choice but to become aware of it. Suddenly I realize—I had this fear even when I was a little girl! That's why I felt such overwhelming gratitude every night I'd go to bed. I would lie tucked in, feeling so happy, so grateful that I was warm, that I had a bed and a roof over my head. How unusual was that for a little girl who never knew any deprivation? That's also why I had a break-down a few months ago during my visit to Santa Barbara. My former boyfriend, who had been storing my things in his attic, had just announced that I had to move all my possessions out of his house. That night, I stared at my boxes in his living room, piled up like orphans, and I broke into tears. But I had no courage then to look at the fear and name it.

Now I'm determined to face it. I'm overcome by dread but resolved not to avert my eyes, not to run away. I'm gazing straight into the eye of fear, deep within me. The eye of fear … like the eye of a cyclone, a spot of stillness in the midst of devastation … the only way to defeat it … look into the eye, the center … and see the light there, a faint glimmer of a spark … and know it to be me. This fear is a part of me. I'm overwhelmed by compassion for myself—my past selves—who had no home, who slept on hard earth and perished in the snow, whose fear had created this powerful emotion.

I stand still and embrace all those past suffering selves. I take their fear into my body and feel it with every cell. I stand and let the fear fill my legs and arms and chest. But I no longer identify with it. *I know you now from the inside … you can no longer have control over me because … you are me. I have embraced your darkness with my light.*

I stand still until the fear is no more.

When I start walking again, my steps are heavy, lead instead of legs, and wonky knees. My whole body aches. Is the fear gone for good?

I arrive home well past one o'clock, feeling numb inside and out. Dwight welcomes me, warm and buoyant. He sweeps me into his arms and holds me for a long moment, his body relaxing into the embrace. "I had fun watching the fireworks," he says with a twinkle in his eyes. "From every balcony people were setting off sparklers at midnight, shouting New Year's wishes to each other across the streets. My, it was festive!"

So Dwight has experienced a different celebration of *Capodinote* in our neighborhood; families, friends, singing and reveling. And I had a lonely and gloomy and freezing walk—plus a duel with my fear. I drink a cup of hot herbal tea, still shivering, my feet up on the radiator.

How very different: the same night, the same event, two experiences poles apart.

"Ognuno a suo gusto," Italians say. "Everyone to his or her own taste."

And everyone according to his or her karma.

New Year's Day rose warm and sunny, with clear blue skies and puffy clouds, a balmy spring instead of a sharp winter. A complete reversal from just eight hours ago. The change in weather is so sudden and so drastic that it feels as though we've traveled in the meantime from, say, Sweden to Greece.

"I have a wish," Dwight announces as we're sipping our hot lemonade in bed. "I'd like to see the best views of Rome today."

What a great way to start the new year! And we can even drive into the center because it's a holiday (on weekdays, the center is closed to traffic). So we get into our Honda, still missing a headlight and the front bumper from our accident in Greece, and set off in search of the best views. From Trinita dei Monti above the Spanish Steps to the Borghese Park to Pincio, we drive and make frequent stops, only to realize that we should be on the other side of Rome, the west side, in order to have the sun behind us.

So we cross the Tiber and drive through Trastevere ("over the Tiber"), in the past a working-class neighborhood of Rome. An unpleasant memory twangs in my heart: this is where I lost my camera, leaving it behind in a cab. We drive up the same street the cab drove that day. And we go to the same place where he deposited us, on top of the Gianicolo hill. How long ago was it?—not even four months but it feels like four years. I feel like a different person now; and Rome feels so different.

"Wow!" Dwight exclaims, swept away by the beauty of the view.

Here it lies, below our feet, the city where all roads lead. The domes, the bell-towers, the palaces glow in the warm afternoon sun, and the tapestry of roofs unrolls seemingly to the white-capped mountains on the horizon. Magnificent Rome. Romantic Rome. The Rome of many a pilgrim's fervor, of many an artist's inspiration. The city that for millennia wove a spell of power, of faith, of glory, of glamour. Eternal Rome.

I remember fondly our first visit to this city, two years ago. We were staying in a modest hotel near the Spanish Steps. Every day was an exciting adventure as we strolled the streets and little *piazzas*, discovering beautiful fountains and fifteenth-century houses painted in those lovely terracotta colors. I was infatuated with Rome.

But when we actually started living here, the honeymoon spell of our first visit gradually wore off. Over the weeks and months, we were discovering the other side of Rome, the side you get to know only in a "married" life: the struggle with traffic, the fight for parking, the ugliness of the modern districts, the noise, the Byzantine postal system. There were days when I felt weary and disillusioned, thinking of divorcing Rome.

"You realize," Dwight begins softly, looking into the distance, "it's quite symbolic...."

"What?"

"Well, to be right here, on this hill, on this day."

"What d'you mean?

"This hill, Janiculum," he says slowly, "was named after the god Janus. And Janus was the god of beginnings and transitions."

"Janus ... that sounds familiar. Is that the fellow with two faces in one head that are looking in the opposite directions?"

"Uh-huh. Symbolically the two faces look into the future and the past at the same time. Back at the last year and forward into the new."

"Oh, how appropriate!"

Then I have a thought. "Let's do the same, the two of us," I suggest. "Let's stand back-to-back and look into the past and future. Which side do you want?"

"What?"

I stand behind Dwight and lean against his back. "One body, two faces. Where do you want to look—into the past or future?"

Dwight laughs. "Future, of course."

It doesn't surprise me. Between the two of us, Dwight is the one who wants to look ahead and rarely thinks of the past. I, on the contrary, tend to remember the past, to reminisce about past events, to cherish memories, but also to ruminate over past mistakes.

"Okay, let's say what we see," I propose.

"You begin, you're the past."

"All right." I close my eyes and pause for a moment. "I see ... I see ... a dry riverbed. It's full of boulders and rocks. It's wide. The banks, though, are grassy and flat. I'm in the riverbed and I'm walking to my destination, which I can't see. I'm faltering and stumbling and have to walk around the boulders and over the rocks and it's very tiring."

"But you don't give up," adds Dwight.

"No. I certainly don't. I won't. But ... why have I chosen to walk the riverbed instead of the soft carpet of grass?"

From behind, Dwight's hand reaches for mine and gently squeezes it. "When you reach your destination, having walked over the boulders, how will your body, your muscles be?"

I imagine myself walking up and down and around, then smile, "Strong, very strong."

At that moment a faint hope rises in my heart—that, maybe, the boulders will get smaller and the riverbed more even, and that in the new year I will get closer to finding my new purpose: how I can bring all the spiritual ideas I've learned so far into the fabric of ordinary life.

Maybe at that moment I should have switched sides with Dwight; maybe then I would have seen how far away I still was from my destination and maybe I would have seen the huge boulders that loomed right in front of me.

Instead, I asked, "And what do you see?"

Dwight clears his throat then begins slowly, "I see a web of light, luminous threads that cross each other like a net. This net is spread over a murky area, but I don't know where it is."

I open my eyes and realize that people are glancing at us. The gorgeous weather has inspired many Romans to stroll out and the Piazza Garibaldi is getting crowded. I detach myself from Dwight's back and face Rome again.

"It just occurred to me," says Dwight, "as the god of beginnings, Janus is also the god of doors and gateways. In a way, he has a similar function to Anubis. He looks after the passages, the beginnings of new endeavors. So maybe you should formulate something for the year ahead while we are here?"

I stare at the rooftops, now turning golden. "It's a good idea, but I'm totally blank."

"What about your book?" Dwight glances sideways at me.

"Oh, that ... I don't know. I haven't had any inspiration. And frankly, I was too busy living and sorting out my fears and taking care of you to be thinking about the book."

"Hum, yes, that's certainly true. But that's over now. We have a fresh start."

I look at Rome below, but can't seem to be able to look into the future.

The whole week passed, quiet and peaceful, a week when Italians take their winter vacation. We'd wake up to a silent building, a silent neighborhood; the air itself felt undisturbed. And we'd go to the center on an almost empty bus, then walk around the normally busy streets without being jostled. This was a period of recovery, both for Dwight and for myself—no events, no problems, no crisis that needed to be solved immediately. And for that matter, no inner work and personal issues to face either! Calm and quiet, for a whole week.

But the expiration date of our visas was approaching, and with it renewed stirrings of apprehension. The apprehension gradually grew into dread as I remembered our immigration ordeal in Sicily. And we were told that the Questura in Rome was even worse. Dwight was bracing for another nightmarish situation, biting his lower lip more and more frequently and becoming withdrawn. He was even contemplating moving to another part of Italy just to avoid the Roman Questura. One evening, in a moment of particular gloom, he even mumbled something about going back to the States.

"You can't be serious?" I asked reproachfully.

There was another mumble and shaking of the head. "Well, no, but that's how I feel." Then he fell silent for the rest of the evening.

"Why do you always become so silent when we have to face something unpleasant?" I finally asked, tired of his silence.

"Oh, I do?" Dwight seemed surprised. "I guess it's because I'm tuning out, so that I don't feel the unpleasantness." He forced a laugh.

"Ah, so you're shutting down your heart again?"

"To a certain extent, yes…." He smiled awkwardly, like a boy caught with his hand in a cookie jar. "But only for the immigration."

A few days later, Noemi arrives from Umbertide to accompany us to the Questura. She is our Italian host who will be a guarantor for us. When she rings the doorbell she is perfectly relaxed and in a good mood. She has even managed to stop by her stylist, the only one who can tame her hair. I can't compliment her on the hairdo because my gut is all tied up in a knot.

"*Ah bene*, don't worry," she says reassuringly, looking at our glum faces. "I did this for my daughter's boyfriend. It wasn't bad. We just go to local police."

The local police office? Not to the Questura? That's different from what we were told. But Noemi is positive. She takes us to the local police station where a friendly receptionist directs us to an office in the basement. We walk into a spacious room with chairs around and only a few people waiting. Noemi takes a number and we seat ourselves to wait for our turn. A perfectly civilized room and a perfectly civilized procedure. I'm actually shocked by the reversal of what I was expecting. No crowds, no squeezing and elbowing, no friends of employees cutting into the line. Dwight, too, is staring around in disbelief. Only Noemi looks completely composed. *"Ah bene*, I told you. Not bad."

No, not bad at all. Actually, it was amazingly easy: a few questions addressed to Noemi, our bank accounts and investment statements presented, a few papers from Noemi, a few forms typed by the woman officer, very polite and friendly—and we were done! We just have to return the next day to pick up our *Permessi di Sogiorno.*

So we are now officially Italian residents ... for one year.

PART 4

CAMPAGNA:
ADVENTURE, ADVENTURE...

CHAPTER 15

NAPLES:

SEE NAPLES AND DIE

At the beginning of March, after a gray and wet winter, we decide to leave drizzling Rome for sunnier and warmer places. We are actually heading to Naples—third time's the charm!

According to legend, Napoli sprang up around the tomb of the siren Perthenope, who had drowned herself after failing to seduce Odysseus (hence its eighth-century BC name, Parthenopean City). So Naples was destined to be the most "tragentic" city in Italy (my term for "tragic" and "romantic"). Many popular Italian *canzoni*, songs, extol its sensuous beauty, its alluring view of the bay, its passionate love stories. "See Naples and die" was whispered from generation to generation, reinforcing the myth of its beauty: see Naples and you can die in peace—you've consummated life to its fullest.

After only a couple of hours on the new, fast *autostrada*, we arrive at the outskirts of the city which I like to call Siren City and which, since my teenage years, I've been "dying" to see. I'm aquiver with anticipation, eyes wide open, taking everything in … ugly and dilapidated housing complexes, dreary industrial areas, truck horns blaring, cranes clanging and rumbling, tugs hooting in the cargo port, glass skyscrapers clustered in a bunch further inland. I clench the steering wheel and can't utter a word. *Bella Napoli,* I cry out silently, *where are you?*

"My God, this is just like Los Angeles," exclaims Dwight, his head swiveling left and right in disbelief. "Had I landed here blindfolded, I wouldn't know I was in Italy!"

We drive for another grim half-hour before we notice a change. Shoddy housing barns are replaced by elegant buildings, huge cargo ships give way to posh yachts, and the garbage-littered road turns into a landscaped boulevard.

We're heading for the central Piazza Trieste where we have arranged to meet Gennaro, a doctor who rents his own apartment as a bed-and-breakfast accommodation (that's the ad I clipped from the *Herald Tribune* when we were in Orvieto last December). Caught in the throes of the afternoon traffic we slowly inch forward, looking for a man with a red scarf on a scooter, waiting for us somewhere on the *piazza*. We are a much easier mark to spot though—a car without the front bumper and one headlight. Finally, just as Dwight is beginning to stress out, I see the red scarf fluttering in the hands of a slightly pudgy and balding man—Gennaro!

With relief, we follow the Neapolitan on his Vespa. I gaze around at the baroque palaces, imposing façades, large squares chock-full of cars, huge palm trees erect as ceremonial sentries. Everything looks grandiose, a striking difference to the flavor of the center of Rome which is all tucked in and cozy. But when we reach the Quartieri Spagnoli (Spanish Quarters), once a working quarter of Naples, the wide, palm-flanked boulevards turn into a warren of alleys and passageways, and *piazzas* disappear altogether.

What a contrast! Dwight and I look at each other with dismay, stuck behind the Vespa in a line of traffic long and slow as a funeral procession, creeping up a steep street the width of a single car. On both sides, the street is lined with sidewalks just wide enough for one person—but where scooters are parked underneath the windows and groceries are displayed and laundry hangs at head height and matrons lean through the upper part of entrance doors, doors that lead into an all-purpose room where the whole family sits and eats and sleeps, and actually ... sings. "O Sole mio-o-o..." "Que bella note..." "Torna a Sorriento...." I hear melodies wafting from shops and bakeries, booming from open windows, and fading out around corners. I can't really tell if Neapolitans are speaking or singing—their speech sounds so much like a song. *This* is the Naples of Pulcinella, the *commedia dell'arte* symbol of the city whose traditional white garb and black mask reconcile the opposites of life and death; the Naples of voluptuous Sophia Loren and the neo-realist movies from the 1960s; the Naples of thriving and throbbing street life bursting with emotions and passions, songs and sins, luscious love stories and rash revenges.

From his scooter Gennaro motions to us to enter a garage squeezed into the corner of two streets atop a hill. "This is a garage?" Dwight suspiciously eyes the tiny space where we have to park our Honda at a dangerously steep angle.

"Sorry," Gennaro says after he tucks in his scooter, "but you can't park on the street in this neighborhood."

Pulling out our suitcases, we walk down to Gennaro's apartment, where we'll spend the next five nights. The long, straight, tunnel-like street is alight here and there with shafts of sun penetrating through crevices between tall buildings. It reminds me of a gigantic Christmas garland, laundry flopping and fluttering from just about every window or balcony. Did the whole street wash its laundry on the same day, I wonder?

We arrive at an imposing, cast-iron gate. Gennaro produces a bunch of huge keys and we step into a large hall in the middle of which crouches the tiny cabin of an ancient elevator, a toll-elevator at that: no coins, no ride. Inside the elevator there is room only for our luggage and a squeezed-in Dwight, so Gennaro and I walk three grim and dilapidated flights of stairs while the elevator rumbles and rattles alongside. I cast apprehensive glances at the peeling paint and dirty railing.

But as soon as we step into Gennaro's apartment, we are hit by an unex-pected contrast—an abundance of antique furniture, Persian rugs, porcelain plates, and paintings of Old Masters. All the rooms are lavishly decorated so much so that, as I look around, I can't find a square inch of empty space. Every corner, every wall surface, every side table, *everything* is filled with things, things, things.

"Wow, this is very … Baroque," says Dwight with a little whistle.

And everything evokes the flavor of royalty: portraits of Neapolitan kings and princesses, heavy double curtains made of crimson velvet and tied with luxurious golden tassels, the *argenteria* gleamingly displayed in the dining room. When I climb to the bedroom perched on the gallery above the kitchen (the apartment is not big), I'm dumbfounded. Like a huge bird with outstretched wings, dark purple swags soar up the wall above the bed, and an exasperating collection of religious porcelain memorabilia *completely* covers the remaining space on the wall—and this in a room that doesn't even have a window! And the boudoir and night tables are buried under framed family photographs, books, collectors' figurines, plates, vases, ashtrays.

All of a sudden I feel my throat tightening. A familiar wave of panic rises from my gut, and a silent scream of claustrophobia wells up: I WANT TO GET OUT OF HERE!

But, wait, I say to myself sensibly, *you conquered this fear in the Great Pyramid, remember?* Suddenly overwhelmed by fatigue, I drop on the plush bed, which feels as if it's made of the finest feathers, and remember the hard granite of the sarcophagus….

The Great Pyramid was plunged into darkness due to a power outage just as it opened for visitors. In the confusion that followed, Dwight and I made our way in right before it was closed again. As we rushed inside, we found ourselves submerged in the dark of a passageway so narrow and so low that we had to walk bent over. Dwight nudged me to go ahead, while he stayed behind. I raced up the long and steep Grand Gallery, the map of the pyramid etched in my mind. *My gosh, I'm practically alone here!* With only a pencil-flashlight in my hand, I climbed as fast as my lungs and heart could take me to the entrance into the King's Chamber—and stopped short. My legs dug into the stone and my body refused to move.

Afraid? You bet. After all, the Pyramid is not exactly a comfortable place, especially when engulfed in darkness. And I'd always been afraid of the dark, actually, of creatures that inhabit the dark. As a three-year-old I had a nanny with a creepy sense of humor. She would cloak herself in a white sheet and lunge at me from behind a door, swaying and moaning like a ghost. Naturally, my screams would rend the air, which seemed to greatly amuse the nanny. Eventually, nanny-the-ghost was sent away, but the ghost scares left a groove in my psyche.

So here I was, enclosed in boundless dark, alone in what felt like a tomb.

"This is crazy! What do you think you're—" Doubt promptly reared its head, but I brushed it off. With a surge of courage and unflinching determination I walked to the sarcophagus, climbed in, then lay down on its cold stone. Finally, I extinguished the flashlight.

In the engulfing silence, the pounding of my heart sounded like the amplified drums at a heavy metal concert. Gradually, my heart quieted down, and the flashes and arrows of different-colored light slowly faded from the inside of my eyelids. I was swallowed by darkness and silence that felt like a gateway to another dimension of being. I felt myself sinking into the Void. And in that Void a realization emerged, or maybe it was the Voice, or my Guidance—one can't tell what things are in a state of mind where nothing is—*you've done it!* To conquer a fear, I understood clearly, one has to "jump" into it without thinking, because it is our thoughts that make us afraid in the first place.

"SVET-LAA-NAA … We're waiting for you!" Dwight's voice floats in from … where was I? Ah yes, in the claustrophobic room in Naples. I smile, looking around in amusement.

I swoop downstairs where our host is hurriedly showing Dwight how the apartment functions. His lunch-break over, Gennaro is rushing to get back to his gynecological practice. As I glance at yet another side table exhibiting precious plates and photographs, I do a double take. Whaaat? Am I really seeing Gwyneth Paltrow leaning over our host, her black-gowned arm sinuously resting on his shoulder?!

"Oh, we became good friends," Gennaro casually says waving his left hand, "when they were making *Talented Mr. Ripley*. You saw it, no? ... Ah, yes, of course, of course, it's beauuutifulllll movie, isn't it? My good friend chose the location and we spent allll of the time together...." And he dashes off, already late, switching off the lights in the entrance hall.

Dwight and I set off for our first walk around Naples—and we almost choke with the exhaust fumes. These steep and narrow streetlets lined with tall houses and surging with a constant flow of traffic, act as perfect carbon dioxide traps. Dwight suffers an instant asthma attack; he's wheezing so badly that I have to go back to the apartment and fetch his inhaler. Dodging people, parked scooters, baby prams, and dripping laundry (not to mention the incessant honking, echoed by the soaring stone façades) is more than enough for gasping Dwight. He's already had enough of Naples. "I want to go back to Rome," he grumbles. "This is hell."

I can't argue but I don't want to give up just yet. "Let's give it one more day," I bargain. "Try the other parts of Naples."

So we stay.

Over the days ahead I discover that Naples is a city of contrasts *par excellence*: from splendor to squalor, from the brightness of Mediterranean light to the darkness of dingy slums, always—contrasts. I wonder if Caravaggio had anything to do with it. Escaping a murder charge, this much-in-demand, innovative artist fled Rome for Naples in 1607 and took the city by storm: his signature style, *chiaroscuro* (light-and-dark), became the official painting style of the day. But Caravaggio had a rather violent—or shall I say, *chiaroscuro* temperament—so he soon fled Naples only to return, pursued, several years later. In the short but tempestuous time that Caravaggio spent in Naples, he left a long-lasting legacy—dozens of exceptionally dramatic, emotionally intense paintings executed in vivid contrasts and with almost painful realism. And he fathered the Baroque.

I find this *chiaroscuro* in yet another pair of opposites. In no other part of the world have I experienced uglier urban sprawl and environmental degradation, and happier people. It is an interesting phenomenon, or rather a paradox: how can such warm, nice people create so much ugliness? Or, turn it around: how can people who live in such squalid surroundings (as are many quarters of Naples) still be happy and singing? Because it's the people, I'm starting to think, who create the myth of the beauty of Naples.

I fully experience this happy energy of Neapolitans one afternoon when I go for a walk alone, leaving the exhausted Dwight to a late siesta. It's already getting dark, and lanterns clothe the streets in sparkling attire. It's the peak shopping time for Neapolitans, as well as a get-together time. I walk by middle-aged couples snuggled together, distinguished-looking gentlemen, boisterous youngsters, smart-looking professionals. I walk by nice stores with lovely clothes and shoes. I walk by cafés brimming with people, chatting and laughing. More and more, I become aware of the energy in the air that makes me feel comfortable and at home.

It is then that I experience a change in consciousness. Instead of being absorbed by, ahem … clothes and shoes, I enter a state in which I perceive everything as a whole—a twirling kaleidoscope of ever-changing shapes and colors. At the same time, I'm aware of every little detail around me, of everyone who passes by, of their feelings, personalities, even life circumstances. An all-encompassing love washes over me, love that floods every cell of my body. I feel as if a great beam of light is pouring through me and I, in turn, radiate that light out—to streets, to people, to buildings.

Dazed and dreamy, I still glance at a store-window to notice this gorgeous dress or that elegant pair of shoes which the ordinary self would very much like to have. A realization swoops over me: by the mere fact that they exist, these objects of desire are already mine. They are part of the same Whole of which I am a part; and this Whole is already in me, just as it is in every little piece that comprises it. Thus I already own everything, not in the sense of physical possession, of course, but in the sense of a field of limitless possibilities.

Later that evening, Dwight offers an explanation of my mystical experience. He quotes Gandhi: "'Renounce the world and enjoy it.' That's what you did, my love." He nods thoughtfully.

Right. I wish I could maintain that attitude of renunciation next time I see an elegant pair of shoes.

"It doesn't matter." Dwight shrugs impassively. "You'll renounce again. And again. And—"

"Again. I know—until it becomes permanent."

It seems so easy to keep this "new vibration," as Dwight put it, here in Naples, regardless of street chaos. There is something conducive about the energy (at least in the city center), a certain feeling of togetherness. Chance encounters in restaurants, people we meet when—hopelessly lost—we ask for directions then remain in conversation for half an hour, helpful but not pushy shopkeepers, polite waiters, families we watch as they take their *passeggiata* at dusk, all exude a certain gentleness of character which is difficult to describe. In fact, it's something unique to Neapolitans, something more than kindness and warmth put together. It's—*gentilezza*. They are famous for it throughout Italy. Compare Neapolitans and Romans, for example, and the difference is immediately apparent: Neapolitans are more relaxed and even walk more slowly; they also look somehow distinguished with a certain nobility of character. Could this be accounted for by the historical heritage of Naples, I wonder? Since the eleventh century a trail of European royal families took turns ruling the city—the Lombards, the Normans, Hohenstaufens, Angevins, Aragonese, Spanish, Bourbons....

"We don't think about negative, what we don't have," Gennaro tells us during one of our engaging chats that always start with music and wander off in many directions. "We see what is good, what we have, *la belleza*! Music, for example ... no? And friends, love, sea...." He sweeps his hand toward the balcony, flooded by the afternoon sun.

"Ah, but you *must* hear this," he says with authority and pulls out one of the thousand (thousand!) gramophone records that completely cover the wall, like some sort of a modern art wallpaper.

Gennaro plays arias from Bellini's *La sonnambula*, accompanying the music with sighs and emphatic back-and-forth movements of his right hand, his thumb and index finger forming an "O." What's more, Bellini, the darling of Naples, is going to be performed at San Carlo the following evening. Ah, we must see the mooost beauuuutifullll Opera house in the world (the hand goes again back and forth to finish with two fingers touching the lips—a gestural exclamation mark).

The following night, we're flabbergasted by the magnificence of the Opera interior. With an enormous Murano chandelier, a sumptuous golden-rimmed curtain, and a flamboyant Royal loge, San Carlo is a real jewel. As proof positive of what I'm becoming convinced—that music has a prime place in the life of Neapolitans—I read that the interior of the Opera house was built entirely of wood and stucco to achieve perfect acoustics.

I feel so perfectly at home at the Opera, as if I've spent all my life among chandeliers and velvet seats and theater binoculars. Granted, I did spend many an evening watching operas and ballets in my youth. We lived a few blocks away from the Opera house, and my mother would take me to hear Verdi just as parents take their kids to the movies today. But I also spent several years on stage as well, before the scoliosis put a stop to my budding ballet career.

During the intermission, as we descend the stairwell to the bar, a sea of shimmering black ripples through a huge foyer lined with mirrors. From where I'm standing, people themselves look like figures in a grand painting. The mingling of black velvet, white collars, naked shoulders, lace and sparkling gowns, the buzz of words and clinking of glasses, give a dreamy quality to the scene and a flavor of an *époque passée*.

The following morning I wake up tired to the bone. My body refuses to move, my senses are dull and numb, and my mind clamors for rest. But we have an agenda for today, and that is to visit the Capodimonte Palace and Gallery perched high in the hills above Naples. So we set out toward the center, in the general direction of bus stops. All of a sudden I feel discouraged by the prospect of having to find a bus stop, wait for the bus, ride for a half-hour to the museum, then walk through countless rooms…. I look at the bus tickets I've just purchased and feel overwhelmed. "I just can't do it," I announce.

Dwight immediately agrees to a change of plan, no questions asked. So we walk back to the Piazza Trieste and plant ourselves at a sunny table on the outdoor terrace. It's Naples' most venerated café, the 150-year old Gran Café Gambrinus, with its Belle Époque décor. Once a salon of intellectuals, dukes, ministers, and writers, it is now mostly a tourist attraction—but who cares? Nothing like a spur-of-the-moment cappuccino in the sun! My body is happy that it doesn't have to walk, and I feel my mind relaxing into a lazy, non-thinking blob.

"Congratulations!" Dwight catapults from behind the pages of the *Herald Tribune*.

"What?" I'm startled out of my blobby state.

"Congratulations for not following your agenda, but listening to your body."

"Honestly, I don't think I had much choice."

"Still," Dwight insists, "the old Svetlana would have pushed ahead, no matter what."

"I guess she would," I admit after a moment of thinking. I've always had "to-do" lists and plans for the day, I've always organized my errands so I'd do them in the most efficient way.

"But you also always had to have it *your way*, right?" Dwight finally lowers the newspaper and looks at me. "Right?" he repeats in another key.

I hesitate. Why is it so difficult to admit our foibles?

"And I usually let you have it your way," he presses on. "And that's why we never get into serious conflicts because I don't really care what agenda we have … well," he laughs, "most of the time, anyway."

I start to fidget. *But I have really good organizational skills and a good sense of timing!*

"And guess what happens when you don't get it your way?" Dwight is just not letting me off the hook.

"What?" I mumble reluctantly.

"You tell me. How do you feel when your agenda is scrambled?"

"Hum … I'm not sure."

"Okay, how do you feel when you don't get the table you want in a restaurant? Now I get it right away.

"Or when they run out of your favorite croissants in the bakery, or when the sweeper is cleaning the beach when you want to jog, or when—"

"All right, all right, you don't have to rub it in anymore, I get it. I feel irritated!" I bark at him irritably.

Dwight is beaming. "But what's behind the irritation?" He fires yet another question.

In all our years of working together, he has always proceeded in this way, question after question, persistent, unrelenting, until I find the answer myself.

"What's behind the irritation?" I sigh in resignation. "Do we have to solve this issue right now?"

"Do we have to? Of course, not." He shrugs. "We don't have to do anything. It's your choice."

And I choose to remain a blob. The sun feels so relaxing, my brain is lazy, and I don't feel like doing a heavy-duty self-inquiry just at this moment. I want to take a morning off. Dwight makes a little coughing noise and returns to his newspaper. I know what he's thinking though, and I'm thinking the same: I'll have to face that question sooner or later.

The last morning in Naples, we are sipping our farewell cappuccino in a petunia-framed outdoor café, while a constant flow of cars belches fumes into our noses. As we gasp for air, I'm thinking that the old saying, "see Naples and die," could actually assume a literal meaning for Dwight who has already taken two shots of his inhaler.

"We haven't seen so much," I sigh as I flip through the guidebook.

Instead of admiring churches and palaces, we have chosen to stroll the streets, sense the energy, and observe the people; in short—to feel the pulse of the city. And even though the traffic is fierce, and even though the smog is thick, and even though it's noisy and crowded and chaotic, the energy is … ahhh, *so* good. Here is the contrast that's been causing my impressions to alternate—the contrast between the Naples I adore and the Naples I abhor; where life is so easy, yet so difficult, filled with songs, but thick with smog; where I would love to live, yet where I couldn't survive.

So we say our last farewell to the old Naples, its hidden courtyards and abandoned *palazzi,* and head for the former Bourbon Palace Capodimonte to make up for the missed visit. (It wasn't my agenda, it was Dwight's suggestion—honest!)

For safety reasons, which are to be taken seriously in certain quarters of Naples, we have decided to follow the advice of our guidebook and splurge on a night in a four-star hotel near the Capodimonte Gallery before heading east to Vesuvius. Away from the maddening chaos of the center, the hotel is a promised haven of quiet, with lovely gardens and sweeping views.

We head for this "easily reached" hotel, only to find ourselves driving through the narrow, meandering streets of one slum area after another where two cars can barely pass. Occasionally I see a poorly dressed man leaning against a peeling wall, beady-eyed and brooding. I become nervous when other cars approach, mostly jalopies, their drivers firing fierce glances at us, like cats bristling at intruder-cats. A sense of unease begins to creep through my body.

Dwight looks at the map for the tenth time to reassure us that we *are* heading for one of the loveliest parks in Naples, the former royal hunting preserve. Nervous, sweaty, and exhausted, we finally emerge from a warren of dingy streets and approach the glistening gate of the elegant hotel. Right next to it huddles a decaying villa, choked with weeds and strangled by vines —the nineteenth century abode of the King's doctor. As we look at cracked masonry with gaping holes, we can't shake off the impression of a haunted house.

When the receptionist hears that we are heading for the Capodimonte museum on foot, he warns me in a grave voice to take off all my gold jewelry, including my watch, before launching on the ten-minute walk.

Normally I never worry about theft and never had anything stolen in my life, unless I left it in open sight. I always believed that we actually draw situations to ourselves; if we fear that we might be robbed, well, chances are we will get robbed. Our feelings and thoughts translate into energy of different frequencies, and since like attracts like, what we fear—or what we desire, for that matter—we attract to ourselves.

Something in the receptionist's voice, however, makes me take his warning seriously and I follow his advice. As we set off to the museum, I feel naked without my rings and earrings and bracelets. And I'm clutching my purse under my armpit so tightly that the buckle leaves an imprint on my skin. The streets are barren, bleak, and deserted. We don't meet a single soul during our walk, and I'm a bit disappointed. Just a tiny bit. I would like to meet poor Neapolitans, sort of the dregs of the society, just to know the other side as well. Dwight looks at me incredulously, probably thinking, *why on earth would you want to invite trouble?*

As we walk through the gates of the royal palace, we find ourselves in the park that drips with luxuriant greenery. I'm tempted to linger among the flamboyant flowers and to lose myself in the View (I will *never* get over my penchant for heights and views, period), but Dwight firmly pulls me away.

When we finally emerge from the museum several hours later, the sun has already dipped behind the trees, the shadows have lengthened, the air has turned brisk, and a sense of peace is palpable—a peace that calms the heart, quiets the mind, and gives a sense of just-rightness. At that moment, the forces of light and dark have attained a transitory point of balance, a point of perfect equilibrium. The equilibrium I'd so much like to achieve within—to stand in the middle, poised, in control of my emotions.

CHAPTER 16

POMPEII AND HERCULANEUM:
EXODUS OF TRAPPED SOULS

The next day, we head toward the Vesuvius National Park for Dwight's big encounter with the volcano. Ever since his "friendship" with Etna, Dwight has been waiting for this moment—to ionize Vesuvius, just as he did with the volcano in Sicily. In Dwight's mind, raising the vibratory frequency of a volcano (or any rock in general) is the equivalent of us, humans, raising the level of our consciousness through meditation. Everything that exists, he explained to me, is based on a spin movement of electrons. No spin, no life. Evolution takes place when the spinning electrons make a leap from a lower orbit to a higher one. The leap can happen on its own, after a long period of gradual geological change, or it can be helped from the outside—through human intention.

The whole morning we've been driving through one densely populated town after another. Even the area designated as a park on the slopes of the volcano is heavily built up with hotels and restaurants. We drive up the winding road toward the crater until we find a solidified lava flow, which we follow on foot. Dwight is silent, withdrawn. I know he's gathering power through concentration and I don't want to interrupt him. After five minutes he stops and looks up, contemplating the lava slope. His face is set in that familiar intense focus on a task at hand; he sees nothing around him, he hears nothing. He turns into a laser beam of determination. I've always thought Dwight would make a brilliant general, what with his uncanny ability to develop strategies, his one-pointed concentration, and the bottom-line planning.

As usual, I'm not feeling any "higher presence" that Dwight says he always feels when he works with Earth energies. I stand by his side kind of lost, like an outsider, a child who is excluded from a game. Why do *I* never feel anything? I watch him dowse, observe his rods swing, cross and uncross, and wonder what is actually moving them. At times like this, I wish I had clairvoyant sight so that I could actually *see* all those different energies that mingle and twine and change frequencies and make the rods move.

After a few short minutes, Dwight is done. I know it because I feel his whole body relax.

"Okay, we can go now," he says.

Wait, just like that—we came, we dowsed, we left? No farewell, no nothing? It just doesn't feel right, I protest.

"Well, what do you suggest?" He turns to me.

I don't know myself, but I *know* that something is missing. I start to twirl a flower between my fingers, a white gardenia I brought with me from the hotel to enjoy its fragrance, my favorite fragrance.

"I know!" It dawns on me. "I should leave this gardenia as our offering." I gently place it down atop the lava, the whiteness of the flower in stark contrast to the dark-gray pumice rock.

As I'm about to turn around, I have a feeling that the gardenia doesn't want me to leave. A few years ago, I would have brushed this off as my imagination. But I've learned so much since then about the aliveness of the "inanimate" world, about energy, the etheric field, the laws that govern the invisible planes of existence. And I have grown to trust my sensitivity to plants. So I tune into the flower and feel loneliness and sadness envelop my heart. I try to comfort the gardenia, to explain the meaning of her sacrifice, but she still won't let me go. I ask her (in a silent communication that takes place on the thought-feeling level) if she has anything to tell me. Immediately, I receive the image of two arms reaching out from her to embrace me. I respond in the same way, like a mother picking up a child to hold in her arms. In the next moment, however, the embrace turns into a strangling. Those two arms are coiling around my neck to suffocate me!

The image is so vivid that I feel deeply shaken and disturbed. Why on earth would the flower "want" to strangle me? Did I do something wrong? Or am I picking up some thought-form of an event that took place here in the past?

Utterly perplexed, I break free and head for the car, where Dwight is waiting. We drive back in silence while the wheels of my brain reel in over-drive. After a while, Dwight stops the car at a spot with a beautiful view of the sea (by now he has become trained to notice the views) and a nearby lava flow. Yep, the ionization has taken, the lava carries the charge, he nods in satisfaction upon checking the solidified path.

Then we seat ourselves on a large, level rock in the shade of pine trees. In the distance, the Bay of Naples glistens with diamond-white sparks of the midday sun. The sky is limpid, not a wisp of a cloud. From this distance, who could ever think that this idyllic-looking bay is the most polluted in Italy; that the fumes in the air are smothering the vegetation; that the noise of the seething traffic is deafening?

"Something doesn't feel quite right," Dwight mutters and glances back at Vesuvius. The volcano, he continues, feels brooding and unhappy to him. Only then do I tell him about the weird experience I had with the gardenia. Dwight listens to me with utmost concentration. Then he moves to another rock from where he can have a better view of the volcano and goes into meditation.

When he comes back fifteen minutes later, he is beaming. For the first time in his life Dwight had a communication with a volcano!

"Yeah, right," I can see eyes rolling. But wait. If you said this to someone in Indonesia, for example, they'd just shrug in response, as if you'd said "I talked to my brother." There, it would just mean you're a medicine man whose job in society is to maintain peace with the forces of nature—in Bali alone, the spirits of seven active volcanoes. Ceremonies are regularly performed, prayers chanted, offerings presented, just to placate the temper of the volcano spirits (or gods, as they see them).

Unlike our Westerner civilization, imbued with the Cartesian mindset of a mechanistic and "dead" nature, ancient civilizations shared the belief in the aliveness of everything that exists. There is *no* dead thing in the Universe. In almost all the Etruscan sarcophagi I've seen, the figures of the deceased held an object in their hands, a round saucer with the raised knob in the middle, called the *patera*. This was a powerful symbol, representing the round germ of heaven and earth, an unborn and undying life-principle found in everything that exists, including human beings.

The civilizations of the "old world," the Mother Goddess cultures, believed the same. The Ageless Wisdom teaches the same; it teaches that behind everything that exists, better still, *within* everything that exists there is a life-force, the Etruscan *patera,* which enlivens every single thing. This life-force consists of tiny creatures or entities who actually *build* all material forms. Everything that exists on Earth—every mineral form, every plant form, every animal form—is inhabited by a different order of consciousness that has created it.

In every single culture of the Mother Goddess world, from Neolithic societies to Celts to American Indians, there were different names to designate this particular type of consciousness that animates everything. This belief has survived even through the Middle Ages, when tiny elemental lives were given names such as elves, gnomes, ondines, sylphs, fairies, or simply—nature spirits. Even Christianity has incorporated that belief in the form of angelic orders. In Hinduism they are referred to as Devas (from the Sanskrit word meaning "the Shining Ones"). But in modern society these elemental lives are relegated to children's literature and dismissed as a figment of imagination. And instead of communicating with the intelligence in nature, we now communicate with the intelligence of operating systems, search engines, and software programs. I want to believe that this too is a part of evolution, but don't know where it's taking us. In fact, I'm afraid to think where it's taking us.

It seems that Western civilization keeps repeating the mistake of a geo/human-centered world view. Christian dogma taught that the Earth was the center of the universe and the Sun and planets revolved around it. And the fire of the Inquisition consumed those who dared to contradict this belief. Now we believe that consciousness is only a human attribute and smirk at the mere thought of a rock having consciousness. But that's exactly what the Inquisitors did to Giordano Bruno and Galileo—how can the Earth move when we *see* that it doesn't move? Burn him at the stake! (Galileo, however, recanted his belief to save his life.) By the same token, how can a rock have consciousness when we *see* that it's, well, just a dead rock?! Obviously, the fact that we can't see something doesn't prove its absence, only—that our perception is limited.

Now theory is one thing, but practical application is another. My mind still can't wrap around the "doing" part. So I turn to Dwight and begin tentatively, "How did you actually talk with *it*?... *him*? *her*?" (Really, what is a volcano grammatically—male, female, neuter?)

"Easy, just came to me," Dwight replies promptly. "I only had to find the right frequency. And once you tune your mind—you know, like a radio station—to the right frequency, you can receive impressions."

In his younger years, Dwight was known to have had "strange" abilities, such as an uncanny feeling for trees, especially oaks, that would come to him as non-verbal impressions of the trees' needs; and he also had a special affinity with fire and all things electrical, a kind of magical touch that would restore dead electrical contacts. So maybe, I'm thinking, talking with volcanoes is just part of his sensitivity to the consciousness of tiny lives that animate nature.

"The spirit of Vesuvius," Dwight continues, "used the flower to communicate the image of how it was feeling—suffocated."

"Suffocated?"

"Well, yes. Just think about it. How did people who lived here feel about the volcano?"

"Probably afraid?"

"You bet! For centuries, no, millennia, people at the foot of the volcano have looked up its slopes in fear, praying fervently that it doesn't erupt. And this created a strong thought-form that was smothering, *suffocating* the spirit of the volcano."

"What about Etna?" I ask. "How come you didn't sense suffocation there?"

"Oh, Etna is different. She is always active, smoking and smoldering, and periodically even burping lava." Dwight glances up the slope, then adds, "Vesuvius, on the other hand, shows no signs of inner activity—except when it erupts. And when it does, which happens every once in a while, the eruptions are devastating."

True. The charred remains of Pompeii and Herculaneum, two Roman cities that once thrived on its slopes, attest to that; as well as the missing side of its cone, which blew out in the last major eruption in the seventeenth century, killing about 4,000 people.

"Wait a second," I have a sudden thought, "what if the image of suffocation was not about the volcano, but the people?"

"What people?"

"Well, all those tens of thousands of people who died in horrible suffering, suffocated by falling ash and fumes. It seems to me their panic would create a collective thought-form of suffocation. What do you think?"

"Quite possible," Dwight nods, then adds after a moment, "But, what if … what if volcanoes have different, say, personalities? Just like people, some volcanoes may be extroverted, like Etna, and others introverted, like Vesuvius."

"Hum … now that's stretching my mind a bit."

"Well, just imagine. It's an analogy. Some volcanoes express their personality by smoldering and spewing pumice on a regular basis—that would be like us humans, shouting and quarrelling. Other volcanoes suppress them, bottle them up, figuratively, but also literally. So whatever is bottled up, sooner or later has to explode … and wipe out entire cities.

"And, imagine one more thing," Dwight continues with mounting excitement, "just as we go to shrinks to ease the pressure of our emotional life, the volcanoes could be 'helped' to channel their eruptions in a less destructive way. After all, that's what the medicine men in Indonesia do."

My head begins to spin—psychotherapy for volcanoes? But Dwight hasn't finished yet.

"Perhaps we humans could cooperate with other forces in nature, earthquakes, tornadoes, floods.... Primitive societies have been practicing this kind of communication as a way of life, something perfectly normal and sensible because they have to live in harmony with nature."

Dwight and I could go on for hours talking ideas. But this time, I feel impatient to visit Pompeii and Herculaneum. Going there, I feel, would clarify our experience with the volcano.

The site of Pompeii stretches over a large area on the southern slope of Vesuvius. In its heyday, Pompeii was a bustling and prosperous trading city with numerous shops, industries, and port activity. Around 30,000 people lived there before the volcanic eruption of 79 AD.

The most vivid and accurate description of the eruption comes from the account of the soldier and historian Pliny the Younger. His uncle, the admiral and historian Pliny the Elder, died of suffocation in an attempt to rescue the trapped population of Pompeii and its sister city, Herculaneum.

That August afternoon, Pliny the Younger tells us, the area around Mount Vesuvius shook with a huge earthquake. The mountaintop split open, and an enormous cloud in the shape of a *pineta*, a parasol pine, continuously changing colors, announced ominously the most disastrous eruption ever to afflict the human population of Europe. During the night, the volcano exploded with a frightening force, spewing fields of hot ash and spitting rivers of boiling lava and mud. It went on the whole night and the following morning: long hours of terror, the earth shaking, sheets of fire and flames blazing atop the volcano. Hot, thick ash and pumice showered the cities for hours and buried the houses.

Due to the twenty feet of ash that buried Pompeii alive we now know how people lived at that time, what their houses looked like, what kind of furniture and decorations they had, how they prepared their food. The ash preserved for posterity the utensils and tools, the wall paintings, even loaves of bread in a bakery oven—in short, a complete way of life, unlike anywhere else in the world.

The ash also preserved the sleeping people in the houses at the very moment of dying. Room after room was excavated revealing bodies coiled around each other like fetuses in a mother's womb, or twisted in agony of suffocation. Imagine all the terror and excruciating pain experienced there. The energy of those strong emotions must have coalesced like a vast cloud over the whole area. But is it still there?

Well, the first thing we notice when we get to Pompeii is—tourists. Hordes of tour groups milling about, laughing and shouting. It's quite difficult to sense the energy of a place in such circumstances. The energy gets so ruffled, like the surface of a swimming pool when many people jump in.

To escape, we run to the Villa of the Mysteries far away from the central area. This patrician residence, shaded by pine canopy, is the most famous villa in Pompeii and houses the most beautiful fresco paintings—some of the finest works of art I've ever seen. I know we've come here to feel the energy, but in the presence of beauty, I forget about everything else. As I stroll through the rooms, I'm awed by the rich, vibrant colors and elegant drawings. The sensual Roman red and the delicate green dance from the walls in the movements of women initiated into Dionysian mysteries. Silence, broken only by the sound of a few cicadas, fills the rooms.

"Well, shall we go?" Dwight's voice startles me.

I sigh. "Already?"

Dwight steals a quick glance at the sinuous curves of a half-naked woman with a billowing red scarf dancing in ecstasy. I know how much Dwight loves art, but I also know that he now feels "on duty." He doesn't want to linger any longer. Pompeii needs cleansing, he emphatically states.

So I reluctantly tear myself away from this villa, from these frescoes, from the beauty, and with a resigned determination start treading the cobbled street back to the center of the city. And back to the tour groups.

The longer we walk the streets, wandering in and out of various houses, the more edgy I feel. I sense a heavy and desperate energy permeating the ruins. As we go along, Dwight is ionizing pavements and walls, temples and tombs, everything made of stone or marble that could take the charge. Until the moment we get to the Forum (the main *piazza* where public life took place in antiquity), when something peculiar happens.

The weather, which has been sunny and unusually warm the whole day, has suddenly turned brisk. Out of nowhere, dark clouds scud and swallow the sun. Just as we reach the Forum, a sudden and violent surge of wind swoops over the columned field. Within a few seconds, the air turns grayish-yellow, whirls of wind lift sand high up, then blow it into our faces. I frantically try to protect my camera first, my contact lenses next. We are caught in what looks like (and feels like to our gritty eyes) the desert sandstorm we had experienced while traveling through Egypt. We run for cover amid a mad whirling of dust. Forget about ionization and sightseeing, this is a serious storm!

But a short one. After only five minutes, as suddenly as it arose, the wind died down. The sky is still cloudy, but the air is utterly still. Dwight and I look at each other in utter bewilderment: what was that all about? Not a breath of air anymore. It feels unnatural and weird.

It took Dwight the rest of the day and a long contemplation in our hotel room to come up with a tentative explanation.

"You know," he murmurs that evening not looking at me, "It could have been the souls who left the place."

"Excuse me…?" I glance at him sleepily over my guidebook to Herculaneum.

"The souls left with the storm," Dwight repeats in a stronger, assured voice. "You see, the storm was an implosion of energy which created an outburst of wind, raised a huge cloud of dust, and roared off—to the south!"

I sit up straight in bed. "What exactly are you saying?" I ask, now totally awake.

"What I'm saying is, didn't you feel all those strong thought-forms of suffocation and smothering?"

"Of course I did. That's what I've been saying all along."

"Right. Many souls were trapped there, still bound to the site of their death, unable to move on because they died so suddenly. And once the ionization took, they were released. You see, what the ionization did," Dwight hurries to explain because I'm staring at him, "it changed the frequency of energy, kind of shook off the energetic chains that were imprisoning the souls."

I still stare at him.

"Don't you remember that south is the direction of elimination?"

I begin to nod tentatively.

"When souls incarnate into the Earth's life system, they do so from the north, while they exit, so to speak, from the south." Dwight pauses significantly.

"This was … a massive exodus of trapped souls," he declares.

I whistle. *Far out, even for Dwight,* I muse—but don't say it aloud.

The next day, however, I get a lesson about my skepticism and doubt.

Naturally, after what happened in Pompeii, we wanted to check out the energy in Herculaneum. The two neighboring cities were both obliterated in the eruption. But unlike Pompeii, which was covered by vast layers of ash and pumice, Herculaneum, which sits on the western slope of Vesuvius, was buried under torrents of boiling mud. As it cooled down, the mud solidified and, like an impression in clay, perfectly preserved everything. In Pompeii, the hot cinders caused fires which burned the interior of houses; but here, furniture, wooden structures, even clothes were preserved—charred, yes, but preserved.

This alone makes a visit to Herculaneum much more interesting. But also, unlike Pompeii, which was mostly a working class city, Herculaneum was a patrician sea resort, like an elite, jet-set club. Hence the houses were bigger, more elegant and opulent. Another major difference is that nobody actually died in the city itself. The residents evacuated the houses and were huddled in the port under the sea walls, waiting for rescue boats which never arrived because the enormous tidal waves prevented them from landing. So entire families met their end by the sea, suffocated by heat and sulfurous fumes.

As we approach the ramp that leads down to the excavated area, Dwight suddenly gets the familiar symptoms of rampant arrhythmia (maybe it was one espresso too many?) and decides to stay in the park above the site. He has seen Herculaneum before anyway, so he delegates his ionizing job to me. MEEE? I don't know if I can do it, I don't know *how* to do it! But he won't have any of my objections, arguments, doubts, reasoning…. So, I set out on my own down the long descending ramp.

The entrance path turns into an underground tunnel before it reaches the outside wall of Herculaneum. This is the very foundation of the city, the bedrock on which it was built. Awkwardly, like the novice that I am, I approach the rock and, trying to look inconspicuous, touch it with the crystal. Again, I doubt. *I can't do this. This is ridiculous, I have no powers, I mean, how can I do this?!* But, like the good pupil that I am, I don't give up.

As I go along the streets, house after house, I realize that I'm moving in perfect timing to avoid the tour groups. Without any conscious effort, I enter a house just as a group is leaving, and step out when a group is about to trample in. It's as if I'm in a flow, an effortless flow and dance. I feel myself gliding, not walking, cushioned by a vacuum that muffles the noise around me. I'm totally open to the energy of the place, in tune with everything around me, and sharply, acutely alert. Come to think of it (except that I did the thinking part later), this must be what is described as the Zen state: being peaceful and serene, relaxed yet alert, in a strange state of watchful meditation.

When I later tried to remember this experience, what I saw that day was also shrouded in a veil; houses, paintings, mosaics, sculptures, were all blurred in my memory. I couldn't even remember seeing the Villa of the Papyri that inspired the design for the famous Getty Museum in Malibu. But—who cares, I'd trade all the memories of ancient sites, of everything I'd ever seen, to be in this state *all the time*.

As I glide around a corner, I see a courtyard shaded by a huge and solitary palm tree that looks inviting. As in a fairy tale I say to myself, *Well, why don't I enter this attractive house and see what's inside?* And my legs take me in. I don't see anything really interesting, but it feels good just to be there. When I try to leave, I feel as if something is pulling me back. I step outside, but then turn right back into the courtyard again. I just can't leave this house!

Then I see a side room I didn't notice before. I feel irresistibly drawn to it. Again, my legs take me there without my head giving a command. The room leads to another small room with an empty altar built into the back wall. My eyes are riveted to the empty space. I stare at this small niche that used to house an effigy of a spirit-protector of the family.

I become aware of a feeling permeating the room, enveloping the shrine. Slowly, the feeling becomes clearer and I *know* there is a presence here. A spirit in the altar? I stare intently, trying to penetrate through (or beyond) the empty air. I can almost see ... but not quite. Then a new feeling forms in my mind—an image of a little girl! A confused and lost little girl, waiting for her parents to come back home. But instead, endless strange people are passing through. The little girl is shivering, helpless and abandoned.

My heart opens at once and I feel a tremendous amount of love pouring through me. I don't know where this love is coming from or how this is happening, but I feel transformed into a ball of boundless, radiant love. In fact, there is no "I" anymore, only—Love. I embrace this trembling little girl comfortingly; I try to "explain" what happened, to reassure her and encourage her to move on. After a while, the presence fades from the shrine, and the altar feels empty. I expand the love to the whole area, brilliant white light washing through and enveloping every building. Then I slowly turn around and leave the house.

"So, you freed the trapped soul of a little girl?" Dwight looks at me in that half-amused and half-triumphant way of his, as if to say, *See, what have I been telling you!*

We are sitting on a bench in the pleasantly warm winter sun. Everything around me looks perfectly solid and normal, thank you very much, and I'm back in my ordinary sense of self. The flow is gone, as well as the cocoon, as well as that relaxed, yet sharp alertness. I'm still alert, but I'm also jarringly aware of the running kids, and the rumbling engines of tour buses, and my fatigue, and the pangs of hunger. I miss it. I knew I would miss it, that Zen state. It felt so ... superhuman.

"Granted, you can never be sure..." Dwight adds in a different tone.

"Of course I'm sure! I *experienced* it."

For once, I don't doubt. Actually I rarely do, when it comes to my experiences. Somewhere I read that only that which is learned through experience is truly learned. We can read about ideas, we can ponder concepts, memorize theories, acquire facts; but only when we experience something do we truly know it—with the whole body, so to speak.

"So, looking back, what do you think about Pompeii now?" Dwight casually asks, but I feel the intense attention behind this how-was-your-lunch type question.

What do I think? I *don't know* what to think. I begin reluctantly, "Well, if I had this experience in Herculaneum, then, I guess, it's possible that something similar happened in Pompeii. But don't you think someone else would have done the cleansing already? I mean it's been two thousand years since the eruption!"

"And how many people lived in Pompeii?" Dwight raises his brow, watching me intently. "People who all died at the same time, violently, in sheer panic. Imagine the population of Santa Barbara dying all at once, in a cataclysm, unprepared. You know what happens in a sudden death, don't you?"

I do know, I read it in many esoteric books. Then I heard it from Kostas who explained at great length the process of dying. In the case of a car accident, a murder, or in a war, whenever death comes suddenly, people don't know they're dead. There is a short discontinuity of consciousness, as if they've fainted, but then they wake up and find themselves in the same surroundings as before. They have no awareness that they've passed to another plane of existence. They try to communicate with others, but it appears that no one hears them. This period of confusion can last for some time, for quite a long time, Kostas said. That's why there are "invisible helpers"—and Kostas was one of them—who during the night leave their bodies and, as consciousness, travel to those planes to free the confused souls, to escort them to where they should be going. "It is like a veil," Kostas had explained, "that exists between this plane of existence and the other side. We, on this side, cannot see the other side. But those from the other side can see us. It is like a see-through mirror."

"If those souls were still trapped," I muse, "it was certainly a very long time...."

"To us. But on the other side there is no time," replies Dwight.

Oh, the relativity of time. I don't think I want to go into that subject just now. I need *time* to digest everything that has happened in these mere two days: the strangling embrace of the gardenia, talking with the volcano, freeing the souls trapped in Pompeii, entering the Zen state, disappearing into cosmic Love, liberating the soul of a little girl.

"By the way," adds Dwight, "I checked the bedrock of Herculaneum ... it's ionized."

CHAPTER 17

SOLFATARA AND CUMAE:

AT THE PORTAL TO HELL

The next day rose clear and sunny, smelling of spring and surprise. To me, days have distinct scents, both physical and emotional. I always inspect a new day by stepping outside and smelling the air. Some days I pick up the whiff of heaviness and foreboding; other days smell of anticipation and the enticing call to travel; still others carry the breath of loneliness, of defeat. And every season, regardless of climate, has its very distinct smells: the scent of sweet, fragrant flowers; the aroma of dry heat; the redolence of harsh winds and grayness and falling leaves; the odor of burning fires, biting cold, and silently falling snow. But my favorite smell is that of adventure; of the unknown that is waiting to happen; of a moment carrying endless possibilities.

It is that kind of a morning when we wake up to leave the Bay of Naples. Today, I've left the itinerary—and the agenda—entirely to Dwight (some victory, I'd say), who seems to have a strong urge to visit the area west of Naples. This region abounds in vestiges of Greek and Roman civilization and has been known since ancient times as *Campi Flegrei* (the Phlegraean Fields). The word *flegrei* ("burning" or "blazing" in old Greek) was given to this area because of intense volcanic and geo-thermal activity that took place from the earliest times. An area of about 100 square miles, extending in an arc along the gulf of Pozzuoli, is studded with small volcanoes, hot springs, steam-jets, and lakes that have filled the craters of extinct volcanoes.

I'm not exactly interested in seeing yet another volcanic crater, dead at that, but Dwight lures me there with mythology—Solfatara was the entrance to Hades in Roman mythology! This is where Aeneas, accompanied by the Sybil, descended into the underworld.

185

So what does the entrance to Hell look like?

Well, imagine first a mud-gray, barren, and desolate area, the size of five soccer fields. This is the crater of an ancient volcano that long ago sank to ground level. The mud field is completely arid with no trace of vegetation anywhere, yet it's alive in an eerie way. Numerous mini-volcanoes, scattered all over the area, emit jets of boiling mud, and the hillsides are "smoking," puffing out plumes of gas, as if the ground were smoldering after a huge explosion. Everywhere a heavy silence reigns, punctured only by the hissing of gas and bubbling of boiling mud. My nose starts to wrinkle in objection as I inhale the first whiffs of sulfur fumes. With my every step, I notice how the ground makes a hollow sound.

Hellish enough?

There is more. As I get closer, I feel the intense heat that radiating from the boiling jets of mud. I smell the stench of rotten eggs and inhale the stifling air saturated with carbon dioxide gases. Wherever I look, the ground is covered with a hoary dust of smoldered poisonous metals.

Get the picture?

And now comes the twist. In all the steam, vapors, heat, poisons, and boiling mud of this infernal landscape—which seems as inhospitable to life as anything could be on our planet (with the temperature of mud reaching 300°F)—there is life! Scientists have discovered rare heat-resistant micro-organisms that live in boiling mud, and also green algae that thrive at the openings of vents or *fumaroles*.

In ancient myths, the region of Hades is reached with the help of the ferryman Charon, who goes back and forth across the River Styx, delivering the spirits of the dead to their eternal abode, or an occasional visitor with a special mission (like Hercules, Odysseus, or Aeneas, for example). We encounter our Charon, the grey-haired Gennaro, not far from the largest *fumarole*, called Bocca Grande (Big Mouth), where he's waiting to give us a tour.

Something about Gennaro draws me in like a magnet. I attach myself to him, while Dwight wanders off to inspect the area for energy currents. With a soft voice and dark eyes that look at me warmly from behind his glasses, Gennaro radiates simple goodness and gentleness. Really, one could not find a more depressing and ominous workplace than Solfatara, and a more kind, warm, and humble worker than this middle-aged Neapolitan.

I'm amazed to hear Gennaro's life story. I don't know how we got onto it, but I find myself gripped by the details of the events that brought him to Solfatara. He tells me (half in English and half in Italian) that several years ago he was diagnosed with throat cancer. After the usual surgical procedure, he was told to inhale sulfurous and arsenic fumes in order to fully recover. (Even that stench of rotten eggs, can you believe it, has healing properties!) So Gennaro took his current job as a guardian of hell—I mean Solfatara—so that he could breathe what for him was a *healing* air.

I find it incredibly humbling to think about the relativity of everything that exists: how what is poison for one person is medicine for another. Every facet of life, it seems, has a function to perform. And even what appears to be useless or toxic in nature still has its role in the greater scheme of life. Deeply touched by this insight, I make a vow to myself, amid all the stink and heat and desolation, that I will never be judgmental or intolerant again. (Then the thought of mosquitoes comes up.... Can I make just one exception?)

Gennaro then suggests something exciting. He will take me beyond the fenced area, into the skull-and-cross-bones danger zone of thin-crusted earth, to demonstrate the hollowness of the space under the ground. He takes my hand to help me over the fence, and we walk amid smoking *fumaroles* (which are like giant pressure release valves) over thin ground, my step strictly following his. It's like walking on thin ice, except it's not cold water underneath—but boiling mud. Through the puffs of smoke, I see the incandescent mouths of the *fumaroles*, where sulfur vapors and red arsenic have combined to form colorful crystals called *realgar*, another rare geological formation.

Gennaro thumps his foot on the ground, and I hear a muffled echo, sounding like the rumbling of a far-away beast or an infernal monster about to attack its prey. Stooping slightly, with his head bent down to the ground, he makes a sound: "Hhhooo-hhhooo...." The ground replies back with the same sound. "You try it now," he points to the baked earth. I don't really want to, his demonstration was quite sufficient, but I don't want to disappoint him. So I do my best to imitate his growl, and sure enough, I get it right back, the echo roaring ominously.

"You know, it's Vulcan, god of fire, who lives here," Gennaro says, sweeping his hand over the landscape. "That was belief in Roman time, that's why they call it Forum Vulcani."

Between listening to the soft-spoken Gennaro and inspecting hissing columns of steam and mud bubbling away like oatmeal in a pot on the stove, plus inhaling the stink of rotten eggs, my senses have by now become totally scrambled. I don't know what to feel anymore. My heart is simultaneously shutting down from the dreariness of the surroundings and leaping forth in compassion for this sweet and humble man. There is something about him that touches me to the core of my being, and I almost feel like crying (the tears I already have from all the vapors don't count).

By now I've learned that everyone I meet has a lesson to teach me, if only I'm open to hear it. And what I'm hearing from Gennaro is his quiet contentment with life. Every day is a gift—it doesn't matter that it's spent in hell. He is happy within himself and by himself; he doesn't need to have a glamorous job, or travel to exciting places, or live in a house with a view (ahem ... as some of us do). All that he needs is within him, the whole universe in this crater.

Really, who is more firmly grounded on the spiritual path, this gentle gatekeeper or I?

"Ah, but you have to see Stufe," Gennaro suddenly says, pointing at the two brick structures in the distance that look like big openings into the hillside. "One is called Inferno, the other Purgatorio," he says and smiles at me as we walk back toward his little cottage.

"Why, Gennaro? I think I've seen enough."

"*Ma comme* enough? Legend says that's entry to Hell. You go underground there. But also," he adds, rubbing his arm, "steams coming up in room are good for skin. How you call it..." he pauses, searching for words, "*ezzema?*"

A portal to Hell that cures eczema? Now we're talking! I'm sold right away as my normally slow-percolating eczema has been burning and searing my skin the whole winter. So I leave my guide/boatman who must attend to other lost souls coming to him with beads of sweat and a disoriented look, and I head for two fumaroles-turned-natural-saunas with a hellish reputation ... and run into Dwight right there. With excitement on his face, he tells me about the energy currents he tracked and of the primitive fire elementals, younger cousins of the volcano spirits, which inhabit this place.

Then it's time to enter Hell. I choose the steam room called Purgatory, identifying with the name which symbolizes the current stage of my life. I'm done with hell, I tell myself. I've served my term there and now is a period of purification for me, both physical and emotional. (I can only smile sympathetically from where I am today, at the naïve self I was then. Little did I know what was to come in the year ahead!)

Following Gennaro's instructions, I take off my blouse to expose the eczema-inflamed skin on my neck and arms, and stoop to enter the brick structure. *Whoa, it's so hot inside! Scorching hot!* And so small, I can't even straighten my back. So stuffy, I can't breathe. And it stinks something awful. Burning-hot drops of condensed vapors are dripping from the low, slimy ceiling—*ouch*—

onto my bare skin. Suddenly, I lose all motivation to treat my eczema. *This is torture. To hell with it!* But another part of me, disciplined and heroic, takes over and orders me to maintain the position.

So I stay, jumping around like an Indian doing a war dance, hopping from one foot to another with a stooped back, just to distract the body, all the while thinking of biting cold nights in snow-covered Utah ... making snow balls with my freezing hands and rolling in the snow ... *Darn droplets!* They bring me back to hell, and I, with due respect to the inner warrior, step out ... ahhh ... side. With relief, I stretch my back and inhale the cool, 70° air!

But as soon as we head back to find Gennaro, I'm gripped by a claustrophobic feeling in the middle of an open field. It's so hot, heavy, hellish, mercilessly baking me from above and from below, suffocating, stinking, dismal, and *I want to get out of here!*

The peaceful demeanor of Gennaro, whom we find by his cottage, immediately calms me down. "I want to give you a present," he says and smiles gently, then disappears inside.

When he comes out, he is holding two beautiful, yellow-orange crystals that form in the openings of *fumaroles*. "Here—*realgar*, to remember Solfatara." He stretches out his hand and I see two incandescent lumps nestled in his palm.

I take these two rocks as if they were the rarest of diamonds. Well, they *are* rare, and precious, very much so. Only here, the sulfur fumes deposit traces of red arsenic on the rock and you have to wait, Gennaro explains, for several weeks before you can "harvest" the crystals. Their beauty is so fleeting, he warns me, that they should be enjoyed only periodically and briefly, otherwise stored in the dark. Exposure to light deteriorates their incandescent colors.

I wrap the two *realgar* crystals carefully in a tissue, and we say a simple goodbye. I'll carry this gift of crystal beauty, offered to me in the midst of the Inferno, to remind me of something I've yet to truly learn.

As we're driving out of the Phlegraean hell, all I can think about is finding a restaurant with a gorgeous view of the sea and resting my desolation-filled eyes on the azure blue. But we don't know any good restaurants around here, let alone one with a view. For that matter, we don't know where to find *any* restaurant. So I just drive aimlessly. Without thinking, I pull over in front of vibrant bushes of bougainvillea enveloping the walls of a small building. There are a lot of parked cars in front of it, so I assume it's a restaurant, and perhaps a good one. Dwight makes a little grumbling noise, sort of "we should check the menu first," but I ignore him and walk straight onto the terrace—and into the view. In front of me explode the colors of a glittering, midday sea in the distance, the sun-drenched marble terrace with blue tablecloths, and the pinks and reds and yellows of potted flowers.

I'm mesmerized. So much so that I don't care what kind of food they have. All I care about is sitting in the sun and staring at the horizon. Actually, it's not just that I care about it—I crave it. It's my fix. I *gotta* have it.

"You know, I've been thinking," Dwight begins as soon as we finish lunch, "if this whole area, from Vesuvius to the Tyrrhenian Sea, is so volcanic with gases coming out of the earth and constant shifts of ground level, I bet the oracle of Cumae must be really special. It's bound to be a strong energy center. That would explain why it was so popular in antiquity, just as much as Delphi was..." Dwight lingers, then adds, "In fact, Cumae might be more interesting than Delphi. We'd better hurry up so we have plenty of time there."

Nothing, but I mean nothing else, would have made me move from this perfect spot, with this perfect view, at this perfect moment. Only the prospect of visiting an ancient oracle where Sibyl used to deliver prophecies, made me forego this beauty.

Cumae, our guidebook says, was the oldest Greek colony in Italy, founded way back in the ninth century BC on the west coast of the Apennine boot. The colony prospered rapidly, extending its rule over the entire Phlegraean area and conquering all the Italic population. This expansion ended in the fifth century BC when Rome crushed the power of Cumae and imposed its rule over the city. For me, however, the most interesting fact was that the Greek Cumeans founded Naples, which they called Neapolis (New City), next to the old city of Parthenope, and introduced the alphabet into Italy (which then the Etruscans picked up and passed on to all the other Western peoples). And, of course, they established the oracle where Sibyl divined.

In antiquity, Sibyl was actually not a personal name, but a Latinized Greek word for "prophetess"—*sibylla*. Dedicated to the sun god Apollo, Sibyls were virgin priestesses endowed with powers of divination and believed to be semi-divine beings. As such they were immortal, or nearly so. There were several Sibyls, but the Cumean Sibyl was the most famous. She was so venerated that Virgil, in his grand epic the *Aeneid*, had his hero Aeneas seek guidance from the Cumean Sibyl before undertaking his journey into the Underworld. Her fame stretched well into Renaissance times, when Michelangelo included her in the composition on the ceiling of the Sistine Chapel (although her looks are far from flattering—he painted her to look like a weight-lifter crone). According to the Latin poet Ovid in his *Metamorphoses*, the Cumean Sibyl lived for about one thousand years.

But here's the clincher. While Apollo granted her the gift of immortality, she forgot to ask for the boon of eternal youth. Ooops … tiny detail. So Sibyl had to live for many hundreds of years as a very old woman, her once-ethereal beauty shriveled into a craggy, haggard face, and her body shrinking with age until, eventually, it was kept in a jar. Finally, only her voice was left. What a fate! Immortality without eternal youth is a rotten deal, if you ask me.

In those ancient days, rulers didn't have senior assistants or cabinets of advisors to help them govern. So when they needed to make an important decision—such as when to attack another kingdom or how to appease the wrath of gods who were ravaging the population—they would go to an oracle. It wasn't easy, however, to understand what the Sibyl divined, crouched over the trance-inducing fumes. Her prophecies were always couched in riddles that yielded various interpretations according to the inquirer's state of mind and level of understanding.

To reach the oracle of the Cumean Sibyl the visitors of antiquity had to pass through a long, vaulted tunnel in the shape of trapezoid—just as visitors do today. At the entrance still stand the same two stones, inscribed with verses from Virgil's *Aeneid:* one describes the Sibyl's sanctuary, the other her prophecy to Aeneas. After more than two millennia, the tunnel is still illumined by light shafts, also in the shape of trapezoids. The impression is awe-inspiring; it's like entering a womb—the dark, mysterious, life-giving womb of an underground goddess.

Dwight and I look at each other in anticipation—we are completely alone! As we enter the tunnel, the silence of the ages settles upon us. We tread the same path trodden two thousand years ago; the same shafts cast rings of light upon the same tuff stone; and we feel the same awe before the powers of the underworld that questers in antiquity felt. Excited and expectant, we reach the end of the tunnel and stand at the entrance to the Sibyl's sanctuary—a rectangular, soot-colored, vaulted chamber, small and completely empty.

And completely devoid of energy!

I don't want to believe my first impression. There's got to be *something* here! I stand in the middle of the room, where I assume the Sibyl had crouched over the fumes, and close my eyes. All my sensory antennae are poised, my mind still, my body immobile. But—no reception.

"Do you feel anything?" I whisper to Dwight, who is—what else?—ionizing the room.

"Nothing. And you?"

"Nothing."

I look at the three empty niches in the walls, the only "things" in this empty room. But they are just plain empty. I look at the volcanic tuff walls, earthen floor, low ceiling. It's as if the cave has been stripped of its energy; like an extinguished fireplace, cold and covered by soot.

"The only explanation that comes to mind," muses Dwight, "is that the energy shut down when the cave was used as a cemetery."

"Cemetery?!"

"Oh, yes," Dwight-the-historian then tells me what happened in the fourth century AD when the Christian authorities assumed the religious reins of the Roman Empire and closed down the oracle. "You see, when you bury bodies in sacred places they decay underground, which lowers the frequency of energy. Anyhow, whatever was here in the past is no longer.

"But look...." Dwight's rods are dancing over the spot in the middle of the room, where I just stood a minute ago. There is definitely a vortex of underground energy, similar to the one we discovered in the *tholos* at Epidauros, but much weaker.

"So how come we're not sensing anything? I mean, if there are energy currents, this place should still be active, right?"

"Not necessarily," Dwight says, shaking his head. "You see, for a sacred site to be active, its energy has to be reinforced through human attention and intention. Remember, this is, so to speak, raw Earth energy that is volatile and changing its flow. To be harnessed it has to be fixed in place and amplified by human attention—prayers, offerings, rituals."

It makes sense. It would explain why ancient temples once considered sacred now feel like empty shells. It would also explain why now-forgotten ancient gods no longer have the power to perform miracles or to punish, the way they used to. It is human attention, or more precisely, *the energy that follows attention*, that amplifies and gives power to the thought-forms of religions and gods. Consequently, the more people who believe in a certain god, the stronger that god will be and the more miracles he would perform.

I remember the temple of Shiva in Tiruvannamalai, in southern India. For almost two thousand years devotees have been praying there fervently, soliciting favors from the deity and celebrating religious holidays, performing elaborate rituals year after year, month after month, day after day, faith permeating every pore of their life.

Our good Indian friend had obtained permission for us—usually denied to foreigners—to attend the ancient worship ritual. We walked barefooted through the huge precincts of the temple-complex, really like a small town, before we reached the main temple. Balu then took us into the subterranean part where sacred rites took place. The energy inside was so thick I felt nauseated. Clouds of incense wafted above a sea of men who were walking around the Shiva Lingam (a rounded hump of granite) and chanting in a trance. A long procession of musicians snaked through the crowd, beating huge drums and blowing trumpets with blaring, deafening noise. The quivering light of hundreds of candles cast a psychedelic hue over the intense reds of carpets, and spooky shadows on the walls shone from condensed sweat. I could swear that ghosts and spirits were hovering and dancing in the shadows, having a great time. It felt hellish to me then, but now I understand: Shiva is the God of power, of fire, of destruction, and the celebration was emulating the energy he represents—and *amplifying* it.

"Let's go, I've had enough of this dead oracle," Dwight says, stuffing his dowsing rods in the inside pocket of his jacket. We walk the tunnel again, this time eager to get out. It feels good to be back in the sun, the realm of Apollo.

"Where would you like to go now?" asks Dwight.

The archaeological site of Cumae is huge; it consists of a lower and an upper town, which is impossible to cover in one afternoon. Naturally, I choose to visit the upper town, the Acropolis, where most of the temples still stand in ruins. In ancient Greece, a *polis* (city) always had a temple area situated on a promontory above the commercial and residential areas. So we climb the staircase near the entrance to the Sibyl's cave and join the Via Sacra that leads up onto the Belvedere and further up to the Acropolis. This *is* my day, I'm telling you, because Belvedere (Beautiful View!) is a huge terrace along the slope of the hill, overlooking the valley beneath and the sea in the distance. And the dazzling sunset.... I won't gush again about the View, but let me just say that it was a sweeping north-south view of the coast, unfolding majestically before our eyes like a lace fan.

"Ah, how I would *love* to live in a place like this!" I throw my arms up.

Dwight eyes me sideways, probably wondering if I've succumbed yet again to my old intention of looking for a home, then says, "Boy, that cave was quite a disappointment. Talk about misleading expectations!" He shakes his head. "Everything was building up, pointing to the cave … just about the perfect setting for something to happen there. Instead, what did we find? A sad, barren, dead room."

"Well, maybe that's the repeat of the same old lesson we have to learn," I offer. "No expectations. I was not expecting to find a restaurant with a view, and look what I found. I was not expecting to find *this* either," I sweep my hand around, "and it's one of the most gorgeous views I've seen in Italy. This all came as a beautiful surprise…" I hesitate a little, then admit, "because I didn't have an agenda, but let things happen.

"Or maybe," I go on, as Dwight is not replying, "that's exactly what we were supposed to experience!" I beam, having a sudden insight.

"What do you mean?"

"That sacred sites shut down when their purpose is violated. Maybe that was our lesson: to experience how human intention affects the body of the Earth."

Dwight looks at me in a way I haven't seen before. "Or maybe," he says reflectively, "it's my turn to learn from you now."

CHAPTER 18

ENVIRONS OF ROME:
A NEW WAY OF BEING

I don't know what's wrong with me. Do I have some genetic defect that prevents me from being happy or do I subconsciously undermine my happiness? Sometimes I wonder if the ability to be happy might be influenced by the energy of planets and constellations under which we were born? Or maybe it has to do with chemical exchanges in the brain? Or something altogether different? I so much can't believe it myself: here I am living in Rome (I mean, *the* Rome!), with the man I love, and I can do anything I want, but I don't feel happy. Is this perverse or what?

But let me go back a little. After we returned from Campagna and our adventures, the heightened state of consciousness to which I got accustomed gradually wore off. No more ancient ruins, no more communications with flowers and volcanoes, no more lost souls and oracles, no more view of the sea! Back to the asphalt and traffic and the four walls and cooking and … the usual.

I know, you're going to say it's a normal reaction after a trip, the famous "dip" after the "high." But I'm talking about something bigger. I'm talking about the lack of vision. A vision of something higher, something larger than the ordinary existence, such as both Dwight and I had had in the past. The first year of our journey our purpose was to learn and explore: meditate in the ashrams in India, visit ancient Egyptian temples, study with Kostas, make new friends in Cyprus. After we decided to stay on in Cyprus, I settled down to writing my book. That accomplished, I was urged by my Guidance to move to Italy, and I put all my energies into making that happen.

After we arrived in Italy and my vision blew into pieces in Ostia Antica, nothing really replaced it. I've been living from day to day, not knowing what I should do with my life or where we should go—you know, eventually, after the journey is over. I'm missing having a vision, something to strive for, something bigger than day-to-day living. A "noble endeavor" as it would have been called a couple of centuries ago, an "inspired service" as Kostas would say, a "Soul's calling" as depth psychologists have put it, in brief—a meaning and purpose of my life.

Really, what am I living for?

Deep down I also feel a bit disappointed. There was so much promise in coming to Italy; the events that happened in Greece (and I still haven't recounted all of them), the preparation for something in the *tholos*, the appearance of Anubis ... what was that all about? Opening the door to creativity, as Dwight said? Yeah, right! More like closing the door to creativity. I don't even remember my ideas for the novel I wanted to write about the Medici. On top of that, my creativity has completely dried up. Keeping my journal has become drudgery rather than something inspiring and enjoyable.

I don't want to admit it, but I also feel uncomfortable about what I'm going to tell my friends and family back in Belgrade when I go to visit them this summer. I was the most ambitious of all my friends. They'd all look at me waiting to hear about my new achievements. And how can I say that I've left the material world behind and embarked on a search for my Soul? How can I explain all the inner work I've done, all the weaknesses I've wrestled with, fears I've faced, emotional patterns I've untangled? Impossible, really.

Oh, people's expectations!

But why do I care about them? Why does it matter what anyone is going to say about me? Dwight couldn't care less about other people's opinions. We're so fundamentally different in that regard. He can stand alone, against everybody, as long as he believes in the higher purpose of his endeavors. I, on the contrary, need the approval of others; otherwise my confidence is undermined and I begin to doubt. How am I ever, *ever* going to embody my role model—the wise and strong Sage?

This was all going on in my mind when we decided to visit the Villa Farnese in Caprarola, the elegant post-Renaissance palace built by the *Gran Cardinale* Alessandro Farnese. I had carefully planned everything, from what we should see to where we were going to have lunch. But in the end, instead of visiting the sixteenth-century palace in the north, we found ourselves in the second-century Hadrian's Villa to the east of Rome!

How did we manage that?

Well, simply by allowing our negative traits to run the show: my Irritation and Dwight's Pouting collided with each other to the point that we were not speaking to each other. So somewhere mid-way to Caprarola, I turned the car around and headed back to Rome.

Then the strange chain of incidents began. Instead of taking the west-bound exit for the ring road, I mistakenly took the east-bound one, so we found ourselves heading in the opposite direction, away from our home. In Rome, this sort of mistake is difficult to correct, because the freeway exits lack U-turns. I failed two more times to find the way to turn around, so I resigned myself to driving the whole circle around Rome—some forty or so miles, instead of only five in the correct direction. But as I was driving on the east side of Rome, nearing the exit for Tivoli, Dwight and I looked at each other and in one of those inexplicable mental agreements said, "How about Villa Adriana?"

So that's how we found ourselves in Hadrian's Villa, a huge residential estate that served as a retreat for Roman Emperor Hadrian. Of course, I have all the wrong guidebooks, I know absolutely nothing about the place, and we are even dressed inadequately: bundled up in warm clothes for the cold weather of the north, whereas it's sunny and balmy here. In brief, everything went exactly the opposite of my plan.

Dwight's gloom dispersed as soon as we got out of the car. "Ah," he exclaims, looking around with that childlike wonder that sometimes takes him over, "this is *so* much better!"

I sit down on the grass under an olive tree and look around, awed by the beauty of the grounds. The silvery glimmer of leaves in the gentle breeze, the juicy greenness of the grass—beauty, everywhere! And joy. What more can one ask for? (A vision, perhaps?)

In the information office we find out that the design of the grounds is so unusual that archaeologists have not been able to identify the buildings or their uses with certainty. "It's because," Dwight leans toward me as I'm looking at the model of the site, "Hadrian designed this place himself and he was a man of great aesthetic and philosophic sensitivity, connoisseur of many things, including sculpture and architecture. Plus," Dwight adds with emphasis, "he was initiated into the Eleusinian Mysteries as well as the Mithraic cult."

As we walk among the well-preserved ruins, Dwight is filling in my gaps in history. Hadrian was a wise and sophisticated ruler who had traveled to every part of his Empire—quite a feat, given the size of the Roman Empire in the second century AD. From these travels, he brought back inspiration and the desire to recreate the most beautiful structures he had seen. Villa Adriana was built, in fact, as a vast open-air museum of the finest architecture of the Roman world. Imagine living in an estate 300 acres in size, where all your favorite buildings and places from around the world are replicated! There were theatres, Greek and Latin libraries, two bathhouses, extensive housing for guests and the palace staff and, of course, formal gardens with fountains, statues, and pools. It was probably the most expensive building project in Antiquity.

We arrive at the elongated, colonnaded pool called Canopus, inspired by the Egyptian town of Canope and its famous Temple of Serapis. Actually, one whole section of this estate was landscaped to look just like the Egyptian site. Beautiful sculptures, replicas of ancient Greek works, are strewn among the columns. The whole estate used to be populated by exquisite sculptures that Hadrian had brought over from Egypt and Greece. But since the time of the Renaissance these sculptures had been steadily looted, and now form major parts of many private art collections in Europe.

"So Hadrian, if I get it right, was the 'philosopher king' of Plato's *Republic*?" I ask as we climb toward the terrace of the Tempe, from where the view opens to the whole complex.

"In a way, yes," Dwight replies, stopping to catch his breath. "He was obviously an emperor, but not a tyrant. He ruled through power, but peaceful power. He was well educated, artistic, spiritually inclined, yet firm. He kept his armies on their toes by constant inspection and regular drills. In fact, he was the first to introduce regular military drills. And he also lived like the soldiers, slept among them, wore military gear, and he was fair. So the soldiers were totally loyal to him. And you know how important that is."

No, not really, but never mind.

"He was one of the so-called five good emperors," Dwight continues after we reach the terrace. "He solidified the Empire, retreated from the provinces he judged indefensible, and built fortifications—the famous Hadrian's Wall, for example—to strengthen the borders. Good strategist," Dwight pauses, looking at the complex of buildings below the terrace. "He did everything I would have done as a ruler."

We continue walking and reach a pool called Pecile. This is the replica of the Stoà Poikile in Athens, from which the Stoic philosophers took their name (*stoa* means "roofed colonnade" or "portico" in Greek). But it's the nearby garden, believed to have been Hadrian's reproduction of the Grove of Academe where Plato gave lectures, that I fall in love with. How quiet it is, and peaceful, under these olive trees! How good for the soul!

"It's sort of ironic…" I begin after leafing through the booklet we picked up at the ticket office. "Hadrian finally finished this beautiful summer residence, the place he built to recharge his soul, and he's stricken with ill-health. How much time did he have to enjoy this?"

"A few years. Enough."

"What do you mean, 'enough'?"

"Well, better than dying before it was finished, isn't it? Just shows how you can't count on anything, on any plan." Dwight casts a side glance at me.

"In fact, here is a lesson for Dwight," he adds. "No hard and fast plans that force me to rush. Avoid rigid framework." Then he takes my hand in his and asks, "How about you?"

"What about me?"

"What's your lesson from today's events?"

"Ah, that!" I feel terribly embarrassed by my outburst of temper and gently pull my hand back. Despite my knowing better, I'm still failing my First Fundamental: practice harmlessness. My speech can still hurt when I let my temper have the better of me.

"Well, actually," I look at Dwight, suddenly having a thought, "I think there's some kind of energy dynamic there: when you behave like a spoiled brat, it triggers my irritation and I explode in the end."

"So it's all right to explode?"

"Nooo, of course not! I'm not trying to find excuses. I'm just trying to understand the mechanism … the 'buttons,' if you will."

"Well, you certainly push my button when you rush me." Dwight now laughs. "And you know why you rush me?"

"Of course! Because we want to get an early start, give ourselves plenty of time."

"Nope." He shakes his head.

"Yes!"

"No!"

I'm lost. "I don't know why else I would rush you."

Dwight takes his time to answer. "The main reason," he finally says, "is your clinging to an agenda. I thought you had already overcome that. I thought we wouldn't need to finish our conversation we started in Naples, when you were not ready to face it, remember?" He eyes me intently.

I sigh. Yes, it seems that every time I didn't have an agenda, things went well, actually better than when I did have one. How many times do I have to be shown this in order to change that habit for good?

"Are you ready now?" asks Dwight.

I gaze at the pool in the distance, the cypress trees that are lining one side of it, and brace myself. "Okay, go on. I'm ready."

"I'm not going to go on. You have to tackle it."

"Tackle what?"

"The issue behind your irritation and making agendas, of course." He looks at me, a bit surprised. "They both come from the same place."

"What place?"

"The need to be in control. Don't tell me you were not aware of it?"

"Oh no, I was," I say quickly, clearing my throat, "but not in that way, I mean … such a clear way."

"Your mother was controlling, wasn't she?"

"Oh boy, and how! Everything had to go through her for approval. She had to be informed about everything—"

"Just like you," Dwight inserts casually.

"What? … I—I do?"

"Of course you do!" He laughs at my surprise. "You always want to know what I spoke about with someone, you always ask me all those questions."

I stare at Dwight as if hit by lightning. *That's because of my control issue?*

"And you always arrange every detail of my life, what shirts I wear, what shoes … which I don't mind a bit," he hurries to add, seeing the expression on my face. "Actually I'm grateful because I don't want to bother with that. But you should be aware that you're doing it … just like your mother was controlling every detail of your life."

"Trying to control," I correct him, finally retrieving my voice. "That's why I kept so many things secret, especially boyfriends."

Dwight breaks into laughter. "I bet you did."

"But why am I doing it now? I don't have any reason."

"No, but you have internalized your mother's behavior. It's now a part of you."

"But why?"

"That's what children do. They watch their parents and imitate them. Not only that, they also absorb their emotional reactions. They are like sponges.

That's how children learn, not through what their parents tell them, but from their parents' examples. Come to think of it, it was probably your defense mechanism also. You emulated your mother so that you could be on a par with her."

"I struggled so much with her, fought my many battles of independence."

Dwight falls silent for a moment. He's leaning against the tree trunk and watching a dove perched on a branch of an olive tree on the other side of the garden. Then he says in a different voice, almost like a reproach, "You should be grateful to your mother."

"Oh, well, I am, she did so much for me, but—"

"It's thanks to her that you've developed your will-power and your strength."

I'm taken aback. "How's that?"

"Because you had to fight. You had to stand up for yourself. You had to defend your principles, your actions, your intentions. This all requires the use of will, persistence, and determination. You have all these qualities—which, by the way, are indispensable on the spiritual path—thanks to her."

I sit silently for a while. I never thought of it that way. I always regretted that I didn't have a mother-bosom friend, a mother-confidante, as so many of my friends did, but instead had to be born to a mother-warrior, who rarely showed affection. It was my father and grandmother who showered me with unconditional love. But mother was always tough, a strict disciplinarian. Now I see that what I thought was a disadvantage, actually served a purpose. When I go back to visit my parents, I have to rethink my relationship with her.

I pick a blade of grass and twirl it between my fingers. After a while I say, "You know, it's actually laughable … look what happens when I revert to the old pattern of making plans. I think I finally got the lesson. No more agendas … from now on, I'm going to live in the moment. How simple, yet how difficult to learn!"

"Everything is simple when you finally learn it. But while you're learning it, it's darn difficult," Dwight says, smiling.

I get a chance to practice this new way of being a few days later when I drag Dwight to the center to help me buy shoes. I finally had to abandon the half-size smaller shoes I'd bought in Perugia last year. I left them next to a garbage bin; maybe they'll find a new owner with slightly smaller feet. Since then I've been looking for a pair of shoes, comfortable yet nice-looking. Then again, it may sound ironic that I'm not able to find shoes in Rome—the world capital of shoes, but that's because of the latest fashion: the shoes are either total flats or absurdly high-heeled, sort of high-rises of shoes. Extreme opposites, no middle way. And I was set on getting the middle-way shoes.

After coming out from the tenth shoe store—all clustered around the Fontana di Trevi, a tourist shopping district, to be sure—I look in exasperation at the massive fountain in front of me. Didn't I make an inner oath not to shop where tourists do? I turn to Dwight to suggest a visit to a café, but don't see him. I look around in alarm. Finally, I notice him leaning against the railing surrounding the fountain. He stares blankly at the water that shimmers with the glint of thousands of "wish" coins covering the bottom of the fountain. I squeeze amid tourists taking photos, lean next to him, and kiss him gently. He manages a tired smile, turns to me, and asks for a coin.

"What for?" I ask, curious.

"To throw it in the fountain and wish that you find shoes so we can stop this ordeal."

I laugh, despite all my weariness. "You're right, I'm fed up, too."

"And how do you think I feel?" His voice sounds reproachful.

"Well, I don't understand why I can't find shoes that are just ... normal. You know, in between, neither too fancy nor too casual."

Dwight raises his brow and sighs. "Because you're too picky."

"Am I?"

"Oh, boy, and how! You always know *exactly* what you want. And nothing else will do."

"Is that so bad?"

"Depends. That's what makes you do everything with excellence. But it's detrimental in shopping ... for those who go with you." He smiles and embraces me. "So what do you want to do now? Where else are we going to look for your shoes?"

On the spur of the moment I say, "In the Doria-Pamphili."

"What?" He takes a step back and gives me a surprised look. "That's a gallery, not a shoe store."

"I know that." I laugh. "I'm just dropping the shopping. Let's do something enjoyable, something inspiring." Then I add, emphasizing every word, "Live in the moment."

Dwight's face brightens up momentarily. "That's a good girl," he says and kisses me.

The Doria-Pamphili Gallery is the biggest, still privately-owned gallery in

Italy. It sits imposingly on Via del Corso, taking up a whole huge block, eclipsing in size and decoration all the other palaces in the vicinity.

"Bummer, I didn't bring my guidebook," I mutter to Dwight while he is buying tickets.

The elegant-looking woman at the counter smiles at me and points to the headphones. "The audio guide is very good," she says in impeccable English. "The heir of the family is more than half British, and an Oxford graduate. It's a delight to listen to Jonathan as he narrates the story of his family."

Jonathan! How strange to hear the English first name together with the Italian surname: Jonathan Doria-Pamphili. I relax into listening to the sonorous voice of Jonathan Paul Andrea as he tells the *story* of this palace. No dry architectural facts, no measures, building techniques, or interminable dates that one usually gets in audio guides, but juicy, amusing anecdotes about different members of the family.

We head for the gallery, housed in the second half of the palace. We pause in front of the portrait of Innocent X (the Doria-Pamphili Pope), masterfully painted by Velasquez, who succeeded in capturing the essence of the Pope—despotic and vindictive, according to his contemporaries. The portrait is so realistic that when the Pope saw it he exclaimed: "It's no good, it's too real!"

As we stroll through the private apartments, we walk through rooms decorated in theme-colors: yellow room, blue room, green room, pink room, then velvet room. I look goggle-eyed at the crystal chandeliers, gilded mirrors and elaborate table clocks, walls covered in silky damask of different colors and patterns, opulent curtains, chairs with gilt frames and upholstered in the same damask as the walls. It's not my first time in a palace like this—I had seen Versailles and Windsor—but this place is different. It feels like a residence, an awfully opulent and resplendent one, yes, but still—a residence. Perhaps it's because the heirs and their families live just on the other side of these rooms, in their private apartments that run parallel to these. And Jonathan himself may pop in any time to see how it's going, as is his habit when he's in Rome.

When we walk into the ballroom, we stand in wonder, taking a snapshot of an eighteenth-century evening: mannequin-servants wearing Doria-Pamphili livery embroidered with gold, instruments of the époque displayed in the corner where musicians sat and played, and the music—some sort of minuet—playing from the speakers and enlivening the room. I feel transported into the past. I see the noble guests whirling on the three-colored parquet, the crinolines swishing at every turn, the fans hiding smiles of intimacy or condescension. It feels so natural to be here; I could just slip into one of those laced gowns and join the ring of dancers as if I'd been doing it all my life. In fact, the parquet is so inviting, the urge to dance so strong that I make a few timid steps.

"Go on, dance!" Dwight encourages me. "Nobody's around."

Since I still hesitate, he adds, "Live in the moment. Do what inspires you."

And I let my body move with the music. I swirl and glide in the arms of an imaginary partner, naturally, effortlessly, and don't even stop when a couple of visitors walk in. They don't seem surprised at all to see me dancing; maybe they think I'm part of the decoration.

Dwight's eyes are sparkling. "Well, this is my reward for the shoe ordeal," he says when I swoop to kiss him.

On the way back home, I make one last—desperate—stop at a shoe store in the vicinity of our home. "You want to ruin this day," Dwight grumbles. "How long does it take you to learn?"

But to his surprise—and mine—I find the shoes I like! And not only shoes, but boots too, on sale. I walk out triumphantly. "The Doria palace brought me luck." I smile gratefully, relieved. I finally have shoes I can walk in that also look good.

"You're amazing," Dwight says, shaking his head. "You never give up until you find exactly what you want."

CHAPTER 19

ENVIRONS OF ROME:

WHAT YOU CAN'T SEE MATTERS

After nine hours of sleep, I awake with the flavor of strange dreams in my mind and a lazy feeling in my body. It's Saturday, and the building is unusually quiet; even the streets, at eight o'clock, are still quiet. Dark clouds are sinking distended from the sky, touching the roofs of the buildings we see from our bedroom. From the other side, the sun suddenly breaks through the clouds and casts a golden shaft on the façades. Caravaggio would have enjoyed this *chiaroscuro* morning.

Then I look around, and somehow everything in the room seems and feels different, with a faint glow of other-worldliness in the air. Dwight, too, senses something. He actually feels like pampering me this morning (I strongly approve of that). So he goes to our café at the *piazza* to get me a *cornetto*. Then he brings it to me with coffee—in bed!

"Are we celebrating something?" I ask. Maybe I have forgotten some important date, although it's very unlikely that Dwight would remember.

"Yes," he says with a twinkle in his eyes. "There is celebration in the air. It's like the whole invisible world seems to vibrate festively. A particularly auspicious full moon. So I felt like doing something for you."

"What a great idea!" I promptly agree, while Dwight props up pillows to make me more comfortable. Then he sits on the bed to enjoy my enjoyment. Purr, I'm lapping it all up: his gentle caresses on my hand, the taste of robust, aromatic coffee and the crispness of the pastry, the golden glow in the room, the feeling of well-being in my body after a good night's sleep. This is more than enough to celebrate the bounty of life.

"I feel like anything is possible today," I say dreamily.

"It is," Dwight nods vigorously. "So what would you like to make possible today?"

I sip my coffee and think.

"Let's practice living in the moment," he nudges me. "Don't think with your head, think with your heart."

"Okay, I'd like to get out of Rome. I feel the need to be in nature."

Rome does that to me; no matter how much I enjoy strolling through the center, after some time I start to feel suffocated by traffic and asphalt (there is not a single tree in the very center). I start to crave vegetation and open space.

"Agreed. So where would you like to go?"

I reach for the guidebook. "Oh, c'mon," Dwight protests, "don't read the guidebook."

"No, I won't, I just want to look at the map and see what calls me. Let's go … let's go … to Bracciano!"

Bracciano is the nearest lake to Rome, twenty-something miles to the north-west. The town of the same name houses a medieval castle that happens to get three stars in the *Michelin Guide*. When we come to the main *piazza*, we're hit by a striking view of the castle that looms, somber and grave, above the town center. My whole body shudders.

"This is so grim! Like a black hole. Like an infected boil full of pus." The words pour out of my mouth. I think I'm becoming something like a canary; all these travels, old palaces and ancient ruins, have honed my sensitivity to the energy of places.

The castle is perched on top of a volcanic rock and commands a superb, *superb*, view of the whole lake on one side and the town of Bracciano on the other. What an incredible position, I sigh wistfully as we climb up to the entrance gate. Standing by the ticket booth, a timid and soft-spoken young man is waiting to give us a tour. Mario tells us that working as a guide is his social service, which he chose instead of doing the military service, an option offered to all Italian young men. He glances at his watch. "It's noon. Time to start the tour."

Just at that moment three couples rush in, pushing prams and carrying babies—three babies! I look at Dwight and roll my eyes. He chuckles, then whispers, "Now, now, remember, it's another test."

So we set off: three babies, three couples, and us. As we walk through the gate into the courtyard, I feel as if we traveled in time back to the, say, thirteenth century. We walk along the walls, following the iron rings mounted there in medieval times to hold the torches. I'm almost expecting to see knights in armor trotting through the gate and dismounting from their horses.

The whole castle is medieval, Mario tells us, as the present owner, the Odeschalchi family, has not altered a thing (a rare occurrence in the country where the Baroque had corrupted the elegance and simplicity of the Renaissance style and all but obliterated the Gothic). The young princess Maria has managed to retain this family property by renting it for weddings, gala parties, and film shootings, as well as opening it up to tourists. (A few years after our visit, Tom Cruise got married to Katie Holmes here.)

What on earth is causing this bad energy, I wonder as we walk through one hall after another, examining the original tile floors from the fourteenth century and the painted wood ceilings from Renaissance times. The castle, Mario tells us, was built in the thirteenth century as a fortress, but was later used as a prison. In the fifteenth century it came into the Orsini family and was then converted into a palace.

"Prison…" I mutter to Dwight as we're walking through yet another cold, damp, fourteen-foot-tall room, "that could account for the bad energy."

It's only when we get to the so-called Orsini hall, which had once displayed one hundred fifty portraits of Orsini family members, that the cause of this dismal energy finally begins to emerge from the darkness of the past. Two portraits hang on one of the walls: Isabella Medici and Paolo Orsini "the Magnificent," wedded for political reasons in the mid-sixteenth century. She was eleven years old; he, a mature twelve. The portraits show a pouting young woman with all the traits of a spoiled brat, and a young man whose eyes reveal unscrupulousness and ruthlessness. He acquired his nickname "Magnificent" not for any intellectual or leadership merit (as did Lorenzo de Medici, for example), but because of his stature: his 160 cm of height bore 160 kg of weight! (I like how the numbers in European measures match; but to convert into the English system, that's 5.3 feet and 352 pounds.)

Then we walk into Isabella's room. Mario tells us that Isabella, who was not in love with her husband (I wonder why?), frequently availed herself of lovers from the working class. In fact, it seems that she had quite a sexual appetite; she'd soon get bored with old lovers and summon new ones.

"When she wanted to dispose of an old lover, she'd send him through this back door," says Mario, pointing at a small door in the corner of the room, next to her bed. "The door," he pauses and looks at each one of us, building up suspense, "led into a small space with a trap door, covering a deep hole, a sort of well. When the out-of-favor lover fell through, his body was chopped up by knife blades sticking out from the walls.

"Finally, the body would end up in a pool of quicklime that would swallow any shred of flesh."

In the aghast silence that followed Mario's words, Dwight wryly remarks, "What an ingenious way to dispose of unwanted lovers."

But Isabella was a pious woman, Mario continues, so after every disposal she would go to the chapel to confess, where, alongside the priest, her husband was listening as well. Finally, when she was twenty-four, Paolo disposed of her. Not because of her adultery, as you might think, but because he fell in love with another woman. The church, naturally, did not allow divorces at that time. (In fact, it still didn't until only forty years ago!) So, in order to be united with his sweetheart, Paolo strangled his wife and hired a hit-man for the husband of his soon-to-be wife. This was a divorce "a la Renaissance." Several centuries later, it would be known as *divorzio all'Italiana,* divorce Italian-style (which, if you have a sense for black humor, is not without advantages: it saves the lawyer's fees and there is no alimony to pay.)

After this grisly story we all feel quite relieved to walk out onto the parapet, breathe the fresh air and take in the view of the lake, which spreads like a cloth of velvet blue under the gauzy blue of the sky. If I were Princess Maria, a trail of thoughts begins in my head, how would I feel living in this place? Well, she doesn't live here, I remind myself. Naturally, who would want to? But still, owning a place with such a gory past....

One of the babies finally bursts into tears; the other two hesitate, then follow suit out of camaraderie. But the visit is over anyway, so we thank our guide and head for the *borgo* that lies contentedly on the southern side of the castle, like a dog at his master's feet. I'm curious to feel the energy there: how much of this gloom did it spill into the *borgo*?

Dwight and I split up and walk in opposite directions, to meet later at the starting point, a tiny clearing—*piazzetta*—in front of a few houses. I stroll around, following the narrow streetlets that meander and intersect at every imaginable angle, ending where they should intersect and turning where you would expect a straight chunk. Delightfully medieval. In front of every door and on window sills, pots and planters with flowers splash colors amid the monochrome beauty of stone façades. On the doorsteps of a house, a cat is lying, curled in a patch of sun. I stop to admire her. She ignores me, of course, dignified like a queen. Then she stretches lazily and minces away. I follow her and, as I turn the corner, almost bump into a woman.

"*Ah, buon giorno, cara, come vai?* Hello, dear, how are you?" The young woman says, but not to me. She stoops and picks up the cat lovingly. "*Que bella!*"

I can't resist. "She knew you were coming," I say in Italian. "She got up to greet you."

The smartly dressed brunette gently strokes her pet. "She does that every day."

"What a beautiful place," I wave my hand at the houses. "Everything is happy here, flowers, animals…."

She looks warmly at me and gives me a smile that says more than words; we chat a little, then part. I head for the *piazzetta* to meet Dwight. He's standing there, in front of a house with beautifully arranged petunias, talking to a cat. I love listening to Dwight when he talks to animals, especially cats. The color of his voice changes and becomes so sweet, the inflection so soft that I wish he would talk to me like that.

"What a friendly town!" he says in his "normal" voice as I join him.

"Amazing, isn't it? And I thought it would be gloomy and unpleasant because of the castle."

"Just shows how you can never know."

We walk back to our car and drive to Anguillara, a small town settled right on the shore of the lake. When I walk up the main street it's as if I walked through an invisible wall and entered a field of sadness. The contrast is so stark and sudden that it hits me like a gust of wind. I'm perplexed: what's so different about this place? I walk the streetlets of the old *borgo* and see the same type of houses, equally old, some restored, others dilapidated. But no flowers at any door. No cats anywhere, no dogs either. The streets, the houses, look forlorn. The people I run into don't return my smile. They gaze at me coldly and indifferently (are they Italians?).

"Oh, boy, this was a textbook example of good and bad energy," I say to Dwight when I return to the bench where he was waiting for me.

"Ah, is that right?" He pockets his pendulum and looks at me with curiosity. "So you got a good lesson in picking up energy?"

I nod. "Couldn't have been more clear—juxtaposition of the opposites.

Even if you're energy-blind you couldn't miss this one.

"But…" I add pensively, "I'd like to know what makes such difference in energy? Is it because of something that happened in the past or because of the Earth energy at this spot? Or because of the people who live here? I guess I'd like to have clairvoyant abilities so I can *see*. Now I feel sort of handicapped; I know but I don't know. You know what I mean?"

"Sure. But I don't think you got such a bad deal. I mean, handicapped, c'mon…" Dwight shakes his head. "Your energy sensitivity is one of the 'super senses,' as Kostas called them. Some people have clairaudience, some clairvoyance—"

"And what do I have? Clairsentience?"

Dwight laughs. "I don't see why you're complaining. You don't want to see or hear on astral planes, it would be torture. Remember Eileen?"

Eileen was our psychic friend in Cyprus, born with 24/7 access to invisible worlds around us. Her healing career began at the age of four (four!), when she healed successfully without any formal knowledge of diseases (obviously, at such an early age). Her "protective walls" were missing, she had explained, so she heard and saw everything that was happening invisibly—in the same space but on different frequencies of vibration. "It's not pleasant, believe me," she said, seeing the expression of wonder on my face. "I'm obliged to live with a mixture of benevolent entities and psychic monsters all the time."

We were visiting Eileen at her home, a modern-day castle built in an isolated and barren part of the island. It took her eight years to find a piece of land that was energetically clean, which meant where no one was killed or died (in other words, where no invisible entities or ghosts were hovering about).

"I can't shut it out," she said wearily, her eyes lackluster. "But this I know for sure," she added in a voice suddenly firm. "Nobody should deliberately try to develop these powers. If you're born with them and can't avoid them, then you have to use them and do the best you can to live a normal life. But it's terribly exhausting, you know…." While she talked her eyes danced from my face to the space next to me, from Dwight's face to somewhere above his shoulder.

"What are you seeing, Eileen?" asked Dwight.

"Well, your guides, of course. They are talking to me."

"What are they saying?"

"That your real life work is only beginning."

At the time, Dwight had no idea how accurate Eileen was when she'd said that. As a matter of fact, he completely forgot her words until his experience with Etna last year. And then it started to dawn on him: working with Earth's energies, that's his real life work.

"Those abilities," Dwight now says in a comforting way, "happen as a by-product, so to speak, of consciousness development, of merging with your Soul. You want to develop intuition, not psychic abilities, never forget that." He looks at me softly, in an almost motherly way, with a strange smile.

"What?" I eye him suspiciously.

"Oh, nothing." He turns away his gaze. "You just remind me of myself when I was young. That same zeal, impatience, wanting it all...."

Rome offers perfect training grounds for honing sensitivity to energy. Just think about it: an uninterrupted flow of life for almost three thousand years! How many thought-forms, "emo-ruptions" (that's short for "emotional eruptions," a word coined by my friend Lyn), and invisible entities inhabit this space! Whenever we walk through a quiet neighborhood of old Rome (preferably without shops), I invariably register the energy. But one quarter in particular feels like a patchwork of good and bad energy—the area between the Corso Vittorio Emanuelle and the Tiber.

The first time I found myself at the Campo dei Fiori—a *piazza* with the biggest open-air market during the day and one of the most popular hang-outs at night—I had the feeling of an annoying itch, like a rough hem rubbing against my skin, psychologically speaking. Something was bothering me but I couldn't tell what. It was a charming *piazza*, lined with picturesque old houses and many restaurants and cafés. But I kept twitching my shoulders, trying to shake off this something bothersome. Then I saw a statue in the middle and my heart lurched: a hooded man with his head bent, caught in the stride, his hands crossed in front as if tied. A haunting sight. And even more haunting feeling.

"Who's that?" I asked Dwight.

"Giordano Bruno. A victim of the Inquisition," he replied gravely.

Ah, Giordano Bruno! I learned about this great mathematician and astronomer in high school. His theory about planetary movements was revolutionary: Sun, and not Earth, he declared, was in the center, and all the planets revolved around it.

"He had turned the known world of the sixteenth century upside down," Dwight continued, standing erect in front of the statue, his hands clasped in front of his heart, as if paying homage to this great man. "Naturally, the church wanted to silence him, so he was kept in prison for years, interrogated, tortured, and finally burnt for heresy there." Dwight jutted his chin toward the statue.

"You mean, right at that spot?"

"Uh-huh. Right at that spot."

Being a cradle of Christianity, Rome is naturally a city of churches *par excellence*. The whole history of this religion is displayed here through churches and their architectural styles:

Early Christian, hidden in the catacombs; Romanesque, embellished by glittering, Byzantine-style mosaics; a few Gothic that have survived (or is it only one?—I'm not sure); Renaissance, having escaped the "baroquization," and of course, the droves of Baroque ones.

San Agostino—the first church built in the Renaissance style—is an example of a shrine that is throbbing with the energy of worship. It is very popular and much frequented by pious Romans because of the sculpture of *Madonna del Parto*. Surrounded by mounds of flowers, lit candles, and photos of children, the statue presides over the church from its throne in the back. It radiates a sense of aliveness as if in some distant past it really were a woman that was turned into stone by a wicked sorcerer.

The best way I can describe the energy in this church is—thick, gooey, glutinous. Like a dough made of fervent prayers, desperate pleas, ardent expectations, desires, demands, favors. I had a weird sensation that all these emanations, these emo-ruptions, were sticking to me, sticking like sweaty clothes in the tropics. I gasped for air.

Dwight, on the contrary, was all right—feeling oppressed—but all right. "You're too open," he said as an explanation, "you don't know yet how to shut yourself off, how to protect yourself."

"But if I shut myself off, would I be able to sense the energy?"

"Well, you don't really shut yourself off, but just don't let the energy get to you, if you follow what I mean?"

"Theoretically, yes, but practically—no."

"You'll learn from experience how to do that," Dwight reassured me.

"You'll be forced to learn," he added after a moment, "or else you'll be at the mercy of whatever inhabits certain places."

That sounded foreboding to be sure.

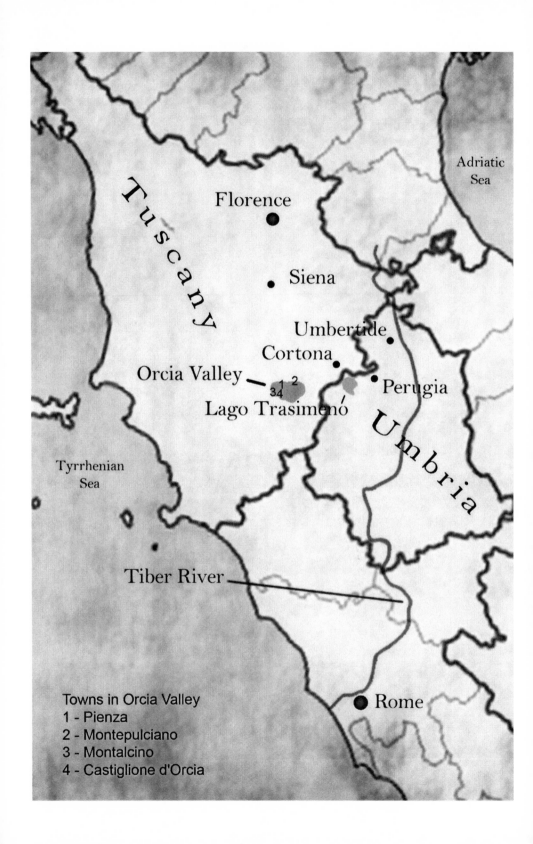

Adriatic Sea

Tuscany

Florence

Siena

Umbertide

Cortona

Orcia Valley — 1 2
3 4

Lago Trasimeno

Perugia

Umbria

Tyrrhenian Sea

Tiber River

Rome

Towns in Orcia Valley
1 - Pienza
2 - Montepulciano
3 - Montalcino
4 - Castiglione d'Orcia

PART 5

TUSCANY:

FREAKY STUFF

CHAPTER 20

FLORENCE:

WHISPERS FROM THE PAST

The best time to visit Tuscany, which I prefer to call by its Italian name—Toscana, is spring. By now, I've truly abandoned my old habit of meticulous planning, making agendas, even reserving hotels. Now I live in the moment. So one morning in April, while I was doing my Qigong exercises on the balcony, I felt the urge to visit Florence. I stepped back into the living room where Dwight was meditating and gently sat on his lap. "Love," I purred, "I feel like going to Florence, say … in two days. How does that sound?"

Dwight stared at me for a moment, dazed, then promptly agreed. "Fine. Why don't you reserve a hotel right now?"

That's when I encountered the weight of mundane reality. It was pre-Easter time and everything was booked. I had completely forgotten. I mean, who thinks of religious holidays when one is working on inner issues! Ever since we came to Italy, I've been living in a world within a world, so to speak, a world of causes rather than effects. Easter simply slipped through the cracks.

So after many phone calls and calculations, at dusk I dropped on the sofa. I was confused and, I'm ashamed to say, disheartened. How could I live in the moment when I had to get all practical and book hotels in advance? Where was the magic? The spontaneity?

Just then the doorbell rang. It was Noemi, unexpectedly here from Umbria for just two days. She needed to get something from the apartment, so I made us some linden tea, brought out sugar-free cookies, and sat down for a little chat. The table was covered with maps, guidebooks, and notes. She looked at the mess and asked, "Are you going somewhere?"

"Well, we wanted to go to Florence, but there is no place to stay!" I said, exasperated.

"*Ah, bene?*" she said casually, then after a moment added, "Gianni's son and daughter-in-law live in Florence … in the very center of Florence, actually. And they are going away, so the apartment will be empty. I'm sure they'd be willing to rent it to you."

Ah, the magic was back!

Two days later, we find ourselves in a beautifully-decorated, spacious apartment only a few blocks away from the Duomo. This is soooo much better than a hotel! We're actually going to *live* in Florence, in this cozy apartment with antique pieces of furniture. I look through the windows at the Renaissance façades across the street, people walking in and out of the stores, everything beautiful, orderly, peaceful.

"You see," Dwight says, "living in the moment did work. I wish you wouldn't get disheartened so quickly."

I wish that too.

Because Dwight has been in Florence several times before, he feels somewhat of a host. He wants to introduce me to this city in the most proper fashion, by having a welcome cappuccino in a café at the Piazza della Signoria. From our table I can see the whole square: across from us the medieval Palazzo Vecchio, also known as the Signoria, the city government during the times of the Republic; in front of it Michelangelo's legendary *David* (a copy, of course), symbolizing victory of the Republic over tyranny. To the right of the Palazzo Vecchio, the Uffizi, a museum with one of the richest art collections in the world (richer than the Louvre or the National Gallery in London), but originally the headquarters of the Medici business empire (*uffizi* means simply "offices"). In the loggia on the right, Benvenuto Cellini's *Perseus* holding the head of the infamous Medusa.

"Welcome to Florence, my love," says Dwight, raising his cup. We toast to Florence, to art pilgrimage, to our love, to Beauty.

It's daunting to write about Florence. How can words, even the most inspired and skillfully chosen, ever fully describe the glory of artistic expression and vitality in this Renaissance-birthed city? Florence is a living museum, studded with churches, palaces, *loggias*, belfries, *piazzas*, inner courts, bridges, all authentically preserved, designed and decorated by the greatest number of geniuses that have ever worked together. (It doesn't come as a surprise that the word "genius"—*ingegno*—originated in Renaissance Italy in order to describe a natural ability for original invention.)

Florence is so beautiful that you feel like flying, not walking. That's why the famous Greek writer Kazantzakis, Dwight tells me in an anecdote, went to a shoe store when he first arrived here and bought a pair of shoes that were one size too small—just to keep his ecstasy in balance. "You see, too much happiness," Dwight explains, "especially when you're aware of your happiness, is *hubris*, Kazantzakis thought. So he walked in the morning in the small shoes and was miserable. Then in the afternoon he walked in his comfortable shoes and was in ecstasy. Perfect balance." Dwight smiles.

Come to think of it, maybe I should have kept the half-size-too-small shoes I bought in Perugia?

But I don't need small shoes to keep my elation in check; there are tourists, tons of tourists to do that. The *piazza* is so crowded, people milling about like ants, that it makes me dizzy simply to walk around. I can't see much, so many bodies throng around me. All of a sudden there is a clearing and I come face to face with a woman on a panel. It's a figure from Botticelli's painting, the famous Venus. I stare at the delicate, sloe-eyed face, swan-like neck, golden curls that flutter in the wind, sensuous lips with a hint of a smile, the languishing, melancholic look that hides peevishness. I'm goggle-eyed, as if seeing her for the first time. I feel a wave of emotion rise from my entrails. Hatred. I hate her with my whole being. I want to knock over the panel to annihilate her naked beauty, so alluring, seductive, enticing, always arousing desire, wistful sighs, endless admiration.

Wait—what was this? What did I just feel?

I look around furtively, as if others could read my feelings and thoughts.

"What's the matter?" asks Dwight, who has retraced his steps.

"I ... I ... hate her!"

"Hate whom?" He looks around.

I motion to the panel.

"Why would you hate this painting?" He asks, puzzled.

I shake my head. "I don't hate the painting, I hate *her*, the model, the woman!" I feel like screaming to release my pent-up emotions.

Dwight looks at me for a long moment. "You seem different," he finally says, "as if something has taken you over."

"Oh!" I look at Dwight, all of a sudden feeling *myself*, as if his words have made me snap back, snap out of that irrational hatred.

I knew very well who this beautiful woman was, the woman who inspired Botticelli, his secret love and muse. The whole of Florence was besotted with her in the last decades of the fifteenth century. In fact, she became known as *the* most beautiful woman not only in Florence, but of the whole Renaissance—Simonetta Vespucci. Married to a cousin of the famous explorer Amerigo Vespucci (after whom America was named), she was also loved and pursued by Giuliano de' Medici, the younger brother of Lorenzo de' Medici. Really, she had it all: beauty, elegance, sophistication, intelligence, charm, wealth, noble origins, and fame. Except for one thing: longevity. She died at age twenty-two, probably of tuberculosis. Strange thing, karma. Sometimes it gives you everything, but not the time to enjoy it.

I'd read everything I could find about the Medici and Renaissance Florence. I was particularly attracted to the time of Lorenzo the Magnificent—the second half of the fifteenth century—known as the Golden Age of Florence. This was the most creative period in the history of humanity, the period that celebrated the glory of Man, that disseminated the ideas, knowledge, and sensitivity of the classical age of Greece and Rome and, above all, of the Neo-Platonic philosophy; the period that was born and reached its zenith in Florence, and from here spead throughout Europe. (The development of the arts during the Renaissance was so remarkable and the achievements so great compared to the previous centuries, that it could be compared only to the sudden explosion of technology in the decades after WW II.)

"So maybe Eileen was right," Dwight says, taking me by the arm and nudging me gently away from Simonetta's face. "She said that you had an incarnation here during Lorenzo's time."

"She said the same for you."

"Oh, I know. I feel so at home here."

"How can we know for sure?"

"I don't think we can. Unless you have a full download of memory from that lifetime."

"Like I had in Dendera?"

Dwight nods. That was the first time I experienced a past life flash-back. It was so vivid and so sudden that it took me by complete surprise. We were visiting the temple of goddess Hathor, some thirty miles north of Luxor in Upper Egypt. It was a clear, calm morning, and the temple was still empty. I climbed up onto the flat roof with a little chapel in one corner. In ancient times, during great annual processions the priests would bring the effigy of the goddess from an underground crypt up to this chapel and display it to the populace amassed below. I climbed onto the ledge and stood facing the interminable expanse of the desert shimmering in golden-red light, feeling the breeze on my face and the gentle heat of the sun. Then I looked down at my feet and saw another pair of feet in sandals, a long thong reaching up to the strip of leather encircling the ankles. My feet! Down below people stood in anticipation, their eyes riveted upon the roof of the temple, upon me. The woman whose body I was in raised her arms and chanted an incantation. The procession then appeared, carrying the effigy on their shoulders, and the people rejoiced.

Our teacher Kostas never encouraged curiosity about past lives. If anything, he tried to discourage us from ferreting through the past. "What you have now," he'd say, "is the greatest achievement of your Soul. Going back in time to previous incarnations, no matter how important they may have been, will not help you to uplift your awareness in this one. You will be going backwards, to a lesser state of consciousness, remember that always."

But what can one do when memories not sought after simply surface?

"Understand what they're trying to teach you, what you can learn from them," Dwight said a while ago, "then move on. If they are popping up on their own, it means you're ready for them and you have the opportunity to balance out your karma."

What do I have to balance out in Florence? Some unfinished business with Simonetta? But I don't remember anything else!

"Don't force it," Dwight says, eyeing me over dinner.

"What, am I forcing it?"

He shakes his head, laughing. "Oh, boy! You should see yourself, you're all tense."

"I'll be darned." I suddenly become aware that my shoulders are hunched and my body tight as if ready to run a race. I've been talking about nothing else the whole afternoon.

"If you 'effort' too much you'll prevent anything from happening," Dwight reminds me. "The energy of 'efforting' will plug up your receptors, so to speak, and you won't be able to receive anything."

"I know that theoretically, but practically… how do you direct all your attention toward solving something without creating a tension, without producing that 'efforting'?"

"It's not easy, I agree. It's a very fine line." Dwight pauses. "But so is everything else on the spiritual path. Every Zen koan carries that message of walking the fine line, the razor's edge. You always have to incorporate both extremes, like—be disciplined and flow.

"So, be focused on your task and open for everything else." Dwight gives me a big smile of support.

There is much to be open to in Florence. Wherever we go, there is something to arouse awe. The city is laid-out in such a way that it creates a perfect relationship between architecture and free, open space. It's hard to imagine that medieval Florence used to be mean, ugly, and stinking, as it was described by contemporaries. But in the fourteenth century, at the onset of the Renaissance period, the city planners met and decided to re-do the entire city. First the streets were widened and straightened, then slum areas were cleaned up, and finally the large squares were redesigned to enhance their usefulness and beauty. I find it remarkable that as early as the fourteenth century, the town planners of Florence were moved by a sense of beauty and an awareness of public good. This is what ushered in the Golden Age of Florence—the striving for order, beauty, and usefulness.

That was the atmosphere that attracted the greatest architects, sculptors, and painters of all time, all of whom were either born in Florence or found their way to this great city: Giotto, Ghiberti, Donatello, Brunelleschi, Masaccio, Filippo Lippi, Fra Angelico, Ghirlandaio, Botticelli, Leonardo, Michelangelo, Vasari, Verrocchio, Alberti, Cellini—a legion of giants in the history of the arts. And to top it all, this is also the city of Petrarch, Boccaccio, and Dante. It was in Florence that Dante wrote his *Divine Comedy*, which subsequently served as a model for the standard Italian language, again based on the criteria of beauty, order, and usefulness.

It is no surprise that Florence gave birth to what we today call the "Renaissance man": a well-rounded humanist and artist who was not a mere specialist in, say, designing churches or sculpting, but was a painter and architect and town planner and engineer (like Michelangelo, or Leonardo, or Brunelleschi). The early Medici, too, were multi-faceted; they were not only astute bankers, but also great connoisseurs of art, philosophy, and literature. Lorenzo the Magnificent, for example, wrote very good poetry. The biggest contribution of the Medicis, however, was their eye for talent, which they encouraged and cultivated. Lorenzo established an art school within the Medici grounds, attended by almost all great Florentine artists, including Michelangelo.

What happened in Renaissance Florence was nothing less than a revolution in art. This was brought about by the discovery of perspective (something we now take for granted) which Filippo Brunelleschi formulated based on mathematical laws. Now, perspective had already been discovered in ancient times, as early as the sixth century BC in Greece, but it had been all but forgotten during the Dark Ages. So when Brunelleschi (re)discovered the principle of the vanishing point and taught it to the young painter Masaccio, the latter revolutionized the representation of landscape, buildings, and figures by introducing a coherent rendering of the third dimension—a complete reversal from the Gothic "flat" or two-dimensional style in painting.

If Brunelleschi had done nothing else but discover the laws of perspective, this would have assured him a prominent place in the Florentine Hall of Fame. But he did much, much more. He designed and executed the biggest dome of Christendom, the dome that is the signature of the Florentine skyline, the dome that crowns the calm, placid beauty of the city—il Duomo. At the time, his feat of raising the vault without wooden scaffolding made him a hero of mythological stature. His brilliance can be fully appreciated only when put into modern perspective: in height and span, the dome of Santa Maria del Fiore had not been surpassed until the twentieth century, and then only thanks to the use of much lighter modern materials such as plastic and aluminum.

I'm thinking about this as I'm climbing the hundreds of steps to the top of the dome where, squeezed among a multitude of bodies, I try to capture the panoramic views of the city. Seeing the interior of the cupola has made it easier for my non-engineering mind to understand Brunelleschi's stroke of genius. The way he was able to raise the dome was by devising an inner circular skeleton, like a series of circular rings, over which the outer octagonal structure was built.

"So, did you enjoy your climb?" Dwight asks brightly as I join him in a café where he's been waiting for me. His heart condition doesn't allow him steep climbs. But he also doesn't care that much for heights and views. I, on the other hand, must scale every bell tower.

"Well, I did and I didn't. The line was absurdly long," I answer tersely, not wanting to admit that his warning was right. I've just worn myself out.

"Mm-hmm," Dwight murmurs, his lips curling into a wry smile. Then he stretches his arms across the table and cradles my hands in his. "I want you to see my favorite church in Florence. Are you up to it?"

"But—didn't we already see it? I mean, wasn't it the Duomo?" I ask, surprised.

But he shakes his head *no*. "The Duomo is too, how shall I put it … impersonal. Too big and cold. But Santa Croce is something different."

Santa Croce *is* something different, yes. As soon as we walk into this Gothic church, I stand as if thunderstruck. In the vast, shadowy interior, all the grandiose works of art are looming from the shadows. I look at the chapels, sculptures, tombs, frescoes, and my heart wells up. It is awesome, it is powerful, it is sacred, it is humbling. It brings tears to my eyes.

I stand and cry.

The immensity of Beauty! I feel like kneeling down, smitten, laying my life at the altar of Beauty. Like a knight of the Round Table, I want to offer my life to the service of beautifying this planet. I want to reach high up and bring down the forms, the shapes, the harmonies that give rise to Beauty. *I'm your servant, take me! Flow through me, infuse my cells, live at my fingertips so that everything I touch may turn beautiful. Open my eyelids in the morning and close them at night. Lead my hand so that what I write may inspire, what I create in space may touch hearts, and what I am may bring light, a tiny little stream of light and joy to others!*

I open my eyes and look up, wishing fervently that someone up there has heard my prayer. In a world that has become so driven by expediency and profit, I want to bring a ray of beauty just for its own sake.

"This church is called the Florentine Pantheon," Dwight's whisper comes from behind me. He gently places his hand on my shoulder. "So many famous Florentines are buried here. Over there is Galileo's tomb, and across from it is Michelangelo's, and further down Machiavelli's, and Dante's cenotaph."

He takes me by the hand and leads me toward the altar. "Giotto's frescoes." He motions with his head toward a chapel in front. "And Donatello's crucifix is over there to the left."

We sit down in the first pew and gape. Now I understand what the French writer Stendhal meant by an overwhelming effect of art. He wrote in his travel book *Naples and Florence* that the magnitude of all the works of art, so condensed in Florence as nowhere else in the world, causes a traveler to break into tears and even swoon. This reaction much later became known as "Stendhal syndrome": a psychosomatic condition of dizziness and heart-racing, even fainting, brought about by particularly beautiful art or by a large amount of art in a single place, reported by many first-time visitors to Florence.

A monk sidles up to us and with his eyes cast downward whispers that the church will close in five minutes. Already? But it's so early! We get up a bit disappointed and take one last sweeping glance at the chapels in the transept.

As we walk along, I notice that I'm actually walking on tombs. Crusaders' crosses, swords and helmets, tau crosses (the symbol of St. Francis), all engravings worn shiny by many feet, mark the burial places of ancient nobility.

"You know," I say pensively as we walk outside, "this church has special energy."

"Yes, a lot of love and devotion. It's Franciscan."

"Oh, so Santa Croce is a Franciscan church?"

Dwight nods. "The largest in the world. The story has it that St. Francis laid the first stone."

"Now I understand why it's your favorite!" I laugh.

We are standing in front of the church, surveying the square of the same name, one of the oldest in Florence. Right here, Florentines have held annual tournaments for eight centuries. In the Middle Ages and Renaissance the jousts were as popular as soccer games are today. The young men from illustrious families fought with lances and swords to prove their skill, bravery, and valor—and gain the favor of their chosen ladies. It was here that Giuliano de' Medici won the jousting tournament in honor of his lady, Simonetta Vespucci. He actually carried a banner with her picture, painted by Botticelli, with the flattering inscription "The Unparalleled One." (Never mind that she was already married.) Giuliano was the darling of the Medici family, handsome, refined, full of joy. He was liked by the whole of Florence; he brought light and laughter wherever he was. *Ah, how regal he is … radiant, glorious.* I feel strange pangs of jealousy in my heart. *I'd do anything to gain his love!*

What—what did I just feel?

I shake my head vigorously as if I'd just walked into some cobwebs. Oh, this city is doing something to me. Where is my home? Where did I used to live? Something is eluding me. The actual memory…. This is tearing me apart, this something I can't quite grasp but just catch the whispers of….

"So where would you like to go now?" Dwight's mellow voice rings in my ears like a breath of fresh air.

I only shrug, my throat strangely tight, unable to form words.

He tilts his head and gives me a long look. "How about getting out of Florence for a bit?"

"But where?" I croak.

"Oh, let's go to Fiesole."

Dwight always says I'm his muse because so many times I gave him just the right book, or took us to a place where he had important insights, or in some other way—usually through questions—gave direction to his own quest. But he does the same thing for me. Bringing me to Fiesole was just about the sanest choice to make. Not only because Fiesole is of Etruscan origin (although that alone is enough for me), and not only because Fiesole is situated up on the hills above Florence (and has gorgeous views), but because it gave me the chance to get some *distance*: it took me out of the cobwebs of the past woven by collective memories that permeate every house, every street in Florence.

Fiesole has a special resonance for me. While still an undergraduate student of world literature, I became infatuated with the famous Serbian poet Milos Crnjanski, who, in turn, was infatuated with Toscana and wrote many beautiful poems about the views of the river Arno from Fiesole. I don't remember his verses any longer, but I remember the rhythm of the poems, the rhythm of contemplative and luxurious indolence. And the moods! ... heavy like summer heat and inexorable like vapors rising off hot asphalt after rain.

That very word, the four syllables *Fi-e-so-le*, rings enchantingly in my ears; it brings back all my youthful dreams, reveries, romantic contemplations. It has nothing to do with reality; it's a pure figment of poetic creation. It stands for an unbridled, exhilarating flight of inspiration, an ultimate freedom, an embodiment of Beauty.

We're riding the bus up to Fiesole, through the hills with wanton vegetation and beautiful villas. This is the Tuscany of the American imagination: mansions surrounded by tall cypress trees, hanging wisterias and grapevines, splendid views of green, rolling hills.

Finally, I'm in the Fiesole of my youthful dreams—and it's getting dark. We can't see anything in the dark, I mumble. Maybe we should have come during the *day*. Dwight doesn't say anything. His face is set and I can't tell what he's thinking. He's looking left and right, trying to orient himself at the main square where the bus has deposited us. Then he takes the guidebook out of his back pocket, looks at the map, and decisively says, "This way."

"This way" is away from all the important sites, including the Etruscan archaeological zone where I was hoping to stroll among the ruins. After all, Fiesole was the most important city in northern Etruria. And it dominated Florence until as late as the twelfth century. But Dwight is striding confidently, looking straight ahead with concentrated determination.

"We are going to the convent!" I exclaim as I spot the sign for the monastery of San Francesco.

Dwight nods silently.

"But this is a bit of a climb … are you sure you want to go up?"

"*Piano, piano.*" He smiles, "I'll make it."

Magic. There is no other word for what we see when we finally reach a small terrace that offers a magnificent vista point. I stare in awe as dusk falls quietly upon the mountains like an enormous theater curtain. The valley is sighing below, a sigh of admiration as if at the sight of dancers on stage. The city lights twinkle, some in clusters, others, solitary lights, sprinkled around like spangles on a tutu. Gently gliding among those spangle-lights is the dark, dark body of the Arno. And above all this, like a decorated theater ceiling, sparkling stars in the sky shaded in layers of lavender, dark purple, and pewter.

Just at that moment the slice of creamy yellow moon appears on the horizon. I let out a scream. "Did you know it was the full moon tonight?!" I turn to Dwight in ecstasy.

"Of course I did, I planned it all," he says in a serious voice, but then bursts into laughter and shakes his head. "No I didn't. I forgot all about it."

The view of the Arno valley and Florence from Fiesole in the moonlight! Is there anything more romantic in this world? I think I might actually faint, this much beauty is hard to take. My chest heaves like a sail in the wind, and blood rushes through my body, thumping in my temples. Then all the gates rip open, and I feel as though I'm bursting into a million tiny cells that explode into this view and become one with the air with stars with lights with the river. Then the cells, like confetti, fall everywhere onto this land, breathe in the life of it all, and thus enriched, fly back to me, into this limp shell left quivering on the terrace. I'm whole again, but this time more fully than before, because I now carry bits of everything around me.

The whole valley glows in the marmoreal light of the full moon. I'll carry this view, this moment in me forever.

"Dwight," I whisper, tucking myself against his chest, "I think I'll go shoe-shopping tomorrow."

Dwight's body tenses up. "Shoe-shopping?" says his indignant voice.

"Yes. I'd better get a pair of tight shoes or else…."

CHAPTER 21

FLORENCE:
DEAD, BUT STILL ALIVE

I have a compulsive need to walk in this city. Just walk without going anywhere in particular: walk and look at the houses, walk and listen to the sounds, walk and smell the air. And, no, I didn't need to buy shoes that were too tight after all. As Dwight wryly pointed out, school kids on their pre-Easter field trips were my totally free and obvious reality check. The line in front of the Uffizi was impossible; the rooms in the Museum of the Duomo were stampeded by countless pairs of swift legs; the main streets were turbulently chaotic with groups of tourists—no, I definitely didn't need tight shoes to balance out too much happiness.

Dwight lets me wander on my own, partially because he gets tired from all that walking, but partially because he feels that I need to be alone, at least some of the time. He also hopes that memories will come back when I'm alone and relieve me from this tension that has built up inside me. I've been feeling increasingly ill-at-ease, and Dwight prefers to stay out of my way when I'm in that state. There are mornings when I wake up with strange thoughts in my mind, thoughts that feel as if they belong to someone else. At times my perception becomes so altered that I lose all sense of orientation. Or I have an urge to walk into a particular house, to knock on a particular door. Weeks later, when I had film negatives from Florence developed (that was before digital cameras), the pictures showed me with slightly altered features. My eyes had an odd glow, as if someone else were looking through them. "You don't look like yourself," Dwight commented as he scrutinized the images.

But this morning I feel perfectly myself, in control of my thoughts and feelings. So we decide to do something educational and head for the Medici

228 • TUSCANY: FREAKY STUFF

library. In a city with so many world-class attractions, this library is a second-tier choice. But it's my first choice because I've grown up surrounded by books; because when I was a child I devoured books at a rate of one per day; because all my life I've dreamt of having a wall-to-wall, floor-to-ceiling library.

The Medici library occupies the northern cloister of San Lorenzo, the burial church of the family. At its inception, it contained only 3,000 manuscripts—a fraction of what was once housed in the famous library of Alexandria, burned down by Christians in the fourth century. But those 3,000 manuscripts were for Florence of the fifteenth century more than what the UCLA library is for Californian students today! It was thanks to Cosimo the Elder, the founder of the Medici dynasty, then to Lorenzo the Magnificent, that priceless manuscripts, such as the oldest known source of the extant tragedies of Aeschylus and Sophocles, are preserved.

The actual building was designed by Michelangelo and it was so innovative, so modern for its time, that it would take a whole century before its influence gave rise to a new style in architecture—Baroque. The *pièce de résistance* of the library is the staircase in the entrance hall: the steps are shaped in the form of waves and their width increases toward the bottom to create the impression of a waterfall.

While I'm gazing in awe at the staircase, a handsome young Italian, as handsome as Keanu Reeves, asks me if we would like a guided tour. (Mind you, as a good Italian he addresses me, not Dwight.) Oh, why not! Nobody else is here and I can linger to my heart's desire. Besides, one can never find in guidebooks all the information these young guides can pass on.

"Is this your military service?" I ask tongue-in-cheek, remembering our guide Mario from Bracciano. But the young man looks at me perplexed, and I mumble, slightly embarrassed, "Never mind."

Then we go up the famous staircase to the Reading Room and stop in the doorway.

Ah!

What a remarkable effect of the perspective: long rows of wooden benches succeed one another in perfect alignment to the opposite wall, some hundred feet away. And what palpable energy! There is a feeling of aliveness and thirst for knowledge and respect for written words.

Young Keanu Reeves begins his story. In Renaissance times the books were huge and heavy, hand-copied and illuminated, bound in leather. Because of their size and weight they were kept in the shelves underneath the reading consoles, he points at the shelves, and the consoles were slanted at a 45-degree angle to accommodate the size of the books. At each row hung a long and narrow board showing the subject matter and indexes of books kept in that row.

He pauses to gives us time to admire the beautiful, highly-polished wood, and the spiral carvings on the benches, also designed by Michelangelo. My gaze slides to the floor, which looks very unusual; I can't tell what it's made of, certainly not marble.

"This is the unique-in-the-world, two-colored terracotta floor," says Keanu, following my gaze. "The earth had been baked until it was glowing red, then cut by hand. The red clay comes from the Arno, and the inlays of yellow clay were designed to reflect the patterns of the wooden ceiling, designed by Michelangelo."

I look up at the ceiling, down again at the floor, around at the beautifully carved wooden rows, and my heart begins to race. Oh, it's too much beauty again…. But our guide continues, "As a motif for decoration of the ceiling Michelangelo used—a goat skull."

"A goat skull! Why a goat skull in a place of learning?"

"This is actually a Capricorn skull," Keanu says with a smile, expecting our expression of surprise. "Because Capricorn is the zodiacal sign under which Cosimo the Elder came to power. Capricorn was regarded as an auspicious sign in the Renaissance because Roman Emperors Augustus and Charles V ruled under that sign."

"And astrology was very popular in the circle of Humanists around Lorenzo," I say, wanting to show off my knowledge. "Marsilio Ficino, the most influential philosopher of the Renaissance, who revived Neo-Platonism, wrote a book on astrology."

I did make the desired effect. Keanu gives me an impressed look. "You know about Ficino?"

"Of course," I say with a wave of my hand as if it's the most natural thing in the world to be familiar with Ficino's philosophy.

"And another rarity," Keanu continues after flashing a warm smile at me, "is the windows." Dwight and I both look up, not having noticed anything special about the windows.

"These are the original windows from 1571!" he says, with a ring of pride in his voice. "The only *painted*, not stained glass preserved from that period in the whole of Italy!"

Wow! The chance of glass surviving all the local wars, games of stone-throwing, street soccer games, earthquakes, and two world wars!

It was a good visit, a particularly educational visit. We've learned so much from the young guide, not only about the library but about life in Renaissance Florence. Our Keanu Reeves happened to be a student of philosophy and the history of art on an internship and not doing his social service. He provided a wealth of information about the trade guilds, everyday life and customs, and told us anecdotes about famous artists. What started my train of thought later that day was his comment that Florence was famous in Europe for *perfect* cloth. (The main Florentine industry was manufacturing wool and silk.) Not only was the manufacture scrutinized at every stage, but the quality control was impeccable. "Experts in detecting stains and flaws"—that was their official title!—examined every piece before it went for sale. If the defects were above a certain tolerance, the cloth would be immediately destroyed.

The search for perfection ran in all the other fields of endeavor. Stone cutters, for example, tested every block of stone before sending it off to building sites. They would strike it lightly with a hammer and listen for the sound. If the stone rang like a bell, it was perfect; if there was a dull thud, it indicated a crack.

No wonder palaces and churches have lasted all these centuries. They were built to last; they were created to bring the ideal of beauty down to earth. I'm not saying this to idealize one epoch. I'm saying this because the Renaissance period actually brought a revival of the ideals of the classical world. And one of the most influential philosophers of the classical world was Plato. His concept about the world of ideas, of archetypes that overshadow the manifest world, was one of the fundamental principles of his philosophy. The primary three ideas were Truth, Goodness, and Beauty. A life lived well and purposefully was a life that embodied these ideas. In fact, our duty, Plato thought, was to bring Truth, Goodness, and Beauty into everything we do. What's more, there is a synergistic relationship between the three: what is good and truthful is also beautiful; and something that is beautiful cannot be evil. So beauty was understood to be larger in scope than mere physical appearance. Beauty was also magnanimity of the Soul.

In terms of all this, I think I belong to a pre-modern world, a Renaissance world. I guess my appreciation for beautiful things was quite obvious even at an early age. I remember my mother and aunts gathered in a sort of family council to discuss my talents, interests, proclivities—in brief, to help me determine my future vocation. My mother looked at me piercingly, tilted her head and shook it somewhat worriedly. "You like beautiful things very much," she pronounced. "You better find a well-paying job." (Notice, she didn't say "a rich husband." In socialist Yugoslavia, women were encouraged, no, *expected*, to have a profession, not to marry well.)

To walk the streets of Florence is to enjoy beauty. To revel in beauty. To stand on the Ponte Vecchio in the early morning, to gaze at the sunlit surface of the Arno as it rolls impassively under the bridges, to observe the simple elegance of the old houses that line its banks, to watch an elderly Florentine pad over the cobblestones to slowly and deliberately open his jewelry shop, is to savor the most beautiful moments life can offer.

I'm not even in ecstasy anymore. I'm just simply, quietly, softly content. The tears of beauty have stopped streaming, only two pearl-like drops glisten permanently in the corners of my eyes. I think this city is doing something to me. But I don't know what.

Yet again, I am out alone, combing the streets in the dark after dinner. I avoid the main streets and seek the silent refuge of empty, shadowy alleys. My body moves on its own. It wants to go west of Ponte Vecchio. It wants to descend to the river, walk along the bank—the Lungarno—up to a little *piazza*, then along one *borgo*, down another *via*, prowling these streets that hide something from me. Something I want to know. A pang of grief stabs my heart.

Empty. It's all empty. Emptiness and desolation. The whole city is empty, the houses abandoned, everybody dead. Doors gape open, fires are burning, the stench is unbearable. Furtive, hooded figures slither from shadow to shadow. My body begins to mourn. It's mourning a terrible loss, of a husband, of a son, of a family, of the whole city. The grief is rending my heart, will it ever be whole again? Tears stream down my cheeks. I've lost ... everything.

Utterly shaken, I ring the doorbell of our apartment.

"What's happened to you?" Dwight asks in a voice that sounds alarmed.

I walk past him straight into the living room, and plunk down on the sofa. "I retrieved something. Not the memory of events, but the memory of emotions."

When I finish my story, there is silence. Dwight is not looking at me, his eyes are turned inward. At long last he says, "My feeling is you tuned into the Black Death. Florence lost more than half of its population then."

His words send a jolt through my body.

"The plague was so bad," Dwight continues, "that Florence had to import slaves because nobody was left to work."

"But was it my memory or was I picking up thought-forms from the past?"

"It's hard to know for sure. What was your feeling? What did you feel in your body?"

Before I have time to answer, a memory flashes. I was five years old, lying in my little bed next to my parents' bed. They were watching a movie and I with them. The TV was still black-and-white, and in the movie there was a lot of black and dark-gray. People were writhing in pain, swollen in pus, then thrown on a pile and burned. Fires were smoldering everywhere, bells were tolling, women crying. I stared at the screen, frozen with terror, then let out a scream and started sobbing. My mother swiftly took me in her arms and stroked my hair. "That's just a movie," she whispered into my ear, "nothing to be afraid of." But I could not calm down. I sobbed for hours.

"It was my memory," I reply with certainty. "But I don't remember any details. Just the feeling that I lost my whole family ... that I, alone, survived."

Dwight takes my hand and gently squeezes it without a word.

"But that plague was way before Lorenzo's, hum ... Simonetta's time. What to make of all this?"

"Well, first of all," Dwight says, "there were many other plagues; they were quite frequent then. Second, you won't achieve anything by trying so hard to put the pieces together. Relax. Just go with it."

I close my eyes and for the first time notice the music that Dwight is playing—one of Mozart's violin concertos.

"Would you like some herbal tea?" I hear Dwight's gentle voice.

I open my eyes and look at him, his calm face, his silvery hair, and all of a sudden I'm overwhelmed with happiness that he's next to me ... *alive*. "You're right," I say calmly now, "I'm efforting again. I should relax."

I get up and light the many candles. Soon the room begins to glow in a golden, dancing light. The antique objects lose their firm shapes, the long shadows assume an existence of their own, and the colors bleed into each other. The violin sings a lyrical, beautiful adagio. I'm so grateful Dwight is alive. I'm so grateful I'm here, now, and not in the plague-ravaged Florence. As if to make sure I'm not dreaming, I start touching Dwight's hair, cheeks, lips, neck, shoulders. I touch him gently, gently like the bow caressing the strings to produce these sublime sounds. My fingers are like the bow, caressing his face, his chest. My lips like feathers touch his lips. Softly, very softly, my skin against his, his lips on my neck. The candlelight casts a strange glimmer over his eyes. They look at me with a passion I have never seen before. The music stops. The sense of time disappears, only the moment is here and this man in my arms.

The shadows dance and sprawl on the white walls. I close my eyes again and drop into abandon. My body is limp, dissolving under his kisses, the kisses of the man in a uniform, the man in a cape, the man in a pleated robe, the French officer, the Renaissance artist, the Egyptian dignitary—I'm kissing Dwight in all his different incarnations, I'm embracing him in the totality of his lives. Like a kaleidoscope, he changes appearance, his hands touch me differently, images flash before my closed eyes, and I feel I'm transcending my body, the confines of this person, to become Woman, archetypal woman, making love to Man.

After we separate, I lie on the sofa in perfect stillness, the sense of time expanded, my perceptions heightened. The veil that separates this world from the invisible one, from Reality, is getting thin. I'm closer ... to what? Slowly I begin to feel something palpitating in the air—an electric field, a different frequency.

Can I ask questions? I address that field.

"What would you like to ask?" I hear a voice in my head, but it's not the Voice from my childhood. It has a different vibration, a different feeling.

About my past lives. What is the cause of this wheel of suffering?

Instead of an answer, I feel myself being pulled into another dimension. The whole succession of incarnations starts to unroll before me in fast motion, like one movie after another. But I want to go even further back, back to the incarnation that caused this wheel. I know I didn't live blindly always. I know I have lived in full awareness of my Soul before. What did I do to cause my fall into ignorance, into suffering? I want to rectify my mistake. I want to put everything aright so that I can be free! I keep going back through time, further and further.

The fall.

I've done something terribly wrong. As a consequence, I had lost all my knowledge, all my powers. With tremendous intensity, I feel my fall. I'm dropping deeper and deeper, away from the light and everything that comprised my world. Anguish, thick like fog, fills my body and I keep sinking into a well. My world, my true world is far up, like a circle of light, getting smaller and smaller, and dimmer as I'm sinking lower ... a fading ring ... a tiny dot ... until it disappears. I lose every remembrance of its existence. O, terrible loneliness! My pain is so deep, it numbs my heart. My Soul aches. Then I hear:

"Falling down was swift, but the way back up is going to be very, very slow."

And so the circle of incarnations began in total ignorance and blindness. With each incarnation I sank deeper and deeper into the quagmire of passions, thrown hither and thither by jealousy and revenge, throwing myself wildly into hatred, pride, cruelty, sacrifice, sinking ever quicker. I was being swallowed by the quicksand of emotions.

Horrified, I open my eyes and gaze into the candlelight. My eyes are dry, but my Soul is crying. How much suffering! Never again. Now is the time of the reversal. To reverse the fall!

The next morning I wake up light-hearted, as if something happened while I was asleep to deliver me from inner torment. The events from the last night are a dim reflection. I get up and walk to the windows. Only a few people are out. There is a feeling of calm and quiet, as if half the tourists have left the city.

"What do you feel like doing today?" asks Dwight from bed.

"Mm, don't know yet. How about you?"

"Oh, maybe go to the other side of the river." Dwight props himself up in bed and looks at me lovingly. "You haven't kissed me this morning," he says in a mock complaining tone.

"I have, but you were asleep."

"Oh, well, that doesn't count then." He laughs and opens his arms wide for me. "Forget about the past for one day, will you?"

I forget about the past while we have cappuccino in our favorite café. But the past is back in full swing as soon as we approach the impressive Palazzo Pitti on the other side of the Arno. The Pitti were the rival family of the Medici, the family that conjured the conspiracy to overthrow Lorenzo. They struck in the Duomo, as the Medici brothers made their appearance at morning mass. Lorenzo managed to escape, wounded, but his younger brother Giuliano was killed, at age twenty-five. The retaliation was brutal, as could have been expected. The conspirators were hanged in the main square and Botticelli was ordered to make sketches of their limp bodies which were exhibited as a warning for everyone.

So this gorgeous palace was begun in the fifteenth century by Luca Pitti, a prosperous banker, but he never finished it. It came into the Medici's hands a century later and became the official court residence of Duke Cosimo I. Today it houses the Galleria Palatina, along with the Uffizi, the most important art collection in Florence.

In a long and narrow room, a portrait of a man catches my attention. "The First Duke of Buckingham" by Pietro Paolo Rubens, reads the caption. As I'm admiring the portrait—ahem, the handsome and noble features of the man—I notice an interesting quality of the painting: from whichever angle I look at it, it seems as if the Duke is looking at me. I move to the right, his eyes are on me; I walk all the way to the left, he's looking me straight in the eye. The longer I gaze at him, the more I have the impression that the portrait is alive; Rubens truly succeeded in capturing the inner qualities of the man. In fact, I can't take my eyes off him, I'm so mesmerized. Is this my imagination or is he actually smiling at me?

"What are you looking at for so long?" asks Dwight from behind my back.

"This painting. It's so alive," I reply without turning to him.

"Uh-huh." He moves on to another painting.

As soon as Dwight turns his back, I feel a surge of energy shooting from the figure in the painting. I stare at the Duke's large, soft, enticing eyes, and suddenly feel like an insecure adolescent girl, secretly and hopelessly in love!

I can't believe my emotional reaction. No, it can't be the real me reacting; it must be some emotional conditioning from who-knows-what circumstances. But the Duke is actually swallowing me with his eyes. I feel his invisible hands touching my hair. I'm starting to blush; I feel shy and embarrassed. This is like an etheric seduction. I am at a loss; I know how to deal with an actual, physical seduction by a man in the flesh, but a seduction by a portrait?!

"Let's go," Dwight's firm voice breaks the spell.

I follow him obediently. After we walk through a couple of rooms, Dwight turns to me and says in a serious voice, "You better go back to the painting and tell the Duke to leave you alone."

"What?" I squeak.

"You'll take him with you, don't you see? You're not yourself; you've been behaving in a strange way, as if you're possessed." And he takes me by the hand and we retrace our steps back to the room with the painting of the Duke. Dwight plants me in front of the canvas, then seats himself in a chair at the other end of the room.

I cast a timid glance at the charming face with a goatee and a long, twirled mustache, framed by hazel curls. The eyes glow sensuously, temptingly. I mentally invite the Duke to communicate with me. Did we have any connection? Do we have something unfinished? But nothing is coming through, no clear impression. *You should go back into your painting,* I send him a thought while gently pushing his energy away. Hell no, he's resisting! I feel a great wave of discontent and resentment coming from him. He's actually rebelling! I push the stream of energy more forcefully until I feel it's back within the frame. I'm about to turn away, but then remember my experience at Herculaneum with the little girl. I explain to the Duke that he should no longer linger bound to the earth, but instead move on to higher realms. I shower him with white light to help him free himself. Mentally, I feel his reluctance. He actually doesn't want to leave, I receive the thought. He's having a great time watching the constant flow of people, eyeing the women, flirting invisibly. Who cares about higher realms?

"It's all right now." Dwight has approached without my noticing.

"How do you know?"

"I felt it from there. He's back in his painting."

"But he doesn't seem to want to go on."

"Well, leave him alone then. Don't meddle. You should never help people against their will."

Much later I found a snippet about the private life of the Duke of Buckingham, which portrayed him as a great seducer and ladies' man. Among his conquests was the Queen of France, wedded to Louis XIII. This affair became fictionalized by Alexandre Dumas in his much cherished novel *The Three Musketeers*.

For our farewell to Florence we go to Piazzale Michelangelo on the other side of the Arno, famous for its postcard views of the city. The terrace around a café is covered with swatches of purple, yellow, pink, white, and red tulips in full bloom. Their colors stand out so vividly against the gray sky that the terrace looks like a vast outdoor painting. The weather has turned cloudy and cold, but we don't mind (too much). We squeeze ourselves into a corner where we are protected from the wind yet can enjoy the view, and sip tea to warm up. We are both pensive and withdrawn. I'm looking at the gorgeous view, the overwhelmingly beautiful sight of Florence garlanded around the Arno, and I feel strangely detached, as if I have already left this city. I think of the past two weeks, of all those extraordinary, peculiar, weird, and freaky experiences, and can't find a firm footing in my memory. It's as if the events are losing their solidity; the memory of them is already hazy and feathery like the mountains in the distance shrouded by this spring mist.

Feeling a bit hungry, I search for a packet of almonds in my purse. My fumbling fingers touch the pulpy surface of bubble-wrap. I take out the little bundle: it's a glass dish I bought in a shop that sells exquisite objects made of blown glass in translucent colors—all *perfect*. I rummage again for almonds and this time feel the hard surface of my new journal I bought in a stationery shop, the handmade covers sporting the traditional Florentine pattern of gold, red, green, and yellow lilies. I place both objects on the table and look at them fondly. These two little objects, *solid* objects, are all that will be left from my trip, from my exceptional experiences. I relegate a difficult task to them: to store my memories and make them available to me when I need them. They are all I have to help me retrieve and recreate this time in the future, when I'm ready to write a book.

In a taxi in Rome the following night, Florence seems so far away, as if it had never happened. How can this be? What an unreliable thing, memory. It's playing tricks with me. The streets of Rome seem unusually lively. At this late hour the city is still bustling. The taxi driver jauntily asks where we came from. When he hears our answer he bunches up the three fingers of his right hand and brings them to his lips, the gesture that conveys something delectable. "*Molto bella,*" he exclaims, whirling his hand through the air. "*Ma un po'…*" the hand goes on whirling, "*un po' morta.*"

A bit dead? His words strike me with full force. *A bit dead….*

When I open the door of our apartment, the interior feels welcoming and "ours." There is a sense of expansion and freedom I didn't feel in that beautiful, antique-furnished apartment where we lived for two weeks. I look around at the familiar clutter, the pieces of furniture that don't match, our modern beds with a metallic, angular frame I'd hit myself against so many times, and I feel back in the present. I feel that time has resumed its stride where I left it off. I'm back from the past, I have just emerged from its shell like Botticelli's Venus from the foam.

Florence—what a play on the perception of time!

In Florence the past *is* the present. Millions of people come to Florence to see the past; thousands of guides talk about nothing but the past. The present revolves around the past events until it gets sucked in and becomes the past. Thus the present continuously feeds the past and keeps it alive. *Le Roi est mort, vive le Roi!* The past is dead, but still alive.

"Well, we've finished our business with Florence," says Dwight, standing by the window and looking out with an air of contemplation.

"You think so?"

"Mm-hmm, I sense the lightness around us. Something that was holding us, holding *you*, has been released."

I feel he's right, but something doesn't let me agree fully. Part of me wants to put everything behind, but part of me, the doubting part, wants to probe further. So I say, "But I haven't found any clear memory. Everything was so vague."

"That's all right. Much has happened on invisible planes. Just by walking the streets you were vacuuming, so to speak, your psychic left-overs, strong emotions you'd left behind."

"But shouldn't I know what it was all about, what the circumstances were and what actually happened so that I can release the karma?"

Dwight doesn't reply right away. He looks through the window at the lights, his hands tucked in his pockets. Then he turns to me and says slowly, "You don't need to know all the details to release the karma. Karma is released by changing your inner attitudes and emotional patterns and raising your vibration, not by knowing the details of an incarnation." He pauses for a while then adds in a different tone, "Don't get too caught up in the business of past lives. Sure, that's important, but it's not *the* most important."

"It's so fascinating, though. You realize what an amazing thing a human being is, so multi-faceted, like, like … a precious but unpolished diamond. All the different surfaces, different irregularities. You want to turn and see each side."

"You don't have to see each side to know what the diamond looks like."

"Maybe *you* don't, but I do."

I don't know why I said this. I didn't mean to be antagonistic or confrontational, but the words came out. Dwight looks at me for a long moment during which the muscles around his lips twitch as if he's about to say something but then changes his mind.

"You do as you wish," he finally says and walks past me. In the next moment, I hear the bedroom door close.

CHAPTER 22

TUSCAN COUNTRYSIDE:
THROUGH THE VAPOR

Two weeks later we are in Toscana—again. On this trip, though, I have no intention of ferreting through my past lives; I've dropped obsessing about Simonetta. Dwight was right: upon our return from Florence I did sense a release. I no longer felt like a prisoner of the past. But also, I've been too busy with the present. It was time again to plan another trip to the States. This time, we both agreed, I shouldn't go to California. Instead, I should explore possibilities for our eventual move to New Mexico. Six years ago on our vacation in Taos, we liked the place so much that we thought of, perhaps, living there some day. We also agreed that I should visit our psychic friend Liana, who lived in Colorado. Maybe the Guidance would come through her and point to where we should go next. So I purchased the ticket for the middle of May. But before I headed for the desert of the Southwest, I wanted to experience the beauty of the Tuscan countryside in spring. You know, those famous landscapes featured on postcards: tall cypress trees lining the meandering paths, gently rolling hills, and meadows carpeted in red poppies.

But we can't see much of those famous landscapes because of the torrential downpours. As we're driving to Pienza, a small town about seventy miles south of Florence, it's raining angrily. Menacing skies, whipping winds, and slaps of rain follow us hour after hour, as if nature has some unresolved issue with me. I'm seriously thinking of consulting an oracle on the subject of placating the gods of weather. Dwight is shaking his head in disbelief, then in anger as I get lost time and again trying to find shortcuts. Finally, exhausted and hungry, after five hours of driving in a steady downpour (a drive which normally takes only two hours), after getting lost three times and ending up in the fields, after being stuck in an apocalyptic traffic jam around Siena, we finally arrive at the *piazza* in front of the old town of Pienza.

Six centuries ago, Pienza was envisioned and built as a blueprint for the ideal Renaissance city. Pope Pius II, one of the great humanists, poets, and diplomats of the fifteenth century, was born here. After he was elected the First Man of Christendom, he decided to redesign his native village according to the ideals of the Renaissance (beauty, order, and usefulness). In completing the cathedral, the Town Hall, and the Bishop's Palace, the commissioned architect exhausted the funds and the work had to be stopped. His over-spending was such that only the beauty of the buildings and the harmony of the square saved the architect from the Pope's wrath.

At this late hour though, and in this rain, all we can think about is food and rest. Forget about the beautiful architecture and the ideal proportions of the town! Luckily, the restaurant recommended by the *Michelin Guide* is right across the parking lot, and we run for the door. Inside it's so warm and pleasantly buzzing with noise that I immediately forget my resentment of this rainy, cold weather at the beginning of May. I look around the cozy room—a tall refrigerator case displaying yummy-looking deserts, plates with mounds of pasta on the tables—and begin to relax. No, we don't have a reservation, I say when the hostess approaches, but yes, there is one table left in the farthest room, she says and takes us there.

We squeeze ourselves next to another couple in the back room packed with people. As I glance around, I notice that there isn't a single Italian in the room, only Brits, Americans, French, Germans. Welcome to Pienza, a model of the ideal Italian town—as the guidebook proudly states—but without the Italians! As soon as I make my tongue-in-cheek remark, an increase in noise behind me catches my attention. I turn back to see a large group of Italian men fill up all the empty seats in the adjacent room. They're young, well-built, and rambunctious.

"Pienza soccer team!" Dwight states with confidence.

"No kidding? How do you know?" I look closely at handsome, dark-eyed faces, and despite the noise I feel better. That is to say, I don't feel like a tourist.

"Simple deduction," comes Dwight's reply. "Obviously they're athletes, a team with an older coach. And what's the most popular sport in Italy?"

"All right, you win," I say after a moment of watching the young men laugh together and slap each other's backs. Their exuberance spills over into our room. This afternoon's horrendous drive, the fatigue, the wet and cold, all are forgotten, and I feel perky and in a good mood. So does Dwight. He's poring over the menu, muttering something like "nothing for my diet," then he puts down the menu and says decisively, "Let's eat normally." Our health has been improving, so maybe it's time to celebrate—together with the Pienza soccer team.

As I am blessing the food in front of me, my eyes closed and the aroma of rabbit wafting into my nostrils, I suddenly feel a different vibration in the room, a rather strong invisible presence. In utter astonishment, I recognize the energy of my Teacher!

Now, this may be somewhat confusing: who *is* my Teacher? Because I'm not talking about Kostas, although I do carry him in my heart and his words in my mind. And, obviously, I'm not talking about Dwight who is sitting across from me, blissfully enjoying his first "normal" meal. To introduce my Teacher (with the capital "T"), I have to go back in time to September of last year, when Dwight and I were traveling through Greece on our way to Italy....

We had just arrived in Mycenae, the fifteenth-century BC city in the middle of Argive plain, on the Peloponnesus Peninsula. This part of Greece swims in myth, legend, and a history of wars. It's embedded in the very DNA of European civilization. We carry those myths, those heroes and gods, in the deepest recesses of our subconscious—in the collective unconscious. The citadel of Mycenae crouches on a large hill, surveying the Argive plain left and right, all the way up to the horizon. Even in ruins, Mycenae exudes power: the power of a prehistoric animal, the power of Cyclopean architecture, the power of a race of demi-gods—the terrible power of dark passions.

It was here that the goriest myths took place. Where Atreus served his brother with the flesh of his children for dinner. Where Clytemnestra killed her husband Agamemnon for sacrificing their daughter Iphigenia to start the Trojan War. Where Orestes murdered his mother Clytemnestra to avenge his father—the whole royal family bathed in incestuous blood for several generations. I was thinking about all this while walking the uneven stone causeways and admiring the massive Lion Gate. I was also reflecting on the qualities of balance and serenity of the Golden Age of Greece, the beauty of art and the harmony between conflicts that later Greek civilization had achieved—like a lotus with its roots in the mud and the flower that opens to the sky. The sky.... My eyes soared above the Argive plain shimmering in the midday heat. The light danced in my eyes, unreal, supernal, filled with longing.

What is so special about the light in Greece? This light, impregnated with fierce opposing forces, divine and visceral at the same time; this light that carries the seeds of tragedy and the seeds of redemption, of Godhood, apotheosis. "In Greece one has the desire to bathe in the sky," said Henry Miller. I have that desire everywhere, but here it was more acute, urgent, intense; it was so intense it became painful.

The light pulsed in my eyes.

What is so special about Greece?

We left the fortifications of the palace and headed down to the Treasury of Atreus, known also as Agamemnon's tomb. This tomb was built as a *tholos*, a round structure hewn out of a hill slope. I stood between the Cyclopean blocks that flanked the long entryway to the *tholos*. The doorway struck me with its geometry: a rectangular opening topped by a triangular one. Four and three, simple and powerful and symbolic: three, the number of spirit and four, the number of matter.

Dwight had made some acquaintances—an Italian family with relatives in Ostia Antica where we were going to move!—and was talking with them. But I … I was drawn to the dark that gaped like destiny through the doorway. Alone, I crossed the threshold. The cone-shaped interior was barren; no decorations anywhere. Yet there was something dignified in this naked emptiness. Around me, people were clicking their cameras. But it didn't matter; I had already stepped into another dimension.

To the right gaped a smaller doorway of the same shape—a rectangular opening with a triangle above the lintel—closed off by a wooden plank. I was drawn to it, irresistibly, irrevocably. I stepped over the plank and faced the grayish, misty darkness of another empty room. Here I was alone. Nobody else ventured into the barred space. My eyes were still full of light and I felt blinded by darkness. Slowly, contours of rocks emerged out of the misty grayness. Slowly, I became aware of something palpitating in the air, some sort of energy moving toward me. This energy carried great compassion and dignity. Almost involuntarily, I addressed a greeting to this energy:

I have come at last. All my life I've been waiting for this. I'm finally here, my Master!

A part of me bowed to my long-lost Teacher; a part of me observed everything, dumbfounded. I received an impression: my Teacher had been waiting for me, imprisoned here all this time. Yet he had been with me all my life. A strange "thoughtalogue" was taking place. Another impression formed in my mind: my arrival would finally free him.

But free from what? Why were you confined here?

"We were together in the flesh in some distant past. You were my neophyte."

"Ah, I was your apprentice! And...?

"Something happened. An error that has separated us."

What error? I asked, horrified. *Was it an error on my part?*

But the energy receded. I felt a wave of great compassion embrace me.

Then it dawns on me. *Were you trapped here because of something I did?*

I felt the energy smile. "Teachers are always responsible for their students and the way in which the students, in turn, use the imparted teaching.

That's not fair.

"That is the law."

At that moment Dwight appeared. Together, we sat on a large stone planted by the entrance and meditated. It was peaceful, very peaceful; no ecstasy, no sweeping bliss, just the quiet, gentle peace of recognition—I'd come home.

After a while, Dwight whispered that he felt the energy as a Mage. A Mage from pre-historic times when the invisible world was seen as the primary reality. I asked the Mage—my Teacher—if he could heal Dwight's heart. I received a vague impression of something solidified, like a mound of crystal, like a giant teardrop. I also had a thought of Rome. But nothing made clear sense. Then I asked to be healed of Candida, that my body be strengthened so that I could do the work that lay ahead. This time, the impression was very clear: "Go to Epidauros."

Before we left, I asked my Teacher to stay with me from then on.

"I'm *always* with you, but we will not be able to communicate so directly, except on occasion."

When we came out, the light cut my eyes like a knife blade, making me recoil. I climbed the mound of the *tholos*, a thin layer of earth covering the round structure of the tomb. Atop, one tree. I sat in its shade and felt strange. Not because of what had happened inside, although that was more than enough to make me feel strange. I felt something trying to come forth. Another memory. And this memory was elusive, like a dream that recedes fast upon awakening, and the harder we try to remember, the deeper it recedes.

What was it about?

I looked around at other mound-tombs in the vicinity; I looked up at the Cyclopean ruins of Mycenae on top of the hill farther away. Downhearted, I lowered my eyes and stared at the earth, the dry yellow grass I was sitting on. The grass rippled like water in a pond, the wave of time rolled through my mind, and I saw myself, as in a dream, sitting at that very same spot. I was nineteen and I was travelling through Greece....

We have just finished a tour of Mycenae. My group was given free time to stroll the site, and I wanted to be alone. I was drawn to this mound away from the fort. My eyes take in the raw beauty of the citadel on the hill. I'm so happy I'm in Greece, seeing the places I've been studying about in my class on Ancient Greek Drama. This morning we visited Epidauros, and now we have the whole afternoon in Mycenae. I'm sitting alone, on the dry grass under a solitary tree. I'm enjoying the peace, this land of stern and sparse beauty. Slowly, a feeling emerges: a sense of inevitability. I had to come here, and I have to come again. This land is magical; it's calling me. I touch the earth and vow to return to this place in the future—with my beloved.

I snapped back from the past and found myself sitting atop the *tholos* on that September afternoon, just two days before my thirty-eighth birthday. I felt profoundly shaken. Almost twenty years had passed since the moment I'd made that vow. How was it possible that I had completely forgotten about that event? How was it possible that the memory had remained locked away all that time? Not even a trace of it for twenty years! I felt like crying. I was stunned, awed at the tapestry of my life. No, not tapestry, more like needlepoint. Who had created it? Certainly, not I; I was but a mere needlewoman, stitching through a design already drawn on the fabric. Just as I did as a little girl: up and down, passing the threads of yellow, green, blue, orange color through a drawing printed on the fabric.

So who has created the design on the fabric of my life?

Your Soul—Dwight would surely say.

True. However ... deep down I sensed that my Teacher had brought me back here because we were supposed to meet in the future. We had a rendezvous at this particular time. Two tears rolled down my cheeks. I felt strongly that from then on, my life would be changed. A part of me that had been asleep was awakened and would never fall asleep again.

That was the point of no return.

The following day we went to Epidauros and I encountered the Anubis-like dog.

So, here I am, eight months later in this restaurant in Pienza, and my Teacher is again with me. After his brief visitation in Florence, the night when he took me through my past incarnations to experience my fall, he has chosen to appear in this noisy restaurant with the Pienza soccer team. I am so taken aback, I sit as if frozen in my chair. Oh, this energy, gentle and comforting, yet powerful and poised, how well I know it! Communication comes easily and naturally. Even before I finish formulating questions, the answers come. He has appeared to me not because the energy of Pienza is special, but because I've worked out a lot of my karma. I'm "lighter" now. I can feel his frequency more easily. He can get *through* to me more easily.

But I still feel lost, my Master, I don't know what I'm supposed to do.

"You are doing exactly that which you are supposed to do."

But ... shouldn't I be writing a book?

"The time is not yet."

When is that going to be?

"You will know; you will feel it."

And how long are we supposed to stay in Italy? What's next? Where next?

"One step at a time."

Why can't you tell me?

"Because *you* have to make the decisions; you have to create your life. Your destiny is not to follow but to initiate."

Emerson's words pop up in my mind: "Do not go where there is a path; go instead where there is no path and leave a trail."

I look around the room, people chattering and laughing. All has become so unreal, so remote. I am sharing the same space with them, but on a different frequency. They seem like ghosts to me. I finally take a bite of my food. The delicious taste of rabbit brings me back into my body, but part of me is still with my Teacher. In that altered state I see more clearly the patterns on the fabric of my life. The design is finally emerging. Grateful, so grateful for all the help I've been given, the presence of my Teacher, and my newly-found health and strength. There is a feeling of closure and a new beginning.

"Dwight," I lean forward, "I'm going to order tiramisu."

Dwight looks up at me in surprise, blinks several times, then his eyes change expression, as if penetrating to the bottom of my heart. "Go for it!" he says with a nod.

This is such a big moment for me; for a year and a half I haven't had anything sweet, not even a piece of fruit. By ordering tiramisu I'm announcing my official recovery from Candida. I quiver at the sight of creamy, coffee-flavored *mascarpone* cake. The tiramisu is ecstatically tasty, and every bite melts with delicate, sensuous flavors. All my senses are rejoicing. I feel my Teacher smiling.

Later that night, we arrive at the *agro-tourismo* accommodation outside Pienza we've reserved through Noemi. I am still in a dreamy state, only half-present in this world. Dwight is too tired for conversation. Actually, he still can't completely forgive me for having taken country roads and getting lost in the rain, instead of hopping on the freeway and driving straight to our destination. The whole afternoon he's been shooting occasional biting remarks about my compulsion for challenges and doing things the hard way.

Now he collapses in bed, while I head for the bathroom. I want to take a long, long shower—it's my therapy, my meditation, my reward.

As the first spray of hot water rolls down my skin, my body begins to relax, muscle by tense muscle. I listen to the soothing sound of the shower water, while in my mind I replay the events of the day. After a few moments I sense the familiar energy of my Teacher. I feel him all around me; he is so close, I could almost see him through the vapor, but not quite.

A sense of accomplishment spreads through me. We're together again. I bask in his energy that offers remembering, belonging, a feeling of having come home. But there is more ... Mentally, he takes me up into another state of consciousness. It takes me several moments to adjust to the expansion, an explosion of light that envelops me.

"*This* is your true identity," he says softly, then recedes.

Slowly, this different frequency completely fills my head and with it an entirely new sense of identity emerges, an identity that is unfamiliar. I am not who I thought I was. The personality with whom I used to identify doesn't feel familiar anymore. This is so unsettling that it's difficult to accept. Throughout all my life I've had a certain sense of who I was, a certain way in which I saw myself, an identity to which I related. This basic identity remained the same during all my inner changes, through all these years of self-inquiry, uncovering truer and deeper layers of me. But it was *me*. Now this isn't me anymore, but a new self. And this is unsettling.

But at the same time, I am feeling peace: the peace of someone who has reached a long-searched-for home, the peace that comes with finding one's true identity. *This* is the real life work. There is nothing else I need to do but maintain this frequency. And in this state, I feel it deeply, there are no personal desires. The only desire is to serve the Higher Reality; to do whatever is according to its Plan. Because I am a part of it.

"It looks like your bad-weather curse is not over yet," Dwight quips the next morning as he opens the shutter-door of our bedroom.

I look up from the bed and can't believe it. Outside, where the hills roll, it's fog. And not just haze or mist, but a thick, autumn fog.

"Fog, in May?" I croak, still in disbelief. "It can't be!" I get up and walk to the French door.

But it is. I look outside and see nothing but milky paste. The drive around the area we had planned for today is out of the question. Even going to Pienza is purposeless; we wouldn't be able to see anything!

"We'd better stay here this morning," Dwight echoes my silent thoughts.

I am utterly perplexed. I thought I was done with fog and what it symolized. My inner confusion has cleared. So what is the fog trying to tell me now?

Try as I might to find an explanation, no answer comes. We eat our breakfast slowly, slowly—there is nowhere to rush to, nothing to see. The Belgians at the next table are talking loudly. The owner, sullen and unpleasant, shuffles through the dining room. When we complain about our runny eggs, he snarls, "If you're not happy with breakfast, eat somewhere else!" Some attitude! Dwight and I look at each other in disbelief.

Back in our cottage we take two chairs outside and tuck them in between the shutter doors to protect ourselves from the wind. Then we sit down and face the fog.

"I think it's clearing up a bit, I can see the outline of a hill now," Dwight says, trying to sound cheerful and encouraging.

I say nothing.

He insists I tell him in detail what happened last night. He is fresh and rested now. When I finish, he remains silent for a long time, then begins reflectively, looking into the distance:

"What you are describing is the state I've known for so many years. It's the merging of your lower self or personality with your Soul. And in this state you don't have personal desires. That's what I've tried to explain to you on several occasions. That's also why it's so difficult for me to make choices about secondary things and I leave them up to you. In the long run, they just don't matter."

"But I had glimpses of my Soul before. Yet now, it was different. Very different!"

"That's because," Dwight says slowly, "before, you experienced your Soul as separate from you, and your consciousness was still identified with your persona. But now, you had a taste of actually *merging* with your Soul—what you've been asking for, right? So your sense of identity was shifted, trying to find a new foothold."

Then he adds in a different voice, almost like a warning, "You got a taste of how it feels to be united with your Soul. Remember it well, because it will not last."

"It won't?"

"No, of course not. You'll go back and forth between the old and the new identity many times before you get firmly established in the new frequency, in your Soul identity. But now, you know where you're going; you know what this state feels like and you can recreate it.

"And that's why your Teacher is back," Dwight adds after a moment in a bright voice. "Because you're ready now to start learning and creating. So far you've been mostly working out your karma, un-learning your past conditioning. But now, that's over—or almost over—and you're ready to reclaim your power."

I wish he were right. But even Dwight, my wise man, couldn't know how far I still was from that goal and how much more karma, dramatic karma, I still had to go through. In fact, it seems to me now that everything up to that moment had just been preparation, a first act leading to the finale.

We remain quiet for a while and watch the fog thinning. We can now see the misty outline of Pienza on top of a hill and the meandering roads lined with cypress trees. Everything is still fuzzy though, as if seen through glasses with fogged lenses. I am trying to find the word that best describes my experience of this sight.

"Vapor!" I exclaim. "Everything seems like vapor in this light."

"This is how the material world appears when you are in an altered state," Dwight says, "like a screen, actually, a projection on a screen. It's not real."

I gaze at the houses scattered around the hills, their white and gray shades slowly acquiring colors. What a wonderful way to impart a lesson: wrapping the landscape in fog to make it seem unreal, so that I can change my perception!

"But when you are immersed in the material world," Dwight continues, "then the inner world seems unreal and vapor-like. Your left lobe takes over and you begin to doubt what you've experienced when you were in the altered state."

As the midday sun burns away the fog, I'm feeling further away from my Teacher. Somehow the mist kept my memory fresh and the experience palpable; it made the inner world feel more real than the material one. But with the sun, with the clarity, with the burst of colors, the "real" world prevailed and pushed the other farther back into the realm of memory—a vaporous memory.

And we set off into the exploration of this world, just a crumb of it, a slice of Toscana.

CHAPTER 23

CORTONA:

I REMEMBER YOU...

*A*rtistico Naturale, I read on the map for the area around the Orcia Valley. We are driving along the loop south and west of Pienza: Bagno Vignoni, San Quirico d'Orcia, Castiglione d'Orcia, St. Antimo Abbey, Montalcino, then back to the other side to Montepulciano. Around us gently rolling hills quilted in fields of yellowing wheat, green oats and burgeoning sunflowers, all dotted with clusters of trees and outlined with curving roads bordered with cypress trees—the hallmark of Toscana. The colors are intense under the blue, blue sky.

"Artistic nature...." Dwight murmurs in that child-like wonder of his. "It's so harmonious, it seems unreal. Just look ...!" He sweeps his hand as far as the interior of the car allows him. "Nature is so harmonized by man that it's like a work of art, a huge canvas. Even the power lines are concealed underground!"

Roadsides are flush with poppies, whole mounds of red poppies. It's riotous. This is the material world at its best. At moments like this I think it's all worth it—struggles with the body, difficulties of the path, challenges and tests.... We stop the car and walk aimlessly. We slip far away from the road into meadows bursting with flowers. No sounds of civilization intrude on the busy life of nature; insects go about their daily business, and birds flit around us. A mere couple of hours after my vapor-induced insights, I've already forgotten the other, invisible world. I'm sensuously immersed into the illusory but—oh, so beautiful—projection on the screen, as Dwight said.

My favorite town on this "naturally artistic" loop is the little village of Castiglione d'Orcia. We stroll the quiet streets that seem happily asleep. In the middle of a *piazza* flanked by sturdy stone houses, an old well marks the center of village life. We sit quietly by the well and listen to silence. We watch silence. A woman opening the shutters on the first floor, leaning out, looking left and right, in silence; withdrawing, then coming back with a pitcher and watering geraniums in the planters, in silence. A girl stepping out of a house, quietly closing the door, throwing a quick, curious glance at us, then walking away, quietly.

But other towns, we discover, are besieged by tourists, and Pienza is the first on that list. We're sitting in a café admiring the harmonious elegance of the piazza and the Renaissance façade of the cathedral. A young Brit, who very politely asks if he may occupy an empty chair at our table, turns out to be an art historian without a job, on a frugal tour of Tuscany. He instructs us that the architectural unity of the square was carefully designed to reflect the balance between the civil and religious authorities.

"Balance," he says, bringing both his hands to the same level in the air, "even in politics and in government, permeated the Renaissance way of thinking. That's because balance is the result of harmonious proportions," he declares in a voice that sounds, well, *balanced*. "And harmonious proportions, in turn, give rise to beauty."

We wish the art historian a harmonious stay in Tuscany and set off for a walk around town. In the nineteenth century, the citizens of Pienza decided to rename the streets around the main square to better reflect the concept of the ideal city. Thus the new names evoke love rather than war: Via dell' Amore (Love), Via della Fortuna (Fortune), Via del Bacio (Kiss). How nice to be living on Kiss Street, for example, and write your address a zillion times! There's got to be a subliminal effect. You would be inclined to kiss more frequently, would you not?

Tired of bumping into tourists all the time, we cut short our stay in Pienza and decide to visit instead the old Etruscan city of Cortona, which has recently become famous as the cherished Italian home of Frances Mayes. As we're driving northwest toward Lake Trasimeno, Dwight and I smile at each other with satisfaction: we've become really good at living in the moment.

Like all the other Etruscan cities, Cortona is perched on top of a hill. There is only one level street in the whole city, the guide book warns. As we slowly progress up the steep Via Guelfa to the main *piazza*, we notice some commotion ahead, costumed people and fanfares.

"Tomorrow is Cortona's Saint Day," a shopkeeper replies to my question. "Today are the first festivities, the pageant of the crossbowmen." She goes on to explain how every *quartiere* (neighborhood) has its own flag and coat of arms, and is represented by a group of crossbowmen that compete in a tournament.

The main *piazza* charms me instantly. It's entirely medieval, presided over by the well-preserved Palazzo Comunale (Town Hall), built way back in the thirteenth century. But it's packed with people, every chair at every café taken, so we continue our walk. We get to another *piazza*, right behind the Palazzo. And another café. And more costumed people. It's exciting to see different garbs and gowns, veiled women and caped men, to hear the beat of drums at regular intervals, to feel the anticipation in the air.

The sound of trumpet fanfares echoes through the street, and I simply can't resist. Leaving Dwight behind, I dash to the square and make my way through the crowd to the front row, just as I used to do on assignment in my journalist days. I position myself in front of the railing to take pictures. I point my camera at various faces: women with laurels around their heads, men with Renaissance hats, girls with colored ribbons plaited in their hair. I shoot couples walking slowly to the beat of the drums, the drummers as they cross their sticks in the air, crossbowmen with their heavy bows resting on their shoulders. Soon, I find myself surrounded by other cameras, big and small, eagerly snapping. I am squeezed, and my angle is greatly reduced. I lower my camera and watch. And listen to the drumbeat: two slow, two fast ... three slow, two fast ... the beat changes with the representatives of each *quartiere*. I feel the rhythm in my womb ... two slow, two fast ... the beat throbs and sends chills throughout my body.

An approaching couple catches my attention, a man and a woman both dressed in black velvet with golden trimmings. He is tall and imposing, majestic really, with long golden curls that flutter in the wind; she is svelte and gracious, her eyes demurely cast down. The man commands attention as he walks. The woman steals glances at him, glances of pride and admiration. Her eyes glow with an image of him. Suddenly, I feel a snap in my heart and my breathing becomes heavy. Something about them, this couple in black velvet, the man trailing power behind him.... Tears roll down my cheeks. The couple is very near me now; my blurry gaze is riveted upon him. Ah, that frowned brow, the expression of irrevocable might in those blue eyes ... and those broad shoulders, the curls resting upon them.

This is my man, my Lord and Master, whom I love more than life; whom I admire more than my father, whom I adore and venerate.... I beam with pride next to him. My eyes drink in his power, his dignity, his magnanimity. The noblest of men....

The drums continue to resonate in my womb, two fast, two slow.... I close my eyes and let myself go with the rhythm. Three fast, two slow....

I am part of the clan, I share the same feelings with everybody else. We belong to our town. And my Lord presides over it, everybody listens to him. This is the call of my town, two fast, two slow.... I follow the call, I can give my life for my town....

The couple is gone. I feel suddenly tired, drained. My camera hangs limp from my shoulder. Slowly, I make my way back through the crowd. Where to look for Dwight? I walk to the small square where I left him and glance around the outdoor tables of the café. Out of the corner of my eye I catch sight of my beloved. He is leaning against the other entrance to the café, a cappuccino cup in his hand, and watching the festivities.

I sidle up to him without a word, curl my arm around his waist, and gently lower my head upon his shoulder.

Today I don't feel like going anywhere. I'm sitting in front of Noemi's house in Maridiana, the alpaca farm outside Umbertide. It's a short drive over the hills from Cortona, so yesterday we decided on the spur of the moment to stop by and see our friends Gianni and Noemi.

No one is up yet, and I'm sitting alone, soaking up the fresh morning sun. My eyes are imprinted with the spectacular view of hills and pastures, fields and forests. Last October we were here searching for a house. That was the beginning of our Italian odyssey—only seven months ago, but it feels like years. Then, the weather had turned cloudy and rainy immediately upon our arrival. Now, however, I am basking in the sun (although a part of me is on guard for some unexpected storm), and can't get enough of the view.

Noemi comes out of the house carrying a tray with *café latte*, homemade apricot jam, ricotta cheese, and fresh eggs from local chickens. Following Noemi, Dwight staggers out, groggy from a long sleep. I look at Noemi smiling, at the tray, at the table she set up, and feel so grateful for our friendship. I want to savor this moment of peace and beauty. I'm almost tempted to succumb to a cliché and emphatically declare *la dolce vita*, but luckily don't. Because in the next moment Noemi tells us that after breakfast she has to go to the office and finish some work.

"But it's Sunday!" I exclaim.

"*Si, certo,*" she smiles. "But there is work to be done. Sunday is the best time because it's quiet."

I only sigh, but say nothing.

After breakfast Dwight retires too. He wants to relax upstairs. Alone again, I sit quietly and close my eyes. Yesterday's events come to mind, and I wonder if that past life had really taken place in Cortona. As I sift through my memories and emotions, my curiosity grows. I can't resist; I reach for my pendulum and start asking questions. The answers come readily and clearly, as if some invisible force is moving the pendulum. And no, the flashback I had yesterday did not happen in Cortona. But where ... in Florence? No. In Rome? No. Somewhere in Tuscany? Yes. Have I been in that city? Yes. Is it Siena? Yes. I wonder how that life ended. Without asking the pendulum, I receive a strong impression that I died in childbirth.

I feel the urge to check all the other memories I had of my previous lives, memories that surfaced at various times and circumstances in Rome, in Florence, in Egypt, in Santa Barbara. The answers flow, precise and definite, and I begin to assemble a greater picture, a mosaic of my Soul's wanderings.

"What are you doing?"

I jump in my chair and turn to see Dwight. He has sneaked up on me.

"You were supposed to be resting. What are *you* doing here?" I shoot back.

"Oh, well, I couldn't sleep, so I thought I may as well enjoy the view and the sun. So, what have you been doing?" Dwight repeats, eyeing curiously my pendulum and the open journal.

"Well, er ... I've been just checking, you know... about my memories of past lives."

"What about them?"

"Well, when they happened, where exactly, you know, er, more in detail...."

Dwight doesn't say anything, just makes a little hum. I know that hum very well. It's Dwight's way of expressing his disagreement. He never says it straightforwardly as I do, just makes that little hum.

"What...?" I look up at him and raise my brows.

He seats himself across from me and looks around. He's still not saying anything.

"WELLL...?"

"Last time I tried to talk to you about this, you weren't ready to listen. You wanted to 'see every facet of the diamond.'"

"Gosh, what good memory you have!" I laugh stiffly. "All right, I'm ready now."

His face lights up. "Oh, good. Then you'll listen to what I have to say." He slides the chair forward, his back erect, and begins:

"I told you back then not to get too caught up in the business of past lives. I know, you want to free yourself from karmic ties. But you won't do it by ferreting through past lives like you're doing now." His chin juts toward my pendulum. "That's tricky. You may pick up memories that don't belong to you, but to people you were involved with. Or you may pick up the collective emotions. Or even be misled by mischievous spirits. Anything can happen on the astral plane. That's why it's best not to fiddle with it."

"But don't you free yourself when you resolve unfinished business from past lives?" I ask, still not giving up.

"Of course you do. But you're not going to resolve it by knowing the details of an incarnation. No. The way you do it is by overcoming the energy patterns of emotions and thoughts from that particular incarnation. Remember what Kostas said—what's important is what you are *now*, what you have become because of *all* your incarnations." As he's saying this, Dwight is tapping his knuckles on the table, as if to hammer these words into my head.

No need for that, because I do remember Kostas' admonitions about past life curiosity. He absolutely refused to answer any questions about past lives. "It will not help you now," he'd boom in his firm, loud voice, "to know what you were in the past. It can even harm you. It can distract you from where you need to go. It can trap you in the glamour of your past glory. Or cripple you with the guilt of your past misdeeds."

"Yes, exactly." Dwight beams, as I repeat Kostas' words. "Ultimately, you will free yourself from karma by not having personal desires, as I said before. Buddhism teaches the same: desires are the cause of our suffering. If you don't satisfy a desire, you'll be unhappy; if you do satisfy it, there will be another one to replace it, and you'll be unhappy again—"

"Oh, wait, I get it! Desires are like precious stones in a cave!"

"What do you mean?" Dwight looks at me, confused.

"I've just remembered a folktale from my country about a man who stumbled upon a magic cave. It's pitch dark inside and he feels a lot of pebbles under his feet but can't see a thing. Then a voice says: 'If you take some, you'll be sorry; if you don't take any, you'll be sorry.' The man decides to take a few. When he came out, he realized those pebbles were precious stones and was sorry he didn't take more. But he couldn't go back."

Dwight laughs. "Great story and even better analogy. So, either way you look, it's a lose—lose situation." He leans toward me and interlocks his fingers on the table. "On the other hand, if you don't long for anything, there is nothing to bring you back to this world, and you'll be free from the wheel of incarnation. Desires are chains that bind you to the wheel. No desires means freedom from incarnation. Granted, you still can and *will* be coming here, but it would be to help others, to serve, and not to fulfill desires and create new ones.

"Take another analogy," he adds after a moment since I'm not saying anything. "You're imprisoned in a house that has many rooms. There are lots of pictures hanging on the walls, covering the openings. If you manage to remove a picture, you can see through to the outside. Well, removing pictures is your working with past lives. Every time you work out an incarnation, you remove one picture, a picture of that particular life, and you see more of the outside, that is to say, of the Reality. But you will still be trapped in the house and even create new pictures! However, if you stop generating desires, not only the pictures, but the walls, the *entire house* will collapse, and you'll be liberated. Because desires are the mortar that binds the walls together."

Dwight stops talking and looks at me. I know he's trying to determine if I got this and whether he should find yet another way to explain it. I must admit, I feel as though an arrow has hit a spot in me. I look at my pendulum, then at the paper with the long list of incarnations—dubious incarnations!—dates and scenarios. What for? What's the purpose of it? Just to quench my curiosity? I'm not resolving anything here. I'm creating a bubble of a big illusion. I've entangled myself in a glamour.

I lean back in my chair and look at Dwight. "I think I got it," I say slowly.

A spark flashes in his eyes, a spark of satisfaction. "I knew you would," he says. "Just sometimes you can be stubborn, perverse."

"Why perverse?" I protest.

"Because you go against your own better judgment, against what you know deep down."

"Yes, that's true," I admit. "But I do have a question."

"Of course you do. Go ahead."

"That evening in the shower, when my Teacher appeared, I had a glimpse of that desireless state. Then it was so clear and I was so much *there*. But it just doesn't last. Seems like I'm back where I was before—"

"Oh no, you're not," Dwight says firmly. "You had a taste of Higher Reality, a taste of what it feels to live as a Soul. Don't forget that. Maybe you feel you're back where you were before, but it's not a circle. It's a spiral. And you always arrive at a higher place, you follow?"

"All right, I can see that. But still, in everyday life, how do you live without desires? I mean, every morning we wake up with some desire in mind, even as trivial as what we want for breakfast, or what we want to do—"

"I wasn't talking about that. Sure, you have desires about your everyday life. But those desires come from the body to shape your day-to-day existence, to let you know what the body needs. I was talking about desires of the personality. For example, to have a nice pair of shoes (Dwight makes a significant pause here, but I ignore his jibe), or a bigger house, or social status—"

"Or a faster car..." I retort just to get even, knowing Dwight's weakness for race cars.

"Okay," he laughs. "You got the point. So, when those desires, through their intensity, create grooves in your emotional body—you know like the old-fashioned records—these grooves, in turn, influence your present *and* future lives. You simply slip into them because that's the line of least resistance."

"So, then, are there desires of the Soul?"

"Yes and no." Dwight pauses. "The Soul doesn't have desires in the way we understand that word. It has *intent*. But we feel the intent of the Soul as higher desires and aspirations, because that's how your emotional body translates the Soul's intent. That's what James Hillman refers to as the 'Soul's calling.' That's what you've been trying to find all this time."

Dwight now looks me in the eye and says slowly, "That's why we came to Italy. It was your Soul's intent."

I turn my gaze away from Dwight and for a moment remain silent. *Yes, that was my Soul's intent. I followed it. But ... I also thought that my Soul's intent was that we settle down and I write a book. And that just didn't happen. Or, if not that, then at least to find out what I should be doing in life. I STILL DON'T KNOW!*

I feel a lump in my throat. *We can't stay here forever. We have to think about going back to "normal" life, finding a job and living just like everybody else.* My throat feels even tighter. *Why haven't I tried harder to write a book? And, come to think of it, was that my Soul's intent or the desire of my personality?*

"But how can you tell," I finally voice my thoughts, "that what you desire is coming from the Soul and not from the personality?"

"Ah, that's a good question," Dwight says with an expression of I've-been-waiting-all-this-time-for-you-to-ask-that. "It's perhaps the most important question on the Path." He pauses to give more significance to what he's about to say.

"It would have to do with the motives, your Second Fundamental. Which, by the way, you haven't been practicing much." He tilts his head in a reproachful sort of way.

"So always ask yourself," he continues, "who wants this—the personality or the Soul? The personality's desires have to do with the good for yourself, satisfying your ambition, providing for your comfort and security, or just simply enjoying the good life. They churn in the solar plexus region. The Soul's intent, on the other hand, which we feel as higher desires or a calling, surges from within the heart and always has to do with the good for all—how you can help, serve, contribute. Does this help?"

"It does. It's very clear when you say it. I understand it, I know deep down it's true. I know that's where I'm headed. It's just...."

"Just what?"

"Well, it's just difficult to apply it. I mean it's easy to recognize a personality desire like, say, I so much want my book to sell because I want to be famous or to make money. But when you have a 'good' desire, so to speak, then it's so much more difficult. Like my desire for views and quiet, that's basically a good desire, isn't it? But I'm not really sure who wants that: I as the personality or I as the Soul. Or a desire that has to do with helping others, how can you know for sure that there isn't also a selfish motivation to make yourself feel good?"

Dwight doesn't answer right away. He's stroking his chin in a manner of that's-a-difficult-question-to-answer. Finally, he replies, "Frequently, there is a mixture of both, and that's perfectly all right. In fact, that's how you begin. For example, your desire to help others is at first mixed with your personal desire for recognition. But gradually, you sift your personal desires through the sieve of the Higher Will, until only the desires motivated by Soul's intent remain. Does it make sense?"

"It does. But again, when it comes to applying it...."

"Of course, of course, that's the most difficult part!" Dwight throws his arms up in the air, laughing. "That's where everybody struggles ... because nobody is perfect." He leans over the table and pats my hand. "Don't worry about that. You try, you do your best, you make mistakes, and you learn. That's how you grow."

I wince. Yes, but I don't want to make mistakes anymore. I'm so horrified of making mistakes. I don't have the strength to start all over again, to stumble, to suffer ... oh, no, I don't want that anymore!

We fall silent. For a while we're just sitting quietly in the stillness of the sun and the soft murmur of budding life around us. An occasional bird chirps and flits above us, a harbinger cicada clicks, insects rustle in the grass, and I can almost hear leaves grow and flowers blossom. Green is everywhere. Life is everywhere. I get up and walk to the meadow. The grass is lush and inviting. I stretch out on my back and pass my fingers through it as if through my lover's hair. I love every facet of life around me. The unbroken vault of blue above me, the warm sun on my body, a breath of wind on my face, the living earth underneath, the peace of a Moment out of Time.

After a while I get up and walk to a linden tree. I lean against its trunk and look at the valley. Balance. The whole world seems in perfect balance at this moment. This must be the happiness of the Soul. I close my eyes. I feel as if I'm in a doorway: behind me, the house with many pictures, the house of my earthly lives. In front of me—freedom, the liberating freedom of my true home, the Reality. I'm standing in that imaginary doorway between two worlds, suspended in time and strangely motionless. I know I have to take a step if I want to free myself.

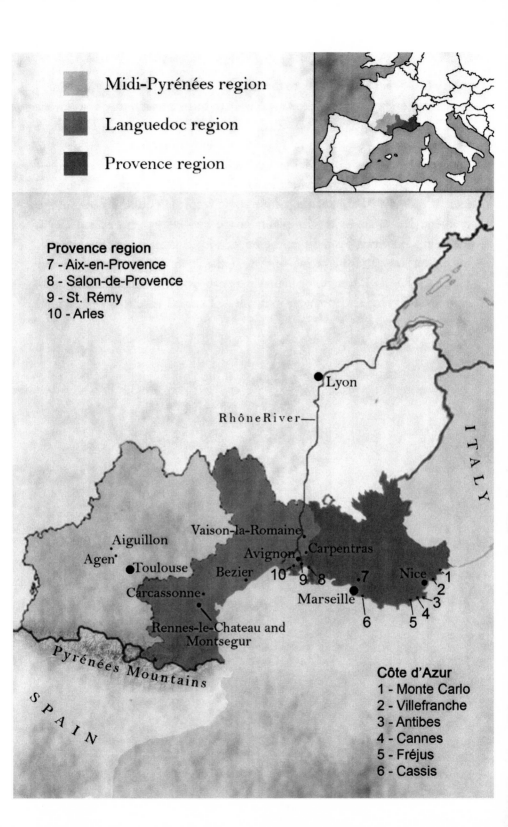

Midi-Pyrénées region

Languedoc region

Provence region

Provence region
7 - Aix-en-Provence
8 - Salon-de-Provence
9 - St. Rémy
10 - Arles

Lyon

RhôneRiver—

ITALY

Aiguillon

Vaison-la-Romaine

Agen

Avignon   Carpentras

Toulouse   Bezier   10 9 8   7   Nice   1

Carcassonne   Marseille   2

3

Rennes-le-Chateau and   6   5   4
Montsegur

Pyrénées Mountains

SPAIN

Côte d'Azur
1 - Monte Carlo
2 - Villefranche
3 - Antibes
4 - Cannes
5 - Fréjus
6 - Cassis

PART 6

SOUTHERN FRANCE:

PRISONERS

CHAPTER 24

VILLEFRANCHE:
COMING FULL CIRCLE

From Dwight's point of view, Italy was my journey, the purpose of which, in his words, was "to work out my karma." It was my Guidance that took us to Italy and led us through many trials, but it is Dwight's life work—revealed to him through a book—that is taking us to France now, at the beginning of June (notice, it's not September!).

Before I left for New Mexico to explore the possibilities of our settling there, I'd bought Dwight a book for his birthday—*The Cathars and the Albigensian Crusade*. The Albigensian, or Cathar, movement (from Greek *katharos*, "pure") was a variant of Christianity that flourished in the South of France from the twelfth to fourteenth century, and embraced a return to the original teachings of Jesus. Since his youth, Dwight identified with the direct and personal faith of the Cathars that rejected the corruption of the Church, as well as with their suffering during genocidal extermination under the Crusade and the Inquisition.

While Dwight was soaring on the wings of insights that the book inspired in him, I, on the other side of the world, struggled in the throes of anguish over the "what next?" question. Santa Fe was expensive and overcrowded with PhD graduates who waited tables or volunteered in galleries just to get their foot in the door. The job market was slim. To my great disappointment, the contact I had at St. John's College, where I intended to apply for a teaching position, had retired! No doors opened at Santa Fe. No peep from the Guidance.

Then, during my visit with our psychic friend Liana in Colorado, Dwight called from Rome. "I got a strong impression from my Soul where we should go next," he announced with a discernible tremor in his voice. "I think we should move to Provence!" *Provence? That came as a surprise...* "It's my new task," Dwight explained, "to cleanse the energy of that area from all the religious massacres inflicted by the Catholic Church. You know, reactivating the energy grid where it's blocked and raising the frequency of the land, similar to what I did in Italy." Then he added in a mellow voice, "And you literally put the answers into my hand by giving me that book."

That's why, in the first week of June, we are crossing the border into France. Finally, we have a new purpose; this is Dwight's journey now, and I'm going for a fun ride. Much later, we'd both smile at how little we knew at the time, and how far I was from having a "fun ride."

But France is also Dwight's journey for another reason: France was actually Dwight's home in the past. For nine years he lived in Paris, Poitiers, and Orleans, studied and raced sports cars, taught at an American military base, and took care of a widow's collection of classic cars while living in a chateau in Moutiers.

We'll begin our French journey at Villefranche, a small town only eleven miles away from the border. Dwight wants to show me where, half a century ago, he boarded the Dona Betta—a British ship that smuggled cigarettes from Morocco to Italy—as her first officer. When Dwight first told me this story, I stared at him goggle-eyed; I tried hard to connect his distinguished appearance with such a shady profession. But it was a very conscious means to heal tuberculosis he'd contracted as an undernourished student in an unheated room in Paris in the middle of winter. "Look at it this way," he said. "I was spending my time in the sun and eating very well. That is a proven cure for TB. And I had a great adventure as well!"

After we leave the border behind, Dwight decides to take the upper Corniche road that snakes high above the coast so that I can enjoy the views. "Gorgeous views," he adds with a smile that sets on his face whenever he does something to please me. My gaze is riveted at the horizon, at the famous azure blue sea; the blue is etched in my eyes. Date palms spread their branches over flaming bushes of bougainvillea below us. Thick layers of rosemary, lemon geranium, myrtle, and mimosa line the road.

"I used to drive my bike down there, along the low Corniche." He motions to the road that follows the coast. "Every night I'd go to the Casino in Monte Carlo. It was so much fun."

"You gambled every night?" I ask, amused.

"Uh-huh." He nods with a mischievous expression. "But I'd stop after I'd win. I made just enough money to live on."

"And you never lost any money?"

"Never. Because I knew when to stop."

I'm looking now at Monte Carlo glistening below us, white high-rises packed tightly next to one another. I love the whiteness of the buildings and the whiteness of the boats that dot the blue cloth of the sea. From up here the city looks like a huge flock of seagulls that have all landed at the same time and are huddling together.

When we descend to the harbor of Villefranche, we find that the spirit of the fishermen's village is still present, but the town has been spruced up for tourists. The houses that line the port are painted in different shades of orange and yellow—apricot, peach, pumpkin, cream, lemon, honey—with green and blue shutters like icing decorations on cupcakes. As we walk along the harbor, Dwight looks left and right, his eyes darting from house to house, from boat to boat. His steps are light, and he exudes a youthful vigor, as if any moment he could jump on a motorcycle and race off to Monte Carlo. He stops and touches my shoulder, pointing to a restaurant on the right. "It's still here!" he exclaims. "Mère Germaine ... this is where I used to eat all the time." His whole face beams. "We'd dock the ship on the other end of the harbor and spend the whole winter here."

"And you weren't afraid that you might get caught?"

"It wasn't that dangerous, really," replies Dwight, "until the captain started to drink more and more, and veer off the safe course. We would miss the police patrol just by a hair's breadth. That's when I thought it was getting to be dicey. My intuition was sending me signals. So this is what I decided to do: I would take a newspaper, open it at random and, without looking, point to a word. Whatever that word was, it would decide whether I'd stay or leave."

"Wow, that was dicey too!"

"Yes, but that's how my Guidance worked," Dwight replied. "So I opened the newspaper and put my finger randomly down on the page, then opened my eyes. My index finger was resting just below the printed word *danger*. That was it. I packed my bags and left as soon as we arrived back in Italy. But my friend the British journalist, who actually got me that job, stayed. On their next trip to France, the captain was so drunk he set course straight for the patrol. Everybody was arrested. And my friend spent a year in jail."

"It's amazing how you were always protected and taken care of," I muse.

"Well, doesn't it work that way? You're taken care of when you're on the right track—doing what your Soul wants you to do."

"Yeah … right," I laugh, looking at him as if he's pulling my leg. "And your Soul wanted you to gamble and smuggle, right?"

Now Dwight starts to laugh. "In a way," he replies, then adds seriously, "Actually, it wanted me to experience life. To be fully, completely alive."

"Always on the edge?"

"Always on the edge," he confirms.

We've come to the other end of the harbor, and Dwight is inspecting the boats docked here. His eyes are flashing with memories. I hear about his other adventures in France: befriending a communist doctor-mayor who performed a breast job on Marlene Dietrich; becoming the confidant of a high-class courtesan who gave Dwight her apartment in Paris and introduced him into high society. I look at his animated face, the glow in his eyes, the expression of spry determination. In fact, Dwight is so vibrant that I catch myself thinking how easily I could fall in love with *that* Dwight—the rebellious, fearless, nonconformist, dashing young Dwight I knew only from pictures and stories. Would the present Dwight be jealous, I wonder?

"So here I am," he concludes, "after fifty years of searching, of discovering who I am, back to Villefranche … come full circle for a new beginning, a new cycle of growth. But this time with you, my muse." He turns to me and embraces me strongly, almost passionately. "You taught me so much," he says.

"And you taught me so much more!" I reply, burying my face in his neck.

With his hands on my shoulders, Dwight moves me away, looks into my eyes, then adds, "That's how it should be in a spiritual partnership—you help each other grow, so you become the best you can be."

In perfect harmony, hand in hand, we walk now toward our hotel, which, perfectly appropriately is called "Welcome." The hotel is small and charming, tucked among the front houses that flank the harbor. From our balcony on the top floor, we have a sweeping view of the Bay of Villefranche. It is the deepest natural port on the Mediterranean Sea, bordered by Cape Ferrat on one side and Cape Nice on the other. As I'm soaking in the view, I also steal glances at Dwight, who is holding onto the balcony railing as if it were a rail of a ship. There is something victorious in the way he surveys the port, or perhaps something of a general who is preparing for the next battle.

"So, we begin tomorrow," he says in a solemn voice, lowering his gaze down to a small chapel right across from the hotel—St. Peter's chapel.

St. Peter's is not an ordinary chapel. It was decorated by Jean Cocteau, the famous French writer, poet, painter, playwright, and cinematographer who was also, speculation goes, a Grand Master of the Priory of Sion. (The Priory of Sion was allegedly the sister organization of the Knights Templar, and, unlike the Templars, continues to exist to this day.) While working on the chapel, Cocteau lived in this very hotel, and I like to imagine that he was sitting maybe on this very same balcony where I'm sitting now, sketching the scenes for the enigmatic murals that adorn the church. When I was a student, Cocteau was one of my favorite modern French artists. But I didn't know then there was this other side to him, the esoteric side.

So we'll begin from the end—the twentieth-century hints that point to a much older, controversial organization: the Knights Templar. Both Dwight and I are drawn to this secretive Order of warrior-monks that wielded its power in twelfth and thirteenth-century Europe. We want to follow their trail because they were closely, if clandestinely, connected with the Cathar unorthodoxy. (I won't be using the term "heresy," because in my opinion Cathar beliefs were closer to the original teachings of Jesus than is the Catholic dogma. And besides, from whose point of view is a teaching proclaimed a heresy?)

"But first things first," says Dwight in a serious voice. "Dinner."

I've been so much looking forward to this moment—my initiation into French cuisine, as Dwight had promised so many times while we were still in Italy. "You don't know what good food is until you eat in France," he declared. "And not everywhere; only in the best of the best." That is, in the restaurants recommended by two gastronomic Bibles, *Red Michelin Guide* and *Gault Millau*. But there is no need to consult the authorities about eating in Villefranche. Mère Germaine is still here.

So we present ourselves rather early at the still empty restaurant. I'm strangely excited, as if I'm going to learn how to eat for the first time.

"You actually will, you actually will," Dwight repeats, nodding with total self-assurance. "Eating is a serious business in France. It's a ritual."

I would learn how right he was when a couple of months later, we became residents of a village in Provence. At half-past noon, outdoor life would stop. The streets would swiftly empty, as if a siren had warned of an air attack. Everyone would retreat into kitchens, dining rooms, or restaurants, and for the next two hours life would be suspended. At times, I really liked that custom, but at other times I'd be annoyed, especially when I didn't manage to finish my errands first.

But right now, seated here at Mère Germaine, Dwight introduces me to the French Menu. I learn that ordering à la carte is not very popular in France, mostly because the meal ends up costing much more than when you choose one of the already-assembled menus.

"Don't look at the prices," Dwight says, reading my thoughts. "This is your first meal. Order whatever you want. But I do suggest you order one of the *pris fixe* menus," he adds as an after-thought. "They know what they're doing. They make the best combinations."

"What about Aldo's—"

My question remains unfinished because Dwight immediately waves his hand. "When in Rome, do as the Romans do," he pronounces. "We're going to eat as the French do."

Thank goodness Dwight's condition has improved greatly over the past months. His asthma has almost retreated, his allergies are on the ebb, and his heart hasn't been acting up at all lately. And thank goodness I'm over the Candida now. Thank goodness, I say, because I don't know how else we would have been able to put away all the cream and butter and wine and *tartes* and mousses that we did. And thank goodness I'm no longer in my vegetarian phase either, because I would have missed out on the great life experience that is French cuisine.

"This is our first romantic evening since Cyprus, do you realize that?" I ask in a soft voice, my gaze lost in the pastel shades of a demure sunset.

"Romantic, how's that?" Dwight lifts his head and swivels it around quickly, as if looking for props that will unmistakably say "romantic."

I laugh. "You're a hopeless pupil! Even after all these years, I haven't managed to train you to notice romantic settings and occasions."

Dwight reaches for my hand in a gesture of apology. "Don't give up, please."

"All right, let's go over it again. Look around—an elegant restaurant, perfect food, a June evening on the French Riviera, a lovely sunset—what else do you need?"

Dwight looks around, following my words and nodding (as if to say, "Oh, yes, I forgot about that"), then turns to me and replies child-like, "A kiss?"

"That's much better!" I smile at him. "Maybe there is still some hope, after all."

I prop myself up and lean halfway over the table, and Dwight leans over the other half. We meet in the middle and our lips join, and through our lips, our hearts.

"May it last forever and ever," he says.

"May it last forever and ever," I repeat.

We smile at each other in a conspiring manner. This has become our anthem from the early days of our relationship when we were so much in love (and so openly), that a woman approached our table in a restaurant in Taos and addressed us with these words, as if giving us a blessing: "May it last forever and ever!"

The first morning in France begins with a deep hoot. *An animal?* My reptilian brain shoots an alarm signal through the last layers of my interrupted sleep. I look at the clock—it's only 6:00! The hooting starts again, this time longer. Now I recognize a ship's warning of approach. It must be one of the cruise ships Dwight told me about last night. I stumble out of bed and onto the balcony. Oh, my God—it's a beast! Like a colossal pre-historic animal bringing sounds of the savannah to the French Riviera.

With this gargantuan greeting, the port below comes to life. The other boats, like small game, begin to wriggle and squirm. Some of them make the first morning coughs and spits of a cold engine and begin to putter through the tangle of other boats. No chance of getting back to sleep, I sigh. So I reach for the book I gave Dwight for his birthday—the book that brought us to France—and start leafing through the chapters. As I read the names of towns, I'm mesmerized by certain combinations of letters and the sounds they produce: Quéribus, Peyrepertuse, Rodèz, Rhedae, Montauban, Moissac ... these names sound so familiar to me. But when I open the page with the genealogy of ruling families in the Languedoc area, my whole body shivers as I read the name: Raimond-Roger Trencavel. Like a secret combination that unlocks the safe, these letters when pronounced in French make a series of clicks in the subterranean depths of my psyche, and a new feeling seeps up from those regions.

Liana's words come to mind, something she told me while she read the energy formations around me during my visit. She saw me as a holy woman of the Cathars, sitting by a fountain in a cobblestoned village. "I" was talking calmly to the agitated villagers that had gathered around. My mission was to retrieve the voice that brings peace and unity and to convey the simple truth of love. Looking past me, she concluded, "And that voice ... you'll find it again through creativity, through writing. This is how you will touch and inspire people. You have to be a translator of the energy that hasn't been fully expressed so far."

The fountain in a cobblestoned village … I wonder where it is … maybe I'll find that village and retrieve my voice … and hopefully dislodge the lid I'd placed on my creativity that distant day in Paris when I stood on Le Pont des Arts—

"You're up already?" Dwight's voice suddenly rings above my head.

I turn, startled, and the book falls down. "The cruise monster," I say, jutting my chin toward the port.

"I told you … they arrive early and dock here for the day. I bet the tourist cargo has already been transported to Nice." For a few seconds he examines the immense cruise ship whose size looks oddly out of proportion in this small harbor, then adds briskly, "Let's have breakfast."

My first French breakfast, I shiver delectably in anticipation of scrumptious and crispy croissants. We decide to find a good bakery, buy pastry there, then enjoy it with *café-crème*, the French version of cappuccino.

We plunge into the *pénombre* (I love the sound of this word that means "half-light" or "semi-darkness," depending on how you like to look at things), which reigns in the warren of streets behind the port. Dwight takes me through La Rue Obscure (The Dark Street), the passageway that crawls underneath the front houses. This is where Cocteau filmed scenes for *The Testament of Orpheus*. La Rue Obscure is the oldest street in Villefranche, dating back to the mid-thirteenth century. We climb the dank, slippery, stone steps, turn left, then right, and spot a sign for a bakery.

In the months ahead, I'll grow to like French bakeries—*boulangeries*—best of all. The comforting, homey smell of freshly baked bread, the rows of neatly arranged plain croissants, chocolate croissants, almond croissants, melt-in-your-mouth brioches, flaky *palmiers*, delicate *madeleines* (immortalized by Proust in his *Chronicle of Lost Time*), and of course, ubiquitous baguettes stacked up like timber in imposing mounds or sticking erect out of deep bins like soldiers, would all give me an inexplicable sense of well-being.

The cafés in the square above Cocteau's chapel are mostly empty. The yellow umbrellas hover over the tables like huge birds. We choose a table at the end of the square, looking down on the chapel. Dwight disappears and comes back with the *Herald Tribune*.

"Don't tell me you're going to—" I sputter through my sip of *café crème*. "The first morning in France and you'll read the paper?"

"Just the stock market report," Dwight says calmly, taking off his glasses, then burying his head in the pages.

I don't like the clicking noises he makes, accompanied by little twitches of his left shoulder. "What's the situation?" I can't hold in my curiosity any longer.

"Not good," he simply says. "Our biggest stock has dropped down."

No, not good.

"Have to keep an eye on it more frequently," Dwight concludes and puts down the paper. "Now, let's enjoy...."

Cocteau's chapel, which we visit right after breakfast, is an astonishing work of art. Even to a layperson's eye, it is obvious that his murals are laden with symbolism. The two tall candle-holders with facial traits and wide-open eyes, (the Candlesticks of the Apocalypse, as Cocteau called them), flank the entrance door from the inside, while many other eyes, big and small, peer down from the walls. Figures of dancing gypsies, guitar players, and zodiacal signs are interspersed among the modern-looking figures of St. Peter and Jesus. All sorts of water creatures swim on the walls because the chapel is dedicated to St. Peter, the protector of fishermen. It's wild and enigmatic, this mixture of modern and religious. Cocteau's symbols allude to the Age of Aquarius, sacred geometry, Masonic rituals, the Jesus and Mary Magdalene saga. And almost hidden among many geometric figures are Templar crosses.

"If Cocteau really was the Grand Master," Dwight muses in a low voice, "why did he bother with this tiny chapel in an insignificant fishermen's village? I mean, it's obvious with the Templar church he decorated in London. But here? What's so special here?"

"Maybe somehow the location," I speculate, "or perhaps some Earth energies we're not aware of. "Or, maybe, he simply liked the place?" I add as we walk out, back into the sun and the glittering blue of the sea, but I'm not really convinced.

We leave the Côte d'Azur and head for Provence to meet friends of a good friend. Pierre and Monique, both respectable retired physicians, have restored a modest chateau in a village nestled under the wild beauty of Les Dentelles de Montmirail, an hour's drive north from Avignon.

Les Dentelles de Montmirail is a small but impressive chain of mountains, whose name means "lace-like admirable mountain." They were given this poetic name because of their dramatically jagged peaks that look so ferocious, as if ready to rip apart any cloud that dares to drop too low. I like the juxtaposition of their fierce look and the impression of delicate femininity their name suggests. Can something be delicately fierce? Or fiercely delicate? An interesting oxymoron. So these Lacy Mountains braid their spikes and crochet their sharp-edged ridges right above the village of Suzette. There is only one street in the village and a handful of houses, so we have no difficulty finding the Haour residence.

"*Bonjour, bienvenus,*" Pierre greets us in an amiable way, standing by the fence that nonchalantly surrounds the property. Flanking his thigh is a portly, hairy creature. I have a hard time telling its front from its back end, but logic says the dog is looking in the same direction as his master. Pierre helps us with the luggage, although I'm afraid to let him carry *my* suitcase. (No matter how many times I've tried, I've *never* managed to travel light.) He looks a bit frail, our host, with his white hair, short stature, and somewhat stooped shoulders, but behind that façade are a certain resilience and vigor that show when he speaks.

We've skipped over polite formalities and are now chatting in the living room as if we've been friends for years. Pierre is so cordial he doesn't even address us using the formal *vous*. I'm amazed. The French people I knew in my youth, when I used to spend my vacations at a friend's house in Paris, were much more formal and uptight. Dwight immediately takes to our new friend, who is a holistic doctor and closely follows cutting-edge scientific discoveries. The conversation naturally moves to the subject of energy, sacred sites, Cathars, and Templars.

"I have a book that might be of interest to you," Pierre says, then gets up and with short, spry steps walks to the *bibliothèque*—shelves with books that cover a whole wall in a niche off the living room—and starts to rummage through. The interior of the chateau has retained the original look; no plastering, no paint, no wall papers, just plain, cold, rough stone. With a little apprehension, I eye the stone stairs that lead up to the bedrooms. They are so uneven and worn slick (and slippery) by centuries of use that I fear Dwight might tumble down.

Pierre now returns with a book and hands it to Dwight, whose eyes immediately light up: it's a book on Templar sites in France, with detailed maps.

"If you're going to follow the Templar trail, you'll need this book," says our new friend. "There are many, *many*, Templar sites in France, more so than in any other country. But the greatest number, in fact one third of all estates that the Templars owned, were in Languedoc."

"The land of the Cathars," says Dwight.

Pierre nods. "The land of sorrow," he says gravely.

"But before you head there," he adds in a lighter tone, "you should visit

Glanum. If you're interested in sacred sites and Earth energies, that's a place for you to explore."

When the following day Dwight and I approach the site of the seventh-century BC Celtic settlement, we feel shivers running up our spines. The natural setting of ancient Glanum is disturbingly beautiful. I feel a mixture of awe before the majesty of the Alpilles Mountains that tower over the ancient ruins and a strange feeling of well-being. Scattered columns rise like a fragment of Greece under the skies of Provence, confusing my brain. It's as if many different feelings are stirred up in my body, clashing like ocean waves moved by different currents. In less poetic terms, it's as if I'm in the middle of a strong magnetic field, and both poles are exerting a pull on my senses, which makes me feel disoriented. One thing is certain—this was, and *still* is, a sacred site. It doesn't matter that the original settlement built by the Glanici, the native Celtic-Ligurian tribe, was destroyed and taken over by the Romans. The feeling of sacredness still permeates the air.

There is more than one source of Glanum's sacred energy. For one thing, the town was positioned at the foot of a natural pass through the mountain range that stretches in an east-west direction. The buildings and temples were built along a north-south orientation, roughly the direction of the path that cuts through the jagged peaks. If the range were a dam for a lake, and this pass a sluice that was suddenly opened, imagine the power of the water that would gush through it. There is something of that feeling in Glanum—a feeling of an energy thoroughfare.

For another thing, the capital of the Glanici tribe grew around a spring that was renowned for its healing properties, and the town had many shrines dedicated to the Mothers of Glanum, ancient Earth goddesses. Springs were sacred to the Celts; they built all their shrines next to water sources.

And then there is the stone of Glanum. As Pierre had told us the day before, the stone in this area has special properties. It's soft when sculpted, but hardens with time as it is exposed to air, qualities that make it a perfect building material, easy to work with and weather-resistant.

"I haven't sensed a power spot of this magnitude since our visit to Epidaurus," I tell Dwight excitedly as I descend from the original Celtic sanctuary on the nearby mound. "It's so powerful yet so nurturing. What an unusual mixture."

"Not unusual, just natural," says Dwight, while we stroll among the ruins.

"What do you mean?"

"Well, just look at the setting … the mountains are very masculine, aren't they? And the spring is feminine. So you have a natural blend of two opposite qualities—yin and yang." Dwight stops and grates the surface of the stone with his fingernail. "Limestone," he pronounces.

"So? …"

"Didn't we read that limestone has feminine energy? It's formed by the sedimentary action of water, as opposed to 'masculine' stones, such as granite and basalt, which are of volcanic origin." Dwight is referring to the writings of Freddy Silva, who delineates seven principles of sacred sites, stone being one of them.

We've come to the café that offers a view of the whole site all the way up to the Alpilles Mountains. Tomorrow, we're going to visit St. Rémy, known as the gateway to the Alpilles. In that little town just north of the mountain range was born, if not the greatest alchemist and seer of Europe, then certainly the most famous one—Nostradamus. While I was still a little girl, my father bought a leather-bound edition of Nostradamus' predictions and occasionally read excerpts to me. I wonder if the Earth energies at St. Rémy had something to do with Nostradamus' exceptional clairvoyant abilities.

"So where do you want to start your work?" I ask Dwight after we seat ourselves.

He doesn't answer right away, only strokes his chin with short movements, looking at the mountains in the distance. I call this pose of Dwight's—*Penseur* (Thinker), after the famous sculpture by Rodin, except that unlike Rodin's thinker who is looking down, Dwight is always looking up, head slightly cocked back, as if to take in the whole future.

"You have that book with you?" he finally asks. "The book that Pierre gave us?"

The bag I usually carry on our expeditions is, modestly put, massive. It doesn't have the slightest resemblance to a female purse. Inside are a portable office, a portable restaurant, and a portable emergency room all together. I rummage through these three compartments and produce the book. Dwight takes it with pronounced deliberation and opens it very slowly, his gaze flattened, as if he's not really watching what he's doing.

"Don't tell me…" I say in disbelief, "you're doing the newspaper thing from your smuggling stint?" I'm at the point of bursting into laughter.

He looks at the page, then at me, and shrugs. "Why not? If you're totally neutral and receptive, you'll get the answer."

I lean to look at the page he opened to. It shows Templar sites in former Gascogne, an area in the southwest of France. "Well ... where to? There are so many."

Dwight scans the map, glances at the text, then says, "Since we're sort of going backwards in time, maybe we should start with Agen. That's where the rumors began that eventually brought down the Templars."

CHAPTER 25

SOUTH OF FRANCE:
THE TEMPLAR TRAIL

/// "As with the sacred places, so with the murderous spots,'" Dwight quotes Henry Miller while we're walking around Agen, "'the record of events is written into the earth.'"

At first sight, Agen is just like other towns in the southwestern area of France: a well-preserved medieval nucleus surrounded by more recently built neighborhoods. But at the energetic level, the town feels as though a heavy cloud hovers above its roofs. We've just learned from a young Frenchmen, a specialist on Templar activities in Agen, that the area around this town was the epicenter of all major religious conflicts and wars in France: first of all, a campaign against the Templars which eventually led to their abolition in 1307; then the Hundred-Years' War, which broke out thirty years later between France and England; and finally, a century later, the protracted and gory war between Huguenots and Catholics—a long and sad history of bloodshed that began twenty miles from this small town in the Aquitaine region.

"No wonder," Dwight mutters while we walk to the post office, built over the destroyed Templar commandery.

"No wonder what?"

"No wonder I opened the Templar book to that page. See how my Guidance works?"

"I'm beginning to see, yes." And I'm finally beginning to understand Dwight's mission in the South of France: to draw forth the Earth energy where it's blocked and stabilize it where it's chaotic.

We stand in front of the modern building that takes up almost the entire block. Eight centuries ago there stood a huge compound, the main Templar

275

commandery for the whole region, where Knights were admitted and trained, where food was grown, where accommodation for travelers was offered, and where a treasury operated as a modern bank. And where the fall of the Templar Order began.

We stand and look, but have a hard time visualizing any of this. Dwight takes out his pendulum to check the energy. He walks slowly along the walls, shaking his head. The pendulum moves erratically, as if pummeled by invisible forces from all directions. Similarly, toward the end, the Knights were pummeled with grievous accusations of heretical beliefs and satanic rituals. Very odd, considering their title, the Knights of Christ, powerful defenders of Christianity for two hundred years.

Among many controversies that surround the Templars, one thing is certain: there is much more to this Order than just the story of the warrior-monks whose mission was to protect pilgrims on their route to Jerusalem. If anything, the whole history of the Knights Templar is strewn with mysteries and incongruities, even the exact year of their foundation, which may have occurred earlier than 1118, the date usually given. Led by Hugues de Payen, the Order began as a group of nine nobles who went to Jerusalem to protect the pilgrim routes within the Holy Land. Nine men, patrolling what is nowadays roughly the area of Israel, and for nine years? They must have been supermen to keep all that territory safe—and in their spare time. I say spare time, because most of the time they spent digging under the Temple of Solomon. When they finished their excavations, nine years later, they returned to Europe with their find. A treasure? Secret documents? Both? We'll never know for sure.

The full name of the new military-monastic organization was the Order of *Poor* Knights of Christ and the Temple of Solomon (and I emphasize the word "poor"). Yet they soon grew to be the major financial power of Europe, the first international bankers who invented the prototype of the credit card and banker's check, the Wall Street of medieval Europe. Travelers would get a "note of hand" from a Templar center in their town of origin, then cash it when they reached their destination. That way, they didn't have to carry money and risk being robbed en route. Templars also lent enormous sums to popes, kings, princes, and merchants. In fact, it could be shown how the Templars' commercial skills ultimately led to the development of capitalism! The financial system we now have, we owe to them—for better or for worse.

Only a couple of decades after the first nine Knights returned from Jerusalem (with a treasure!), a revolution in architecture happened—the Gothic style was *suddenly* born. The Templars initiated a building boom of cathedrals that were so radically different from anything built before and so technologically advanced that it would be, for example, as if present-day architects *suddenly* designed skyscrapers the height of Mt. Whitney. As documents show, the Templars were behind the formation of builders' and stonemasons' guilds, acting not only as major "developers" who provided finances, but also as master architects. They had both the means and the knowledge. The cathedrals of Amiens, Rouen, Reims, Bourges, Paris, Chartres, to mention a few, rose one after another, astonishing in their height and their feeling of lightness. Within only one century, 150 cathedrals and churches were erected!

With all their knowledge, wealth, and power, Templars were accountable to no one else but the Pope. Which meant they had more power than the King. This astonishing independence proved to be a double-edged sword. There are many speculations about the cause of their demise, but it is very plausible to assume that resentment and envy were behind the decision of the French King, Philip the Fair, to abolish the Order and seize all their property, especially when we know that he was heavily indebted to the Templars and had no means to pay back his debt.

So secret orders were dispatched from the throne and at dawn on Friday 13, 1307, the Templars were arrested in every corner of France *at the same time*. Which, again, is somewhat mystifying because the Templars were highly trained warriors, something like the Foreign Legion of the day, and they were rounded up by local policemen. It's almost as if they handed themselves over voluntarily, without any resistance. Meanwhile, their treasurer had managed to slip away (with all the coffers, to be sure), and the entire Templar fleet had disappeared without a trace. The legacy of that tragic day when the Templars met their demise survives in the common belief that Friday the 13th is an unlucky day.

For the following seven years, the imprisoned Knights were systematically tortured and forced to "confess" heresy and idolatry. Finally, the Grand Master of the Order, Jacques de Molay, was slowly roasted to death in front of Notre Dame Cathedral in Paris. (Incidentally, while turning on the spit, de Molay prophesied that both the King and the Pope would follow him within a year. Which indeed happened: they both died that same year.)

Since we really don't like the sad, heavy energy of Agen, and since there are many Templar sites in this area, we decide to set our base instead in a nearby small town called Aiguillon. Up until the fifteenth century, Aiguillon had commanded a position over the confluence of the Lot and Garonne rivers, which met there at a right angle. But then the rivers changed course, leaving the town stranded.

I like the quiet stillness of Aiguillon, so still that my breathing feels like a workout. The town is only a handful of miles away from Agen, but I feel as if we've come to the end of civilization. The only hotel is a charming, turn-of-the-century building, empty and quiet. Our room is upstairs, cozy with rustic furniture and an old-fashioned lacy bedspread. A little balcony overlooks the main square, also empty and quiet.

Something about the energy of this hotel, or maybe the whole town, fills me with memories of my childhood, of summers spent at my grandma's house in a town in southern Serbia. The house was old, with thick, thick walls, cherry-wood furniture, a massive dining table, the smell of solitude and dry sage, and the feeling of mystery in the shadowy corners full of forgotten memories. An oil-dip hung underneath the picture of St. John—the family saint-protector—the only contact with religion I ever had as a child. My grandmother cooked on a wood-burning stove, and we bathed in a tin trough outside, hiding behind a fence swathed by morning glory. There was no comfort, really, but I felt protected and safe unlike any other time in my life, tucked in the cocoon of my grandma's love. There was no television (not even a telephone), so I roamed behind the house, through a neighborhood of abandoned storage buildings and military barracks, and hopped along the dead-ending rails of the nearby train station. Every now and then trains would trundle through, rending the air with self-important shrieks. They carried passengers somewhere, to other cities and countries I imagined. As I caught glimpses of various faces through the windows, I amused myself imagining their life stories. I could stay by myself for hours, never bored.

All of this flashes through my mind as I look around this cozy room. A sudden flicker of nostalgia. But Dwight whisks me off, not leaving me any time to indulge in my memories (which I like to do).

Before we begin our time-travel visit to the medieval part of Aiguillon, we locate the tourist office. Over the weeks ahead, I'll learn that tourist information offices are very useful places for making contacts and getting valuable information. A woman *d'un certain age*, as the French delicately refer to a woman whose age is anywhere between forty and sixty, is the only employee in a spacious and welcoming room. As we inquire about the locations and regional history of the Templars, she shows growing signs of embarrassment. She has no answers. But her face lights up at the sight of a tall man in a suit who presents himself at the door.

"*Ah, Monsier le Maire,*" she fires at him with relief, "here are some questions for you."

The Mayor of Aiguillon, who has just walked in, to our delight happens to be a history professor and knows the answers to our questions. Not only that. He knows other historians who can be of help to us, and so we walk out with names and telephone numbers of new contacts. We're particularly happy that we have an introduction to call on a well-known specialist on the Cathars who lives in Albi.

"Doors are opening," Dwight comments, hardly able to restrain his excitement. "Finally."

Yes, I have to admit, it does feel good to be in the flow of synchronicity again, to be helped rather than hindered, as I felt I was in Italy.

We're getting used to this: wherever we go, we meet someone who gives us a piece of information that makes us change our plans and hotel reservations. I had roughly outlined our itinerary in my calendar when we left Suzette. But I had to cross out every single stop so far and cancel every hotel reservation. We're finding ourselves zigzagging through the South of France, following hints that sometimes send us in the opposite direction from where we wanted to go. It has become obvious that this really is Dwight's trip. He has become so one-pointed and determined that he exudes a quality of energy totally different from usual. Sometimes while he's driving I feel as though I'm sitting next to a missile, so great is the feeling of focused power around him. He has definitely turned into a man on a mission.

Since his work with the volcanoes in Sicily and southern Italy, Dwight has honed his sensitivity to the Earth's energies. It was in Aiguillon that he discovered he didn't really need the little pumice rock—"the charger," as he nicknamed it—given to him by our friend Andreas, the Ayurvedic doctor, who introduced Dwight to "ionization" in Cyprus. Initially, Dwight had used this rock to pass on the higher vibratory rate to the bedrock. By the process of entraining frequencies, the lesser charge would rise to meet the higher charge—

what Dwight called "tightening the spin radius of the electron." But in the little square of Aiguillon, Dwight made an accidental discovery. It was enough that he focused his intention on raising the spin and bored this intention into the stone. The effect was the same as when he used the charger stone.

"It wasn't the stone," Dwight said that evening, marveling, "but my *intention* that did the job!" His face was lit up by this sudden insight. "You realize what this means? The power of the human mind can alter the environment, just as it can alter the inner environment, our own bodies."

In the last town where we stopped, La Villedieu du Temple (there are many places in France whose linguistic heritage reflects their Templar past), there was no tourist office, so we went to the modern art gallery instead. The curator was obliging about finding us a book on the history of this area. It happened to be a Saturday afternoon when the libraries and bookstores were closed, so she took us herself to the author, who, amazingly, was willing to receive a visit at home by total strangers, and foreigners at that.

Monsieur Turzac was recovering from an attack of sciatica and he couldn't move much. So he told me to get refreshments from the kitchen, and soon I was serving tea and cookies as if it were my own home. How come we never met anyone in Italy in this way? What is different in France? Is it only our fluency in the language or are we really being guided on this trip to places where we normally wouldn't go? Because it was thanks to Monsieur Turzac that we found ourselves at Notre Dame de Livron—by "mistake."

When I got out of the car, I stood rooted to the spot for a good while. The place looked familiar somehow, as if I'd seen it before, no—as if I'd been there before! I surveyed six huge plane trees, three on each side of a forecourt that led to a small shrine with a white altar-stone shining in the sun. The morning light filtering through deep green foliage dappled the forecourt with bright, sparkling patches. The contrast between the light and the shadow was so sharp that it gave the space a two-dimensional feeling, as if the third dimension— depth—had been flattened. It looked magical; it felt magical.

It looked ... just like a place from a dream I'd once had, and right down to the tiniest detail!

I started to feel dizzy. The line between the real world and the dream world felt blurred. Have I walked into my dream? Or has my dream crept into the world of waking?

To the left was the chapel of Notre Dame de Délivrance. The energy inside was gentle, oh, so gentle ... *la douceur suprême*. The light, soft, seeping through the stained-glass windows. The figure of Notre Dame, bathed in red and yellow and blue light. Her posture, graceful. Her face, gentle, oh, so gentle. Her gaze cast down. For the first time in my life, I felt I could actually kneel and pray. Pray to be awash in this same gentleness, this same compassion, this boundless love and infinite peace. As if this little golden statue of a graceful woman shrouded by a veil had the power to forgive all atrocities, to appease all suffering, to soothe all pain, and to understand … everything. The true Mother of the world.

Behind the chapel there was a spring surging out of a cave and more openings in the hillside. A nun noiselessly slid out of an enclosure and walked toward us, as if she knew we were there. The little woman smiled at me with that same gentle, compassionate, forgiving smile of the statue. I smiled back. *"Bienvenus,"* she greeted us simply, looking at me with eyes calm like a mountain lake, in which I saw total surrender. Her hands were tucked behind the brown scapular of her habit, rounding up all of her, self-contained.

Just then Dwight ruptured the dreamy fabric that permeated the air. He asked if we were at the right place, the Templar church of Notre Dame de Livron. He must have been a little suspicious of the "templarness" of this sanctuary.

No, came the answer.

"I thought so," said Dwight. "We've made a mistake."

A mistake? I winced. *How can this be a mistake?*

The nun, we found out, belonged to the Carmelite order, and this monastery was a spiritual retreat. She waved at the openings that dotted the hillside. "Hermits," she explained.

What did I do in this place in my dream? Was I a hermit in a cave? And why am I here now?

"But there is a Templar chapel in the fields," the nun murmured. "It's near the village of Lacapelle Livron, where there is also a Templar church."

"Ah, that must be where the historian had sent us!" Dwight exclaimed. "We took the wrong Livron sign."

The nun's face assumed a Mona-Lisa smile.

CHAPTER 26

SOUTH OF FRANCE:

MYSTERIOUS PAST, SPOOKY PRESENT

The Templar chapel of Notre Dame des Graces stands small, lonely, and forsaken in the middle of a hilltop that surveys the rolling hills. As we're driving up the narrow country road, the rain starts. All along, we haven't passed any car, any living creature. We're completely alone in this remote corner, somewhere in the region of Midi Pyrénées. Because it's raining when we get to the Templar chapel, we sit in the car, waiting for the rain to stop. Through the blurry windshield we gaze at the old, weathered stone cross in front of the church and the equally weathered shrine behind. It's so perfectly isolated that I wonder why the church was built in such a solitary place. Monsieur Turzac had mentioned this chapel as a place with a mysterious reputation.

Dwight was immediately intrigued. "In what way?" he asked.

"There were rumors in this area," the historian said slowly, hesitating, "that something had been hidden there just before the dissolution of the Order. Something that was of great value to the Templars," he paused, then added in a low voice, "which they buried under the door."

Dwight and I both gaped at the historian, then looked at each other.

"Would that, perhaps, have to do with their devotion to Mary Magdalene?" Dwight inquired.

Monsieur Turzac looked at him as if deciding how much to say. "Perhaps," he uttered, lowering his voice even more, "her very remains. But I don't think they are still there," he added in a different voice. "Personally, I think they have been removed and hidden somewhere else."

Following the Templar trail in France is inseparable from following the cult of Mary Magdalene. For one thing, the whole area of southern France is steeped in Magdalenism. According to the legend, this is where Mary Magdalene escaped after the death of Jesus. She landed on the shores of Marseille, where she started preaching. The Basilica at Saint-Maximin-la-Sainte-Baume claims to possess her remains, since proven fake. Other churches have made similar claims, but the truth is, her remains have not been found—at least not officially.

The Knights Templar, too, gave a special allegiance to Magdalene. And that's another oddity about this organization. Although the Templars were officially called the Knights of Christ, all their cathedrals and many smaller churches were dedicated to Notre Dame. Except that, contrary to popular belief, the Lady whom the Templars venerated was not Mary the Mother—that was just a convenient cover—but Mary Magdalene or, as she is also known, Mary the Beloved of Jesus.

The rain has stopped and we crawl out of the fogged car. The air is brisk, smelling of grass and wet soil. The silence is unbroken; not a bird or an insect is to be heard. It's as if we have stepped into a sealed chamber.

"What a site!" Dwight exclaims, heading straight for the church.

I stay behind and look around. It is definitely imbued with power, this solitary place. It reminds me of an old, battered soldier who still stands guard and will do so until he drops dead. The weathered stone of the church has darkened with age and is covered with lichen. It has a feel of a place where magic has been wrought. Dwight is inspecting the wooden door, its sill definitely slanted.

"The ground could be hollow underneath," he says, dowsing the energy.

"But how can we know for sure that the door is not slanted simply because of the soil shifting?"

"Well we can't, obviously, unless we dig under the door. But you know, where rumors exist, there is usually a reason. Something must have gone on here, otherwise there wouldn't be rumors.

"And don't forget," Dwight adds after circling the chapel, "wherever Templars built churches, you can be sure those are power spots." Templars, it has been postulated, were keepers of the old knowledge of the Earth's energies. In fact, their first mission—to protect the pilgrim routes to Jerusalem—was really about making sure that the Earth energy channels remained open and functioning.

At that moment the shower starts again, an angry downpour, as if someone has ripped open a distended water bag right over our heads. I want to run for the car, but Dwight insists we take shelter at the other end of the church, where we're protected from the wind. But soon the wind is whipping up the rain with such force that we do have to run to the car—only to find that I had left my window rolled down, in the direction of the wind. Inside, everything is wet. I sit down in a puddle of water, and my jeans immediately get soaked.

After ten minutes, the sun comes out innocently, as if there never has been any downpour.

"See, I told you, this place has spells woven around it," I say testily. I don't have any spare clothes in the car, and wet jeans feel awfully unpleasant on my butt and thighs. "Whatever is hanging around here, it didn't like what you were doing."

"Mmm," is all Dwight says, as he turns on the engine and drives back to the village of Lacapelle Livron.

We enter a deserted street, sullen stone houses brooding on both sides. They look medieval, thirteenth century or older. Not a single soul. We park in front of the Templar church and walk inside. Empty. On a Sunday? The shadowy interior has an unpleasant feeling about it, like a cantankerous old man who doesn't want to be disturbed. Dwight is too busy dowsing to feel anything, but I definitely sense a presence in the gallery above the entrance. The sensation I'm getting comes close to what psychics would describe as ghosts. I sit in the last pew trying to meditate, but the cold is creeping into my feet from the stone floor and my wet jeans feel so clammy that soon I begin to shiver.

When we walk outside, we notice a sign for the Templar enclosure. All that is left are the walls, now on someone's fenced-off property with a closed gate. So we get back to our car and drive through the village, following the walls. It feels spooky, this village with empty streets and somber houses. On the other side of the property we see another gate, gaping open, rickety and ramshackle. Behind it is a driveway, overgrown with weeds and leading to a house in the back.

"Doesn't look good," Dwight mutters.

"No, it doesn't," I agree. "But I'm curious."

Despite the creeps this place gives me, I get out of the car and walk through the gate. To the left is another building with unhinged doors and broken windows, weeds crawling up the walls and sprouting out of the cracks. Decay, nature's powerful force, has reclaimed this estate. But the feeling is not of nostalgic solitude or melancholy; rather of an assembly of invisible entities, sinister, creepy, and menacing. Behind every gaping window I feel ghosts lurking. I slink toward the main house further down the driveway, trying not to step on any twig or kick any rock. With every silent step, I feel as if my feet are pulling ghosts out of the very soil. Pretty soon they are trailing behind me like those warriors that rose from dragon's teeth in ploughed furrows in the myth of Jason and the Golden Fleece. I stop in front of the former mansion. A two-sided, curved staircase leads up to a heavy door flanked by two lion's heads. There is something so eerie about those heads that I can't muster the courage to go up the stairs.

I hear Dwight approaching and turn to him with relief.

"I couldn't let you go in alone," he says in a hushed voice.

Dwight is very good protection against ghosts because he has no fear of them. For many years he took his students on field trips to Krotona, the Theosophical Headquarters in Ojai. There was a room in the main building (since then remodeled) known for its resident ghosts. Visitors invariably reported sensations of clammy cold that crawled into their guts, a symptom of the presence of ghosts. So Dwight challenged his students: whoever managed to stay in the room for twenty minutes would get a passing grade in his class right away. One after another, the boisterous teenagers would scuttle out of the room, ashen-pale and holding their tummies. Some of them vomited. Dwight would then walk in, stay for a good twenty minutes, and walk out cheerful and smiling. For this feat, he got himself a reputation as a hero. The secret, he had explained to me, was to laugh at the creeping entity at the first onset of clammy cold. "Laughter is the best protection," he'd said. "It shields you from the frequency of fear."

Standing in front of this creepy house, neither of us feels like laughing at the moment. A question is hanging in the air: Should we walk up the stairs? We look at each other and shake our heads. Better not. As we turn to go back, I sense a presence right behind me. I feel its energy on my right shoulder, on my exposed neck and ear, like an animal panting on my skin. I shudder, trying to shake it off. But no, the ghost is obligingly walking me back to the gate, in the manner of a well-groomed doorman.

Escorted to the car, we drive away through an empty, ghostly village. Not a single person in sight.

Rennes-le-Château is another tiny village in the South of France near the Pyrénées Mountains, and a village with a great mystery attached to it.

The mystery goes something like this: there was a local priest called Abbé Saunière, who lived about a hundred years ago. One day he decided to renovate the tenth-century church where he preached. During the course of renovations, he discovered something that made him immensely wealthy overnight. As a result, he built a posh residence which he called Villa Bethania (where he entertained famous visitors who would regularly come down from Paris), plus a medieval-looking building to house his library. This crenellated edifice he named the Magdala Tower.

Further deepening the mystery of the priest's sudden wealth is the bizarre way in which he decorated the old church, with a contorted demon at the entrance and the inscription carved over the door: *Terribilis est locus iste* ("What a terrible place this is"). The church is dedicated to none other than Mary Magdalene, whose statue watches over the entrance. In the light of this dedication, the names of the other two buildings assume a different meaning: the *Magdala* Tower, after Magdalene, and Villa *Bethania*, Bethany being the biblical home of Mary Magdalene.

This is just the tip of the iceberg of the Rennes-le-Château mystery. The rest goes back to the times of the Merovingian dynasty (mid-fifth to mid-eighth century), Jesus' bloodline and the Grail story, secret treasures, the Masonic origins, the Priory of Sion, and everything that could be termed "underground Christianity." (This term covers all the "heretical" disciplines condemned by the Church, from the practice of alchemy, astrology, and sacred geometry, to cabalistic studies and the cult of the feminine—Magdalenism.)

Rennes-le-Château and the surrounding area in Languedoc were hotbeds of underground Christianity, and that's why we decided to come this way. It's a thrill to drive up a steep hill on a narrow road, and to feel the anticipation build as we get higher above the Aude valley and closer to the village.

I don't want to superimpose speculations I have read about this place, but there is an odd feeling here. It's still early in the morning and the village is empty ... or not quite. As we walk by the famous esoteric bookstore, out of the corner of my eye I catch a glimpse of a body swiftly moving behind the bushes. I walk back, pretending to be interested in the books displayed in the store window. Surreptitiously, I cast glances at the bushes. Someone is definitely lurking behind there, I can make out the blue-black colors of a shirt through the foliage. I resume my walk. Suddenly, I stop and shoot a glance at the bushes, just in time to catch two eyes glaring intensely at me from between the leaves. In that one second, sensations of suspicion, mistrust, and dark curiosity are downloaded into my bodily awareness.

"What else would you expect here," Dwight shrugs when I catch up with him and tell him about this encounter. "

"But it was the gardener who was spying on me, I saw him afterwards watering the lawn. Why would he be so … so suspicious and hostile?"

"Well, this is not exactly a hospitable, friendly place, is it?" Dwight says, pointing at the inscription *Terribilis est locus iste* above the church door.

We've come to the (in)famous church where the Rennes-le-Château mystery was born. I'm surprised to see how small it is and how garish the decorations are. I can think of only one word to describe it: weird. As I survey the interior of the church—the hideous-looking demon crouching by the doorway with the holy water basin on his shoulders, the white-and-black tiled floor, the jumble of colors (but a gorgeous blue ceiling), the clutter of plaster and gilded decorations, the beautiful bas-relief of Magdalene on the front of the altar—a feeling of discomfort rises in my body, as if something is seriously amiss here. I close my eyes and tune into my body. In slow motion, I feel goose bumps forming on my skin, one by one. *If I hadn't read all those books about the mystery of Rennes, about the secret documents that had been passed down through the noble families of the area from the time of the Merovingian dynasty, about the secret treasure and mysterious murders, about the Masonic symbolism in the interior of this church, about graves being dug out and inscriptions on tombstones changed, if I were here without knowing any of this, what would I feel?* I open my eyes and look around anew. Creepy, it just feels creepy, as if something invisible is crawling—

"Let's go to the tower." I hear Dwight's voice. From behind, he puts his hand on my shoulder in a protective sort of way. I nod, but don't move. He nudges me gently, then turns me around and looks into my eyes. "You look weird. You don't look like yourself. What have you been doing?"

I find it hard to formulate words. I stare at him, my mind suspended.

"Let's get out of here," Dwight says decisively.

When we get to the edge of the cliff from where the view bursts over the whole valley, I feel much, much better. I retrieve my ability to think. Dwight eyes me occasionally with a little shadow of worry in his eyes. "That might be dangerous, what you were doing," he finally says.

"What?"

"Well, opening up like that. It's like hypnotizing yourself—anything can get to you. Your body is like a canary, you feel everything through it. That's why you can pick up so many impressions about places, but … you have to be careful. You have to learn how to protect yourself," Dwight now looks at me for a long moment, "because I won't be around forever to do that."

"Oh, c'mon, you worry too much. Look at this view!"

To the right, the crenellated roof and turret of the Magdala Tower poke into the air, hanging over the sheer drop of the cliff. In front of us, the whole valley rolls out, all the way to the mountain range of the Pyrénées. We gaze at the trees and roads that intersperse the valley, houses and hamlets that dot the landscape which, on this day in June, is painted in many different shades of green and patches of brown. The air is clear, the vast sky a soft blue, the silence uninterrupted; yet I don't feel the sense of peace I would expect before a view like this.

"Would that be Bézu?" Dwight asks, stretching his arm in an imaginary line that ends at a tiny village in the distance.

"Could be, not sure."

"Well, this is certainly a remarkable location. You can survey the whole valley from here, and from there," he motions to the Magdala Tower, "send signals if need be."

Henry Lincoln, one of the first authors to write about the Rennes-le-Château mystery, put forth the hypothesis of a pentagonal geometry that connects the most significant sites in this area. According to this theory, a mix of sacred sites and churches built on hilltops are connected in the shape of a perfect pentagon. And allegedly, within it is the hiding place of a long-lost treasure. Nostradamus himself hinted at this connection in one of his obtuse quatrains.

We stand in silence for a while, then Dwight starts to make little coughing noises, the sign that he is thinking intensely and has made a new decision.

I turn to him inquisitively. "What do you have in mind?"

"Well, I'm just getting this feeling to go to Bézu. I don't think much is here in Rennes, at least not much left by now. This whole thing about Abbé Saunière could be just a smokescreen to attract attention to this village and divert it from the real thing."

"What 'real thing?'"

"I just have a hunch that other places in this pentagon might be of more importance than this one where everybody flocks to. Bézu has deep Templar roots. It housed the main commandery for this area, along with a treasury. Remember, that was the *only* commandery in the whole of France from which the Templars fled before the dawn of their arrest. And the treasury was found empty."

So we set off for Bézu.

Driving across the valley, I enjoy the simple and frugal beauty of the landscape: expansive fields of wheat that have already turned golden, an occasional hill, sparse trees and farmhouses scattered randomly. There is a sense of intense peace, a certain tense equilibrium, as if something could explode at any moment. But maybe it's just the configuration of the Earth's energies that gives rise to this peculiar feeling. The road is narrow, the width of a car. Of course, no tourists are heading this way. As we're driving, completely alone in this countryside, a feeling of tension is rising in my body.

All of a sudden, from behind a curve appears a car—a big, brand new, glistening black BMW. The posh BMW is so out of the place on this country road that both Dwight and I stare at the driver as we gingerly roll by. Our curious stare is met with the same; a middle-aged man glares at us with unhidden scrutiny that borders on suspicion. For a good moment, we eye each other through the windows of our cars. We are so close that I can see a stubble on the man's distrustful face and catch a momentary flash of a who-the-hell-are-you expression in his gimlet eyes. Then we pass, but the BMW lingers purposefully on the road behind us. I feel the driver's eyes riveted to the rear-view mirror.

Dwight shakes his head. "Not exactly a type of countryside where you would expect to see brand new, expensive BMWs."

When we get to the village which, just like Rennes, is perched on top of a hill, we encounter signs that it is all but abandoned. The main street is torn apart, discarded cars lying overgrown by weeds, houses falling down. One house, though, shows normal signs of life: open windows, curtains fluttering in the breeze, even a sign, *Honey For Sale*. For sale—to whom, I wonder? When we come to the village church, things get even weirder. From the outside, the small church is in a state of ruin, with pigeons nesting in the portal and fluttering away with cries of protest when we approach the door. I try the heavy wooden door, but it's locked, just as I expected. I stoop to look through the keyhole and can't believe what I'm seeing. Candles, half-burned in candle-holders, chairs lined up neatly in rows, the altar dressed up for a service—the interior looks as if it's being used regularly and by a lot of people, judging by the number of chairs. Yet from the outside the church looks abandoned, just like the village.

"Things are not what they seem," I say, remembering what I read in one of the books on Rennes-le-Château.

We continue uphill, toward a newish-looking, wooden house that rises above the village. The house faces in the direction where the Templar lookout post and a chapel once stood. I leave Dwight behind and head for the mound to survey the area. As I'm climbing up with my back to the house, I have a distinct feeling that I'm being watched ... through a pair of binoculars. The feeling is so uncomfortable that I turn around and look back.

What the hell is that thing in front of the house?!

I squint in disbelief—a big Indian wigwam!

A *wigwam*, in the nearly-abandoned, tiny little village buried in this remote part of Languedoc? And it's so positioned that it can't be seen from the village, only from up here. How much weirder can it get?

I don't find any ruins but get myself entangled in weeds, and my pant legs velcroed with burrs. But it's worth it, because from the top of the mound there is an exquisite view of the setting sun, the dark Pyrénées in the south, the Aude valley shimmering in the honeyed light, and to the northwest, as if connected by an invisible bridge, Rennes-le-Château.

Back where we started from, Dwight and I stand uncertainly in the middle of the street, the village around us enveloped in the profound silence of decay. We're pondering where to go next, when out of nowhere fast-beat music ruptures the silence. This is so unexpected that I jump in surprise. It's a modern song all right, with the pounding rhythm of enhanced bass. Gingerly, we head in the direction of the music—a shoddy-looking, polyvinyl-roofed structure—and peer around it.

A horse stable! Big and modern at that, with many horses. In the middle of the ring, poised, a beautiful white stallion; a lanky man dressed all in black is adjusting a saddle.

Dwight and I look at each other in complete confusion. We quickly duck behind the building when the rider lifts his head and looks in our direction. It wouldn't be exactly wise to let ourselves be seen nosing about (which is what we are doing). As we steal back to the car, I notice that all the street signs are written only in the local Occitan language. Standard French (that is to say, the Parisian dialect), which was legally enforced as the linguistic norm in France at the beginning of the twentieth century, has not made it to this village.

"Things are not what they seem," Dwight says slowly as he unlocks our Honda.

CHAPTER 27

LANGUEDOC:

KILL THEM ALL!
GOD WILL KNOW HIS OWN

fter we left Bézu and went back to our hotel in Quillan (in the mystery pentagon), I had the strangest dream.

Dwight and I were sitting near a spring, in a small group of people drawing Tarot cards. There was a sanctuary in a cave below the ground. Dwight drew the card of a King; an unknown woman drew the card of the Magician. I was sitting next to her, looking at the stack, my hand suspended in the air. In my heart I felt a twinge of foreboding—what if I got a bad card? I withdrew my hand and declined to draw.

This dream is lingering in my mind as we're driving away from the mystery pentagon and toward the Cathar lands. I have a feeling it was a strong warning from my subconscious. The feeling of my unwillingness to draw a card ... am I refusing to see something in the future? Had I taken the card, what would it have been? Now I wish I had chosen one. And the sanctuary near the spring? Am I supposed to find that fountain Liana has mentioned?

One thing I'm sure about—I'm glad we're leaving this area of treasure-hunts, mysterious tombstones, the unexplained murders of priests, gardeners who lurk behind bushes, and villages that seem abandoned but are not.

An hour later, we reach the northern end of the Aude valley. In front of us rise the donjons and ramparts of Carcassonne, one of the former Cathar strong-holds in the Languedoc region. I've been anticipating this visit with a mixture of apprehension and eager curiosity. Carcassonne was the capital of the county governed by Raimond-Roger Trencavel, the twelfth-century Languedocian noble whose name sends shivers up my spine every time I read it. The first time

Dwight told me about the history of Languedoc and the Cathar movement, I was so overwhelmed with the horrid accounts that a deep sadness choked me with tears.

The feeling was this: something so beautiful and pure—like a rose, or a nightingale singing, or a white mare galloping through a meadow—was brutally squashed, crushed, trampled. I kept seeing two colors: white and dark red. The white of purity and the dark red of blood mixed with earth.

I throw my usual attempt at objectivity out of the window now; my heart is gripped with fitful pangs of sorrow. As we survey Carcassonne and the Aude valley from the rest area by the road, my entire body begins to shiver. Cone-shaped donjons, crenellated towers, and massive ramparts rise from an escarpment overlooking the Aude River. The city was perfectly restored in the nineteenth century and now looks just as it did in the thirteenth century, at the time when the Crusade was mounted against the Cathars (also called Albigensians).

The course of the Aude River outlined the main route between Narbonne in the south and the northern provinces as far back as Roman times. Along that same course the Crusaders marched to stamp out the Albigensian faith. This was the second time in the bloodstained history of Christianity that a Crusade of Christians was called against *Christians*. (Five years earlier, the Fourth Crusade changed its course and instead of fighting the "infidels" in the Holy Land, unleashed its greedy ferocity against Constantinople—Orthodox, true, but Christian nevertheless.)

Along this very road we've just driven barreled the army of the Albigensian Crusade. Interestingly, no Knights Templar took part in it. In the summer of 1209 this army had just obliterated the city of Béziers; the whole Christian population was massacred. When the soldiers asked their commander how they could tell Catholics from Cathars, he replied: "Kill them all. God will know his own." And all were killed—20,000 citizens. Children, women, priests, butchered or burned alive as they took refuge in the churches. Truly, the first genocide in European history.

Carrying enormous booty, the Crusaders marched on, having set the *whole* city on fire, just for good measure.

Carcassonne was next.

We enter the city through the Porte Narbonnaise, the gate that received travelers from the coastal city of Narbonne. I sense a dome of heavy, dark energy encapsulating the city. I'm actually starting to feel dizzy and sick to my stomach. The nausea subsides a little as we walk the cobblestone streets besieged by tourists and lined with sickening souvenir shops that sell trinkets commercializing the Cathar heritage. But in the chateau of Raimond-Roger Trencavel I'm so nauseated that I'm not sure I can endure the visit.

It was from this sturdy, stone castle that the young Viscount directed the defense of the city. Two massive donjons tower protectively over the gate and the barbican bridge. Next to them, wooden galleries shielded the crossbow archers stationed there. At the time of the siege, Raimond-Roger was only twenty-four, abandoned by his overlord the King of Aragon, forsaken by his uncle the Count of Toulouse, and his offer to submit refused by the Church prelate. After all, if the Church made an agreement with him, where would the soldiers pillage?

In the church of St. Nazaire, where we go next, I stand motionless, over-whelmed by sadness congealed in the walls, in the stone floor, in the ribbed ceiling, in the very air. My heart is raw, my body drained.

Carcassonne was crammed with refugees—the entire population of surrounding villages took refuge here, including the whole Jewish community of Béziers. The heat was merciless, the wells dried up, and what little water remained was contaminated. Disease broke out, animal carcasses rotted, stench everywhere, yet the garrison defended the city with dauntless courage. But no water....

The entrancing colors of the stained glass Rosetta dance before my eyes. The aquamarine, peacock, and lapis blues glow in the sad, shadowy interior. The petals of the rose begin to spin slowly at first, then their whirl becomes one blurry motion—or is it my tears?

The Crusaders wanted to capture the city intact; it was the military key to the region. But they also wanted to loot. So they offered the Viscount safe-conduct to negotiate the terms of the surrender—to spare the inhabitants if they walked away from the city in only their underwear. When the agreement was reached, the Crusaders—in the name of Christ, of course—seized Raimond-Roger in flagrant breach of his safe-conduct. He was put in prison. Carcassonne, the strategic prize, now empty of people, was taken over and looted. Raimond-Roger died in prison several months later, poisoned. His city now belonged to Simon de Mont-fort, the ruthless future commander of the Crusade, the terror of Languedoc.

I'm so sick to my stomach I can no longer stay in this church, beautiful as it is. So much sadness.... I take Dwight's hand and pull him toward the door. He follows, no questions asked. We walk away in silence, we walk through the crowded streets in silence, we walk out of the gate in silence. Words are useless now.

How did the Cathars feel, for half a century chased like game in a hunt and cornered into ever smaller areas of their country, marooned in castles on top of tall and steep crags where only goats could climb?

"They had unshakeable faith that surpassed all suffering, so nothing that happened in this world really mattered. Because this world didn't matter," Dwight tells me as we're driving to Lavaur, one of the Cathar castle/fortresses where four hundred Cathar holy men and women were burned at the stake during the Crusade.

"This world was just a vale of tears," Dwight continues, "and the body was considered the prison of the soul. Death was a great liberator. They welcomed it."

I glance at him. "You said that as if you were talking about yourself, as if … you were one of them."

Dwight nods vaguely, then tells me a story: "When I was living in France in my late twenties, I went to Montségur. I'd read about the last of the Cathars taking refuge there, in the stone citadel on top of the steep mountain, then refusing to turn themselves in and convert to Catholicism. When they couldn't hold out in resistance any longer, they descended from the fort and walked into the fire the Crusaders had built below. All of them, over two hundred men and women, chose to burn rather than betray their beliefs." As he pronounces those last words, I detect a tremor in Dwight's voice. I cast a quick glance at him again. It's so unusual to see Dwight overtaken by emotions.

"When I got atop the steep rock," he continues, his voice composed again, "about five hundred feet tall, nobody was there. A man appeared out of nowhere, middle-aged and distinguished-looking, and approached me. He told me details about the Cathar faith and pointed out the place down in the valley where the pyre had burned. Then he showed me the side of the mountain down which a few of their holy men, called *perfecti*, had escaped the night before the capitulation. They carried away something that was of utmost importance to the Cathars. The man looked at me with a strange glint and said, 'Welcome. At long last.'

"At that moment I didn't pay much attention to those words, the energy of the place was so powerful. I gazed at the peaks of the Pyrenean foothills that surround Montségur, then down the sheer drop of the cliff where I stood, wondering how on earth could anyone go down those sharp crags in the middle of the night…. When I finally turned to look for my new acquaintance, he was gone. I looked down the trail, but it was empty."

"You mean, he just disappeared … just like that?" I ask.

Dwight nods.

"But maybe he took another path that you couldn't see from up where you were."

"Maybe … but there were no other paths. One would have to be a mountain climber, with a rope and special boots to negotiate those cliffs, not dressed in leather shoes as he was."

I'm silent for a while, trying to imagine Dwight's experience, trying to find plausible explanation. But nothing comes to mind. "So what did you make out of it?" I finally ask.

Dwight shrugs. "It has remained a mystery to this day."

The province of Languedoc, although nowadays poorer and more backwards than other regions in France, used to be the most prosperous in the High Middle Ages. Its name comes from the medieval Occitan word for "yes"—*oc*. The language spoken there—*la langue d'oc*—was regarded by Dante's contemporaries as finer than either the Italian or French languages. For some reason, the name of the language has stuck as the name for the southern region right up until today. So we're now travelling through the Land of Yes, so to speak.

At that period in history, Languedoc was almost three times larger than it is today. The society prospered due to its trade with the Mediterranean, and the nobility were more cultured and refined than their northern counterparts. Languedoc consisted of many vassal lands governed loosely by two major families, the Counts of Toulouse and the Viscounts of Trencavel. Because the smaller lords were semi-independent, they all built castles that housed their courts. And in those courts was born and flourished what is now known as "the twelfth-century Renaissance"—the art and poetry of the troubadours.

The troubadours were itinerant poets who travelled from court to court performing their poems accompanied by music. It is hard for us to imagine the revolutionary role that these men of mostly humble origin played in the history of Western civilization. Yet the troubadours marked the birth of modern European consciousness.

Before that time, European civilization was plunged into the darkness that followed the collapse of the Roman Empire, as if someone had pressed the rewind button on the tape of European history. Brutal, short, and coarse was the life of people who tilled the land, which would be ravaged by mercenaries every so often. Individual life meant very little; murders, wars, and diseases were everyday companions. Art as such was non-existent. Love, as we understand the concept, was unknown. People married in order to procreate and marriage was the basic unit that kept society together. As strange as it sounds today, passionate love was not part of human experience. So when troubadours began to sing about the beauty of their Lady, about the flames of love that burned in their heart, about the misery and pain they felt when away from their Lady, this was a totally new concept, a new way of thinking and *feeling*. It marked the birth in medieval Europe of consciously registered emotions of love, known as "courtly love."

And this happened at the courts in Languedoc, where life was regulated by laws different from those in the North, where women could (and did) inherit and govern land and took an active part in courtly life. Because of their sophistication and education, these noble women became the source of inspiration for the troubadours. Later it became more clear to me how the troubadours and the ideals of courtly love were intertwined with the Cathar movement.

We're headed for Toulouse, the capital of this whole region called Midi-Pyrénées. This city, the fifth-largest in France, lies almost midway between the Mediterranean and the Atlantic, straddling the Garonne River. In the past, Toulouse was the capital of the old Languedoc province and one of the three most important Cathar centers, along with Carcassonne and Albi. Because it was the seat both of the Catholic bishop and the Count of Toulouse, it also became the seat of the Inquisition for the South of France. As a result, it acquired the reputation for being one of the most intolerant cities in France.

That mere word—Inquisition—makes me shudder in horror. Even Dwight, usually tolerant and non-judgmental, talks about it with open hostility, because this organization was the darkest product of Christian fanaticism.

The Inquisition was established in 1184, as an attempt to eradicate Catharism. The task of the new organization was to root out the Cathar beliefs from the South of France.

And so began the reign of repression and terror that would last for the next six centuries and spread to other Catholic countries (and was particularly successful in Spain). Anonymous accusations, secret depositions, confiscation of property, denial of the right of appeal, sophisticated torture mechanisms were the order of the day. The Inquisition established an insidious system whose tentacles reached into every nook of life in order to control the beliefs and the behavior of entire populations.

The Inquisitors were given immunity from secular laws and were at once detectives, prosecutors, and judges. They could arrest whomever they pleased and hold them in prison indefinitely. They could work secretively, never opening the trials to the public. They could adjourn the proceedings indefinitely. They had unlimited power. They were the thought police.

It was in Toulouse, in the cloister of the Basilica of St. Sernin, that the Dominican Inquisitors set up their headquarters and torture chambers. Thousands of Cathar believers and sympathizers were interrogated, imprisoned, tortured, and burned there.

Naturally, this is where we're headed. I say naturally, because Dwight suspects that the Earth energies are either blocked or severely disturbed at that church due to so much torture and suffering of innocents. As we leave the hotel in the outskirts of Toulouse, I arm myself with protective shields, which I visualize around myself. We're going into the lair of dark forces after all, and I have to be on my guard. But when we leave the car in a parking garage and walk through the pedestrian zone of the city center, I'm so surprised that I stop every few steps to look around and check the sensations my body is processing.

"Dwight," I say, tugging at his sweater that hugs his shoulders, "what are you feeling?"

"Uh … what?" He stops and looks at me as if interrupted while deep in thought.

"The energy, what are you sensing?"

Dwight blinks several times, then swivels his head from left to right, surveying the narrow Taur Street that leads to the Basilica of St. Sernin. "It's fine," he finally says. "Why?"

"Right, my point exactly. The energy actually feels good!"

And so the modern Toulouse has taken me by surprise. Picturesque streets swarming with students, cafés filled with the buzz of their chattering and giggling, attractive shops—overall, exactly the opposite from what I expected. The dark energy of the past seems to have already been purged.

"Perhaps it's the university," Dwight muses, "it's one of the oldest in Europe." Perhaps. I've read that students make up one-tenth of the city's population. The famous Renaissance Italian poet Petrarch studied law here.

When we arrive at St. Sernin we discover that the infamous cloister/torture chamber has been demolished, and a high school now stands in its place.

Dwight and I linger in front of the gate, looking at the beautiful garden that fronts the building. Cheerful. Lovely. Dwight makes little coughing noises as he runs the pendulum along the fence. "No need to do any cleansing here," he says in a surprised voice. "The energy is fine."

Looking at the flowers on a sunny, peaceful morning, it's hard to imagine what suffering transpired in this very place. It's hard to imagine the psychological and physical torture of tens of thousands of Cathars and their sympathizers that took place for over a century. If I were a visitor from another planet, how would the story of Christianity and its secret police appear to me? I think as the story of the ultimate winner. Because in the first few centuries after the death of Jesus hundreds of different variants of Christianity proliferated. The one that became the official religion succeeded only because it suppressed the others through systematic propaganda and meticulous brutality. It was three hundred years after the life and preaching of Jesus that the Council of Nicea chose a mere *four* gospels out of *fifty* as the true ones. The rest were rejected and proclaimed heretical. The Christian story we know today is basically the story of the sect that won. All the others—Manichaeans, Paulicians, Apollinarists, Gnostics, Arians, Docetists, Mandaeans, Ebionites, Euchites, to name only a few—were viciously fought and exterminated. And so were the Cathars.

But if the Cathar beliefs had won, how would Christianity have been different today? And life in Europe? And, consequently, in America?

For one thing, the Cathars believed in direct communion with the divine. The faith was not a doctrine to be believed, but a way of life. Hence no intermediaries were necessary—no Church and no priesthood. The Cathars preached the return to the original teachings of Jesus, the lifestyle of simple living infused with faith—as opposed to the greed and opulence in which the priesthood lived.

The Cathar version of priests were *Bonshommes* and *Bonnesfemmes* (Goodmen and Goodwomen), also called *perfecti*. Contrary to their Catholic counterparts, they were not intermediaries between God and humans, but merely teachers and holy men—and women—who traveled extensively to preach and heal and to deliver spiritual baptism. They lived lives of complete renunciation: celibacy, poverty, and frequent fasting. St. Francis was so inspired by their exemplary lives that he modeled his order of mendicant friars along these same lines of absolute poverty, chastity, and direct faith.

The ordinary folk, called simply "the Believers," were not expected to follow such strict rules and live in austerity. They were only expected to live good lives and to receive spiritual baptism at their deathbed. *Consolamentum* was performed by *perfecti* by laying on of hands, which transmitted the blessing of the Holy Spirit and insured that all believers found their way into the world of a beneficent God, avoiding reincarnation into the body.

It wasn't only in religion that Catharism caused change by calling for the return to direct faith. In Cathar communities women were regarded as equal to men. This was light years away from the rest of Europe, where women were considered property, and the only two choices that existed for them in life were marriage or the monastery. In the light of that, to consider women equal with men and to allow them to preach the Cathar faith was truly revolutionary. Old documents show that almost half of *perfecti* were women.

To fully appreciate this, we need only remember that a century later, when the Cathars were stamped out, when the Templars were also disbanded and burned at the stake, the torture and pyres of the Inquisition turned against another enemy—women. For several centuries to come, all over Europe, fires consumed "witches" ... an estimated 200,000 women (and a sprinkling of men) expired in what could be called—a "*gender*cide."

And now I come back to the poetry of the troubadours. It is no coincidence that this new art sprung up in the lands of the Cathars. Many troubadours were secretly Cathars, and that also explains why the troubadour movement was repressed by the Church. Troubadours, it has been pointed out, used a language that could be read and understood on several levels. The very word "troubadour" derives from Occitan *trobar*, which means "to find," but also to use words in a different way from their normal meaning. To give you an example—when troubadours (those who were also Cathars) sang of their Lady, on the surface level they extolled the ideal of courtly love; but on another, hidden level, they sang praises to their Church of Amor (or "Love," which is "Roma" spelled backwards.) This is how they managed to venerate openly their Church. In their ballads their own church is often symbolized as a *mistress* who is the true source of light and inspiration, as opposed to the nagging and dangerous *wife* (the Church of Rome) whose meals one shouldn't eat (a counsel against taking of the Eucharist).

After visiting many places connected with either the Cathar movement or the Knights Templar, I begin to glimpse that the South of France is an enigma. All the books I've read, the wealth of facts and various theories, our experiences, all of this has been swarming in my head as we have traveled through the Midi. For the past several days, I've been distinctly feeling that I'm missing a unifying thread that would tie all the pieces of the puzzle together.

Now that we've finished our visit to the Basilica (Dwight did some stabilizing of the energy grid in the church itself), we've come for lunch to a boat-restaurant on the Garonne River. As we're waiting for our meal to arrive, I'm idly gazing at the city of Toulouse on the river banks. Images of places I've seen and stories I've read about float on the surface of my brain as our boat gently sways on the river. I face the old bridge, built of red brick and trimmed with white stone. The bridge is rather low and stodgy; it doesn't leap over the river, but instead lumbers to the other shore like a hippopotamus. As I'm gazing at this bridge that connects the two halves of the city, a spark of eureka insight suddenly flashes through my mind.

"Dwight," I scream, reaching forward across the table and clasping his hand, "I think I understand!"

Several heads turn in my direction, but I don't care; I'm so excited. "Dwight," I repeat, squeezing his hand even harder, "it's all beginning to fall into place!"

"Well, go ahead. Tell me."

"It just occurred to me," I lean forward and say in a burst, "that Cathars, Templars, troubadours, the cult of the Holy Grail, the cult of Mary Magdalene and the Black Madonna, all of them appeared and thrived in about the same period—the two centuries between 1100 and 1300. And all of them were interconnected! I had this image of different threads braiding into a fabric of beliefs that is based on some crucial piece of information. That information the Church either didn't have or was trying to suppress. Most likely it had to do with historical details of the life of Jesus and his relationship with Mary Magdalene. Because it was Magdalene who continued to preach his original teachings, here in the South of France."

I stop to take a deep breath, then continue:

"So when the Church clamped down on the Cathars and Templars and troubadours, they all had to go underground. Cathar beliefs subsequently turned up in the Tarot cards, which appeared in the fourteenth century, right after the last Cathars had been eradicated. See, their very teaching is stored in the symbolism of those cards! Then the Templars from Bézu who escaped the arrest took refuge in Scotland, and soon afterwards Freemasonry was born. Then there is the cult of Mary Magdalene, conveniently covered up as the worship of the other Mary, the mother of Jesus. I can't remember who said that when an important event is too dangerous to be talked about, it is turned into a myth...?"

"Denis de Rougement," Dwight promptly reminds me.

"Ah, yes. So there it is. Something very, very important—Mary Magdalene as Jesus' beloved bride, perhaps a child they had, and who knows what else— was too dangerous to discuss, so it became a story."

"Of course that's what the authors of *Holy Blood, Holy Grail* argue."

"I know, but there may be much more than that; I don't think they have the whole story. My point is that it all converges here, in the South of France, in Languedoc and Provence! Remember, Pierre told us that most of the Templar commanderies were in Languedoc. We read that many Cathars also became Templars, and many Templars came from Cathar families; that the majority of the nobility in Languedoc were either Cathar believers or sympathizers. When you think about it, Catharism was an unusual combination of grass-root movement, supported and protected by the ruling class. It means that there was something very, very important there."

As I finish, Dwight begins to stroke his chin, not looking at me. Then he says slowly, "The rumors of a Cathar treasure smuggled out of Montségur the night before all of them walked into the pyre would fit into this. And, of course, the story of the treasure the first nine Templars found when digging under Solomon's Temple ... and the treasure of Rennes-le-Chateau."

"And don't forget the search for the Holy Grail. It was too dangerous to talk about this treasure, so it was turned into a myth. Remember, the earliest Grail story appeared only a few decades after the first nine Templars returned from Jerusalem, the same time when the Cathar religion flourished. In the German version the Guardians of the Grail are called Templars. And Montségur was alluded to as the Grail Castle.

"You see, they all knew something we don't know!" I finally let go of Dwight's hand and lean back.

"Which was probably found in one of the gospels that were proclaimed heretical," Dwight muses. "Or some other ancient document the Knights found while digging under the Temple."

"It's all beginning to make sense ... now our own trip here seems different to me." I glance again at the bridge.

"How so?"

"Well, you had your purpose from the beginning. You knew exactly why you came here. But I didn't. I just followed where you felt you were supposed to go. For me, it was an adventure trip. But now, it's beginning to feel like a part of me."

"Could you be more specific?" Dwight eyes me.

I don't answer right away. I'm still trying to understand fully what happened when that insight flashed into my mind. I'm struggling to find words to describe what was downloaded into my brain awareness. I gaze long at the bridge connecting the two halves of the city.

"For one thing," I begin tentatively, "I looked for connections, where things overlapped, how interrelated they were," I try to explain, while Dwight watches me with an expression that has become tender.

"What I'm trying to say is that I didn't just passively read books to get information, but, but...." I sip my Perrier and gaze at the bridge. My mind is laboring. It's easy receiving the eureka revelation, but putting it into words is so much more difficult.

"You're not helping me," I complain.

Dwight starts to stroke his chin, looking at me patiently. "Your struggle," he finally says, "is to translate what you received at the level of intuition into the concepts and language of the concrete mind. And this is always difficult, for anyone. You're stepping down, so to speak, the higher frequency of energy, the frequency of intuition—through which your Soul communicates with you—into the lower frequency on which your brain operates. Naturally, something gets lost in the translation." He smiles.

"That helps," I say, watching the cars, buses, and trucks traverse the bridge, the line of uninterrupted traffic filing from one side to the other in both directions. "I think I know how to put it. It has to do with my personal experience, what these historical events—the story of the Cathars, of the Templars, of Mary Magdalene—mean to *me*."

"You got it!" Dwight beams. "What they mean to your own quest. So, what is it?"

"No intermediaries," comes my reply even before my brain has formulated the thought. "I have to find my own way, forge my own path to the Divine, and not take anybody else's. And I have to create it *myself*—not wait to be shown it or given it ... *synchronistically*." I let out a deep sigh and smile. It's a tired smile, but content and happy.

Our fish arrives, and in the next moment we put aside our conversation. No matter how much I admire them, I could never be a *perfecta*. I too much enjoy this sensual world.

CHAPTER 28

PROVENCE:

THE BLACK BRIDE

We have decided to treat ourselves. We're staying in an elegant, eighteenth-century chateau-turned-hotel in Géménos, way out of our financial league. It's absurd how much we're paying for the demi-pension, but the restaurant serves refined cuisine, the Relais (French for a luxury-hotel-plus-gastronomic-heaven) is surrounded by a park of lavender and olive trees, and the guests can use the library replete with antique books and dine under the candle lights on the terrace flanked by pine trees.

But the true reason for this extravaganza is to celebrate our arrival in Provence. As we crossed the non-existent border between Languedoc and Provence, everything felt different. There is a new feeling in the energy that surrounds us; I'm picking it up just as a dog sniffing the air would pick up a new scent. Deep down I'm sensing a feeling of renewed hope, of a fresh start, of new vistas opening before us. Somewhere around these green hills, among this fragrant vegetation, we're going to find a home.

It's the middle of summer, almost the end of the year (my personal year, mind you, that began in September), and I'm feeling what I frequently do in summer—that anything is possible. While I was a student in my hometown of Belgrade, every summer I had a feeling that my life could change radically in the year ahead. There was no sense of limitation in my mind—my life situation could make a flip and I could end up in another part of the world. And eventually I did. I went to do graduate studies in California. The feeling continued. I met Dwight. After several years we left California and I found myself in Cyprus, then India, then Egypt. Still the same feeling. We left Cyprus and I experienced life in Italy. The feeling never left me. Now we're in Provence. *Anything is possible.*

The hills above the Côte d'Azur where the Relais is nested are one of the most attractive areas of Provence. Only fifteen minutes to the south and we're in Cassis, on the Mediterranean coast; twenty minutes to the west and we're in Marseille; half an hour or so to the north, we're in Aix-en-Provence. And just ten minutes up a narrow, mountainous road is the cave at St. Baume, where Mary Magdalene spent the last years of her life as a hermit. But the cave was closed when we went to visit, to my great disappointment.

Since we left Languedoc and the lands of the Cathars, we've decided to visit places that are connected with the story of Mary Magdalene. So this part of our trip is under her auspices—naturally, because Provence was her country and in many ways still is. According to the legend, after the death of Jesus, Magdalene escaped Jerusalem on a tiny boat, accompanied by her brother Lazarus, sister Martha, and the little black servant Sarah the Egyptian. The boat landed some miles west of Marseille, in a town called Saintes-Maries-de-la-Mer, and Magdalene spent the rest of her life preaching in Provence. Hence the South of France carries her legacy. Very appropriately then, we're staying in a hotel named after her—Relais Madeleine.

The major pilgrimage spot for Magdalene is the place where she used to preach—Marseille. So this morning as we're finishing breakfast on the terrace, I'm leafing through our guidebook while the cicadas start their chirping chorus all around us. Marseille is a huge city, the second largest in France. Where exactly do we start paying homage to Mary Magdalene? If anything, the whole city of Marseille is under the protective umbrella of feminine energy. Towering above the city is Basilique Notre Dame de la Garde, with an enormous gilded statue of the Virgin mounted on the belfry; above the Old Port is the former Abbey St. Victor, where Magdalene and Lazarus have been venerated throughout the centuries; on the other side of the port, in the old district where poor people used to live, is the eleventh-century church dedicated to Mary Magdalene, and flanking this small, crumbling shrine is the enormous new cathedral Sainte Marie Majeure, erected a century ago to replace the old one. So where to start?

Without a clear idea, we drive off to Marseille and take a tunnel, built under the maze of city streets to speed up transportation. It's unusual for Dwight not to have studied the maps and outlined the road; it's unusual for me not to stress out when I don't know where I'm driving. It's unusual that we are both so mellow and relaxed in the midst of a major traffic tangle. It's as if some other navigator has taken over the driving, and it's not the GPS system. Effortlessly, we follow the tunnel in the general direction of the historic city center, take the exit to the Old Port, and somehow find ourselves deposited in front of St. Victor Abbey, on a promontory above the Old Port. There is even a parking spot in front of the church. My parking luck, says Dwight in disbelief.

The first breath of air I inhale carries a scent of vague familiarity. My first glance at the Old Port from the terrace stirs something in me. I gaze, mesmerized, at the two fortresses flanking the entrance to the harbor, the church domes, the high-rises, the mass of houses packed tightly on the hill across from us, the harbor full with boats, row after neat row, masts like porcupine quills spiking the air. *It's good to be here ... so, so good.* My body quivers a little from such a great sense of well-being; a frisson of recognition touches my skin like a sea breeze.

Behind me rise the massive crenellated stone walls of St. Victor, the saint-protector of sailors. Its architecture is so military; if I didn't know this was a church, I'd think it was a fort. Before this fortress-church was erected in the eleventh century, the original church from the early fifth century stood in its place. And before that one, a little shrine where Magdalene's brother Lazarus was said to have been buried.

When we walk inside, the shadowy interior is so charged with energy I feel tingling around my head. My perception changes, as if I switched into an altered state: everything looks sharper, shapes and colors stand out, and I can almost make out a slight halo, the etheric field around objects. I've never felt so much charge in a church.

And the crypt—huge and ancient, with catacombs, pagan and Christian sarcophagi, chapels and shrines—feels even less Christian than the church above. The crypt is saturated with spirit; it feels *solid* with spirit. My heart is strangely aflutter, and in my head a mounting pressure, so great is the energy pouring into me. We're all alone and we hush our voices.

So it was in these catacombs that Magdalene and Lazarus were worshipped in the early days of Christianity.... We walk to the cave-like chapel dedicated to Magdalene. Something very ancient, primeval, hovers in this place, energies that belong to remote times, old, so old, they make me shiver. In the middle of the crypt is the altar, a carved, white stone altar, and next to it—the Black Madonna with the black child in her lap. This is the fifth Black Madonna we've seen so far. Very often the two—Mary Magdalene and the Black Madonna—are found together in the same place.

The Black Madonna. What did she really represent? With the Jesus child in her lap, she is reminiscent of the Egyptian goddess Isis, who was also portrayed with the child Horus in her lap. The Templars, too, worshipped the

Black Madonna. For them, she represented the gnostic Sophia, the Mother of Wisdom, black symbolizing wisdom in ancient Egypt.

I look at this black statue, gently standing in her corner, unassuming. Her features are unmistakably European, the blackness is obviously symbolic, just as the color black symbolized wisdom in ancient Egypt. She is kept down here in the crypt, underground. Once a year, on Candlemas, the procession carries her above ground, up into the sun. Small cakes called *navettes* (boats) are baked and eaten to commemorate the arrival of Mary Magdalene and her siblings in Provence. For this occasion, the black statue is cloaked in green, and people carry long, green candles—all of this symbolizing the renewal of nature, the impatiently awaited green shoots of spring.

The Black Madonna. She looks at me through the dim light of the crypt, gentle, ever so gentle, her right hand raised to her right breast. What is she conveying through this gesture?

A memory comes to mind. The statue of the Egyptian goddess Hathor was also kept in an underground crypt at her temple at Dendera. Dwight and I sneaked inside past the fence, in complete darkness. The crypt was narrow like a passageway, dank, and carved with wall-to-wall hieroglyphs. From there, once a year, the statue of the goddess was taken up to the roof of the temple to bestow blessings upon the people before being carried to meet Horus, the Sky god. He too, was making the journey from his temple at Edfu to meet her. Hathor and Horus, reuniting once a year, in a spring ritual that re-enacted the cyclic tides of life force in nature.

I stand, entranced, looking at the blackness of the woman and the child. Sophia, Isis, Hathor.... What is common to all of them? Sophia, the mother of wisdom; Isis, the mother of Horus; Hathor, the fertility goddess. I look around the dim crypt. The crypt! Of course, that's the womb of the earth, which feeds and nurtures. The womb of the earth is ... black, naturally.

In the darkness of the crypt, an insight flashes into my mind and illuminates all these thoughts. The blackness provides the link with the primeval religion of the Mother Goddess. In these statues of Black Madonnas, then, was compressed and hidden the ancient worship of the feminine principle! The Black Madonna is the dark mother, the body of God. She represents the blackness of a pregnant womb, from which light will burst out.

I look around for Dwight to share my insight. I'm strangely excited, *electrified*. But I don't see him; he's somewhere in one of the catacombs, checking the energy. So I sit by the altar, next to the Black Madonna. There is a certain softness that radiates from the statue, something like an embrace, protection. It's so good to be in the presence of this feminine energy. I feel as if the energy is murmuring inaudibly: *"All is well. Rest in me. Your strength is rooted in me."* And I feel my body becoming heavy, grounded safely and strongly, like a tree. At this moment, in this shadowy crypt, I feel as if I've truly and deeply understood the feminine principle. Because I've *felt* it.

How can people live without this embracing, grounding energy, worshiping only male gods? Jehovah, Jesus, Allah ... all lopsided religious systems. The past two thousand years of human history devoted to the male principle only. And now we have a world that is out of balance—*koyaanisqatsi*.

Whereas the ancients knew better. All ancient traditions believed that the feminine principle was *inseparable* from its polar opposite, the masculine. The ancient religions wisely united the two, worshipping both male and female deities. The very fabric of the manifest world was reflected thus: one life force permeates this world, but that life force is dual. Two opposite energies braid together—male and female, yang and yin, sun and moon, day and night.... To worship an exclusively male image of god is distorted, and in a sense, unnatural.

Fortunately, there were pockets of people in all great religions that secretly paid homage to the Feminine. In Christianity, the Knights Templar were one of those groups; they gave special allegiance to Magdalene disguised under the worship of Mary the Mother. It was really convenient they both had the same name, because Mary Magdalene, as every Christian soul has been taught for 1,500 years, was a sinful prostitute who repented.

At a mere thought of this I bristle. I want to shout—IT'S NOT TRUE! It's a Christian tabloid. I feel suddenly hot. The softness and gentleness in which I've been basking are gone, replaced by revolt and fury. I'm ready to fight. That's how I feel whenever I think about what the Church had done to Magdalene's name, to women in general.

The casting of Mary Magdalene as a repentant prostitute is perhaps one of the greatest smear campaigns in the history of Western civilization. It was 600 years (!) after her life time that Magdalene was arbitrarily slapped with the libel of "penitent whore" by the then Pope—and this, despite the complete lack of evidence in the Bible to support it. Even when the gnostic gospel of Mary Magdalene was discovered in the late nineteenth century—the gospel that clearly showed that Magdalene was the favorite disciple of Jesus—it did little to change the situation. It was as late as 1969 that the Catholic Church officially removed the stigma of prostitution from Magdalene's name.

In the South of France, however, Magdalene was all along venerated for what she really was—the beloved of Jesus and a spiritual teacher in her own right. Thus the continuity was maintained of a much older tradition, that of the Divine Feminine. And the Divine Feminine has two aspects—both mother and mistress. Hence the Black Madonna and Mary Magdalene were worshipped in the same place.

I see it so clearly now, in this crypt under the ground, in this dark vault lit dimly by a few bulbs on the ceiling: the worship of Mary Magdalene insured the survival of the ancient Great Goddess in her sexual function! The very archetype of the feminine principle that has been reviled and suppressed by the "Churchianity" for centuries ... centuries of burning pyres that consumed thousands and thousands of women....

In this moment, in this awe-inspiring place, I'm paying homage to all the women who perished on the pyres of men's paranoid pursuit of power.

I stand up and look closer at the black statue, the walnut wood out of which it was made nine centuries ago. "I'm black, but comely," a line from Solomon's Song of Songs comes to mind, the most popular love song ever written. The black bride ... the female principle gone underground.

Back up in the sun, outside the church, I feel exhausted, and so does Dwight. The energy in the crypt was so powerful, he tells me, it drained him. It was like a tightly-knit invisible fabric, protecting the crypt from any interference. I'm dazed in this bright, warm June sun, having just emerged from the darkness of the Earth's womb—the two worlds juxtaposed.

The nearby stairs lead down to the port, and we take them. We don't know where we're going, but we follow where it feels right to go. The stairs deliver us not only to the little marina of the Old Port, but also to a brasserie, charming in its blue and white décor. A boat's helm hangs above the door, and the ropes line the flowered planters that surround the patio. We seat ourselves and order the menu of the day. Everything seems so beautiful—the boats, tranquil in the marina ... the view of Marseille hugging the port ... the mighty fort of St. John that guards the harbor entrance ... Chateau d'If on a little island out in the sea, where Alexandre Dumas imprisoned his two fictional heroes ... the sun and sea and fragrant, briny air ... our lunch, delicious.

A feeling gradually grows in me: I've come home. I've come to a place I've been searching for all this time. I'm so moved, a few tears roll down my cheeks.

"You've been unusually quiet," remarks Dwight when we finish our lunch.

He's right; I haven't said a word, very unlike me.

"What's going on?" he insists.

I open my mouth but don't know where to begin. All of a sudden, a torrent of words is rushing to get out. "It—it feels like I've come home." My voice surprises me; it sounds thick and hoarse. But then all the emotions I felt, all the insights that flashed through my mind, everything that stirred, simmered, swelled, and surged in my heart down in the crypt comes out in one big wave of words.

Dwight is taken aback. He looks at me at first surprised, then probing; then he begins to nod. "So," he says when I stop to take a breath, "you're reclaiming your heritage."

"Heritage? What do you mean?"

"Mary Magdalene, what she stands for, it's about you, your own voice, your roots. Before you can find your path and your mission in life, you have to know your origins, where you come from."

In my head, wheels are turning. I stare at Dwight, emotions choking my throat. When I have my voice under control again, I utter, "It's about my past lives, isn't it?"

Instead of replying, he asks, "What does she represent to you, Mary Magdalene?"

I pause for a moment to think but don't need to, the answer comes from my entire being, my body and heart. "She unites spirituality and sexuality," I say quietly, strangely certain. "She represents Sophia, the deeply feminine wisdom which incorporates the sexual aspect."

"And you were her priestess, in some distant past," Dwight adds, "serving the Goddess of Love/Wisdom. You know the ways of the body instinctively. You were born with that. And now you know the ways of wisdom too. You've been retrieving it rapidly."

After all the emotional upheaval, calm has settled in my heart. Dwight's words came as no surprise. I've known it all along, but not consciously. Even in my youth, making love was a ritual for me; it required a special setting: music, dance, candles, fragrance. There was beauty to be created in that coming together of a male and female body, and I was the conduit; I created the magic of love that transported my lover beyond himself. Even then when I didn't know anything of what I now know, I was dedicating the sexual act to the union of a god and goddess. In my body, I enacted the goddess; my lover, I consecrated as the god.

"In the past, the temple priestesses were the sacred servants of the love goddess," Dwight continues. "They initiated men into the mysteries, they opened for men the way to God. Those ways were rendered sinful by the moral judgment of the Church. Even though Jesus himself was partaking of them."

I look at Dwight with gratitude. There is something—I grew to dislike this word but there is no other way to say it—*empowering* in reclaiming your past heritage. It's like finding a missing foundation. Knowing where you come from gives confidence, a sense of inner poise.

Dwight takes my hand and squeezes it gently. "I know it's become corny," he smiles, "but you *are* my goddess." In his eyes there is so much love I feel dizzy.

"You notice I'm not avoiding your eyes any longer?" he asks.

In the early years of our relationship, I frequently teased Dwight, and sometimes reproached him, that he never really looked me in the eye. Even when we embraced, he would quickly avert his gaze.

Now he pours love into me, his eyes shining. "Back then I was afraid I'd lose myself in your eyes. It was dangerous."

"But now, are you losing yourself now?"

He squints slightly and laughs. "Yes, but I'm also finding myself—and a much better self, more complete."

I lean forward and touch his lips. Even my love for Dwight has changed, I sense deep down. The quality of worship that used to color it, the desire to please, has imperceptibly changed into a quality of a strong, steady love of equals. He was my teacher, he *is* my teacher, but now I've reclaimed my own wisdom too.

Out of the corner of my eye, I notice a figure standing by our table. I turn to face our waitress, who is standing relaxed, watching us, a smile of approval on her tanned face.

"I see you have each other," she says, winking, "but maybe you'd like a dessert too?"

"By all means," exclaims Dwight, and with that we launch into a conversation.

Thinking back to this encounter, I recognize in Annie the spirit of the Marseille woman—cheeky, uninhibited, straight-forward, strong. I find that spirit in the iconic painting of *Liberty Leading the People* by Delacroix: the figure of a robust woman, her face aflame, bare-breasted, the flag of the French Revolution thrust in one hand, while with the other she's brandishing a bayonetted musket. The figure of the warrior-goddess. (Sexy, at that!) I find that spirit also in the Marseillaise, *the* song of revolution (later to become the French national anthem), the epitome of the fight against tyranny and oppression.

Annie has something of that warrior spirit. She's used to dealing with sailors from all over the world. She's strong and feminine at the same time. It's the strength that comes from knowing her femininity and fully accepting it. I immediately like her.

"So you would like to live in Marseille," she slowly repeats my last sentence. By now, we've invited her to join us at the table. It's very late and we're the last guests. I admire the line of her shoulders that makes a strong curve into her arms. Her skin is glistening. I remember the line from one of Pablo Neruda's love poems, "… the fine and firm feminine form." I'm looking at one. Every now and then she tosses her black hair and makes a little sound, something between a brief, throaty laughter and a giggle. How does she do it? It's so sexy.

"You have to know where to look for apartments," Annie continues. "There are sixteen *arrondissements* in Marseille. In some, you don't want to get lost. Others, there is no way you can afford." She tilts her head and looks at me, then at Dwight. "I'll help you find an apartment. If you come back here, I'll bring the paper with rental ads and we can go through them together."

Oh, heavens, am I dreaming or is it finally happening? The long-awaited help … to lead us where we're supposed to live!

Dwight jumps at the offer right away. "When should we come back?"

Annie frowns for a second, counting on her fingers, then says, "Thursday. The paper comes out on Thursday." And she makes that throaty giggle, gets up, and straightens her tight, very tight black skirt.

Because we have a couple of days before we go to see Annie again, we're doing a little sightseeing. I insisted on visiting Arles, even though this city was not on Dwight's list of places that needed cleansing. But it was in Arles that Van Gogh took refuge from Paris and lived for two years, and Van Gogh is one of my favorite modern artists. He strove, just as I do, to express happiness by creating beauty. I love his powerful, wide, passionate (Dwight says "disturbed") brushstrokes; I love his intense colors and the quality of light in his paintings. It's the light of Provence, vibrant, revealing, bursting, the light famous among French artists.

But Arles also has a long history. It was a prosperous city in the Roman Empire; the first-century amphitheater still stands intact in the middle of present-day Arles. In fact, during the Middles Ages, a small town was built *inside* the amphitheater, complete with two hundred houses and watchtowers.

Arles is situated at the tip of the Camargue, the marshy delta of the Rhône, where the river forks and continues its dual course to the Mediterranean Sea. The city marks an unofficial border between Languedoc and Provence, and energetically that border is very pronounced. Arles is a good-energy place, a place that feels quiet and happy. I don't sense any feelings of desolation and poverty that permeate so many Languedocian towns we've visited.

This is my first encounter with the famous Provençal colors and motifs. Street after street is lined with shops that sell tablecloths, napkins, cushions, pillows, mats, pottery, and all sorts of home accessories in gorgeous yellows, blues, purples, and golds, the hallmark of Provence. Whole fields and orchards are transported onto the cloth and clay: lemons, olives, lavender bouquets, rosemary branches, bunches of sunflower .... This is joy itself, these colors, this sun that drenches the vegetation. I can't get enough of these colors. I enter every shop, I browse through hundreds of tablecloths of various shapes and sizes and colors and motifs. They make me feel so happy, these golden-yellow tones full of sun.

Dwight is unusually patient with my shop-hopping. I think he enjoys the colors too. The tablecloths that flutter in the wind in front of every shop are like paintings. The whole city is a like a big work of art. The shutters on many houses we pass are painted sun-yellow, pots vibrant with flowers hung on the inside of the open shutters. As we stroll the streets, we see Roman ruins strewn everywhere, incorporated into the fabric of the city. Two Corinthian columns supporting a fragment of the temple architrave are inserted into the wall of a nineteenth-century building. We take our *café-crème* at the Place du Forum, which Van Gogh painted in his famous canvas *Café Terrace at Night*.

Is it the proximity of the Camargue marshes, famous for their cowboys and white horses galloping unbridled through shallow waters, is it this hot and sharp southern sun, or is it some other invisible quality of energy here that infuses Arles with this artistic and passionate energy? Dwight takes a picture of me in the courtyard of the old hospital, now the Van Gogh gallery. The courtyard offers a riotous sight of colors exploding in the midday sun, the flowers frolicking and reveling, the trees swinging genially over them, the bougainvillea branches shooting up the walls, untamed, in one frozen motion of pink and purple. Abundance.

It's just as Van Gogh painted it.

While driving through Marseille the following day to meet Annie, I carefully examine the suburbs we pass through. Which area of Marseille is Annie going to recommend? I suddenly remember my visit to Liana in Colorado.

"Dwight," I exclaim, "this is just what happened when I spun the globe at Liana's, remember? This is where my finger landed, on Marseille!"

"Well, your Guidance is working," Dwight says with conviction.

But this time it's much harder to find a parking place. I drive around and around the neighborhood of St. Victor. "Where is your parking luck?" Dwight mutters in a half-joking and half-frustrated tone of voice. I have to park a considerable distance from the steps that lead down to the port and the brasserie.

"Cheer up." I take Dwight's hand. "This way we'll get to see more of Marseille."

Dwight casts a displeased glance at me because walking the city streets amidst the car fumes triggers his asthma. But his expression changes as he looks me over. "You look very pretty today," he says with a tone of admiration. "Any special occasion?"

I blush a little. "Well, you know, for coming home," I mumble. But it's really meeting Annie and reconnecting with my feminine roots in Marseille that has inspired me to put on my long black skirt and black top, my sequined black sandals, sparkly white necklace and long metal belt that gives my outfit a touch of a romantic, pre-twentieth-century look.

It's mid-morning, and the brasserie has just opened but is still empty. We go inside, looking for Annie. She's arranging glasses at the bar. When she sees us she lets out a little squeal.

"We've come," says Dwight, "just as we agreed."

There is a flicker of embarrassment on Annie's defiant and self-confident face. "I'm really sorry," she begins awkwardly, "but I didn't get the paper this morning. They always deliver it before I leave for work. I don't know what happened this morning...." She shrugs and spreads her hands, as if to say, "not really my fault."

A moment of silence fills the space between us. The counter that divides us seems to erect a line between our two worlds. Three days ago, I had the impression that our worlds were intermingling; now, they seem fully apart, without any point of contact. Annie stands behind this counter-wall in her gorgeous insouciance, and we are on the other side, two foreigners brought by the wind in one second and gone with the wind in another, just like hundreds of other customers, without leaving a trace.

When she speaks again, Annie's voice has already assumed a neutral, breezy tone. "Would you like some coffee?" she asks.

In unison, both Dwight and I shake our heads *no*.

"Well, all right, then," says Dwight, who doesn't seem as defeated as I am. "Goodbye." And we leave the brasserie and my crushed hopes.

Looking back, the obvious solution of going to a newsstand and getting the paper simply didn't occur to us at that moment of shattered expectations. Dwight took the whole episode as a sign; I, on the other hand, sulked, feeling let down.

"So where to now?" Dwight looks around the harbor, then turns to me.

I don't care. *We may as well go back to the States.* I shrug.

"Oh, you're letting this get at you—"

"WELL, HOW NOT TO!" I burst out. "We were led here, LED TO HER—and it's another dead-end!"

"I know," Dwight says calmly. "It just means this is not where we're supposed to live."

I say nothing, feeling deeply hurt, worse—betrayed. If I can't rely on my Guidance, on my deepest feelings and impressions, what can I rely on then? A strange emptiness gradually settles in my heart. In a flat voice I ask, but don't really care if I get an answer, "And where do you think we're supposed to live?"

Dwight doesn't reply right away. He gazes at the other side of the port but he's not really looking at anything. "We'll find out, when the time is right," is all he says.

Aimlessly, we begin to walk around the Old Port. We go to the famous Canebière, the long, wide avenue that every sailor dreams about while at sea. Then we drive to the old church of Mary Magdalene, sadly truncated to make space for the new, cavernous cathedral that looms in an out-of-place Byzantine style above the new docks. Then we go to Le quartier du Panier, the oldest part of Marseille—ancient Massalia—where the Greek settlers built temples. This is where Magdalene used to preach in the public square long gone. This area is directly across the harbor from St. Victor and the brasserie. We have a different view of the harbor now, a view that doesn't feel familiar anymore. We sit on a bench that faces the harbor and St. Victor, where I had my epiphany a few days ago. I look at the massive church impassively, with strange detachment. I no longer feel at home in Marseille.

Dwight takes my hand and plants a kiss. "Well done," he says.

"Well done, what?" I feel a stab of shame in my heart. "Not being able to control my emotions? Having an outburst just like in the past?"

"True, but you've bounced right back. In the past, you would have been complaining all the time. And look at you now—already composed."

"All right, you have a point. It is progress. But I'm certainly totally confused. What was all this about with Annie? I have Guidance or I don't have Guidance? And what happened to my first impression of Marseille—coming home? Was that an illusion or some kind of a test?"

"You'll find out, just be patient." Dwight pats me on the knee with complete assurance. Then he looks up at the high-rises in the distance and says after a moment, "At least we know that Marseille is not the place for us. It's just another metropolis, noisy and congested."

At the end of the day, Dwight takes a detour road back to our hotel. He wants to show me Cassis, a charming coastal town. But he also wants to inquire about less expensive hotels to stay in. Cassis reminds me of towns on the Dalmatian coast of former Yugoslavia where I spent many summers in my youth. The streets are steep and charming, lined with oleander and rosemary bushes. Pine trees spread their crowns above flat roofs of houses painted white. We meet a couple, British expatriates, who give us helpful tips on life in Cassis, rentals, prices, and good restaurants. *This would be a nice place to live....* But when we come down to the main promenade, where cafés are lined up facing the marina, I have only a few short minutes to take in the beauty of the bay, then the fog skids in and envelops us. The milky, clammy shroud hides everything from view—just like in Italy. Dwight shakes his head in disbelief: such thick fog, in mid-summer....

"Just means this is not where we're supposed to live," I say tongue-in-cheek, but actually deeply serious inside. I look around as if to catch sight of an invisible escort who has power over the forces of nature (my Teacher perhaps?), and who follows me everywhere to make sure I don't make wrong decisions just because I'm enchanted by the view.

When I wake up the following morning, I'm not surprised that I had this very vivid dream:

I'm by the sea in an unfamiliar town. The sea is very close, intensely blue, inviting, but when I try to get in to swim, it starts to move away from me! The farther I walk, the farther the sea recedes, until it becomes almost like a mirage, shimmering in the distance, unreachable....

I don't need Dwight's help to interpret this dream. But I feel like having a word with my Guidance. I'd like to ask, "Could you please explain what's going on? Why do you send me these teasers to get my hopes all up, then crush them—"

Just as I write these words in my journal, sitting on the terrace after breakfast, a thought gets downloaded into my brain, and all of a sudden I realize: I was completely wrong in the way I interpreted the "coming home" feeling! I understood it literally as coming home to Marseille, while it had to do with coming home to my roots, the Magdalene heritage.

I put down my pen and stare blankly. I've done the same thing that people had done for centuries with the Grail myth and the story of the treasure— understood them literally as physical objects, whereas they were metaphors for inner treasure. I drain the last sip of my second cappuccino, still staring without seeing anything. The purpose of going to Marseille seems so clear now.

Dwight emerges from the hotel with a map and a piece of paper. "I had a nice talk with the receptionist," he says, "and he gave me some suggestions where to look for a *gîte*. That's the best way to have a base while we look around for a house."

A *gîte* is the French version of agro-tourism: a restored and fully-furnished old house in the countryside. In France, this is the most popular way to travel— renting a *gîte* for a week or two or longer—much less expensive than staying in hotels, plus much more picturesque.

Surprisingly, in the first village we go to, Vernègues, we find a *gîte* we like. A two-story, stone cottage, beautifully furnished in Provençal colors, with a spacious garden, high up in the hills above Salon-de-Provence. We like its solitary location, no neighbors on either side of the traffic-less road. It takes a while to locate the owners (through the receptionist's contact, then her acquaintance, and finally her friend), but when we do, the owners are very efficient. We sign the contract for a month's rental and move in the next day.

"You see," Dwight says in a somewhat victorious voice, "we were not supposed to live in Marseille."

"Nor Cassis," I add, scanning the space behind me, still a bit suspicious.

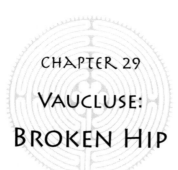

CHAPTER 29

VAUCLUSE:

BROKEN HIP

Two weeks later, we feel like semi-residents of Provence. We've learned our way around Salon, we've found a health food store that sells *produits biologiques* and had quite a few *cafés crème* and croissants in local cafés.

We've also explored the surroundings, visiting many picturesque villages and the two biggest Provençal cities: Aix-en-Provence, just half an hour to the east of Salon, and Avignon, about the same distance northwest. I fell in love with Aix, which is known as "the Paris of Provence." I was charmed by the Cours Mirabeau, the main boulevard with three gurgling fountains, flanked and shaded by old plane trees, and lined with cafés full of students. I fell in love with the lively spirit of the city, stately and elegant buildings, specialty shops and bookstores with the most beautiful stationery I've ever seen, shoe stores that compete with the Italian ones (I found a beautiful pair of sandals in the first shop I entered—a good omen).

Avignon, on the other hand, didn't charm me. Perhaps the main reason was the mistral, which had been blowing for a whole week and was at its strongest the day we went to Avignon— sixty miles an hour. The mistral is a murderous wind, and I mean it literally. It is known to drive people crazy (literally, like the whole family of Les Beaux, the extinguished local nobility), to cause accidents, and even worse, to drive people to suicide. The milder effects are those of irritation, lethargy, and depression. Dwight says it's because of the positive ions this wind carries as it funnels and pummels through the Rhône Valley. (Positive ions are air molecules that have lost an electron and adversely affect our mood and even our health.)

All the places along the course of the Rhône River, from Lyon to Marseille, suffer the havoc of the mistral. Folk wisdom has it that the mistral blows in threes and sevens: if it doesn't stop after three days, it will blow for seven days; if it doesn't stop after a week, it will blow for three weeks! When we visited Avignon, the mistral was in its eighth day. Which meant we were in for another two weeks of this relentless pounding. Just for my birthday! What kind of omen was this?

Granted, there is a positive side even to the mistral. The wind sweeps the air clean and gives that famous luminous quality to Provençal light, so prized by the artists. Nowhere else in France does the sky don so many shades of lavender-blue, and nowhere else is the light so crisp, delineating the landscape in its minutest curves and details.

We celebrated my birthday with a fabulous lunch in St. Rémy. Just a year ago, on this day, we were on a ferry, crossing the Mediterranean Sea over to Italy. Only one year, and it feels like a decade. Dwight suggested I formulate the most important goal I wanted to achieve in this next year. "To find what I'm supposed to do in life," I answered without hesitation.

"What about your book?" he then asked. I averted my gaze. *I've been too busy living; I can't write a book when moving all the time and without a home....*

A few days after my birthday—the days I spent calling about rental ads and all the contacts we were given by our French and American friends—the mistral delivered a huge blow of destiny. Or perhaps it wasn't the mistral, but my karma. Or Dwight's. Even many years later, I can't completely understand how that accident happened, and why I stood as if frozen, watching everything unfold in slow motion.

I once read in Dwight's journal some interesting notes about memory. According to new scientific research, memory is *not* stored in the brain. No localized memory centers have been found; rather memory seems to be every-where and nowhere in the brain. So the conclusion was that the brain is more like a TV receiver than a DVD recorder. If that is so, I imagine all the events that ever happened floating all around us as waves, as holographic images. And our brain, much like a TV set, picks up a wavelength and reproduces the images on the screen of our mind, and we say that we *remember*.

While I'm writing this my inner TV is picking up only fragmented images of what happened in Vaison-la-Romaine that fateful day: grass in the courtyard, ancient stone walls, a stone throne, a concerned male voice calling *les pompiers*, Dwight lying motionless on the stone floor behind the sarcophagus ... and I ... standing rooted to the spot.

What helps me to recreate the whole event from the waves floating around me are my emotions. I remember how I felt every moment that afternoon, so re-experiencing those feelings helps me to conjure up images from thin air.

We'd made an appointment to see a house for a long-term rental in Beaumes-de-Venise, a village in the northern region of Provence called Haut Vaucluse. Since we were to drive quite a way north, we decided to visit Vaison-la-Romaine, a town with extensive Roman ruins, an intact medieval hilltop town, and a Romanesque cathedral, parts of which were built during Merovingian times in the eighth century, a true rarity.

As soon as we entered the cathedral, Dwight was drawn to its apse in the back. I lingered, looking around the austere nave, built all in stone. It looked so ancient, in a way primitive, and it felt as if all the past ages—the medieval, the Merovingian, the early Christian, the Roman, the Gallic, perhaps even more ancient Celtic—were still present at this site where sacred temples succeeded one another.

The apse too, looked ancient, unusually set at a lower level than the rest of the church. What drew my attention was a stone chair at the opposite end, called the Bishop's Throne. There was something spooky about that stone chair. It was empty and cold, but felt as if it were inhabited. On both sides of it, along the walls, stretched semicircular benches, like long steps cut in stone. Dwight walked over to me and murmured that the chair must be much older than the Middle Ages, perhaps a remainder from the Gallic shrine, perhaps a chair used by Druid priests. Two lines of Earth energy crossed right at that spot, he said, creating a powerful node. Then he went back to the chair. I saw him take out his pendulum again. As the pendulum began to bounce and swing wildly in Dwight's hand, my memory of what followed is recorded in slow motion.

I stayed back and watched as Dwight moved from one side of the chair to the other, his concentration solid like a rock. He climbed up the steps to the left, his back now turned to me, the pendulum still in his hand. His movements slowed down; he made one step backwards, following the movement of the pendulum. I still watched, noticing how close his foot was to the edge of the step. I watched as Dwight's right leg made another movement backwards and his foot neared the edge. At that moment I could have yelled to warn him, I could have run to stop him, I could have ... but didn't. Instead I stood frozen like a slab of stone. His foot continued the trajectory toward the edge of the step and in the next moment landed on it partially, only to slip off the worn, shining stone surface and send his entire body toppling down onto the hard, hard stone floor.

It was only a second, but it felt like several minutes, before I ran down and kneeled by my beloved's immobile body. He looked at me, somewhat confused, somewhat apologetic and said, "I can't stand up. My leg feels like rubber. I think I've broken my hip."

I've just walked into our *gîte* at eleven o'clock at night, alone. I look around the kitchen and dining room where dishes have remained, unwashed, from this morning. I see Dwight's sweater, casually left on a chair. The book he was reading, his pencil and notebook, lie on the side table by the sofa. His slippers are waiting by the door. The air is impregnated with his presence, and I can feel him, even if he's not here.

I drop down a blue garbage bag I was given at the hospital. It contains Dwight's clothes and a few valuables. It strikes me: this accident is like a rehearsal for his final departure. This is how it's going to feel when he really leaves—the terrible sense of emptiness. A pang of remorse fills my heart. This morning in bed Dwight was very affectionate and wanted to make love. But I refused. We had an agenda for the day, an appointment to meet. "Tomorrow we can stay in bed as long as you want," I promised.

Now I can't forgive myself. Tomorrow ... there is no tomorrow for anything. Today is all we have.

I drop onto the sofa, exhausted. The whole afternoon I've been frenetically busy. After my initial shock at the church, while I was following *les pompiers* carrying Dwight to the hospital in Carpentras, I pulled myself together—or something helped me pull myself together. A reservoir of strength had suddenly opened like a secret vault in a bank, and I could tap into it as much as I wanted. I had no idea so much power was at my disposal; I had no idea I could focus my will so sharply. I felt the inside of my body turn into a pillar, stable and strong, and I galvanized all my powers into one single aim—to provide the best care for my beloved.

As soon as Dwight was well placed in the emergency room, I called the woman with whom we'd had an appointment about a house for rent and apologized for not showing up. She warned me that my husband would need a good doctor to operate on his hip if he wanted to walk again. And she dropped the name of a surgeon—but he's the best in the whole area, so he's very busy, with a long waiting list. It would help to have a connection....

I immediately jumped into the car again and bolted to see our friend Pierre in Suzette. I drove fast, very fast, taking curves with a screech of tires. Our Honda Prelude responded like a pet horse. "Good car," I whispered.

Thank goodness we have Pierre here. Together, we made a plan of action, and I returned with his personal note to *the* surgeon. Pierre will go to the hospital the next morning and make sure Dwight is given the proper care. And thank goodness my French is so good. I spoke with nurses, receptionists, the x-ray technician, the emergency doctor, the night-shift doctor.... A lot of questions, explanations, requests, legal forms, paper-signing. When I left, around ten at night, everything was organized to the best of my abilities.

I don't know what took over me as I was driving back to the *gîte*. The events of the day flashed before my eyes like a movie. I replayed every scene, wondering if I did the right thing. There was a certain detachment in this movie-watching, except for one scene. Confusion mixed with guilt twanged in my heart every time I replayed Dwight's fall. I could have done something—why didn't I? I had stood unmoving in the church, as if under a spell.

I turned on the radio. As it happened, the station played Queen's song, "I Want to Break Free," my personal anthem in a way. As Freddy Mercury's voice boomed, imploring in all urgency to be free, I too begged my Soul to set me free from all karmic bonds, from the chains of emotional hang-ups so that I can become clean and pure, clear like a spring. And thus pure, to serve where needed.

I now cast a weary look around the room where Dwight's things are scattered. With great effort I push myself up, unpack the blue garbage bag, and put his things away. Then I go to bed without even removing my make-up.

It's lonely, so lonely in this big, empty bed. Suddenly all my strength is gone, and I feel weak and helpless. Loneliness, heavy like a tombstone, settles in my heart. I cry silently. After a long time, I finally go to sleep. The dried-up tears have traced salty paths on my face.

Our *gîte* is an hour away from Carpentras. For the next ten days I'd be commuting, sometimes twice a day, leaving early in the morning and returning late at night to an empty, dark house, solitary in the dark hills. At times, when I would get out of the car to open the gate, I thought, *what if somebody is lurking here, or behind a tree in the dark?* I'm not the bravest person when it comes to being alone in a remote house, in an unfamiliar country, and at night. I'd conquered the fear of darkness several years ago in the Great Pyramid, but the residue is still lingering. I'd furtively glance left-and-right, then dash to the door, my fingers slightly trembling while turning the key.

I'm grateful that the mistral has stopped. There is no more howling around the house, no more thrashing of trees, clanging of shutters, whistling through crevices. I can finally hear the silence at night, finally feel the stillness. The mistral actually stopped all of a sudden, the night after Dwight's fall. I had this weird feeling that the forces of nature had achieved their goal and could now relax. The tension that had been building up with every day of the mistral blowing was released.

The night before Dwight's surgery I couldn't sleep. I had the worst attack of discouragement yet. Feelings of weakness and complete loneliness washed over me, suffocating me. I felt as though everything had been pulled out from underneath my feet—home (our *gîte* rental would expire in a week, and we had no home to go to), finances (the stock market had just crashed; we had lost a lot of money, and the insurance wouldn't cover the cost of Dwight's hospitalization), even Dwight's support (I was all alone here in this cottage). I was left with nothing else to rely on except myself. I was stripped down to the bone.

Around four o'clock, after a couple of hours of fitful sleep, I got up and went to the bathroom to take a shower. As the hot water rolled down my tired body, a feeling of misery weighed over me like heavy storm clouds. I mustered the last crumbs of strength and said to myself, *You have to be there for Dwight. And you have to be there, strong and cheerful.* As I made that decision, a thought flashed through my weary, struggling mind … *this is a test. A test concerning your attitude—how are you going to cope with this crisis? Are you going to fall apart or remain strong?*

Then I screamed. I screamed from the bottom of my lungs, madly almost, until my voice was gone. But in that scream I expelled all the fear, I flushed out the helplessness, I shook out the defeat. I exorcised them all, my inner demons … at least for the time being. I chose to be strong.

At the end of the day, I actually congratulated myself. I managed to resolve one problem after another—an unexpected change of schedule due to an emergency, the doctor being late, a complication with the anesthesiologist, Dwight's request for a room change, and finally, billing problems. To my astonishment and disbelief, the hospital did not accept credit cards. No amount of indignant arguing ("this is Europe for heaven's sake, not a third-world country, you *have* to accept credit cards!") or logical reasoning ("but it's impossible to produce so much cash in one day!" and "I don't have a bank account here to write a check") changed the situation. I had to make several trips to ATM machines (at intervals of two hours) to withdraw enough cash to pay the first part of the bill. The rest of the money I have to have wired from the States.

But Dwight's operation went well, and that's what matters most. I don't care that receptionists in the hospital have developed a strong dislike for me; I'm not even ashamed that I threw a fit at the supervisor; I don't feel guilty that I've used my charm to get the doctor to operate on Dwight right after his emergency. Dwight's health was my priority. After all, he's seventy and his heart is arrhythmic. A slight mistake in the dosage of the anesthetic and he may not wake up.

As I was driving back to the *gîte,* I had a feeling of a job well done, a sense of accomplishment—just as I used to feel when I'd pass an exam with an "A" grade.

But now I have the next big problem to solve—finding a house where I can take Dwight to recover after he gets out of the hospital in ten days. Now I'm in a real panic. I'm even thinking of taking him back to Rome and Noemi's apartment. It's our last resort if I don't find anything here.

Why should it be so difficult to find a house to rent? Do other people have so much trouble renting? I'm starting to think that this ludicrously tenacious house problem might be in a way symbolic of my life situation. I mean, seriously—in dream analysis, a house is a symbol for oneself. For the past year and a half, ever since we came to Italy, we, *I,* couldn't find one; everywhere we lived was just a temporary solution. And what has been going on at the same time on the inner planes? I have been trying to find my mission, what my Soul wants me to do. So, really, it's not that far off to make a connection between the two: just as I can't find out my true purpose in life yet, I can't find a place to live—my house—either.

I did go to see the rental in Beaumes-de-Venise we were supposed to check out the afternoon of Dwight's fall. The house was acceptable, the rent reasonable, the village charming, but ... if ever I had a gut feeling telling me *no* it was that time. I think it had to do with the landlady, Madame G. Over the phone, I liked her; she was quite sympathetic about Dwight's accident and helpful in giving me information. But face to face, I felt drained in her constantly chattering presence, bombarding me with details of her personal life and gossip about the neighbors. I felt as though all my vitality were sucked up by her eyes, large brown eyes that burned with intensity as she fixed them upon me, never turning them away for the whole two hours. After I left, I decided that this was not a good rental situation for us: the landlady lived in the house right in front of the one she was renting.

But a week later, I still haven't found anything else. I have a few promises from friends of acquaintances who would be looking around, but that's all tenuous. I was supposed to move out of our *gîte* in a couple of days. I implored the owners to extend the rental for one more week. But they had other guests scheduled to come, so they gave me only a three-day extension.

I'm almost numb from house-worry. I feel as if I'm buying my time, life itself, day by day. Dwight will be released from the hospital in five days. I have to move out in five days. I HAVE TO FIND SOMETHING. My homelessness issue resurfaces big time. Why are we put in a homeless situation every time Dwight's health is in a serious condition?

I have no choice. Two days before Dwight's release from the hospital, I reluctantly call Madame G. and say that we will take her house. In the afternoon, I go to sign the contract.

Our future landlady is waiting for me at the dining table, two dozen sheets of paper spread out. My heart sinks. Page after page, she reads the contract, clause after clause of "if"s and "when"s and "in case of"s—totally inhibiting for someone as uncomfortable with legal matters as I am. Actually, it's plain frightening. My French doesn't cover all these legal terms; I don't understand legal jargon in any language, even in my native Serbian. I just understand that we have to buy insurance for our stay in the house, for possible fire, for guests coming to visit and accidentally toppling down the stairs—it seems to me, insurance for every step we take in the house, including taking a shower and flushing the toilet. I didn't know the French were so obsessed with safety. I wonder if it's the same all over France, or perhaps only a Provençal quirk. Or Madame G.'s obsession. Because for all her insistence on taking precautions, she has a disastrous history of accidents: two car accidents, numerous house falls, broken bones, surgeries, you name it. I'm given a detailed account of each one.

With my heart sinking ever lower, I sign page after page of the never-ending contract. It feels as if I'm signing my prison sentence. When we're done two hours later, I feel angst paralyzing my body. As I'm getting up from the chair, I stumble.

"Attention, Madame Johnson," comes a warning from our new landlady, "don't fall down the steps like your husband!"

My "husband" (we have to present ourselves as husband-and-wife in these foreign countries to simplify the paperwork) doesn't share my premonitions. He thinks, based on my description, that the house is a good deal and he likes the fact that the village is protected by a hill from the worst attacks of the mistral. And that we will be only ten minutes away from Pierre (Beaumes and Suzette are neighboring villages). Dwight doesn't feel any foreboding as I do. Naturally, because Dwight is in his own world right now. The fall has totally shaken him out of his usual way of thinking and feeling. (Which is what accidents generally do, I'm told.)

But this accident also disconnected his etheric body because, for the first time in his life, Dwight had an out-of-body experience. While lying on the cold table in the x-ray room right after his fall, there was a "snap" in his head and he suddenly saw his body from above. At the same time he also had a strange vision which opened for him the invisible world of nature spirits.

As Dwight tried to explain to me that very evening, there were entities imprisoned in the stone chair in the church, bound by the magic spells of an ancient priesthood. Dwight had first encountered this practice—still alive in today's modern world—during his sailing trip in Polynesia. There, local shamans still wage psychic wars and many souls are trapped in Tikis (large wooden carvings in human shape). So in the Bishop's chair at the Vaison church were imprisoned nature spirits whose power was harnessed by the priesthood. Druids were renowned for their magical powers throughout the ancient world, even traveling to Egypt to compete with Egyptian priests. (Ancient documents say the Druids won.) It could be, Dwight speculated, that they secured their power in this way, by enslaving nature spirits. Something like the genie in the bottle—I tried to find a familiar analogy.

In his out-of-body state, Dwight went back to the church, concerned that the freed entities might be a threat to other people. What he saw in the apse of the church was a swarm of black, maggoty forms circling around the chair, unable to get back in. Dwight felt great compassion for those entities, trapped and abused for such a long time. In the out-of-body state, he knew what rites he had to perform to release them from the chains of the past.

And just like the handsome prince trapped in the form of a frog and then transformed by a princess' kiss, out of the black cloud emerged four large golden forms, heart-shaped and shimmering, and surrounded Dwight. They looked angelic in the beauty and love they radiated. As he faced these shimmering beings, Dwight was struck by a violent shaking. His body convulsed on the table in the hospital, and he abruptly dropped back into it. But the angelic beings stayed with him and returned the favor: they opened for Dwight the glory and beauty of the inner life. There and then, on that x-ray table, though in agony from pain, Dwight sobbed with love and joy.

Later he would joke that the fall had not only broken his hip, but had also shattered the wall that was encasing his heart, the wall of congealed tears that Aldo had sensed back in Rome.

When I'm in the room with Dwight, I, too, sense a different energy in and around him. For one thing, he is a transformed man. Every time I appear at the door of his room, his eyes mist over and he starts to sob. From sheer gratefulness that I'm there, he says. When I sit on his bed, he looks at me with an intensity of love I can't describe. It's as though his electrical circuitry has been rewired from 110 to 220 volts and perhaps beyond. When he takes my hand in his, I feel that electrical charge passing into me, and my fatigue and worry go away. Sometimes I have a vague impression that I also sense these spirits, these angelic beings—I don't know what to call them really—there is so much love around Dwight's bed.

The morning when I have to move into our new home, I wake up with a burning feeling of anxiety in my stomach, making me sick. The fear, a heavy boulder of fear is pressing on my chest, and I can't breathe. All around my heart I feel a prickly sensation, like hundreds of tiny needles poked into my flesh. Am I having a heart attack?

This is insane, I say to myself. This is irrational. You really have no *objective* reason to feel like this. Okay, Madame G. is not the most comfortable woman to be around, but she was accommodating, I continue the inner dialogue, trying to persuade my body to see reason. We are moving into a spacious house decorated in those gorgeous Provençal colors, in a picturesque village, and with a very reasonable rent. We'll finally have our crate shipped from Milan, and we'll have our things again; I'll have my clothes and *shoes* back. Not that bad of a deal, really.

But my body doesn't give a damn what my head is saying. It's shaking uncontrollably. I take a double dose of valerian to calm it down. But as the morning progresses and I continue to pack, the panic spreads from my body into my head. I can't think clearly any longer. A silent scream wells from my chest, as if I were being dragged to a dungeon: NOOO, I DON'T WANT TO GOOOO! PLEASE, LET ME FREEE....

In desperation, like a drowning person clutching at a straw, I call our acquaintance from the hospital one last time; she has friends who have friends who know somebody who might have something for rent.... *Maybe in the last moment she'll find something ... I'll cancel the contract ... just lose the deposit ... who cares about the deposit ... anything, just to escape!*

The acquaintance calls back after making a round of calls. Bad news. Nothing available.

I remain in the chair, crumpled and numb. I wasn't really expecting a miracle, was I? Yes, I was. But there is none. My entire body is flooded with a sense of foreboding. I suddenly remember my dream with the Tarot cards. That same sense of foreboding! What card would I have drawn, had I had the courage?

As I take the last bags to the car and sweep my gaze around the yard, the trees, the stone cottage, I feel as though I'm saying farewell to freedom.

CHAPTER 30

BEAUMES-DE-VENISE:
THE WAR BEGINS

Some events in life happen because we set them in motion; others because we're swept up in the motion set forth by others. But there are those situations that, in hindsight, seem triggered by a greater force outside ourselves. Only after they transpire do we hopefully realize their purpose and see their role in the wider framework of our lives.

There was no way I could have grasped what was truly going on while caught up in the events that followed our move to Beaumes-de-Venise. I was too deeply embroiled in the unbelievable vicissitudes and drama of those eight months we lived in the house behind Madame G. It was only several years later, as the patterns I had to outgrow and the lessons I had to learn played themselves out, that I fully understood my "home saga." At last I clearly saw why I couldn't find a home anywhere *but* behind Madame G.'s house. An unseen force, the will and plan of the Soul, orchestrates our external life events with infallible precision, to provide exactly what we need to learn our lessons. Assuming we learn, of course.

And so it was that after we moved in, I was given two months of reprieve from inner work to attend to practical duties: taking care of Dwight while his broken hip was mending, unpacking the crate of our household goods that had arrived from storage in Milan, and finally setting up our home and my study where, with renewed hopes, I planned to write my book.

But my Soul had other plans for me, yet again.

One late afternoon in November, our landlady appeared at the door. In a voice that tried to sound calm, she informed us that we had miscounted the rent money. One hundred Euros was missing.

Dwight said nothing. I stood between him and Madame G. trying to figure out how that could be. I had personally counted the entire sum three times. Dwight had taken the envelope the day before and given it to her. But she hadn't opened it until now. Dwight should have asked her to count the money there and then, I thought, and I was a bit upset by his oversight.

"The cleaning woman was there yesterday. Could she have taken the money?" I inquired. "No," came the answer.

The situation was getting awkward. Dwight and I stared at her while she stared back at us with her unrelenting, intense eyes. I was now really annoyed. Madame G. seemed to enjoy creating trouble; she had done it already several times. And now money is missing!

I looked at Dwight but he sat in his armchair, saying nothing. In those few seconds between Madame G.'s dismissal of the last question and my fated suggestion, many thoughts passed through my head and many feelings swept through my body. I'm not trying to excuse myself or rationalize my behavior; no, I take full responsibility. But in that moment before I spoke, something foreign appeared in my head, an interference of a sort, which put a thought into my head—*maybe her son took the money*. Madame G. was divorced, living alone, but her younger son visited frequently, helping her with the property. So the money from the house we were renting was his income.

The truth was, I very much liked the fellow. In fact, the first time Xavier showed up to fix the shower, my jaw dropped. He was stunningly gorgeous, so gorgeous it took my breath away: a beautiful yet masculine face, perfectly regular features (eye lashes twice as long as mine!), shiny black hair, well-built body, kindness, a lovely smile. I immediately took to Xavier, not because of his looks (well ... somewhat), but more so because of his kindness and unpretentiousness.

For a fraction of a second, as I stood between Madame G. and Dwight, I felt that perhaps I shouldn't put forth that question. But I couldn't help it. I heard my voice say, as if it belonged to someone else:

"Maybe your son took the money?"

Oh, Lord—all hell broke loose!

An avalanche of words was hurled at me, an explosion of fury, threats, and indignation. I instinctively thought I should correct the misunderstanding—I was *not* implying that her son was a thief; I did *not* think she was dishonest. It was a silly thought that he may have needed the money and she didn't hear him say that he took it. But I said nothing. Again, that same force that led me

to say those wretched words prevented me from saying the words of apology.
I stood mute.

And Madame G. stormed out deeply offended, furious, and vengeful.

The tomahawk was dug up.

That's how my life turned into a prison. I'm feeling Madame G.'s gimlet eyes
spying on us from behind the curtains of her back windows, which face our
living room, kitchen, and my study—practically all the rooms where I spend
my waking hours. If I lift my head up from the computer in my study, I can't
avoid seeing her house, the back windows and the white curtains. I can gaze
at the driveway, or the garden that separates us, or the adjacent house that
also belongs to her, rented to a young man with a sad dog, but eventually, my
gaze drifts back to her windows. There, behind those unmoving curtains, is
my jailer.

Maybe I'm imagining that she's watching us continuously. But I can't shake
off her energy, even the very thought of her. She haunts me all the time I'm in
the house. I forget about her only when I fall asleep or leave.

On second thought, I don't think it's my imagination. On that fateful day
when Dwight went over to give her the rent, he stayed long enough to look
around the house. He was struck by a certain feeling of austerity, loneliness,
and grimness. The only pictures on the side tables and hanging on the walls
were of her deceased pet, her beloved bulldog. Not a single photograph of her
family, of her sons. Not a single family member, except her younger son, was
on speaking terms with her, she had told Dwight. Her only companion was a
ferocious terrier, who had to be tied up at all times and who would launch into
mad barking anytime someone would approach the house.

After the incident (and after the interference in my head had vanished), I
wrote a polite and sincere letter of apology. But Madame G. didn't hear my
apology; she wrote back wrathfully, as if she didn't read my words. I wrote
another letter, explaining myself and apologizing again, but with no result. Since
then she's been slipping venomous notes into our mailbox with the obsession
of someone who lives to maintain the memory of the offense.

"You better learn your lesson," Dwight warned me one morning over breakfast. "Because if you don't, you'll be put in an even worse situation than this
one, and worse still, until you learn." Then he said in a teasing voice, "But don't
count me in. I have no desire to go through that with you...."

"But what do I have to learn?" I asked anxiously. "I'm not trying to deny it or to get out of it. I'm just not sure what my lesson is."

Dwight looked at me seriously, then made a muffled grunt. "How about learning your First Fundamental to begin with—Do not offend?"

I take my inner work seriously; it's my full-time job at the moment. So not only did I decide to confront my tendency to offend, as Dwight had suggested, and practice harmlessness, but I also made a firm resolve to change all the other negative traits of my personality. So I sat down and made a list: criticism, short temper, impatience, irritability.

Proudly, I showed my list to Dwight. "See," I said to him, "I've put down everything I want to change. I meditated and vowed to my Soul to eradicate these shortcomings."

He took a look—a long look—blinking several times, then he turned his concerned gaze upon me. "Don't you think you've taken on a bit too much, all at once?"

I took the list back from him and glanced again at the "Limitations to Overcome," as I have titled my endeavor. Reluctantly, I nodded. "I don't know where to begin and how to go about changing them," I confessed.

"Take one limitation at a time," Dwight suggested. "Assign a certain period of time—a day, a few days, a week, you decide—during which you're going to be mindful of that tendency. But," he paused significantly, "rather than fight the flaw, cultivate its opposite—the positive trait. Then go on to the next one."

That sounded like a sensible plan of action. So I decided to tackle impatience first, because it seemed to me that impatience is the source of everything else. For days I was mindful, watching my reactions, repeating silently my current mantra: "Practice patience." And invariably, I would fail. Somehow, wherever I'd go, I'd run into a "slow" situation: an obstinate driver obstructing the road, unwilling to move; a shopkeeper closing his shop for "ten minutes," which turned into twenty; interminable lines in the *hypermarché*—and irritated, I complained.

After a week of trying hard (but to very little effect), Dwight suggested we go to Aix to have a little break. Oh, do I need a break! Not only from this new practice, but also from Madame G.'s jailer energy.

We've spent a lovely day in Aix strolling the pedestrian streets lined with beautiful shops, sitting in a café on the main boulevard and watching life, having a delicious lunch in one of the best restaurants. I admired the French women dressed ever so chic, marveled at the harmonious architecture of palaces that flank the Cours Mirabeau, indulged in specialty stores. On our way back home in the late afternoon, I'm replaying the whole day in my head.

"Dwight," I say dreamily, "that was the best day I've had since your accident. I really enjoyed myself."

Dwight looks at me for a moment then says, "You really did, didn't you?" He laughs, then adds with a slight concern in his voice, "Perhaps too much."

"What d'you mean—too much?"

But he doesn't answer; instead he looks ahead at the road that is being enveloped in dusk and says, "Don't follow that car with the trailer too closely. Leave some space."

I slow down for a while but my excitement is bubbling from inside and I can't keep my foot off the gas pedal. Or maybe it's that espresso and cappuccino mousse I had in the *patisserie*? I chatter about the lovely stores, my new journal, the gorgeous winter coat I found on sale…. All of a sudden, I notice that the trailer in front of us is getting awfully close. I slow down, but then realize that the car has stopped—in the middle of the road! I have no time to stop our car, I'm too close. The only thing I can do is swerve and go off the road. In the next moment there is a bang, then a crash. My body is slammed against the steering wheel and my head hits the windshield. I remain unmoving.

As if through a fog, I hear voices, a door opening then slamming. Then somebody opens my door. "Are you all right?" comes a male voice.

"Let's call the ambulance," another voice joins in.

But I can't move, I can't utter a word. I start to shake.

"Svetlana!" I recognize Dwight's voice and feel his hand on my shoulder. Slowly, I lift my head and turn to face him. He's stooped through the door and is looking at me carefully.

"You're not hurt," he says very calmly, "you just hit the windshield." I continue to shake. I still can't get out of the car; my legs won't support me. Dwight turns to the two men who are standing by our car. "No need to call the ambulance. She'll be all right. It's just shock." His voice is composed, and his body exudes a certain monolithic poise. He helps me get out of the car, and I stand on wobbly legs, uncontrollably shaking all over.

More cars have stopped and Dwight is now talking with a group of men. I finally understand what has happened. A car had stopped to turn left onto the side road; the car with the trailer in front of me had stopped too, but I couldn't see that because his stop lights didn't work. In swerving, I've hit the trailer then smashed our car into a tree. My heart sinks when I see the damage—I have totaled the Honda.

Dwight has decided to take care of everything without involving the police—sensibly, because we don't have residence papers for France and I, the driver, with my Yugoslav passport should have a French visa (which I don't). My brain is still in a state of shock, so I don't follow all the details of the discussion. The man who began the chain of events by stopping in the middle of the road (which he had to do to let the cars from the opposite direction pass before turning), invites us to his house, just up the road. While we're riding in his car, Dwight turns to me from the passenger seat and says, "I told you to be careful, but you weren't listening. This is a two-lane country road, houses all along, you have to anticipate turns and stops."

"It's amazing you weren't hurt," the driver comments, shaking his head. "You must have good protection." He swirls his hand in the air, as if to say— guardian angels.

Only then it dawns on me that he's right. Neither Dwight nor I were wearing seatbelts, and Dwight is unscathed. I have bruises and cuts, but nothing major. It was a miracle of a sort, as if we were held back. Because at the speed I was driving, smashing into a tree should have sent us through the windshield.

In the house, the wife starts to fuss over me, cleaning my cuts, making tisane, putting ice on my bruises, while Dwight and the husband take care of the practical details: calling a tow truck to get our Honda transported to the car dump, then our insurance agent in Cyprus, and finally a taxi to take us home.

That night I'm lying awake in bed, disgusted with myself beyond words. Now we don't have a car. We'll either have to buy another car or rent one for the rest of our stay in France. It's going to cost an arm and a leg, and our finances have already suffered badly because of the hospital bill and losses on the stock market. Then I summarize the events of the past month and get even more disgusted—positively dejected. I'm not making any progress with my inner work; the landlady has sent us a note that she won't renew our lease when it expires in a month (we had a six-month lease); and all my efforts to find a teaching job back in the United States have failed. (After his recovery, Dwight had assessed our financial situation and informed me that we have to think of going back to the States to find a job. So I've been sending my résumé to different schools, but with no results.)

In the morning I wake up to Dwight's stony silence. I glance at him periodically, but feel too ashamed to say anything. Finally, I muster courage. "Are you angry with me?" I pipe.

He waves his hand as if to say, what's the point of being angry.

"You better get on the phone and find us a rental car," he says icily. "You crashed the car, you take care of finding another one. I'm not getting involved." Then as an after-thought he adds, "And when you're done, think about what lesson you have to learn from this."

I don't mind going through hell, I don't mind living in an energetic prison, I don't mind fighting obstacles or battling my fears, as long as I have Dwight on my side. But to have his support withdrawn and him angry on top of everything else, that's just too much for me.

"Can we first talk about the accident and my lesson, please?" I ask in a small voice. I know he can't stay angry for long when faced with my sincere efforts to improve. The teacher instinct, the desire to help when help is requested, is too strong in him. I know him well.

"Hum," comes the grunt. "What do you want to talk about?"

"Well, what I have to learn."

"So…? *You* have to figure it out. No good if I tell you."

"True, but you can give me a hint."

Dwight remains silent for a few moments, probably weighing whether to give in. Then he replies, "The hint is the previous day. How did you feel in Aix?"

"Great! I mean, I had such a wonderful time!"

"That's my point. You were enjoying yourself *too much.*"

I stare blankly at him. "Are you saying that the accident came as punishment for having fun?"

"No, not punishment, just an immediate karmic balancing."

"But wait, you're not saying that we shouldn't enjoy ourselves, are you?"

"No. I'm just saying that it's the law of cause and effect. Every 'high' is followed by a 'low.' Opposites define each other. So when you have a great time, you have to be prepared that sometime in the future you'll have a bad time. In your case, the karma worked instantaneously."

"So how can I avoid the retribution or, as you call it, balancing? Because…" my voice sinks, "I would like to enjoy myself occasionally."

"I don't think you can avoid it, but you can certainly prevent the karma, not cause it in the first place."

I perk up. "How?"

"You're ready to hear?"

"You bet!"

"We've already talked about that ... in Italy. It's about personal desires." My face must have shown total confusion, because Dwight now shifts into his teaching mode. "Whatever you do, you have to act impersonally. Because as long as you have personal desires you will continue to create karma and you'll bounce up and down on the see-saw of life."

"I remember now, yes, we've been over that before. But I don't know how to act impersonally. That's the problem."

Dwight looks at me, thinking, then replies, "It's all in your Second Fundamental."

"Examine your motives?" I raise my brow since I'm still not getting it.

"Exactly. You have to examine the motives behind your actions: are they personal or impersonal? Ask yourself: 'Is this a personality's desire or Soul's intent? Who is having a great time in Aix, the personality or the Soul?'"

I think of my delight in the stores, how I felt when I bought my new coat, and I have no doubt who was having fun in Aix.

"So, the key is my attitude," I say slowly. "When I'm personally involved in having fun, something opposite has to happen to balance out the pleasure I experience. I get that, but ... what does the impersonal attitude really look like? I mean, how do you *impersonally* enjoy yourself?"

Dwight smiles. "Okay, I'll put it this way: being impersonal means being detached. And detachment means that you don't identify with the experiences."

"Now it's starting to make sense!" I exclaim. "If I identify myself with an event, either good or bad, I'm getting personally involved because I generate reactions, either positive or negative emotions. And those reactions, because they're personal, will have to be balanced out."

"Yup. Cause and effect." Dwight nods. "The law holds true for everybody, just that in general, the balancing is not immediate—as in your case—so people don't see the connection."

"But why is it instantaneous for me?"

"Well, it's obvious, isn't it?" Dwight tilts his head and squints in disbelief I'm not getting it. "You're on the path, you're working on your shortcomings, you made a pledge to your Soul! For you, experiences are quickened because you have consciously committed yourself to becoming a better person, because you're striving to unite with your Soul.

"Put it this way," he concludes in a voice that sounds definitive, "whenever you sincerely invoke something, there is a response. That's the Biblical knock on the door. And you'd invoked your Soul two months ago, when you launched that plea to become free from karmic chains."

As I was meditating in the evening, after the whole day on the phone with rental companies (I finally found a good deal on a Peugeot 3), I went over my morning conversation with Dwight. I also went over what I wanted to achieve.

I'm quite determined, I said to my personality-self. *You* have *to change, whether you want to or not.*

To turn my decision into a command, it occurred to me to visualize my personality-self as the starship Enterprise from the *Star Trek* series. So I imagined three decks on *my* Enterprise: deck E (the lowest) stands for the etheric body, deck A (in the middle) represents my astral body or my emotions, and deck M (the highest) stands for the mental body or my thoughts. Then I went further and decided to assign an officer to each deck. These officers are going to be named after the qualities I want each body/deck to achieve.

First, I put Officer Stable Strong in charge of deck E—my etheric body has to become impervious to outside interferences such as loud noise or barking dogs. Then I chose Officer Serena Calm as head of deck A. My astral body, my emotions, have to shape up; enough of tempestuous reactions and flare-ups, of whining and feeling sorry for myself when things get difficult. Finally, I selected Officer Poise Still to control deck M. My mental body has so far been allowed to run rampant, churning thoughts overtime. I want Officer Still to order everybody on the deck to stop working when it's time to rest.

These officers are going to report to me in my ready room on the Bridge, located in the middle of my head. I made it clear to all my bodies/decks that I am the chief-commander (Jean-Luc Picard), and that a general maintenance of the ship is going to take place. Some engines on deck A, old and worn-out, are going to be permanently shut off (and I immediately thought of the engine "Impatience"); others are going to be replaced with newer, better models. I summoned the crew to help out because we all, as a starship, report to the Admiral—my Soul-self.

All of you, I announced to all decks over the speakers, *as the crew, have to work in unison. All of us have to become aligned with the will of the Admiral. There's no other way.*

My thoughts then shifted to the immediate goal: to achieve detachment from personal desires. I thought of things I still clung to—a croissant breakfast, for example, and surprisingly, I was able to dismiss it easily and effortlessly. *It doesn't matter!* Then I thought of having a cappuccino in a café, enjoying a moment of idleness. I had the same response—*that, too, doesn't matter.* Living here or there, Europe or America, doesn't matter either. Shoes ... I stumbled at this thought, my heart making a little thump of panic, but then I said to it comfortingly, *you can have all the shoes you want, just don't be attached to them.*

Very pleased with my work, I went to bed. *Accidents serve a purpose,* trailed my last thought before I fell asleep, *because they point to what needs to change ... out of something bad, the good will come....*

I've just finished writing the overview of my most recent learning experience in my journal—as well as rethinking my whole life in the light of this new attitude of detachment—when I discover that the battery in the Peugeot we rented yesterday, has gone dead. And that's because I accidentally left the key half-turned in the ignition after cleaning the car.

My emotions flare up. *These car troubles just don't end! Why this now?*

Then a thought appears. Yesterday, I snapped at that really nice girl in the rental car agency just because she didn't give us the model she'd previously promised. I was mean and bitchy, Dwight told me.

So now I'm faced with the dead battery. Instantaneous karmic balancing. My Soul is really watching me carefully.

I don't know if Dwight is feeling sorry for me or empathizing with me, but he's been really kind and supportive. He calls me to sit next to him, takes my hands in his, and looks long into my eyes. His gaze is peculiar, a mixture of love and concern, but projected intensely, almost fiercely. "Don't give up," he finally utters, "Do not get discouraged. You have to persist."

"I know," I sigh in resignation. "It's just that sometimes I feel like Sisyphus; the rock keeps rolling back. I'd like a little break."

He shakes his head doubtfully. "You've taken on a major task. You've invoked, you've set things off into motion. Now you have to take on what's coming."

So, it's war!

It started rather innocently....

This morning, I drove out to the nearby village of Caromb, which has the best bakery in the area, to get our favorite croissants—*impersonally*. But when I got there, the door was tightly shut, and the piece of paper attached to it said, "*Fermeture exceptionelle.*" Ha! These small businesses in France will sneak in an "exceptional closure" when you could not possibly expect it.

But this didn't disturb me in the slightest. I'm watching my reactions all the time now. Completely unperturbed, I walked away and drove to the bakery in our village. I repeated to myself, *it doesn't matter, one way or the other.*

I came back home, parked the car in the driveway in front of the garage, and got out with arms full of croissants and baguettes. As I closed the gate to our garden, I saw, to my horror, that the car was rolling backwards! Shock, anger, worry, surged like a storm in my heart, and wild thoughts whirled in my head for a second before I leaped to action. I threw down my bags and ran after the car to pull on the emergency brake (which I'd forgotten to do in the first place). But the Peugeot was gaining more speed, and just as I reached it and touched its hood, the car swerved sideways into a rosemary bush. In the next moment, it hit the landlady's fence.

I couldn't believe it ... I just couldn't believe it! The fourth car problem in two weeks! With thoughts colliding in my head, violent emotions shooting their first arrows, I went up to call Dwight for help. I'd had it! This lesson ... or punishment, or whatever it was, just went overboard. One can take only so many "learning experiences" in a short period of time, and especially of the same kind. I was definitely feeling taxed by my Soul or whoever was behind this "pedagogical act." I was positive I hadn't failed anywhere, either in my motives or my reactions. So why then?

"WHY?" I ask, perturbed, as we entered the house after rescuing our rental Peugeot. Luckily, the car wasn't damaged as it was cushioned by the rosemary bush. The bumper made only a slight dent in Madame G.'s fence, and I only hope she wasn't at home to see what has just happened, or else she'd charge us for the replacement of the whole fence.

"All my efforts and determination and sincere motives," I fume, really distressed, "and what do I get? Another accident! Not fair! What's the point in continuing this horrendous work of taming my lower self if this is what I get?"

While I'm ranting, Dwight sits silently, his eyes riveted to the floor. The only response on his face is a slight frowning of his brow. After a long while he looks at me and says simply, "This is a normal reaction."

"NORMAL!?"

He nods. "It's a normal reaction from the threatened aspects of your lower self. What you're facing is their counter-attack. It's a well-known psychological phenomenon, explained in many spiritual teachings."

"Ah! Right...." I sigh, but don't feel any better for knowing this.

Dwight explains: "When you make a resolve to overcome certain tendencies, they will intensify as soon as you make that resolution. Don't you see, they're trying to remain where they are; they'll make any effort to keep themselves in place. Their very survival is at stake!"

"Wait, you talk about 'them' as if they're alive, as if they're human beings."

"They are alive, you bet!" Dwight laughs. "They are strong thought-forms you have created. When you repeat certain emotional reactions or thoughts over and over, you energize them. Gradually, as you direct more and more attention and energy their way, they assume a life of their own."

"Oh, just like Alexandra David-Néel's companion?"

Everything suddenly clicks into place. I've read about this French explorer and writer, the first foreigner—and woman at that!—to travel to Tibet when it was forbidden to foreigners. To make bearable the long, freezing nights away from any human settlement, she created an etheric "companion" by using visualization. This genie eventually became so strong that she had enormous trouble dissolving it afterwards.

"So, this is a good sign!" Dwight now beams. "You're doing a good job in your self-observation and controlling your emotions—except right now," he says laughing, and I immediately realize that I've lost it again. I've just had an outburst of temper. Oh, this is so hard.

But Dwight continues cheerfully, "Your lower self feels that it's losing ground, so it's striking back in a desperate attempt to reclaim its territory— your emotions—don't you see?"

I begin to see, yes. I've just thrown a fit at my Soul, whom I saw as unjust and unfair. What's worse, I was on the verge of giving up—which is exactly what my ego wanted me to do!

Thus, I finally saw my enemy—the creation of my own intense thoughts and emotions I'd been generating throughout my life, and most likely over many lifetimes. This bundle of mental and emotional energy now has an independent existence, feeding off my emotional reactions, and is determined to keep it that way. Hence I can expect many more attacks—probably not with the car since

I'm now prepared for that, but where I don't expect them.
A mutiny has broken out on the Enterprise.
It's going to be a fight for life.

CHAPTER 31

CÔTE D'AZUR:
REBORN IN ANTIBES

One day in March Dwight said we needed a change of frequency. We were too bogged down by *the events* (that's how he refers to my car accidents) and Madame G.'s energy. Besides, he said, he needed a little break too, from his own work. Because in between the *events*, Dwight had been checking out Earth energies in various locations and re-activating the shut-down energy grid at massacre sites. So he suggested we go to the Côte d'Azur to relax and get away from everything. On this trip, he promised, there would be no work on the agenda, no forlorn churches and grim villages where the houses of the whole Huguenot population were burned down by their Catholic neighbors. None of that. We're going to be simple tourists: visit Cannes and Nice and Grasse (the world capital of perfumes), stay in Antibes, dine in the charming Eze village, and gamble in Monte Carlo (well, maybe just take a tour of the Casino).

While packing, I'm watching myself and my thoughts with doubled attention. I've also assigned support crew to Officer Serena Calm in charge of deck A. She has to report to me at the onset of the slightest *personal* desire or anticipation of enjoyment. I don't want to crash this rental car or have some other kind of accident. Going to the Côte d'Azur, the epitome of glamour, is my big opportunity to practice enjoying myself *impersonally*. I can see many of you smirking, "Yeah, sure … good luck!" But I'm determined. Big victories are won in big battles.

The morning of our departure, I'm surprised to see myself going about preparations in a calm, even relaxed way. As I turn on the engine, after getting everything packed even earlier than planned, I say to Dwight, beaming, "I have a formula for success!"

Then I explain, since he looks at me confused. "The key to taming my irritation is to slow down. In my normal mode of functioning I do things too quickly. And when something gets in my way, a slow car, a slow person—"

"A slow Dwight," Dwight says dead serious, but I see a twinkle in his eyes.

"Yes, unfortunately, even a slow Dwight...." I laugh.

"Then you get impatient and sometimes—frequently—explode," he finishes my analysis.

I'm so glad we first went to Cannes and then came to Antibes; it's like first eating frozen vegetables, overcooked and bland, then savoring a gourmet dish and keeping the delicious taste lingering in your mouth. From a distance, Cannes looked glamorous; but when we went for a stroll we were almost the only people in the streets. Later we learned that Cannes comes alive only during the film festival and summer months; otherwise, the houses are locked up. No life, no soul—as Marie from Ostia Antica would say—just one big film set, an illusion of life.

But Antibes! In Antibes I see and feel and smell life in its meandering streets, in its many squares, in bakeries and *charcuteries* (sounds so much nicer than "butcher shop"), in little restoration stores, fabric stores, even in quiet residential areas. We're staying in a modest, *really* modest hotel, but with a priceless location: right above a square where life—not traffic—takes place. Our balcony looks down on the cafés and restaurants, tables and chairs of different colors spread like a quilt over the whole square.

As soon as we unpack, we go to do what we enjoy most—watch life.

We position ourselves at a café on the corner of two pedestrian streets and order a couple of pear *tartes*, just to fortify ourselves. Then we begin to watch. We watch friends run into each other, put down their grocery bags then engage in "manual" conversation. We watch old men stroll by with hands crossed behind their backs, berets pulled down to their brows. We watch young men with rolled newspapers or art portfolios tucked under their arms debate with each other, frequently stopping to make a point with the other free hand; and young girls casting inspecting glances at their reflection in the store windows, then adjusting their tops to hang just so.

Then we get up to stroll and watch some more. We go to the promenade above the sea. It's the end of March, but the weather hasn't warmed up yet. We bundle up against the chilly wind. It's good to be alive and be aware of life itself. No need for heavy talks, self-analysis, ideas, plans for the future, no need to dissect energetic impressions of places, as we so often do. Antibes makes me aware of that simple feeling we take for granted: the feeling of being alive.

In the morning Dwight eyes me strangely over breakfast.

"What's the matter?" I have to ask. I don't like that look of his.

"Oh, nothing."

"Oh, yes, there *is* something!"

"Well, not really, just, you know...."

"Know what?"

"Well, we're going this morning to Cap d'Antibes, the most elegant, the most luxurious—"

"Oh, I get it!" I start to laugh. "You're worried that I won't resist the temptation to have personal desires, right?"

Dwight nods, a mixture of embarrassment and concern reflected in his eyes. "It is a big temptation," he says. "The most beautiful villas with the most gorgeous *views* (and here he pauses, eyeing me again), are scattered among pine trees and lush vegetation. And the famous hotel where all the stars and royalty flock. And now we have a rental car which—"

"I promise I will watch myself carefully," I say solemnly. "I'll be conscious to a 'T.' And you can also remind me from time to time, just in case."

When we get to the first wall of vegetation that hides somebody's paradise, I understand Dwight's concern. Cap d'Antibes is like a forest of sumptuous private estates, where billionaires from all over the world come to spend the summer months perfectly protected from the unwanted attention of paparazzi and the envy of paupers. As we drive along the main road that follows the coast, we can see very little of those luxurious villas, hidden deeply in the forests of pine trees, palms, cypresses, and assorted hedges.

I admire the beauty that reigns supreme on this little promontory: the famous azure blue that fills the eye with a sense of deep calm; the lush greenery that is so bursting with life force you can almost hear leaves growing and buds forming; the contentedness which fills the space, that quiet contentedness which only moments of leisure can beget. But I don't desire any of it. And I'm not fooling myself; I'm not pretending. I really am ... neutral. Or better, *detached*. I'm not even coveting to be invited to one of those villas, not even to enter behind those green walls for a visit. I'm perfectly fine where I am—in the passenger seat of our rental Peugeot. And I'm not even smug about my achievement.

We continue to Juan les Pins, the Mecca of night life, the setting of extravagant parties, jazz concerts, in brief—*joi de vivre*, according to the brochures we picked up in the Tourist Office. Scott Fitzgerald and his fun-loving wife Zelda discovered this village with pine forests and white sandy beaches in the 1920s and introduced the crazy years to the Côte d'Azur; then the Jazz Festival was established in 1960. But places have their life span just as people do. Juan les Pins, as a party town, has aged; the exuberance of its youthful years is now replaced by the shabbiness of mass tourism and the proliferation of tacky apartment houses, cheap night clubs, and tawdry souvenir shops.

Next to Juan les Pins is Golfe Juan, best known as Pablo Picasso's two-year long residence after WW II. He came here with his new mistress, the forty-years-younger Françoise Gilot. He was then invited to establish his studio in the Grimaldi Castle in Antibes, which had by then become a museum. This is where I want to go after lunch, to this castle that is now the Picasso Museum. But Dwight is tired and needs a nap. "Besides," he says, "I've had enough of Picasso and his angular, distorted women. They don't inspire me." So I leave Dwight at the hotel and head to the château that used to belong to the same famous Grimaldi family that now resides in Monaco.

The Grimaldi Castle looks just as its name sounds—grim. With thick, gray, windowless stone walls, a tall medieval tower, also windowless, the structure is enclosed upon itself, built for protection. But the location makes up for its stern appearance: it rises right above the sea, its large terrace like an altar where you come to bow to Poseidon. I learn that at this very place stood a Greek acropolis 2,500 years ago. Antibes was colonized by the same Greek settlers that founded Marseilles—the Phocaeans. To their new settlement they gave the name of Antipolis, the "city across." But I'm not sure what the "across" referred to: the island of Corsica, about a hundred miles out in the Mediterranean Sea, or the town of Nikke, nowadays Nice, only seven miles to the east.

Even though the works Picasso created during his stay at the château were inspired by the renewed joy of living after the war ended, I find little of that joy in the murky, dull colors and the light without luminosity that permeates his paintings exhibited here. I'm actually much more interested in the story of Picasso's stay at the Côte d'Azur and the photographs which document that period of time. I look at his bald head with tufts of white hair on the sides, the eyes that burn with an uncanny, fierce fire. There is so much animal power and passion in his intense eyes that I feel uncomfortable looking at them—almost as if he can bewitch me with those eyes. Which, come to think of it, he may have been doing to those numerous lovers and mistresses and the two wives he had during his 92-year long life.

In the museum, I'm shocked to learn that Picasso's first wife, a Russian ballerina Olga Khokhlova, ended up in a mental institution, and his last wife, Jacqueline Roque, shot herself after his death. Marie-Therese, with whom he had an enduring relationship and who bore him a daughter, also killed herself after his death. Another lover, Dora Maar, was plunged into a state of emotional trauma after Picasso left her. Françoise Gilot, with whom Picasso came to Antibes and with whom he had two children (Claude and the now famous Paloma), had to flee Antibes to escape his abuse. Quite a disturbing trail for a man to leave behind!

But I'm no judge of other people's love lives. What do I know about Picasso's true motives, his intentions, his inner battles and demons? In fact, as I again examine his paintings and drawings, I have this impression … of a Soul struggling to express itself, to come through, to communicate, but in vain…. It's not the images themselves that speak to me; it's the energy *behind* them, as Kostas said. And the invisible imprints I sense in these paintings speak of inner labors, endured in the hours of night, in solitude. A man wrestling with himself.

I move on to the artwork of Russian-born Nicolas de Staël, who painted in Picasso's studio several years after Picasso had left. Again, I sense that same struggle, the cry of a lonely, unhappy, struggling human being, cut off from his Soul. De Staël committed suicide (according to art historians) or lost his life falling off the balcony in a state of total inebriation (according to the old Antibois).

The visit left me sad and deeply moved. With tears in my eyes, I walk to the road above the sea from where I so much enjoyed the view the day before. I look at the sea, now becoming gray, and in my heart I feel the eternal pain of all human beings who have struggled to express themselves, who have struggled to make some sense out of a senseless life. Pain pierces my heart. So much suffering on this planet, so much groping through ignorance, stumbling in the dark. Miserable human beings at the mercy of their emotions, tormented by their passions.

No, it's not the fate of other people I'm weeping for. I'm actually recognizing what could have happened to me had I not met Dwight, had I not made the effort to awaken, had I not stepped on the path.

I look at the sea, then the sky, as if I'm going to see my Soul there, outlined in the shapes of ever-changing clouds. *Why is it such a struggle to find you, my Love?* From the bottom of my heart, I launch these words to my Soul. *Why does it take so long to merge with you?*

There is so much longing in my heart, in my body, that I feel like tearing open my chest to expose my fledgling heart. I scream silently to my Soul—

I'LL DO ANYTHING, A-N-Y-T-H-I-N-G, JUST TO UNITE WITH YOU!

To seal the vow, I throw a ring into the sea, the ring I bought in Santa Barbara the year I met Dwight. My vow is now irrevocable. Nothing will make me retreat.

Slowly, I walk back to the hotel.

Around midnight, the noise from the square below our room wakes me up, and I suddenly become aware of a sharp, piercing pain in my left foot. Earlier that evening, as we were walking back from a restaurant, I stumbled on a curb and twisted my ankle, but there was no injury. Before going to bed, I slathered my foot with arnica gel, which is good for bruises. Now I realize that I won't be able to sleep with this throbbing pain, so I get up to take a sleeping pill.

As I take the first step in the dark, the pain becomes so intense that I can't stand on my left foot. Hopping on my right foot and holding onto the bed, I drop onto the chair by the table. I know Dwight keeps the sleeping pills in his kit, for emergencies. As I'm fumbling through bandaids and files and floss and combs, I begin to feel woozy and weak. And it's getting worse very fast, as if my very life force is being sucked out. I try to reach for a glass of water, but it takes tremendous effort to lift my arm. I don't manage it. My body is rapidly stiffening, becoming paralyzed, and I can't move my legs or arms any longer. I try to call Dwight, but only a gasp comes out. I glance, desperately, at his sleeping body, but the whole room begins to blur, then to swirl. I feel light like a feather ... darkness closes in on me like a pall....

The first sensation I have a minute—or an hour, or is it two hours?—later is a sensation of the bones in my shoulder dancing. Dwight's hand is vigorously shaking my shoulder. The consciousness plops back into my limp body. I become aware of the chair I'm slouched over, my head cocked back and my mouth gaping. With my return to consciousness, the same sick, nauseating, paralyzing feeling comes back and washes through my body. I barely make it back to bed with Dwight's help. He's not saying a word. In the glow of the street lamps that suffuse the room, his face looks pale. I actually see fear in his eyes.

Then the cramps start, excruciating, unbearable cramps that are stronger than my strongest menstrual pain. Something is pulling out and ripping my whole womb. The diarrhea urge stabs. Leaning on Dwight and squirming on my aching foot, I reach the bathroom. Bent forward with my forehead on my knees, I stay on the toilet for a whole, long hour.

Dwight helps me back to bed, and I lie in pain, exhausted. I'm feeling chilled to the bone. I can't warm up. Dwight layers over me all the extra blankets he finds in the armoire, plus his heavy winter jacket. Finally, curled up against his warm body, I doze off.

It's nine o'clock when I wake up. Dwight is sitting on the chair, watching me worriedly. He has a crumpled look. "How are you feeling?" he asks and comes closer, seating himself on the bed.

I direct my attention to my foot, then my stomach, then my whole body. Not a trace of pain! "I feel fine," I say, incredulous. Then I get up and I walk perfectly fine; overall I feel perfectly fine—as if nothing has happened the night before!

"This is *so* weird. How could this be possible?" I pace back and forth, swinging my arms and twisting my feet just to make sure everything is okay. "I don't understand … whatever caused that amount of pain both in my foot and my stomach had to be a serious disturbance. Yet it's all gone now."

Over breakfast in a café, I look around at people, our waitress, the croissants and cappuccinos she brings, as if seeing all that for the first time. I notice every tiny detail on the passersby; I *feel* what they're feeling—as if I can merge with them, as if there is no separation between me and my environment and I'm one with everyone and everything around me. Something in my brain is altered. All the colors appear sharper, more vivid. I feel vibrantly alive, as if … I'm living a new life.

"So what do you make out of this?" I turn to Dwight, who has been unusually withdrawn.

"I've been thinking…." he begins, slightly biting his lower lip, but he doesn't continue right away. After a moment, he pronounces:

"I think you were attacked by your lower self that tried to kill you."

I gag on my sip of coffee. "*Kill me?*"

I'm not sure whether to take it seriously or to laugh.

But Dwight is dead serious. There is no twinkle in his eyes. He says, "You threatened its very existence by making that vow yesterday, don't you see?"

"Yes, but still ... to kill me, that's *huge*."

"If I hadn't woken up to empty my bladder and found you unconscious, who knows what would have happened to you. You were totally gone, and for quite a while."

"But had my lower self really killed me, that would have been the end of *it*, too."

"Not really." Dwight shakes his head. "Even with you dead, those elementals still survive in the astral and mental planes. Next time around, you would have to pick up where you left off. Meaning, you would have to face the same negative tendencies and fight the same battles. Death doesn't magically erase our limitations. Remember, death is not the end, just the continuation on a different plane of existence, on the other side of the veil, if you wish."

I begin to seriously consider what Dwight is suggesting. That's a deadly mutiny on my Enterprise!

"Do you think," I ask, slightly anxious, "that my lower self will continue to attack me like that?"

Dwight shakes his head. "I don't think it will ever be able to pull an attack of this magnitude again," he says. "Its forces are now permanently weakened. It will still try, for sure, but you're now well over the critical point." Then he looks at me with a big smile, takes my hand, and pronounces:

"You went through a not-so-symbolic initiation rite—death and resurrection. Welcome to your new life, my love."

I blink several times, suddenly grasping the wider implications of this event. Death and resurrection ... "You have to die in order to live"—the enigmatic injunction I had read in mystical literature. I always understood it symbolically, as a process of dying to your personality in order to be born to your Soul, but actually, those words may have a literal meaning as well.

"I know it sounds corny," Dwight smiles awkwardly, "but this is the first day of your new life. And it coincides with Easter too." He kisses me in a solemn sort of way.

"Well," I raise my cup with a few sips of cappuccino left at the bottom, "let's toast, then, to my new life." Just to dispel seriousness, I add, "And to being saved from death by your full bladder."

Life continued to glisten around me that whole day. To celebrate, we went to the Matisse Museum in the hills above Nice. Since we came to Provence, I've rediscovered Henri Matisse, Picasso's contemporary and friend, who painted vibrantly alive scenes with child-like freshness. Now in his museum, I delight in canvases on which stylized figures dance in a circle holding hands and birds swoop from the sky and flamboyant colors efface perspective. In his canvases I truly sense *joie de vivre*.

It strikes me how different the two masters were, not only in their attitude, but in their artistic gifts as well: Picasso was born with an innate skill for drawing, and started painting while still a child; Matisse, on the other hand, discovered painting late in life and had to work very hard to achieve a relative mastery over lines and shapes. To Picasso, the use of the brush came naturally and effortlessly; for Matisse it was always a struggle.

I'm not surprised when I read that Matisse had deep reverence for life. His paintings, beliefs, and creativity were permeated by this reverence, by a spiritual outlook on life. Looking at the photos of him, I see compassion and gentleness in his eyes, very different from Picasso's animal-like, magnetic eyes. Now I understand why I sense this energy of pure joy behind Matisse's paintings. They sing an ode to life. How appropriate to be in his museum *today*, the first day of my new life.

But it's not only Matisse's paintings that are infused with life and that make my spirit soar. The ancient olive grove that surrounds the museum is a very special place also. Actually this whole hill, Cimiez Hill, is replete with ancient Roman baths, houses, an arena, roads.... The city of Nice itself is one of the oldest human settlements in the world. Archaeologists have found remains of early humanoid life and the first crafted stone tools dating back to the Old Stone Age. So we are walking here on a continual stream of life that has flowed through this area for the past 400,000 years!

This is a special place, indeed, to celebrate my rebirth.

We walk through the olive grove, the trees gnarled with age. I read in the information booklet that these trees are several hundred years old. The energy is thick with nature spirits; I can't see them, but I certainly feel them. They infuse me with a sense of well-being, of love, and I feel I'm gliding rather than walking on this grass. I see the same reaction in Dwight's eyes. He's hobbling on his crutch (after his hip operation he still can't walk without it) twice as fast as he normally does. "The energy," he tells me when we reconnect after strolling on our own, "reminds me of what we felt in Hadrian's Villa. Remember?"

"How could I forget?" I smile. The energy of nature spirits, the energy of Life itself.

The whole next day—the *second* day of my new life—small obstacles are thrown at me from every side, as though my Soul wants to see if I can live up to my reborn-self of yesterday, the self that glowed with calm and serenity, the self that was loving and compassionate, the self that was *patient*.

I'm patient as we get lost many times in the unexpected turns around Vence, a little town in the mountains where Matisse decorated a chapel that we want to see. I'm still patient and calm after we find that the chapel is so crammed with tour groups that we can't see it, after the weather changes and becomes cold and windy, after we have the worst lunch so far on this trip, after I get a parking ticket in Eze while unpacking the car in front of our hotel—but patience is hard work.

So when we go to Monte Carlo, and Dwight delivers me to the park in front of the Casino, I feel as if I'm finally given a reprieve. I can relax in these opulent and fragrant gardens, admire the carpets of red and yellow and pink tulips, lush palm trees that flank the path, and the fountains where jets of water splash down in the shape of fireworks. And past all this beauty, at the end of the garden path, rises the elegant, art nouveau Casino.

"Is this where you gambled back when you lived in Villefranche?" I ask, curious.

"Uh-huh," Dwight nods with a mischievous glint in his eyes. "But only the roulette."

"How did you know which number to bet on?" I'm still amazed at Dwight's gambling luck.

He shrugs. "I just knew it. And I knew when to stop so I didn't lose the money I had gained."

And in Monte Carlo, one can smell money everywhere: in the lines of cars parked in front of the Casino (nowhere else have I seen so many Porsches, Lamborghinis, Ferraris, and Bentleys in one place); on the streets lined with posh boutiques, liveried doormen, and perfectly manicured flower beds (without a single wilted flower); and mostly, on the corners planted with policemen who are continually on watch for any intrusion of irregularity, mess, or ugliness. Here in Monaco we've seen more policemen than in the whole of Provence during the past several months!

By the time we reach the cliff where the old Monaco and the Royal Palace are perched, the sun is already setting and the wind is picking up mercilessly.

As we stroll around the empty, barren square in front of the Palace, as we glimpse the modern part of Monte Carlo and the now gray azure sea, as we try to see the cathedral in biting gusts of wind, and as I venture down the slopes of a park, I have to use all my power of imagination to picture how nice all this would be on a warm and sunny day.

Thoroughly chilled and hungry, we make our way back to the garage through empty streets. As we drive out onto the road that will take us back to Monte Carlo, we suddenly face the unctuously fat full moon staring at us haughtily from above the sea. I stop the car to take in this remarkable view. The gold orb of the moon rises slowly in the royal-purple sky, casting a silvery pathway of sequins on the dark sea, and the entire scene is bejeweled by the shimmering lights of Monte Carlo in the background.

Dwight's suggestion to catch the evening in Monte Carlo was perfect. If the city looks beautiful and elegant during the day, at night it's enchanting, as if touched by a magic wand. We drive back to the Casino and—gasp!—the building is transformed. Light and shadow, like two eternal lovers and enemies, kiss and clash, caress and combat along the walls, on the roof, under the windows, in the park that leads to this scintillating illusion.

Today is our last day on the Côte d'Azur. Just as well, I'm so tired I can hardly get out of bed. The previous day was so hard on me—as well as cold and bitterly windy—that I've used up all my reserves of energy. I'm lying in bed like a puppet abandoned by its puppeteer, unable to move my legs, my arms. I really need a day of rest at this point. I shudder at the thought of our plans for today: visiting the old town of Nice, going to the Chagall Museum in the hills above, then on to Fréjus before heading back to Provence.

I'd love to see the old Nice; so far we've only been to the famous promenade by the sea, Le Boulevard des Anglais, and the legendary Hotel Negresco. The old town is so much more charming and cozy. But I can't face driving through the maze of streets and getting lost again and again. I have no strength left in me to deal with stress, no energy to maintain patience and calm.

I grope under the blanket for Dwight's hand. I find it atop his belly. I know he's awake; I heard the little noises he makes when he wakes up, but his hand lies unresponsive to my touch. I can't even turn to kiss him. I squeak a weak "good morning," and am alarmed by my own voice.

"Do you really want to do all those things today?" comes Dwight's question instead of a greeting. His voice sounds worried, worse—dispirited.

"I'd love to, but don't know if I have it in me."

"I sure don't." Dwight's hand finally twitches a bit, and his fingers tentatively stroke mine. But he's not turning to kiss me.

"I think we'd better skip Nice," I suggest.

Dwight's fingers now definitely stroke my hand, and in their touch there is a sense of relief.

Nevertheless, we decide to make one stop before heading back to our village in Provence. We want to visit Fréjus because, according to our guidebook, this sea resort is a perfect blend of beautiful sandy beaches, ancient monuments, and charming, modern architecture (I'm curious about this last one—normally, "charming" and "modern" are contradictory terms). For us, Fréjus is also of interest because of the Chapel Jean Cocteau and because supposedly a relic of Mary Magdalene is kept in the church of St. Maximinus.

But we forget these points of interest when we get to this town, about forty miles west of Nice, because of an incredible festival of flowers that fills the square and the main church. Hundreds of thousands of roses and lilies and calla lilies and gerberas and tulips and daisies and dahlias and hydrangeas—*all white*—braiding and unbraiding, cascading, looping and swirling, creating a living floral temple in honor of the Easter celebrations. I stand gaping under the canopies of entwining ivy and calla lilies and orchids; I'm in awe before a huge cornucopia-shaped "flower-fall;" and my senses are completely aroused when I enter a space framed by columns of gardenias. My chest swells like a sail in the wind, inhaling the warm, sweet, fragrance of love—my favorite fragrance—that brings back the memory of Ettore and Sicily.

I move to the next flower space. White daturas hang from a dark ceiling like stars; in the corners, lilies-of-the-valley demurely protrude from the walls of white tulips; and I walk along the path lined by daisy-covered trellises in the shape of hearts. In a chapel, bird-shaped hydrangeas swoop down the walls. How is this done? How is it possible to fasten the flowers in such a way to make them look like they are floating in space? What size army of florists did it take to create all this magic?

And then I start to notice ... a wilted petal here, a yellowed leaf there, a limp branch elsewhere—the first faint signs of decay. All of a sudden I feel overwhelmed by sadness. Sad to feel the dying energy of thousands of cut flowers. Sad to see beauty so transient, fleeting in a blink of an eye—almost.

I look for Dwight and find him in the courtyard, sauntering over a wooden footbridge that crosses a pond covered with white water lilies. The pond, the little footbridge, are so Monet-esque. I stand in the cloister and watch. Dwight stops and looks down at the water lilies, then slowly turns around, as if sensing my gaze. He sees me by the door and his whole face lights up. Then he walks to me, takes me in his arms, and presses his forehead onto mine. "I missed you," he says softly.

I can't manage a smile. "The flowers..." I begin, trying to find the words. "All those flowers will wither in a few days. Beauty..." my voice chokes, "so short-lived."

Dwight plants a kiss on my forehead. "The real beauty is within," he says and looks deeply into my eyes. "That beauty never withers because it's not of the material world." He takes me by the hand and we walk out, away from the church and the mounds of white flowers. We walk to our car, ready to head back home, a couple of hours drive north. Our Côte d'Azur get-away is ending on a strange note, with this taste of sadness.

By now, I should have learned this pattern in my life—that fatigue is my second enemy, right after haste (the source of my impatience). I should have learned this, but I didn't. And so when we got caught in bumper-to-bumper traffic and I missed the turns to Avignon, I was suddenly overcome by exhaustion, as if the very last drops of energy were drained from my body. As I made two more wrong turns unable to find our way, I lost it—I exploded in a fit of anger. At no one in particular, really, just venting my frustration. And in the same instant I knew it: my painstakingly-gained victory over my temper was lost. My lower self had tricked me again.

CHAPTER 32

BEAUMES-DE-VENISE:
BREAKING FREE

Coming back to my prison-home felt like descending from Mt. Everest into an underground cave. The expansion, the sense of freedom, the glimmer of a different, better me I had experienced for one day in Antibes, all of that was erased in one broad sweep when I laid my eyes upon the narrow driveway to our house. For one day I had embodied my Gandalf/Dumbeldore/Ged role model: I was strong, serene, poised, even patient.

For one day, I thought that I had made it.

Now, it's all gone.

But Dwight has a different take on this. He says that now I've experienced what it's like to *act* like a Soul—even more, now I know what it feels like to be united with my Soul for one whole day. Then he reminds me about the first time I experienced my Soul-identity in Tuscany. "It was short, wasn't it? A mere hour or so?" he says. "And now you had one whole day. That's progress, don't you see?"

"How can you have so much patience with me?" I ask, amazed but enormously grateful.

Dwight looks at me warmly, his eyes shining and full of love. "Because you never ever give up until you reach your goal. I admire you for that. And I'll stay to help you as long as I can." He adds the last sentence in a slightly different voice, the voice I don't like.

Since we came back from the Côte d'Azur, I've been sensing this unexpressed cloud of worry around Dwight. I know he's deeply concerned about our financial situation and the possibility that he may no longer be able to provide for us. This worry has insidiously penetrated our life, adding an extra gloom to the already glum feeling in the house. Dwight is tired; I sense it. Not tired in the usual way, but tired of life, of "having to struggle," as he put it, with the body, the landlady, the finances. Even though he is so in touch with the invisible world, with his Soul, the material world is still a challenge.

Struggling with the body has used up a lot of his energy reserves. After the hip surgery, it took him almost two months of diligent exercising and therapy to start walking again. Meanwhile, due to the trauma of the surgery, his heart condition had become more erratic. For several months his heart was permanently arrhythmic, with occasional fits of tachycardia. Finally, on the advice of a cardiologist, Dwight underwent an electric shock treatment. It was risky, having the high-voltage current jolt his heart in order to force it to resume the regular beat, but Dwight is the kind of person who always takes risks. And it paid off—he now has a regularly-beating heart.

We've also spent a couple of weeks looking for another house, a short-term rental, since our six-month lease was about to expire and the landlady wanted us out. And *we* wanted us out. At the risk of being repetitive, I'll say that yet again I went through a by now perfected house-hunting routine. This was the sixth time since we left Cyprus roughly eighteen months ago that I had this "part-time job." I was beginning to think that I had a serious case of "house karma."

After a couple of weeks of futile searching, we received a note from Madame G. She would extend the lease for another month or two. Dwight and I looked at each other, perplexed. Then Dwight said, "I bet she can't find new tenants, and the summer season starts in two months. She doesn't want to lose money on an empty house."

So we accepted. Now I can concentrate on job-hunting back in the States, and Dwight on his energy work.

The energy work is the only thing Dwight is not tired of. We've combed this part of Provence, Vaucluse, visiting the grimmest, most dismal corners and villages, so that he could re-activate the points in the energy grid that were shut down due to religious massacres.

Sometime after his "hospital-awakening"—when the world of nature spirits opened up to him—Dwight fully understood the purpose of his work. He was shown the image of the Earth as a luminescent grid made up of threads of light (similar to the web of light he saw on the New Year's day atop the Janiculum hill in Rome, when we stood back to back to face the past and the future). Strewn around that grid were patches of darkness. No light flowed, no scintillating threads passed through those areas. His task was to repair the grid by reconnecting the threads and to re-establish the flow of light and energy in this little corner of the world. By doing this, he would be helping build the foundation—the energy matrix—for future generations.

"What do you mean, 'for future generations'?" I asked, perplexed, when he first shared his insight with me.

"You see, raising the energy frequency of the Earth will make it easier for more advanced Souls to incarnate. It will also make it easier for others who are just starting on the path to raise their own consciousness."

"Big task for one person."

"I'm sure I'm not alone doing this," Dwight replied. "Many others are dedicated to the same task—changing the frequency of the Earth's energy for evolutionary purposes."

I gazed at Dwight for a long moment. Finally, I began to understand what he had been doing since we came to France. The frequency of vibration of our planet is the energy matrix that informs and permeates all life forms. It's like a musical tone to which everything that exists is tuned. Increase the vibrational frequency of the Earth and the molecular vibration of all life follows.

"That's why I need to go to the places of massacres and bloodshed," he concluded.

And there has been a lot of bloodshed in this region for sure. Provence was home to the Waldensians, the Provençal version of the Cathars who appeared in the twelfth century preaching the return to poverty and the original teachings of Jesus. Several centuries later, during the Protestant Reformation, the Huguenots emerged also. The "faith purges," as the Pope referred to the wiping out of entire Waldensian and Huguenot villages, had reached genocidal proportions during the sixteenth and seventeenth centuries. In 1545 for example, a punishment expedition obliterated eleven villages in only six days.

It's not only the slaughter of the innocent that I find so disturbing; it's the way in which the attrocities were committed, with incomprehensible, blood-curdling cruelty on the part of the Catholic forces. Historical records that preserve the details of the massacres choke me. I can't find a trace of humanity in men smashing the heads of little children against rocks or tearing their little bodies limb by quivering limb. I can't see souls in men capable of burying other men alive in the furrows of their fields, then plowing them into the soil. Or forcing them to march to their death with the severed heads of their children hanging around their necks.

Why such cruelty? How is it possible that men are capable of atrocities that animals never commit? Do we carry a cruelty gene in our *human* DNA?

In Mérindol, one of the eleven villages in the Lubéron area that were wiped out, a memorial plaque shines on the ruins of a wall high on a hill. It reminds visitors of the religious genocides committed in the name of the faith and love that Jesus preached. The air is thick with congealed horror. I breathe it in with every breath I take. I watch the valley below, the spring sun searing my eyes. The whole valley was bathed in blood and charred by fire five centuries ago.

What if time were suddenly erased so that all events happen simultaneously? And we could see over our shoulder the horrid massacres, as well as peaceful land-toiling and love-making; torture as well as gentle care of toddlers; cries of agony as well as the laughter of children playing. Would the sight of compressed suffering teach humanity to become more compassionate?

But it's not only the churches and the remains of castles and towers that we visit; frequently, Dwight is led to the countryside, to an apparently "innocent" clearing in the woods or a field by a road. Dowsing with the pendulum would almost always indicate that the energy line was disturbed, scrambled, or completely shut down. By now, I can pick up the distinct feeling of sadness that permeates these places, a "silent scream" as Dwight calls it, a scream of despair and anguish which colors the whole area. Afterwards we'd go to the tourist office to inquire about the local history. Where information was available, we would find out that there had been a particularly bloody battle at the forest we just came from, or a massacre in the field where Dwight had just re-established the energy flow.

I don't want to give you a wrong impression. It's not all grim work and no play for us in Provence. We do visit famous tourist hang-outs, such as breathtaking Gordes, and red-rock Roussillon, and Menèrbes (where the author Peter Mayle used to live before busloads of Japanese tourists forced him to escape to an undisclosed residence). We do make pilgrimages to restaurants Mayle recommended in his witty and charming book, *A Year in Provence*. We make outings to different villages that have either a gorgeous location or a delectable restaurant—or preferably both.

It was on one of those days that I stumbled upon a stone fountain. As soon as we arrived at the medieval village of Crestet, embedded in a steep rock and towered over by a chateau, I felt chills running up my spine—chills of familiarity. Have I lived here in the past, in this tiny village that still looks as it did in the Middle Ages, with few concessions made to modern times?

I observe the villagers going about their business as if tourists didn't exist. I feel as though I'm getting a peek into their lives, into the lives of their great-great-great-grandfathers, a peek into times past.

The little square is irregularly shaped, surrounded by old stone houses, completely asymmetrical—one window here, another there, a triangular façade jutting into the square, a vaulted passage cut through the ground floor, a flight of steps leading to an arched doorway. And in the middle, an old, old stone fountain topped by a tall, cast-iron cross, and four carved heads squirting water into the basin day and night. It is utterly peaceful; no sound of modern times intrudes upon the timeless gurgling of the fountain.

I sit on the octagonal-shaped basin rebuilt of cement—the only sign of the present time—and gaze at the worn-out cobblestones. There is not a single flat surface on the pavement; everything is undulated and slanted, even the steps seem a bit crooked. As the fountain continues to gurgle, feet appear, walking over those cobblestones. Many feet in clogs, and legs clothed in rough, woolen fabric, long skirts and aprons.

I snap back. Am I imagining, am I fooling myself, or is this *the* fountain my psychic friend Liana told me about? Am I really in the village she saw in her reading almost a year ago? My body seems to feel so, shivers crawling up my spine, but my head rejects this possibility. It can't be; there were no Cathars here. And I *know* I had a Cathar incarnation; the purity of their beliefs is in my blood. What did Liana say? The holy woman of the Cathars ... *perfecta* ... bringing the truth of love where the Church was disseminating separation and violence. But she also said something about my voice ... finding that voice of the past that once soothed the villagers ... finding that voice again through creativity to touch and inspire people.

I shake my head. Liana must have been wrong. I don't seem to have any creativity in me, I haven't even thought of my book. All I'm writing about are my inner battles with my "limitations," the attacks of my lower self, torments caused by the *events* with the landlady, in brief—the inner and outer war. And an occasional breakthrough, like in Antibes.

At that moment, while sitting by the fountain and absentmindedly gazing at the cobblestones, the wider perspective of those battles, of *the war*, escaped me. It would take several more months to see the meaningful design of those situations of inner torment and outer hardship, and several more years to fully integrate the lessons and begin to live what I glimpsed during the break-throughs. From a higher perspective, which only the distance in time can give, everything that happened had a role to play in the ingenious curriculum of the path upon which I inched step by slow step.

But in Crestet, I gaze despondently at the gray stones worn slick. It seems to me that I have failed everywhere: after three months of applying for a teaching job, I haven't received a single interview; after a glorious excursion into the Soul-dom, I'm back in my lower, impatient self that throws fits of temper every now and then. During all those months, I haven't done anything creative; and on top of that, I still have a big issue with the landlady. A pretty dismal list of non-achievements.

I'm gazing at the gray stones worn slick, and thinking of all these failures. The stones are of different sizes and irregular shapes, hard to walk on. It must be particularly hard to walk on them in winter, when rain coats them with a layer of ice. How did life look in the past, during bitterly cold winter months? A pair of feet appears, stepping on the stones, feet shod in rugged but fancy Timberland shoes. Nice shoes, I can't help thinking; but in an instant I snap out of my inner monologue and realize that the shoes I'm staring at are Dwight's.

"What's the matter with you?" he asks half-worriedly and half-lightheartedly.

I look up and give him a tired smile. He seats himself next to me and listens to my list of failures without saying anything. When I finish, there is a moment of silence, unusual silence, because Dwight always has words of support for me. Then he simply asks, "Would you like to leave?"

"Leave? No, not necessarily, it's so peaceful here, so soothing."

"I didn't mean that. I meant—would you like to leave Beaumes and Provence?"

I turn to him, surprised. "You mean, move?"

Dwight nods.

"Where to?"

"Well, I've been getting these … what would I call them … promptings, that my work here is almost done. But…."

"But what?"

"There is more work to do in other parts of France."

I stare at Dwight, a stirring of excitement in my heart. "Where?" I ask in a tremulous voice.

"Brittany."

"Brittany? But there were no religious massacres there, no bloody history."

"No, but there are many Neolithic sites, megaliths and alignments, major energy centers."

All my gray thoughts are suddenly dispelled. I don't feel a trace of defeat left in my heart. I ask in a bright voice, "Are you saying we should move there?"

"No, not really. We don't need to live there, besides (and Dwight's voice now assumes a darker tone), we can't stay in Europe that much longer ... a few more months, perhaps."

"Until when?"

"Until ... let's say, September."

This didn't come as a surprise. In fact, I was expecting him to say June, July at the latest. I had no idea how much money we had left. I didn't want to ask those questions. Perhaps I didn't want to know. Dwight made all the financial calculations of our living costs. So far, he's always been remarkably accurate.

"So when do you think we should go to Brittany and for how long?"

"Oh, when it warms up. We'll stay in Beaumes until May, then spend a month or two on the road. We can take our time and visit cathedrals and chateaux on our way to Brittany. Then we'll come back here, stay with Pierre to rest, and then go to Rome. We'll fly back to California from Rome." Then he adds with a smile that can be either ironic or nostalgic, "One-way ticket."

It takes me a moment to understand what he's hinting at. "One-way ticket, you mean, like when you came to France the first time?"

Dwight looks away and strokes his chin. He makes a slight, almost imperceptible nod.

"Life unfolds in cycles," he says after a while, "shorter and longer, cycles within cycles. But there is always a completion to each cycle."

So there it was. The end and the beginning, the sadness of the end of our journey and the excitement of the beginning of a new—although last—leg of it. I sit with this mixture of feelings in my heart, thoughts racing, questions popping up. Now it's all laid out. We have a direction—*a renewed purpose*—until September. And then ... wait, I don't want to think about "then." I want to enjoy what's coming before "then," all the new places I'm going to see—cities, chateaux, streets and people, museums, lovely architecture—but above all, the mysterious Druid country in the north of France. Ancient Neolithic sites. Dolmens. Menhirs. Alignments. Like candies in colorful wrappers, all these places shine in my mind's eye. I shiver in delightful anticipation of unwrapping them and tasting each one of them, tasting their energy flavor. I want to savor the last treat of our six-year-long journey before we have to go back to "real life."

But before I could enjoy any such sweets, my Soul sent me a message about a forthcoming trial through a dream:

I'm about to board a plane to the States. The airport policeman sends me to a special security checkpoint. I come face to face with a middle-aged, white-haired customs officer, and put my suitcase on the counter. He examines the contents very thoroughly. I'm relaxed because I have nothing to hide, but I do worry if I'll make my flight on time. On a bulletin board behind the officer I notice, among other papers, a photo of me with my friends. I'm greatly puzzled that he has my picture and wonder why he keeps it there.

Then the officer informs me that he has to take me to another building and orders me to follow him. I'm still calm, but I sense that something is wrong.

The building we walk into could best be described as Kafkaesque: an air of secrecy, weirdness, and threat hovers in the deserted corridors lined by doors with peeling paint. The officer ushers me into an empty room. A girl appears and greets him with extreme respect and admiration. He seems to be a person of great authority. He gives her instructions, then takes me to another room, and another, each room getting more and more somber and sinister. As we progress, the feeling of the building becomes darker and more constricted, just as in Kafka's novel The Castle; but at the same time, the officer becomes more radiant, and I don't feel afraid.

Finally, we reach his personal office where, on the bulletin board, I'm astonished to see another picture of me. There is something peculiar about the photo: it doesn't look solid—the image is fluid and changes into another image, like photos in the Harry Potter books. I ask why he has my pictures, but he only shrugs and says, "Well, you know, everyone has a lower self."

Then he takes me outside the building to an area that looks like a Roman amphitheater. All along the round wall, there are small openings with hanging rubber strips instead of doors. They remind me of openings for wild animals, like the ones I saw in the Colisseum in Rome. He shows me one opening and tells me to go inside. For the first time since we started our passage through the building, I raise the question about my flight, but he ignores it. Instead, he motions for me to go in. In that gesture, there is a sense of inevitability, as if I had no choice but to obey. Still, I trust him.

As I crawl inside, he suddenly shuts a door behind me. In that moment when the door slams and I'm plunged into total darkness, I'm overcome by an indescribable sense of panic. I start to slide down to the bottom, along a steeply-slanted floor. A scream mounts from my entrails. I'm imprisoned in a tiny, airless, pitch-black space in a state of complete sensory deprivation. LOCKED IN THIS DARK LAIR FOR ETERNITY!

At that moment of sheer horror, when the feeling of panic is starting to consume me and push me into madness, I hear these words: **"The only way out of this prison is to reach up, reach to your Soul—transcend this entrapment."**

Instantly, I switch into lucid dreaming. This can't be real … I must be in a dream … I am in a dream….

As I think this, the prison dissolves like a mirage. A great sense of relief washes through my body and I wake up.

A few days after this epic dream, we had the second head-on conflict with Madame G. In response to Dwight's note that our deposit money was to be used as the last month's rent, we found the lock on the garage door changed. A note followed: if we don't pay the last month's rent we won't get the key to the new lock. Which meant we wouldn't be able to get our wooden crate stored inside and pack our belongings that we now have to ship to the States. The reason Dwight decided on such a move was that he had misgivings about the landlady's willingness to return our deposit. After all, we were going to leave the area, we were foreigners (without legal resident permits) and we couldn't do anything if she kept the deposit of one thousand Euros.

We went to consult with a lawyer, recommended by a friend. When she heard who our landlady was, she shook her head with an expression of doubt. Madame G. was well known to her, as she was to the whole village and beyond, for her revengeful and aggressive behavior. The lawyer's forecast was gloomy: our landlady would be capable of putting up a tenacious fight. She relished fighting; it was her only *raison d'être.*

From the lawyer's office we walked out with this piece of advice: best not to be at war with Madame G; best to forget about the deposit and preserve peace of mind.

We listened and dutifully paid the rent. In two days we got an envelope with a key to the new lock. Now we could begin to pack. Now we also have to meet with the landlady who wants to inspect the house.

Mind you, I haven't seen Madame G. since our falling out five months ago. If there was an issue to solve, I'd send Dwight as an emissary. He had no problem dealing with our landlady. I, on the other hand, would get heart palpitations just thinking of her. These last days, however, in expectation of our encounter, the sporadic heart palpitations have become pretty much a permanent condition. I had to face it: I'm living in a state of constant anxiety … all right—*fear* of the landlady. My heart actually hurts from an invisible hoop that squeezes it. I can't escape from this fear even at night. A few fitful hours of sleep are interrupted by nightmares. I actually can't recognize myself. I look in the mirror and meet two blue eyes that return my gaze with a hollow, ghostly stare. The face I scrutinize looks downright haggard.

Dwight is not exactly the example of cheerfulness either. But from time to time he gives me pep talks. He's actually assuring me that this is the best thing that could have happened to me (is he in his right mind?); that this is a lifetime opportunity to work out my "authority issue," as Dwight has dubbed it, and break free from my karma—exactly what I'd been asking for all this time, right? So I should be grateful to Madame G. for providing me with the opportunity to do this. "Remember," he'd repeat like a refrain, "our enemies are our best teachers."

When we're away from the house, when we escape for a few hours to a café, and when I feel fortified by a *grand café crème*, I admit that he's right. I mean, really, I'm overreacting. Sure, it's not going to be pleasant meeting the landlady when she comes over, but to be in this shaky state with a hole in my stomach—that's a bit exaggerated, wouldn't you agree? Obviously, I have a big issue with authority and now I'm given the opportunity (thank you, my Soul) to work it out. And, yes, I know the rule: if I don't do it now, the lesson will be repeated in the future, only in more drastic circumstances—just as happened to Bill Murray in *Groundhog Day*.

So here we are, on the day when Madame G. is due to come over and inspect the house. I'm working on the last adjustments, filling the holes I made in the walls for pictures and removing my beautiful, Provençal-yellow curtain I put in the bathroom to replace the hard-to-slide closet doors. I was very fond of that Provençal-yellow color. Every time I walked into the bathroom, the golden-yellow greeted me like the sun. The whole room was suffused with a subtle glow reflected by the fabric.

I climb on a ladder to take down the curtain. My insides are paralyzed by fear. I'm fumbling because the palms of my hands are cold and clammy, and everything slips from my fingers. I so desperately don't want to be here, in this village in Provence. If only I could fast-forward this moment in my life, skip this afternoon…. I stare at the sun-yellow fabric and every cell of my body cries out—*I don't want to be here!* Two more hours before she comes over. The panic mounts to my throat and chokes me. My brain is going into a paralysis mode; I'm utterly unable to control my emotions.

Just when fear gushes into my brain and engulfs the last cells that were putting up resistance, the image of a little girl with her nose glued to the window appears on the screen of my mind. In my head I hear the words: "Who is afraid of Madame G?"

In astonishment I recognize the Voice from my childhood!

I'm so stunned that the Voice is back after all these years that all the wheels in my brain suddenly come to a halt, and I have no thoughts, no feelings. I am in a vacuum state. Of its own accord something snaps in my head, and I experience a shift in perspective. I am out of my body, looking down at this scene as if it were a dream. As if it were the tiny, pitch-black prison cell from my recent dream.

Again the Voice speaks: "You have identified with a dream."

From the high, dry, and safe place where I am, I look down at the bathroom, our house, the driveway, and Madame G. Our lives, I see it clearly now, are made up of dream-scenes with which we identify. We take them as real and consequently suffer.

I invoke our landlady's face. I look at her short, hazelnut hair, her troubled eyes that burn with intensity, her round face, and I blink.

What is there to be afraid of?

Instead of fear, I feel an overwhelming compassion for her struggling little self, for all the people in the world who are grappling with life because they have forgotten their true identity, because they are living blindly, with no recollection of their immortal selves—their Souls.

It's so simple. All that suffering could be avoided if only we would wake up and see this life as a dream, one in a chain of many we, as Souls, go through. It's just like our dreams that seem real at night while we're dreaming them, but dissipate like smoke upon awakening. When we die, this life too will evaporate like smoke, and we'll awake to our true life.

I embrace Madame G, wishing that her suffering might lessen. *Thank you, my teacher.*

Awash with gratefulness, I turn my attention to the Voice. A flicker of recognition flashes though my mind, but I'm not able to catch it. I'm immersed in a sea of love, sweet, ecstatic, timeless. I remain in that state for a long while, my brain suspended.

Slowly, I become aware of the yellow curtain before my eyes and the curtain rod I was struggling to dismantle. I take the fabric in my hands and bring it close to my face, to my cheek. I rub my cheek against the firm but fine, delicately ribbed cotton. *Thank you.* I kiss it.

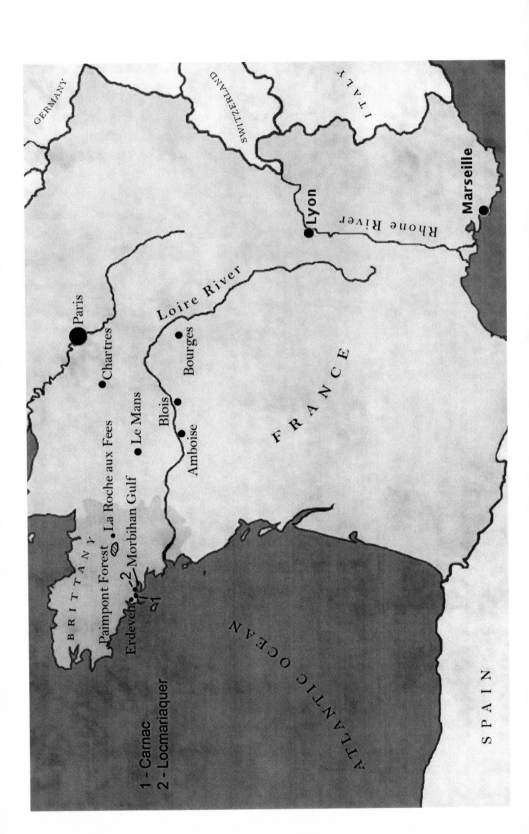

PART 7

BRITTANY:

RITES AND PASSAGES

CHAPTER 33

CENTRAL FRANCE:
ALL BACK ROADS LEAD TO LEONARDO

Everything is packed. The crate has been picked up and is now in Marseilles, scheduled to be shipped to California in a couple of weeks. The luggage for our month-or-so-long trip through France is also ready. I'm ready too. I feel like I've brought a sense of closure to this experience with Madame G. When the landlady came over a week ago, my heart was beating normally, and I even managed to talk to her in a friendly manner as if nothing had ever happened between us. I've passed the exam; I've overcome the paralyzing fear of authority.

What a wonderful feeling—to be free from the chains of the past, free from fear, from the conditionings of the personality. With that sense of freedom comes strength, a natural outcome of freedom. With every fear overcome, with every old conditioning dissolved, we reclaim bits of our consciousness that were trapped in those thought-forms. Bit by bit, we make ourselves whole again, and that wholeness has power.

I'm gliding through the house serenely, finishing the packing. I'm even so much more loving, and Dwight is the recipient of this fuller, stronger love. Out of the corner of my eye, I catch his glances. He looks at me with such relish and so much satisfaction, just as a ballet teacher would look at his protégée who finally becomes a prima ballerina. He also looks at me with admiration, with an abiding love, so solid that it feels rooted in the very foundations of time. At one moment he even commented that of all the students he'd ever had in his long career and whom he was helping and steering through life, I was his masterpiece. He has taught me everything he knows. Now I have to apply that knowledge and live according to it.

As for Dwight, he's on to a new learning experience, a new cycle in his life. The type of energy work he's going to be doing in Brittany will be different from what he did in Provence, although he doesn't really know in what way. Unlike me, who had a teacher (him) to guide me through the dark regions of my own psyche, Dwight does not have anyone to teach him. He has to find out everything for himself.

With one exception. Dwight has stumbled upon a British dowser, Hamish Miller, through a book I brought him from Santa Fe, and has been in touch with him since our last weeks in Italy. The work with Earth's energies that Hamish has done both in England and throughout Europe has been a source of inspiration for Dwight and has served as pointers on the road.

According to Miller's investigations conducted over many years, major energy lines flow through or over the surface of the Earth. Those energy lines are made up of two intertwined strands: a male or *yang* strand and a female or *yin* strand. Hamish and his collaborators have followed a double energy line from England through Europe to Jerusalem. They've dubbed it the Apollo/Athena axis. This line happens to go through many of the places that Dwight and I plan to visit. The first one is Lyon.

Lyon is the capital of the Rhône-Alpes region, about 130 miles north of Avignon. It's a major economic and industrial center, as well as the capital of gastronomy in France. We've already heard a great deal about this city from our friend Pierre, who was born there. Pierre insisted we had to visit Lyon if we were interested in esotericism because Lyon was the alchemical hotbed of France in Renaissance times and a center of Egyptian Freemasonry (the first Lodge was created there by Count Cagliostro in 1782).

"Lyon has a past," Pierre said significantly one day while visiting. "An alternative spiritual underground. You won't find that in the books." He waved his hand dismissively toward the guide books and other assorted brochures lying on the coffee table.

So we are well prepared to look beneath the surface when we arrive on top of the hill where the Celtic city Lugdunum used to stand 2,000 years ago, and now Notre Dame de Fourvière rises protectively above the city. Good thing we're prepared to look beneath the surface, because one needs to do that when facing this late nineteenth-century church. The edifice resembles something William Randolph Hearst would have built—a jumble of styles and a flashy display of the-more-the-merrier pieces of art.

We first descend to the crypt where the statue of the Black Madonna is venerated. In addition to Marseilles, Lyon is one of the biggest centers of her worship and perhaps the most ancient. But the crypt is so full of people and loud organ music that my senses are overloaded. I can't feel a thing in here.

We walk outside and stand facing the sweeping view of old Lyon, the River Saône, and the modern city beyond. Behind us, from the summit of the Basilica, rises the statue of St. Michael. He is poised atop a dragon, the symbol of terrestrial energies. According to Hamish, St. Michael—the Christian equivalent of ancient sun gods (the Greek Apollo, for example, or the Celtic Lug)—reigns over the hilltops, which are associated with the sun. Those high places mark the passage of the masculine or Apollo energy current. The female counterpart, the Athena line, usually flows through valleys, springs, and caves—in general, low or underground places. But here, it passes through a statue of the Virgin, which tops the side tower of the church. With outstretched arms, the gilded statue gazes in a motherly way at the city, as if to say, "Here it is, the blessed spirit ... it's passing through me and I bestow it upon you."

There has to be some energy here, because Lyon seems to be associated with light in many ways. Old Celts named their capital after the sun god Lug; the present-day nickname of Lyon is the City of Lights; there is also an annual celebration—the Festival of Lights—in remembrance of the protective influence of the Virgin Mary who (it is said) spared the townspeople from the plague in 1643. It is only befitting, then, that the brothers Lumière (again—"Light!") invented the cinema in no other city but Lyon.

There has to be some energy here, but I'm not sensing it.

I'm eager to descend to Old Lyon at the foot of the hill and experience the "hotbed of alchemy." Vieux Lyon, Pierre had told us, is a honeycomb of traboules, narrow passageways built in medieval times to connect parallel streets through the houses. In that way, during religious raids, the alchemists could quickly escape through the warren of passageways not visible from the streets.

So we walk down to the Quartier de St. Jean and ... can't believe what we're seeing. All along the main street, groups of punks, clochards, or gangs are loitering, sitting on doorsteps, spitting, smoking, yelling at each other. Esoteric and alchemical energy? I don't even feel safe here, let alone feel any kind of spiritual energy!

Other streets are better—emptier. So empty in fact, that I'm overwhelmed by a feeling of angst which I can't control. It's worse than angst actually; it's the feeling of despair that washes through my body. Unfortunately, one of the highly recommended restaurants is in this very area. We walk into the elegant décor of an empty restaurant. We eat alone at a round table decked in a starched damask tablecloth and imposing crystal candle-holder. Beautiful artwork covers the walls. But none of this can cover the feeling of desperation that permeates this old house and, it seems to me, the walls themselves.

Back in our beautiful hotel in the affluent part of Lyon on the other side of the river, I read about the history of the old town. From Renaissance times, Lyon was the most important center in Europe for currency dealings. The advent of the silk industry ushered in a true golden age, and Lyon thrived. This is also the time when all things occult and alchemical thrived too. But in the eighteenth century came the reversal. International banking moved to Genoa, and the rich and powerful deserted Lyon. The silk industry declined as well. Impoverishment, overcrowding, and despair oppressed the once-affluent city. In the mid-nineteenth century, destitution reached such a point that silk workers staged two major uprisings to change their situation. But it's only in the last forty years that decrepit Old Lyon has gradually been restored.

"You're like a canary," Dwight marveled, "I've always said that."

I don't exactly like being a canary, but I was certainly pleased that my impressions were confirmed. Old Lyon helped me to understand *experientially* what Tom Graves wrote about the energy of places in his classic book *The Needles of Stone*. Imagine, says Graves, each emotion having its matching color, even shade (big difference between bright red and brown-putrid-red, between golden-yellow and sickly lime-yellow-green). And imagine that each time you walk into your house you throw a bucket of paint onto its walls. Over time, the walls are going to assume a predominant color that will match your most frequent emotional states.

So what happens if you live in abject poverty with no hope of betterment? If you have to watch your children starve? The "colors" of misery, despair, and hopelessness will permeate the air and "paint" the walls. And those colors would, in turn, reinforce your emotional states.

Decades and centuries of misery, however, cannot be stripped off by simply repainting the walls. The energy of emotions penetrates much, much deeper than the thin layer of paint; it can be stored directly into the fabric of the place, even in the thick layer of brick. The only way to energetically "re-paint" a place is through positive emotions.

"So, instead of spiritual energy, we found the energy of misery," I said, putting down the book on Lyon. "What a let-down."

"No," said Dwight firmly, "it's not a let-down. You had an important lesson. Do you believe now what I've said so many times? That you're extremely sensitive, even though you don't have etheric and astral vision, as you've always complained."

Slowly, I nodded. I had to.

"You don't need clairvoyance or clairaudience. Those are astral reactions. 'Powers and abilities of the past,' as Kostas said. We're in the age when we need to develop intuition. And only as we become more spiritually aware, can those old astral powers be re-activated ... if necessary. But then it will happen on a higher turn of the spiral, when we won't misuse them to hurt others."

For the remainder of our stay in Lyon, we didn't return to the old town. We sat in cafés on the river bank, enjoyed the view of Notre Dame, and strolled the bustling and colorful streets of the nineteenth-century Lyon. The energy on this side of the river felt really good. Perhaps it was the benediction that the Virgin bestowed so lavishly this way.

From Lyon we drove about 200 miles north through Auvergne to the central region of France and its exact geographic center—Bourges. We also went back in time as we arrived in this beautifully preserved medieval town with half-timbered houses. Bourges is like a doll-house town; reduce it in size, and you'd think it was built as a little girl's favorite toy. Everything is clean and restored, with lots of flowers and trees—in brief, perfect. You feel like playing with it, inventing its inhabitants, moving them about, creating stories of their lives.

According to Hamish's investigations, Bourges is one of the places where both strands of the energy line—the Apollo and Athena—meet and actually cross. Those places, for which Hamish coined the term "nodes," are special. There is an energy charge that doesn't exist elsewhere. And the node in Bourges is located inside the famous Cathedral of St. Etienne, one of the masterpieces of Early Gothic style, built at the end of the twelfth century, the same time as Chartres Cathedral.

When we walk through the portal door in the late afternoon, we step into a mind-altering space: the interior of the cathedral explodes like a massive forest of pillars, the canopy of which meets in the vaulting at an astonishing height of 115 feet. The whole interior is bathed in soft, evenly distributed light. And as we walk in, the sonorous notes of organ music reverberate throughout the vast interior. Imagine: space, light, and sound—unified in this architecture—at the very moment we stepped inside.

I'm in such awe, I can't move. Slightly shivering, I take in the immensity of this shrine. Like a huge, elongated horseshoe, the nave extends some 400 feet to the choir. No transepts, no enclosures, only two rows of arcades that extend all along the nave, accentuating the feeling of simple vastness. After a while, Dwight has to take me by the hand and walk me to the place where the two energy lines cross. He seats me on a chair above the node. The deep organ sound soars above my head and the energy of the node streams through my feet and up my legs. The sound around me and the energy below me wash through my body. All thinking stops and I enter a state of pure beingness.

After a while, I start to feel pain in my heart, sharp and constricting. Intuitively, I know that this pain is not triggered by any physical cause. It is the pain amassed over the lifetimes of living in fear, loss, and sorrow. The pain has the shape of a sharp-pointed flint, and it's piercing my heart. I start to choke. My throat feels swollen with a lump of unexpressed longing. All those lives lived under repression, in silence, suffering, sorrow…. I want to rip out that constriction, that tight-binding collar, so that I can breathe freely, so that in this life I can express who and what I truly am.

I've lost track of time. I might have been sitting there for five minutes, or fifteen, or fifty. When I again become aware of my surroundings, it's because a large group of tourists has walked in and piled up right behind me—in the otherwise empty church! I can't believe it. A priest is serving as a tour guide, shouting over the sound of the organ. I feel so disgusted that I'm boiling inside—*this is not fair! You have the whole church in front of you! Why have you encroached upon my space? Why have you ruined my mystical experience?*

Just as I launch this silent scream of indignation, I have an unmistakable feeling that this is a test. The test of my ability to control my temper and irritation. I take several deep breaths and let go of my indignation. It's not easy, but I curb my irritation. These people have the right to be here, just as I do. Calmly, I sit on my chair, centered in my heart. When the priest ends his talk and the whole group disperses, I'm alone again, but my altered state has vanished. Never mind. Something else is gained. I deeply sense my own victory: self-control trumped irritation, compassion replaced selfishness. I feel warmth around my heart where before there was the pain of that sharp, cold flint.

"You have to see the windows," I hear Dwight's voice behind me. I turn to him and look at his strong face and broad chest, and my heart wells up with love. I take his hand and pull him toward me. With surprise in his eyes, he leans forward, and I touch his lips softly, gratefully. A kiss beyond centuries.

Then we walk to see the stained glass windows. The earliest ones, from the thirteenth century, are the most beautiful. The colors are so rich, intense, and lit from within, that they seem other-worldly. Both the stained glass master and the master mason who designed this cathedral remained anonymous. Such an incredible achievement of architecture and its creators have not signed it! One thing is known though: the Knights Templar were the force and the mind (and the coffers) behind the Gothic revolution in architecture. It has been postulated that they brought the principles of sacred geometry from their initial sojourn in the Holy Land and applied them in building Gothic cathedrals. (Sacred geometry, simply put, is a blueprint of geometrical shapes found at the root of all creation in nature. It reflects the metaphysical postulate "as above, so below," which means that geometric order on earth is a reflection of the celestial geometry.)

Sitting in the interior of this cathedral, one cannot but feel the effect of those principles—that particular proportions embody a resonance with divine harmony.

God, taught Pythagoras, talks to humankind through numbers.

I could stay in Bourges longer, much longer than the two days we have planned. As I walk the streets alone the following day, I feel so perfectly content. No impressions of misery, desperation, or angst jar my nerves. Peace and calm permeate this place. Perhaps this is because Bourges has always been a prosperous town of merchants and bankers, never plagued by poverty. Or perhaps because there never were any religious massacres here. Or both.

I'm walking back to the hotel, basking in this peace and thinking of the lovely dinner we're going to have in an elegant, exquisite restaurant we discovered the day before. All of a sudden, my cell phone rings from the cavernous depths of my purse. It must be Dwight; we don't have that many friends in France who'd be calling us when we're travelling. I dig out the phone, glance at the number, and feel a short stab in my heart. It's Madame G.

I feel strongly that I shouldn't answer. But I disregard my hunch and push the "talk" button. The shrill voice shoots into my ear: Why haven't we left the house properly cleaned? I remain calm and answer that we did clean the house.

But no, we left food in the refrigerator, comes a holler. Other accusations are hurled at me in what soon becomes a fit of rage.

I stand rooted in the middle of the street. I can't believe what I'm hearing. I can be accused of various faults, of course, but accusing me of leaving the house dirty and damaged—me, an ultra-conscientious Virgo!—that's just plain false. I try to explain; I try to argue; I even try to defend myself. Nothing makes any impact on the intensity of rage gushing from the phone into my ear. I can't take it anymore. With a shaking hand, I press the red button and the wrathful voice disappears. So does my peace.

The next morning as we are driving to the chateau of Blois, I still can't shake off Madame G.'s voice. I feel as if the arrows of her wrath are stuck in me. I complain at length about her unjust accusations. Dwight is periodically shaking his head and making little "hum" noises, until he bursts out, "Oh, c'mon, stop wallowing in your indignation!"

"But, but … I was unjustly treated!" I protest.

"And what else would you expect from an unreasonable, irrational person? It's like expecting a dog to behave like a cat."

I'm so surprised by his words that I don't know what to reply.

"You can't go through life open like that," Dwight continues in a calmer voice. "Reacting so *personally*. People will hurt you all the time."

"So how can I protect myself?" I ask wearily.

"By becoming impersonal and detached." He pauses for a moment than asks, "Who gets hurt, anyway?"

"What do you mean?"

"Who feels unjustly treated?"

I see now where Dwight is going. We're back to my old lesson, my Second Fundamental. "The personality, not the Soul," I answer with a sigh.

"Exactly," Dwight booms. "When you identify as a Soul, when you *act* as a Soul, people's attacks can't hurt you. The frequency of their emotions can't find anything matching in your own field, so their arrows just slide off. It's the emotional patterns of the personality that attract those arrows and keep them inside your energy field."

"I still have so much to learn," I say with a much deeper and longer sigh.

"You've already learned," Dwight declares with certainty, "this is just additional practice. You see, when you're breaking up an old pattern of behavior, the tests are repeated in different circumstances. It's like taking a picture of a sculpture from different angles; it's one and the same sculpture, but it looks different depending on your position. You have to know the sculpture from every side."

A half-hour later, we're in Blois, on the north bank of the Loire River. Dwight didn't really want to come here because he didn't like the chateau on his earlier visit while living in France, but I insisted that we come, although I didn't know why.

The weather is cold and gray when we park the car in the vicinity of the chateau. I'm wearing my Roman winter gear, with a shawl snuggly wrapped around my neck—and it's the end of May. The chateau returns the gloom of the day. The courtyard is barren, bordered by wings that were built in different centuries: from the medieval fortress, through Flamboyant High Gothic, to Renaissance, to Classicism, the chateau tells the story of its different owners.

"Well, which wing do you want to visit?" Dwight asks, surveying the buildings without enthusiasm.

I hesitate. The Renaissance wing looks the most interesting, with a magnificent staircase-tower in the shape of a spiral, all lavishly carved. But I don't go there. Instead, I head for the oldest wing that was a part of the thirteenth-century medieval fortress. Dwight follows. We walk into the Hall of Estates General which, the brochure says, has preserved its original layout. The so-far-grumpy Dwight suddenly perks up. With decisive steps, he strides to the huge fireplace supported by black marble columns with golden trimmings. The upper part of the fireplace is covered in a *fleur de lys* pattern, the emblem of the House of Orléans that subsequently became the symbol of the French monarchy.

For a long while, Dwight stands in front of the fireplace, his back turned toward me. Something is happening, I can tell. He takes his right hand out of his pocket and places it on the column, then the mantel. He's not doing any energy work, I don't think, but he's communing with something. I stay behind, not wanting to interrupt whatever is going on. I, too, start to sense something unusually alive in this medieval hall with arcades and wooden barrel vaulting, all painted in deep-red tones. I take out our books and start to read about the chateau.

Out of the corner of my eye, I catch Dwight turning. Slowly he walks toward me. He looks different. His face is troubled and ... am I imagining or do I really see his eyes beginning to mist? I stay put and wait.

"I ... I," stammers Dwight, looking away from me, "I had a strong past life flash-back."

I raise my brow in surprise but remain silent.

"I saw myself walking into this hall, standing by the fireplace, talking with other guests and warming my hands at the fire." Dwight now turns his gaze upon me and says simply, "My Templar incarnation."

"Ah!"

We look at each other for a long moment. Dwight has always felt that in some past life he had worn the white garb with the red cross on his chest.

"I was overcome with sadness," he continues softly, and again I see his eyes misting over. "I saw Templar commanders and Masters gathered here to discuss matters of importance. There was so much promise then. So much aspiration for the regeneration of humanity.... All that went astray, destroyed. All the hope for the new path of spiritual growth, corrupted. The spirit, gone...."

At these words, my heart quakes. I'm not sure what he's talking about, but I understand in my heart. I make a step forward and embrace my beloved. I embrace him tightly, and open my heart so he can take whatever he needs. He returns my embrace with uncertainty, as if wavering. Then he bends his head and rests his forehead on mine. From my heart pours so much love, I don't know where it's coming from. I feel bottomless understanding. I can give—endlessly.

Then we part. Dwight is strong and composed again.

We walk back into the courtyard.

"Are you ready to hear something?" I ask, glancing sideways at him.

"What?"

"I just read that Blois was one of the centers of Templar activity."

He looks at me, startled. "So the vision I had was correct."

I nod. "And not only that. Blois played an important part in the French esoteric tradition. One of the counts was the patron of the first Grail story written by Chrétien de Troyes."

Dwight stops and looks at me, his eyes aglow. Then he takes my hand and plants a kiss. "Thank you."

"For what?"

"For bringing me here." Then he adds with a smile, "My muse."

We have reserved a room for tonight in Amboise, just twenty miles west of Blois, along the Loire River. Our hotel is on the same bank as the chateau, and the windows of our room look at the ramparts. I can see the balconies with wrought-iron railings from which the Protestants were hanged in one of the bloody episodes of the War of Religion. Others were hanged from the battlements, or from iron hooks, or were strung from the town walls, or simply thrown into the Loire in sacks. The stench of the rotting corpses was so bad that the Court had to leave town for a while.

Surprisingly, I don't detect any negative energy when we go to visit the chateau the next morning. Perhaps my sensors are tricked by the magnificent view that opens from a terrace in front of the castle. The Loire is meandering sensuously through the lush valley, and on its other bank is nestled the town of Amboise. Like a crop of corn stalks, blue-slate roofs sprout up from within the walls. Beyond the houses stretches the undulating land, tame, gentle, inviting. No wonder the French aristocrats flocked here to build their chateaux. This is a beautiful land. Soft like a woman's skin, lush like spring rains, abundant like a starry night. Along the 200-mile course of the river from Orleans to Nantes (the nicest part), I've counted no fewer than seventy chateaux worth visiting. But if you look at the entire course of the Loire, some 600 miles, you can no longer count the aristocratic residences; you have to take the guidebook's word for it—a thousand chateaux!

Inside Amboise castle we breeze through different halls, mostly empty, all looking new and clean. Then we go to a little chapel, the only structure that remains of the buildings that lined the ramparts centuries ago. The St. Hubert chapel is a tiny but beautiful piece of late Flamboyant Gothic architecture. Now, I don't really care for late Gothic, ornate and spiky, but this little chapel has attracted me because Leonardo—*the* great Leonardo da Vinci—*may* have been buried here. That's a curious state of affairs, if you ask me. Leonardo was such an illustrious mind that the French king François I called him "father" and sat with him on his deathbed. A man who was so famous in his own time, and yet his burial place is not certain!

From here it's a short walk to another royal mansion, the much smaller chateau Clos-Lucé, where Leonardo lived the last three years of his life. We walk along a strange-looking street. On one side, houses are built into the rock spur which dominates the town of Amboise. Chimneys protrude out of the vertical crag; stairs lead to glass doors that, in turn, lead into the rock face and—inside the rock. It looks surreal. But the doors are new. These rock dwellings have been recently remodeled. This is like a French—and modern—version of the cliff dwellings of Mesa Verde.

Somewhere along these rocks, or *under* these rocks, is the secret passageway that connects the main chateau to Clos-Lucé, the passageway which François I used on his visits to Leonardo. The French king avidly absorbed the knowledge which the aged master had accumulated during his intense and very full life. Good for him. I'd do the same. Leonardo is one of my artistic and intellectual role models. The notion "Renaissance man" may have been coined after him (and if it wasn't, it should have been).

Leonardo was a grand package: a painter, sculptor, musician, poet, architect, engineer, inventor, town-planner, and philosopher/scholar. He was so ahead of his time that some of his inventions, such as the bicycle, took five centuries to manifest. Leonardo was a precursor of most of modern science. He was the first to practice anatomical drawing; he studied acceleration and the law of falling bodies before Galileo, and the balance of liquids before Pascal; in physiology, he discovered the function of the valves in the heart; in astronomy, he explained the twinkling of the stars; he invented the photometer, the hygrometer, the dredging boat, the vapor pump, the breech-loading cannon, the steam cannon (please don't ask me what all these things are), as well as the clock pendulum, city sewers, and the parachute; he established experimental science before Francis Bacon, and created the basis for geology, optics, and mechanics. Oh, and I forgot to mention—he established the High Renaissance style in painting before Michelangelo and Raphael, and invented *sfumato* (atmospheric perspective, created by the "smoky" treatment of the background). Wait, he was also an accomplished musician who not only played harp and lute beautifully, but who also redesigned those instruments in new shapes that produced fuller sounds.

As much as this seems impossible for one man to achieve in a life of sixty-seven years, this is not all Leonardo did. He was also heavily involved in the underground esoteric current of the Renaissance, and is believed to have been the Grand Master of the Priory of Sion. His paintings are studded with mysterious symbolism and his drawings reflect the concept of sacred geometry. Whatever he drew—men or machines, horses in movement or falling draperies—embodies the tenet that there is a meaning in patterns, and harmony in proportions. The drawing that most explicitly illustrates the concept of sacred geometry through the use of the Golden Mean is his *Vitruvian Man*, the famous drawing of a male figure in two superimposed positions enclosed within a circle and a square.

To call Leonardo a genius would be an understatement. In my eyes he was a superman, an evolutionary model of what human beings could—should— become in the future.

So no wonder I'm excited as we walk into the courtyard and stand before the red brick building highlighted with white stone (Flamboyant Gothic again). No wonder I hush my voice as we walk inside, just as the other handful of visitors do. No wonder I walk with reverence through the Renaissance reception room, the salons, the basement that houses the museum of Leonardo's fabulous machines (a collection of models made by IBM), even the kitchen with its monumental chimney. But when I walk into Leonardo's bedroom and studio on the first floor, I feel such awe as if I had entered the most sacred of sacred places. I stand before his bed, a four-poster, with dark-red velvet curtains tied with golden tassels to the posts.

I approach the bed as far as the rope allows. Here, the king sat by the dying Leonardo and held his head. I take it all in, standing alone in the room. Everything is peaceful, impregnated with an energy I cannot describe. Something is touching my heart right to its core, and I don't know what it is. My heart flutters like a birdling that is anxious to attempt its first flight. *I … I … want to do…*—my heart doesn't dare finish its thought, but I know what it wanted to say. A few tears roll down my cheek; tears of longing to express the unnameable, to give shape to the invisible, to manifest the Beauty I sense, vaguely, when I close my eyes. To expand and be more than I am, to take the whole world inside me, merge with it, then return it fuller, brighter, more beautiful.

The energy is … awesome.

In the Renaissance garden where we go next I feel the same energy that permeates the chateau. Is the soul of the great Master still here, I wonder?

"I rather doubt it," Dwight answers my question while we're sitting in the garden café, amid red roses and perfectly trimmed hedges. "Leonardo was a highly advanced soul," he continues, "who had incarnated to give humanity a lead, the guidelines for the next several centuries. He wouldn't be hovering around his deathbed." Dwight firmly shakes his head.

"Besides," he adds, hesitating, "I think there is something else you were picking up."

"What?"

"Well, I'm not sure, but the wall text in the house and the booklet gave me sort of a clue. You see, the curators who worked on the restoration of this building, they are very devoted to Leonardo's work; you can tell that from what is written and how it's written. There is so much love, respect, and admiration for the great Master that I think this is what you were picking up."

I take the booklet Dwight has placed on the table and leaf through it. There is an article on Leonardo's work by a member of the private organization which carried out the restoration work. As I skim the pages, I feel that Dwight is right. This is not a scholarly treatise, but a heartfelt address.

"With Leonardo da Vinci, expansion becomes the rule," reads the first page, and I immediately shiver. "There was no aspect of life which did not interest him and fascinate him to the point of wanting to conquer its every feature, to taste all its joys, to experiment with all its grandeur."

I look around at the pine trees, the hedges, the roses that hug the pond in the middle. A sense of perfect peace and harmony pervades the air. This garden, this mansion, is like an oasis. A place where you come to be inspired, a place where you come to commune with your Soul.

I read Leonardo's quote at the end of the booklet:

"If man's body seems to you a wondrous work, consider that it is nothing in comparison to the soul. In truth, whatever the man, he contains always the element of the divine."

CHAPTER 34

BRITTANY:

OF FAIRIES AND GIANTS

Visiting the Chateau d'Ussé (the famous Sleeping Beauty chateau), and even the Chateau de Villandry, with the most famous gardens in France, felt anti-climactic after my experience at Clos-Lucé. Granted, the Villandry gardens were exquisite: over twelve acres of colorful flowers, herbs, and vegetables planted in the most intricate geometrical shapes or grouped under different themes, such as unrequited love, passionate love, broken love, all faithfully recreating the formal Renaissance style in gardening adopted in the fifteenth century. Granted, the Château d'Ussé was so well restored—with all the furniture, mannequins, and costumes telling the story of *Sleeping Beauty*— that it felt as if we were walking through the fairy tale itself. (According to tradition, Charles Perrault chose this castle as a model for his fairy tale.)

But those were mere tourist visits. During our journeys, I've gotten so used to having inner experiences as well—insights, inspirations, past life flash-backs, energy imprints—that an ordinary, perfectly fine tourist visit doesn't do it for me anymore. It's like riding in a Ferrari on fast roads for a long time, then switching to a Chevy in a residential neighborhood. You'd feel the difference, wouldn't you?

With those two chateaux, we completed our visit of the Loire Valley. It was time to move on to Brittany.

Bretagne, the northwest peninsula of France, is considered one of the six Celtic nations which remained independent until as late as the sixteenth century. But even after its annexation to France the region has preserved its strong Celtic heritage: the Breton language is much closer to Welsh or Irish than to French, and the mores and character of the Breton people are distinctly different from those of the French. And then there is the folklore. The Celts left a strong legacy of magic, beliefs in spirits, and unforgettable legends. Some of the most famous ones, such as the legend of the Round Table, Merlin and Viviane, Tristan and Isolde, all sprang from here. Hence Brittany is also called the "Land of Legends."

That is why going to Brittany feels like leaving France and traveling to another country. It also feels like traveling back in time to the remote past of the Neolithic civilization that thrived here several thousand years before Christ. The Neolithic people left a fascinating heritage—gigantic blocks of stone, called megaliths, strewn all over the peninsula.

Our first stop is the Neolithic site of La Roche aux Fées (the Fairy Rock), just on the other side of the "border" with France. The branches of huge, old plane-like trees hug the massive slabs set up in the shape of the Greek letter *pi*: two vertical megaliths are topped by a horizontal one, many π's lined up to form a corridor that ends in a semi-circular chamber—a structure called a dolmen ("stone table" in Breton). The forty-two stones are so heavy, each weighing forty tons, that it was believed that fairies brought them to the site, hence its name.

Peace and quiet reign at this solitary—*fairy*—glade when we arrive. It's the kind of peace that makes you stand before the glade as though it were a temple; a peace that fills you with reverence. The sun is filtering through the foliage, dappling the surface of the rocks in patches of dancing light. Wood and rock—the essence of nature. The glade feels alive with nature spirits; I feel their presence around me, dancing and hopping, greeting me in a way. In awe, I walk around the massive monument. I touch the cold surface of the stones, my fingers gliding over patches of lichen. They are rocks, but they feel alive.

I'm beginning to understand now why the Bretons are so inclined toward the "dreamy, the fantastic, and the supernatural," as our guidebook states. Brittany is studded with megalithic sites where you can literally feel the fairies, and where the colossal size of stone blocks evokes the mythic presence of giants. At these places the notion of reality becomes slightly blurred, as if it's been only partially superimposed over the invisible world that shows through. In a way, the two worlds co-exist in Brittany, and the visible world cannot be explained or understood without taking into account the invisible world. The latter informs the former.

I watch Dwight move around with a pendulum in hand. He's following one of the currents, his pendulum swinging wildly. Then he places his hand on a nearby tree trunk to commune with the tree. It feels so ... well, *natural* to talk to nature in Brittany, as if the channels of communication are much more open than in other places. Here, in this Celtic country, we have entered a different world, a world where other laws and beliefs are in place, a world where people consider nature alive, and magic is a part of reality.

I feel very, very much at home in this world.

Choosing the hotel Auberge du Sous-Bois in the little town of Erdeven as our base was one of those decisions Dwight made based on his pendulum. He dowsed the map of Brittany, holding the question of our lodging in mind, and the pendulum swung wildly over Erdeven. That's why we're going to spend the next six nights here, even though this hotel wouldn't have been our choice: it's too close to the main road, the rooms are too small, and the owner is, to put it mildly, odd. With furtive eyes and terse words, he reminds me of a dark character in a Roman Polanski movie, and I can imagine him tormented by a secret obsession.

In the half-empty hotel, the quirky owner selected a room for us on the second floor at the back of the building. Why did he assign us this room when there were so many other options? I was going to request the corner room, a little more spacious than this cramped space, but Dwight stopped me. He called me to the window and pointed to the garden below, where three megaliths stood in the corner.

"This room," said Dwight, "is right on the energy line. That's why the pendulum sent us to this hotel. This energy is conducive for our work."

Well, "our" work is not exactly one and the same. Unlike Dwight, who is very clear on what he needs to do—re-activate the energy centers that have been shut down due to the breaking of menhirs ("long stones") or the building of roads through the alignments, I'm not sure what I am supposed to do or learn here. (It has become the usual pattern with us: Dwight always knows exactly what his work is, whereas I have little or no clue about mine.)

As if to confuse me even more, my Soul sent me an odd, odd dream the very first night in this "specially assigned" room.

I'm in a place I don't recognize. I'm wondering what I'm supposed to be doing there, when my mother shows up out of nowhere. For whatever reason, at the moment when she appears, I am bent forward. She approaches me, puts her hand on the middle part of my back, right where the two curves of my scoliosis meet, and announces (in Serbian of course): "Well, now is the time for you to find out why you were born this way and why you had to go through everything you did. You are finally ready to hear...."

While she is talking, she keeps me in that same, bent-over position, not allowing me to straighten up. She continues: "You should know that you were born into the Order of St. Germain, and all the difficulties, illnesses, and my disciplinarian attitude toward you was a set-up, a part of your training—"

Then she stops talking before revealing the crucial piece of information and the dream changes into another one.

I wake up in the morning and can't believe my bad luck. Did my mother really stop short of disclosing my life purpose or did I forget the end of the dream? All these years I've been searching to find out exactly that—what I am supposed to do in life. And now that crucial information is withheld from me! I replay the dream again. This time I get a distinct feeling that my "mother" was not really my mother but somebody else using her image to contact me. But who? My Soul? And why didn't "she" allow me to straighten up? And what the heck does St. Germain have to do with me—or rather vice versa? What is this Order of St. Germain anyway? True, I've always been fascinated by this mysterious French Count who had extraordinary gifts and skills, and about whom many legends have been told, but I've never been interested in the hype about him in recent decades.

As we go down for breakfast, I can't shake off the strange feeling of the dream. We walk through the empty reception area, oddly quiet; we walk into the huge dining room, completely empty. The owner is lurking in the corner and jumps promptly at us as soon as we step inside. He takes our orders for *boissons* and motions toward the self-serve buffet. We haven't even managed to get back to our table with food, when he plonks down our coffee and promptly disappears without a word. Just so we don't face all the empty tables, we seat ourselves to face the windows. This place gives me the creeps, regardless of how "conducive" the energy is.

Our first exploration is the alignment of Kerzerho, just outside of Erdeven. Alignments are collections of menhirs that stretch in more or less straight lines through the countryside. Menhirs are single upright stones, phallic in appearance. There can be anywhere between a hundred and a thousand menhirs—which can range from small to really huge—in a single line.

The alignment of Kerzerho consists of ten rows of over one thousand menhirs of different sizes. We start from the so-called "head" of the alignment, a semi-circular formation of stones that used to mark either the beginning or the end of an alignment (explanations vary, depending on the sources you read). At Kerzerho the head has been destroyed by a road that passes through. So we examine what's left of it—megaliths as large as houses, scattered without any order, some of them toppled down. The rocks used for this alignment are granite with quartz crystals, a very masculine type of rock which gives off an electrostatic charge, according to Freddy Silva. I wonder what it might feel like to live in that house right behind a huge menhir.... The house, painted ice-white with a gray roof, blends in with the rocks.

I feel dwarfed by the sheer size of these megaliths. They loom above me, stern and reproachful. I touch a menhir that has been knocked over and is now lying like a wounded animal. A feeling of hurt rises in my body.

"How interesting," Dwight mutters, his eyes glowing with intensity while he's dowsing.

"What's interesting?"

"Well, the energy here. It's like, how to describe it, like energy scars. This place has been scarred ... which is obvious." He motions to the road that shoots by the fallen menhirs.

As I'm walking around these huge stones, obviously placed here for a definite purpose, I cannot but feel humbled by my ignorance of that purpose. A whole mindset of an ancient civilization—a civilization that existed in various parts of the globe—is impressed in these stones, in their size and formation. And our modern civilization, so technologically advanced, knows nothing about it.

Fortunately, there are researchers who are exploring these mysterious structures, and I remember what the antiquarian John Michell wrote about what he calls, "the science of megalith builders." In the very distant past, over ten thousand years ago, there existed a unified system of knowledge (a true science—although completely different from ours) about the ways of the Earth spirit, symbolically represented as a dragon in folklore and in early Christian imagery.

For ancient people, the spirit was a formative cause behind the world of appearances. So the Earth spirit—in modern terminology, electromagnetic currents or telluric streams of energy—flows through the countryside on certain routes and on certain days, governed by the cycles of the celestial bodies. By placing large menhirs on particulars spots, the Neolithic people increased the flow of energy—just as acupuncturists do by placing needles on the meridians in the human body. The increased energy flow, it was believed, increased the fertility of the Earth. But the megaliths also had an effect on human conscious-ness. By amplifying the magnetic charge of the Earth energy, these megaliths made it easier for ancient people to establish contact with the spirit world.

Exactly what the difference was in the effect of a menhir, or a dolmen, or an alignment on Earth energy has not been established with certainty. But one thing does seem certain: these megaliths were used to mark the places where terrestrial currents were particularly active.

Nowhere else is this science of the megalith builders more evident than at Carnac, Brittany's prehistoric capital and namesake of Egypt's famous temple, Karnak. Situated near the Gulf of Morbihan, Carnac is probably the largest megalithic site in the world. It consists of three alignments—Menec, Kerlescan, and Kermario—which total up to about 4,000 menhirs. The alignments are arranged in ten to thirteen parallel lines that stretch through the countryside in variable length, from 300 feet to almost a mile. The stones also vary in size. From the largest of about twelve feet, they gradually decrease to about one foot. As researcher Pierre Mereux has discovered, these alignments were placed over the fault lines (thirty-one fissures in all) of this most active earthquake region in France. Moreover, these stones are electromagnetically active—in the state of constant vibration.

The alignments, however, are closed off for free strolling, as we discover when we arrive at Menec. There have been too many feet trampling the soil, too much destruction of vegetation, which has led to soil erosion. So we stand behind the fence surrounding the alignment, alone, and look over the vast moors where menhirs extend in almost straight lines. I close my eyes halfway and gaze at the rows of stones positioned there like soldiers in formation. The silence envelops the moors, the mute silence of forgotten purpose. Stone after stone, the lines march toward a distant target. As I gaze at them with half-closed eyes, they appear to me like ... like a huge drawing, a diagram of a sort! All of a sudden I remember the schematics of electrical circuits my father used to draw for huge cargo ships on which he worked as an electrical engineer. These stones in front of me are just like the lines of electricity my father used to chart!

"Could very well be...." Dwight nods when I share my insight. "These align-ments most likely mark the flow of the electromagnetic currents of the earth."

We change our vantage point and now observe the stones from the side. I'm amazed by the different view, as well as the impression they now offer. From the head of the alignment, the stones conveyed the impression of immutable order, succeeding each other with the regularity of a perfect design. But from the side they resemble a herd of living creatures, silently milling about the field.

After lunch, we plunge into the forest to visit the giant menhir of Manio. This is Carnac's largest menhir, almost three times my height. It exudes awesome power. The cracks and irregularities on its rough surface give the monolith the appearance of a living creature, almost like facial features, with a long horizontal crack at the bottom for a mouth. The giant menhir commands respect in everyone who approaches it; it's like a king that reigns over a kingdom populated by lesser menhirs.

I leave Dwight to his dowsing and venture deeper into the forest. I walk under thick foliage, so thick that the sun can barely penetrate. The light is magical; the shafts of sun powder the air like a fine shower, sprinkling the muddy soil with bright drops. Deeper in the woods, the sun doesn't penetrate at all. I seat myself on a stump to absorb the silence. After a while I notice that the forest is a very busy place; birds are chirping, branches creaking, various insects crawling on the ground, and the wind humming through the foliage. Not that silent after all!

The clouds must have covered the sun because all of a sudden it gets dark, very dark under the trees. I feel a twinge of discomfort. I've never felt at ease in dark, damp forests. I feel unprotected and vulnerable because I can't *see* what's beyond the trees. An unknown danger might be lurking, wild animals or enemies. I feel like prey, robbed of my powers. And the nights ... I shudder. *There is no shelter, no safety in a forest. To sleep means to be exposed to attack. No, sleeping is impossible ... I have to be on my guard, always. And on the move ... so I'm not found ... move and cover my tracks ... confuse my pursuers ... never stay in the same place, never fall asleep. On the move ... MOVE!*

I'm startled by my own thoughts. Where is this primeval fear coming from? I feel as if there is a split in my head and I'm in two different times and in two different bodies. I try to assimilate the other body and its thoughts and fears. I impose *my* vision of the trees as they are in this moment, serene and majestic; I enforce *my* feeling of the forest as a peaceful, friendly place. *There is no danger here*, I assert. Slowly, I visualize moving through the other body, reclaiming it bit by bit. But the "other" thoughts resist. They don't want to be assimilated. They want to continue their existence and they fight with all their power. As soon as I corner them, they wriggle out and bounce away from me. And fear—my old fear of dark, enclosed spaces, which I thought I'd overcome in the Great Pyramid years ago—pokes up its ugly head again and sneers at me defiantly.

"It must be some deep-seated fear from a past life," Dwight offers as an explanation while we're having dinner in a local restaurant.

"But which past life? The Druidic one, with my Teacher?"

He doesn't answer right away. Instead he takes an oyster from his plate and slurps it down. The oysters are alive, just harvested from the sea. Brittany is a seafood paradise; sea creatures are abundant and unpolluted. I look at the slimy mollusk with hesitation. It looks repugnant to me. Dwight slurps down another oyster with such enjoyment that I finally decide to follow suit. The cool, squishy texture at first surprises my tongue, but then explodes with the taste of sea plankton and the freshness of ocean waves.

Dwight lifts his eyes off his plate and looks at me with a little squint. He has taken off his glasses and I can see the depth of his eyes, all the new layers of feelings I haven't seen before. He looks me straight in the eye and I sense deep power mixed with radiant love. Ever since his "heart opening" on the x-ray table in the hospital in Carpentras, the expression in Dwight's eyes has changed. His whole energy has changed. It's the energy of a man who commands much more power because he has reclaimed regions of his consciousness previously suppressed.

For a long moment, Dwight looks at me with that new, penetrating gaze. "That fear," he finally says, "could very well have been from your Druidic incarnation. We all carry deep fears from past lives—that's unavoidable. Fear is the strongest emotion on this planet, the dominant astral energy that affects our psyche. But ultimately, it doesn't really matter where it's from. What matters is that it's there, in your psyche."

"So how should I deal with it when I don't know where it comes from? It was different with fears of homelessness and of authority—they were specific. I knew what I was up against."

"Doesn't matter," Dwight brushes off my concern. "The principle is always the same: to defeat a fear, you have to lift your consciousness above it. Remember, the higher must always be called in to deal with the lower. So look at this fear from the Soul's point of view—what is there to be afraid of?" Dwight smiles, then adds, "Remember how you did it in Provence? How you overcame the fear of the landlady that day in the bathroom? Do the same with this fear. Go above it."

Yeah, it sounds easy now, but in reality....

"Fears are not rational," I object, "so telling myself there's nothing to be afraid of doesn't help much. I know it in my head but that doesn't have any effect on the actual emotion of fear."

"No, it wouldn't. You have to be centered in your Soul, obviously," Dwight replies and slurps down another oyster.

The next day we decide to visit the Paimpont Forest, also known as the Enchanted Forest of Brocéliande. This is *the* legendary forest where Merlin retired to spend time in isolation and solitude, but instead fell in love with the fairy Viviane. (It just shows how no one, even a great magician, can ever know what life has in store.) But get this: the gorgeous Viviane was so enamored with Merlin that she wanted to keep him forever. Hence she cast a spell around her beloved—a prison of air!—so that he would never leave her. And Merlin, being the great magician that he was, could have easily overridden the spell of his sweet enchantress and freed himself. But he didn't; instead he joyfully accepted his captivity.

Today, not much is left of the once vast, lush forest that used to cover the whole of central Brittany. Continuous logging of ancient trees and a big fire in 1990 have reduced the magnificent forest to a mere twenty-seven square miles. When we leave the car at the parking area before the trail to the Vale of No Return, I'm prepared for another encounter with the forest—and a magical forest at that! There is another legend that tells the story of the sorceress Morgana, who cast a spell so that no men (her lovers?) could escape, hence the name—the Vale of No Return. But Lancelot, who was longing for his beloved Guinevere, managed to break the spell and leave the forest. Hopefully, all these captivity spells are no longer potent, and we'll be able to find our way back.

We walk deep into the forest and darkness, over fallen trunks and vigorous brooks, but find no Vale. We realize that we must have taken a wrong turn, so we retrace our steps through thick foliage and around ubiquitous mud puddles (it rains a lot in Brittany). When we get to the little lake called Fairies' Mirror, we declare ourselves lost. Dwight has had enough of walking through the muddy, damp forest, so he heads back to the parking area, the only clearly marked direction. I, on the other hand, decide to continue.

Now that I'm alone I look around, wondering where to go. I'm determined to face my fear again and obliterate it. I go through my options: I can go around the lake, although I don't know where the trail is going to take me; I can try again to find the Vale, hoping that this time I'll find the right turn; or ... I notice a narrow path through the bush going uphill ... I can follow this trail.

I climb for quite a while until I find myself high above the forest and the lake, among sparse pine trees and scattered red rocks. I emerge from the woods at the summit of the hill, where I stop, ecstatic and breathless (but not from climbing). In front of me is a magnificent view of the whole forest and the surrounding villages and fields, all the way to the horizon. I gaze in rapture at the space, the clouds, the green mass of trees below, the tiny white houses peppering the fields. The contrast between the dank, dark depths of the forest from which I just ascended and these heights where I suddenly find myself above everything is so sudden that I experience a jolt in consciousness. An image appears on the screen of my mind: a woman—*une magicienne*—standing high above the world. She extends her power, like a gossamer cape, over the whole of nature. This cape covers the forests and brooks and valleys and little nature spirits—everything, as far as her eye can reach, is under her control.

I feel compelled to look at my hands. They are burning ... as if some force is flowing through them. I raise them to the level of my chest, palms facing the horizon. Then I shake my head. *What on earth am I doing?* I squeeze my fists several times, but the sensation persists: my hands *are* burning. Something is passing through them. I stand still, alone, above the world, in perfect silence and poise. There is a distinct sensation in my body that sometime in the distant past my hands wrought magic. Traces of memory are in my cells. My hands *remember* the motions. It feels so natural to move them in this way, to direct the power out, to focus that power like a laser beam to whatever I want to create—or uncreate.

My body feels strong and strangely full. I look at nature below and have a new sensation. I actually am *becoming* that nature; I am merging with the trees and streams and fields and grass and clouds. I know everything from within because I am one with everything. I know what every life form needs, what I have to do to help it thrive. From that place of at-one-ment, my power pours forth to change, move, speed up, create, undo, alter.... Since everything is in me, all the changes also happen *inside* of me, inside my huge, gossamer body that covers the whole of nature.

Then I withdraw my consciousness, and it returns to its ordinary size and back into my physical body.

I stand, alone, above the world, in perfect silence and poise, filled with awe.

No, not alone. In me, around me, I now feel the distinct frequency of my Teacher. His energy permeates the clouds, the forest, the wind that gently flutters my hair, the sparrows that flit around the sparse trees. I open my arms to embrace the air so that I can feel him. I close my eyes. *Master, I ask, were we together in this land in the past? Was it here that I was your neophyte?*

I wait. Will I get an answer?

After a while, words appear in my head: "Here or there is everywhere. That which matters is to retrieve the quality, not the location."

But you've come here. You must have something to tell me?

I feel him smile. "I have not come. I always am around you. Only you do not perceive me."

Oh! So you were with me in other past lives?

"You were not ready then. The time is now."

The time for what?

"The time to retrieve. This life of yours is your time of reckoning with the past, so that free and light, you can step into your future."

But what is my future?

"That which you desire above everything else."

What I desire above everything else ... What is it? I feel a little embarrassed to put forth this question. I should know it myself, shouldn't I? Then I remember Antibes and instantaneously I know: above everything else, I desire to merge with my Soul.

I do know, yes. But there is still that other question ... of my life work. What should I do?

Instead of words, a wispy image of a dark cavern comes through—a cave with a deep well. Then it dissolves. And with it, the energy of my Teacher.

It was a few months later that I fully understood the nature of our relationship. After our return to Santa Barbara (in September), on my fortieth birthday, my Teacher made his last appearance. I was lying in bed at night after the birthday dinner, when the whole bedroom suddenly throbbed with his energy, much more radiantly than I'd ever felt it before. His presence felt luminescent, mighty, awe-inspiring. That was because, he explained, he was free now to reclaim his true nature. *I* had freed him by resolving our mutual karma, which had been binding him to this level of existence. Our ties have been untied. Our "contract" was fulfilled. It was time for him to move on. With tears in my eyes and a smile on my face, I wished him farewell.

Standing above the Paimpont Forest, I sweep one last glance at this magical land where I may or may not have lived before, but where I have retrieved so much of my past. Deeply grateful, inspired, and infused with the energy of my Teacher, I get ready to leave.

The descent takes me back into the forest. The horizon disappears, as do fields and villages. Thick foliage blocks the view of the sky. I enter the dark, damp space again, and find myself enclosed in a sort of prison. I have no idea where I am going. I can't see further than a few trees. Oh, how uncomfortable! Memories take hold of me again. I have a sensation that my magical powers could not extend into these woodsy, earthy regions, that in the forest I was powerless…. A vague memory of something horrible I did in the distant past flutters through my heart. Losing my powers was a punishment. With my whole being I know: *that* was the fall, the memory of which I retrieved in Florence! My fear of dark, enclosed spaces was born from having perished in a forest. But strangely, I no longer feel that fear. In its place I find a smile, the well-known, familiar but elusive smile of my Teacher. I look around the forest and still feel uncomfortable, but to my amazement, the actual fear is gone.

Rain. It's been raining on and off for the past several days, the weather cold, gray, and dismal like in the fall. We've moved to another hotel so we could be near the other sites we wanted to explore. Our new hotel, very comfortable and perfectly *normal*, is located in Locmariaquer, a village that commands the channel into the Morbihan Gulf. I'm so glad we've changed hotels because after we return from our wet and windy expeditions, I can take a hot bath and turn on the heat (in mid-June) in our large, cozy room.

Over the past several days we've combed the whole southern area, visiting Les Pierres Plates (Flat Stones), Er-Grah, Le Grand Menhir Brisé (Big Broken Menhir), and several other dolmens. The weather is still cold and gray, but I don't think it's because of the weather that this whole area feels to me heavy, depressing, and somehow dead. I sense a different energy here, as if this region has been dedicated to the souls of the dead.

We can't wait any longer for the weather to improve to go to the island of Gavrinis, home to the only fully decorated Neolithic monument in Brittany, proclaimed a masterpiece of universal art.

So one drizzly morning we take a boat to the middle of the Morbihan Gulf to visit this tiny island. The Gulf is actually a small inland sea dotted with islands, created by the land settling only tens of thousands of years ago. Even though the weather is moody, with snatches of sun and spits of rain, the boat has filled up: twelve people, the maximum number allowed inside the cairn, are on board. I sit shivering next to Dwight, glancing at the sky and water, trying to spot those "most delicate light effects" the guidebook has promised. But it's all gray. Gray and windy.

As we land on the southern point of the islet and walk toward a huge mound of stones, the sun pierces through the clouds and shoots an arrow of light on the cairn. The wet stones shine with a golden glint. This is so sudden and so dramatic that I stop in my tracks. It's almost like a welcome of nature, a smile of elemental forces that have finally let up.

So here it is, the most outstanding monument from the Neolithic era, lying before us like an enormous turtle-shell of dry stones. This huge mound hides in its bowels a narrow passage and a tiny chamber. Gavrinis is remarkable for the disproportion among these elements. The outside tumulus is 20 feet high and 160 feet in diameter, yet the chamber is a measly eight square feet. Why did the Neolithic people need such a huge mound to cover such a tiny space?

The entrance is also small and quite low. One has to bend to get into the narrow passage.

It's like entering a womb, a vagina, a dark, damp place of fecundity that waits to be fertilized by the seed-thoughts of visitors. What am I going to fertilize this place with? What seeds am I going to leave behind? I feel awe as I walk this corridor made of rough-hewn stone slabs, carved in intricate designs of semi-circles, double-edged axes, croziers (fern-like coiled staff), and horn formations, all symbols of the Mother Goddess culture. The carvings are of exceptional beauty.

Our guide chatters constantly and in a tone of voice that lacks any respect for the sacredness of this place. His voice booms and rings with vigor, as if he's guiding a tour in a big city. I interrupt him to ask a question about the low entrance. Is it because of the short stature of Neolithic people?

"That was not the case," his answer comes, loud and ringing. "The low entrance and ceilings forced people to walk bowed, which is a sign of respect."

His words hit me like a bolt of lightning. Bowed. Bent-over. Just as I was in my dream, just as my "mother" forced me to be by keeping her hand on my back. Despite our guide's loud voice, I don't hear anything else. In a flash of a second, I realize the message of my dream: the reason I've been struggling so much with my temper, criticism, irritation, impatience, and indignation is—my pride!

A watershed of insights swooshes through my head, all my life condensed into a few moments. Since I was young, I took pride in my intelligence, then pride in my beautiful body and graceful dancing, then pride in my success as a journalist. My Soul chose to incarnate me in the very country where pride was a national trait—the hubris that brought suffering and demise to its people many times in the past. Pride ... the root cause of my personality limitations. And what does the bent-over position in my dream symbolize? The need to develop humility, tolerance, compassion. Not just to feel them *occasionally,* as I have been so far. No. They have to become *permanent* features of my character. These traits have to become new threads in the fabric of my personality. That's why my "mother" was not letting me straighten up.

My heart is so full, I feel like crying. Crying from gratitude for all the help I've received, for all these years of journeying that were given to me so that I can learn and become a better human being. In this dark, beautiful place where the Mother Goddess reigns, I want to leave seeds of respect and humility. Let them fertilize the collective psyche of humanity so that men may walk the Earth with light steps and with heads bowed in respect to nature, to other people.

Respect ... humility... I bow my head in deep gratitude.

CHAPTER 35

LE MANS AND CHARTRES:
THE WAYS OF THE WOUIVRE

After two weeks in Bretagne, I'm more than ready to leave this country. I've had enough of rain and wind and cold in June. With apprehension I'm eyeing Dwight, who is pouring over a map in our heated hotel room, studying megalithic sites.

"Haven't you done enough energy work?" I finally ask, barely containing a tone of complaint. What I really wanted to say was—*Let's get out of here, out of this heavy, cold, harsh land!*

How did my elation with the energy and nature spirits turn into this sensation of oppression? Did it have to do with the rain? Or coming down to the southern part of Brittany? Because at some point, the initial feeling of lightness and magic was buried under this bleak and dour mantle of gray.

Dwight lifts his eyes and turns toward me. "Almost," he says curtly. "Why?"

"Oh, just that the energy of this place is starting to get to me. It's so ... cheerless here."

I remember reading about the poverty and backwardness of Brittany throughout the ages. Even monks in the monasteries, which in the dark Middle Ages were the only beacons of literacy and culture, could not write or read. They were so wild and unruly that the famous medieval scholar Pierre Abélard had to flee for his life when he tried to discipline the monks of his Abbey. He had been exiled to Brittany in the first place as a punishment for seducing his pupil Héloïse and fathering a child with her. But before exiling him, the offended uncle took revenge for the soiled family honor by castrating the seductive tutor. This drastic revenge and the flurry of letters that followed between the separated lovers gave rise to the first love story of European civilization—that of Abélard and Héloise.

I gaze through the window at the gray trees, gray grass, gray sky. Gray drizzle. Somehow, Abélard's fate seems gorier now than when I read about it in the warmth and light of our Provençal house. Can climate shape the character of a whole nation? Does the sun make the Mediterranean people exuberant, loud, and warm? And does the lack of sun and the cold, make northern Europeans subdued, reserved, and aloof?

"We can leave in two days," announces Dwight. "I want to finish one last thing tomorrow and then we can go. How's that?"

I clap my hands in cheer, shaking the whole bed where I've curled under the blankets.

Leaving Brittany did bring relief from the rain, but now I'm sensing clouds of another kind. They are subtle, very subtle, and just barely taint the clear sky of our zeal to explore; but they are there nevertheless. I first sensed them a week ago when I looked at my calendar to reserve a hotel and realized how close we were getting to our return date. And by return, this time I mean our final return to the States. That's when I felt the first pang in my heart—anxiety, no point denying it. I've asked Dwight if he felt apprehensive about going back, and he nodded without saying a word. He didn't need to; I know him so well that I can read his body language, the occasional biting of his lower lip and the little constricted coughing noises when he'd look at the calendar.

We've booked the flight for—naturally—the beginning of September. I will celebrate my fortieth birthday in Santa Barbara, back where everything started: my American life, my love for Dwight, my spiritual path, our journey. A circle closed. A cycle finished. Inevitably, the question arises: how will it feel to go back to the same place? Back after this long journey and everything I've seen, learned, and experienced?

I dread to think about it.

From my point of view, the apprehension is well justified. What are we going back to? Nothing, really. No home, no job, no money in the bank. We have to start our life from scratch. And worst of all, I'm no closer to knowing what my Soul wants me to do. I have every reason to feel apprehensive and anxious. And depressed, if I so choose.

The only thing that saves me from these gloomy thoughts is our exploration of new places and all the things I'm learning. I don't really have much time to dwell on our bleak future. There are moments during our visits to ancient sacred sites when I enter a different state of mind. I feel much more integrated, focused, centered. I even feel poised and strong. At those times it seems to me as if the neural pathways in my brain are being rewired to create a new frequency, a new state of consciousness—a new me.

This is exactly what I'm experiencing in Le Mans, a city about a hundred miles north of Paris, best known as the motor-race capital of France. When Dwight first suggested that we go to Le Mans, I didn't take him seriously. I thought he was getting a nostalgic prod from his car racing days. "So you want to see that famous twenty-four-hour auto race, is that it?" I laughed. All I'd heard about this city was that Le Mans was the birthplace of the first French cars.

But Dwight was quite serious. He opened Hamish's book and showed me the page on Le Mans and its famous Gothic cathedral, St. Julian. "There is the Apollo line passing through the church. A beautiful church, by the way, with the original stained glass windows. And the city is quite charming too, famous for its good food." And he pronounced the last words with special emphasis.

So it was a done deal; energy, art, and good food—all the requirements met, as far as I'm concerned.

We start our exploration of this ancient Gallic settlement from the Place des Jacobins below the Cathedral of St. Julian. As we look up, the cathedral surges dramatically from the hill above Le Mans, as though it's about to take off. The flying buttresses are so intricately designed—tall, slender, and Y-shaped—and they completely surround the far end of the church so that in the foggy weather the church could easily pass for something you'd see on *Star Trek*.

Inside, the cathedral is bathed in light. In the chancel it assumes a soft pink hue, colored by the stained glass windows in which reds and pinks predominate. It's so soft, this pink hue; it creates a sense of lightness and peace. The vaulted ceiling is painted in different shades of red, a very unusual choice of color for a church. And on that red background, various angels are flying, playing instruments, and reading or carrying scrolls.

I'm smitten by the sensation of gentleness. I feel as if the church is embracing me with love; not a nurturing, motherly love, but bridal, sensual, yet timid love. It's as if the church is a young maiden who has just consummated the first nuptial night with her beloved groom, and is now resting, perfectly content, perfectly happy in her body and heart, her every muscle throbbing with a new sensation of love. Which is an unusual impression to get in a church, and on top of that, one where the masculine Apollo energy line passes through.

Dwight walks toward me, having checked the energy with his pendulum. "This is the friendliest and happiest church I've been to," he says, seating himself next to me. "I feel so inspired here." He flings his arm around my shoulders and brings me close to him in a cuddly sort of way, a gesture that doesn't come naturally to him. We sit embraced, bathed in quiet happiness. Soft pink permeates the air and settles upon everything like a fine dust. Soft pink—the color of the heart center on the astral plane; the color of higher love. This cathedral in Le Mans will remain in my memory for years to come as the soft pink church.

So imagine my surprise when, as we walk outside, I see a menhir tucked in the right corner of the west doorway. A menhir unlike any other. Resembling a torso of some broken Greek or Roman sculpture, it's covered in folds as if draped in a toga—of a pink color! Dwight is taken aback too. For a long moment he just stands in front of the giant stone without pulling out his pendulum. Then he whistles. "A pink-veined sandstone! How about that?"

Yes, how about that!

The stone is leaning to one side as if wanting to take a step, caught in a forward motion. I can't shake off the impression of looking at a living being that has been petrified under molten, pink lava folds. It looks primeval, this stone, a remnant of the Earth Powers, of the times when giants walked the Earth.

I look around the charming, quiet square, lined with beautiful Renaissance mansions. We are completely alone, and the air itself is quiet, peaceful, happy. Are we still in the twenty-first century? Or had we accidentally stepped through a time portal and found ourselves in the past? I almost expect to see a lady with tall, conical headware on her plucked forehead open a grilled window and lean out.

As we walk along Queen Berengaria Street we discover that the old town also feels peaceful and contented. We pass perfectly preserved half-timbered houses from the fifteenth century, occasionally interspersed with a Renaissance town house. Queen Berengaria, after whom the street was named, was the wife of the most famous warrior of the age, Richard the Lionheart. We saw her tomb and effigy in the cathedral; the queen was honored as the wise and firm ruler of the County of Maine which she governed after her husband's death in 1199. We walk into the courtyard of her museum, and I feel a shroud of stillness envelop me. My whole body becomes still, my thoughts arrested midway in whatever idea they were trying to form. I stand still and look around.

Peaceful. Happy.

Then we come to the square that looks down on modern Le Mans—the same view that the Celts had, but without the sprawl of civilization. Le Mans was the capital of a Gallic tribe that inhabited the territory of Sarthe, to the east of Brittany.

Dwight is the first to break the silence. "If the Celts chose this hill to build their settlement and temple," he says slowly, looking at the modern Le Mans below, "that means the energy here is special. The Celts would know that, they knew the ways of the Earth spirit."

"More precisely, the Druids did," I say, my voice sounding raspy, as if I hadn't spoken in hours. "The Druids had the knowledge of the invisible world, nature lore, Earth energies … using nature spirits to work magic."

"True. The Old Knowledge," adds Dwights.

"The Old Knowledge," I repeat wistfully. "What a shame we've lost that knowledge."

"Well, not quite. There are so many dowsers who work with Earth energies."

"What I meant was that collectively, as a civilization, we've lost the knowledge of an alive nature. It's not part of our world view anymore. But imagine if it becomes a part of mainstream science, or better still, a new science that would combine the best of modern technological discoveries with the Old Knowledge of Earth energies. Where would we be as a civilization!"

Dwight looks into the distance. "We, as a society, may have lost the knowledge of Earth's energies," he says reflectively. "But there have always been groups that have preserved it and passed it on. Benedictines, Cistercians, the Knights Templar, Rosicrucians, Masons, they all kept that knowledge alive, although not publicly. Just think about all the Gothic cathedrals built at the energy centers and using the principles of sacred geometry! One church could have been an accident. But one hundred fifty? … Hardly." Dwight shakes his head in a very definite "no."

"And think of the use of prayer, ritual, chanting, meditation. We don't give it a second thought, but these are all techniques for working with the energy, for increasing the rate of vibration of the Earth in order to raise consciousness … or as Kostas would say, to 'uplift the awareness.'" Dwight cracks a smile as he mentions our teacher with whom our whole journey began. Then he adds in a conclusive voice:

"*This* is a true spiritual science: a precise knowledge of universal harmonics, proportions, and rhythms, as well as how to use them to create desired effects on the human brain."

"In other words—magic," I say, smiling. Really, what is called magic is nothing else but science, although the science of the invisible laws. If we don't know and cannot observe those laws, we label the resulting phenomena as magic. Just as medieval people transported to the future would consider the telephone and TV magic.

After a long silence Dwight finally turns to me and says, "Now you know why I'm doing all this energy work." He is looking me in the eye, and his gaze is serious. "It's my final life work to help build the energy foundation for future generations. Just as it has been done throughout history by the custodians of the Wisdom tradition."

At that moment the sun emerges from behind wispy clouds and shines in full strength upon the city below, the River Sarthe, and the Gallo-Roman ramparts that rise above the river embankments. Just then I notice that from a distance, those ramparts, a unique landmark of Le Mans, glow in pinkish hues.

Even though we have begun our return trip to Provence and are moving in the general direction of the south, we're now backtracking toward Paris in order to visit Chartres, some sixty miles northwest of Le Mans. Of course, we could have included Chartres on our trip up to Brittany, but we didn't. It's a big deal for us, visiting this most sacred of sacred sites in France. We wanted to do it right, to be in sync with the phases of the moon and all the other forces that pull the strings of our lives and this journey in particular. And since we can't divine from the flight of birds or quivering livers of sacrificed animals as the Etruscans did—not even from coffee dregs or tea leaves or Tarot cards, as modern-day diviners do—we had to use the pendulum.

And the pendulum indicated the third week of June as the most auspicious time for a visit. That's why we're barreling to Chartres this afternoon, when the sun is playing hide-and-seek, and the clouds are piling up dramatically in massive heaps ahead of us.

I feel as if I already know the cathedral; I've read so much about it in books by Louis Charpentier, Freddy Silva, John Michell, and a few other authors. I've read that the site was held sacred as far back as Neolithic times, when the mound was dedicated to the Great Mother, and many menhirs and dolmens were erected atop and around the hill. Chartres was the geographical center of the territory inhabited by the Celtic tribe of Carnutes, as recorded by Julius Caesar in his *Gallic War*. The Druids chose this very mound as their sanctuary of sanctuaries, the seat of their yearly conclave as well as their college. Many strands of telluric currents and underground water streams weave and unweave at this site, creating a powerfully charged energy in the cathedral. I've read about the carefully incorporated principles of sacred geometry, using precise ratios in elevation and proportions to give the cathedral properties of a tuned, resonant chamber; about the underground crypt where the statue of the Black Madonna has been venerated since the early Christian times; about the famous labyrinth, walked by the pilgrims of all ages in lieu of a pilgrimage to Jerusalem....

I think you get the point: I already know so much about this cathedral that it's impossible *not* to have expectations of an amazing experience that should—will—await us there. Which is definitely not a wise thing to do. A thought appears that I might be setting myself up for a big disappointment, but I don't pay any attention to it. And for all I can determine, neither does Dwight. He's positively preparing for the encounter with some special energies at Chartres.

Today it's my turn to drive, and I'm feeling particularly calm and inspired after our beautiful visit to Le Mans. We are on our way to experience the holy of holies.... Life is about as good as it gets, I'm thinking while observing the dramatic play of light and shadow on the countryside.

Then we whiz into the city. As we get closer to the center, the traffic thickens in a chaotic sort of way. I feel as though we've been sucked into a bumper car ride, and something is moving the vehicles, and us, in a frenzied way. The traffic signs are confusing; turns are not well-marked; I can't find our hotel; the waves of cars, like monstrous currents, are carrying us along, and I'm unable to extricate us from their course. Stressed out, I shriek into my cell phone, trying to get clear directions to the hotel from the receptionist. But I can't find the turns. I'm listening to his warbled voice, looking around for the streets he mentions, trying not to run into the car in front of me. I'm on the verge of falling apart. My nerves begin to overheat and I'm slightly shaking. Almost instinctively, I swerve out of the traffic line and pull over into an empty parking space.

Dwight casts a glance at me. "Got stressed out?" he asks.

I nod, letting out a long sigh of frustration and irritation. But I remain composed.

"Good girl," he says with obvious satisfaction. "You're learning."

Yes, I'm finally learning. This time, I did not let my lower self trick me again and push me into falling apart, as it did at the Côte d'Azur. I sit quietly for a few moments and breathe deeply. I'm consciously regaining control of my nerves, slowly calming their agitation. Dwight gently pats my knee. "I'll take over the driving."

Somehow he quickly finds the turns I missed, and we finally park behind the Hotel de la Poste. We enter the old, decrepit building from the nineteenth century (my guess), check in, then walk up to our room on the fourth floor. Dwight opens the door and walks in, making a little "hum" sound. I want to enter too, but there is no room. He has to move sideways between two beds to let me in into the sleazy, cramped, dangerous room. Yes, dangerous. The room has a sloping ceiling (being on the top floor under a gabled roof), and a TV set is mounted so low that it's easy to bang one's head against it. I gag on the reek of stale tobacco and the nauseating smell of cleaning products. "What's this stink?" Dwight wrinkles his nose. As soon as I edge into the bathroom, I discover the source of the stink—a chemical toilet, the kind you get on the buses or on construction sites. I hurry to open the window (and bang my head into the TV set), but the street noise is horrendous. Dwight and I have to shout to hear each other from a few steps away.

But—the room is facing a square with a breathtaking view of the cathedral. And this is what I asked for when I reserved the room and why I chose this hotel in the first place.

"Well," Dwight mutters after emerging from the stinky bathroom, apprehensively scanning the space for sharp corners, "sometimes you have to be careful what you ask for."

I plunk down on the narrow, squeaky bed and bury my head in my hands. Really, the contrast between our elegant hotel in Le Mans and this squalid dump could not have been more pronounced. And so is the contrast between the calm of Le Mans and the hellish traffic of Chartres. I feel as if I'm being jerked, like a yo-yo, between extremes. I get up and take two steps to the window and stare at the cathedral.

It's late afternoon and the light has become spectacular. Pewter gray clouds are piled up in the east behind the church, but on the other side, the setting sun has ripped the clouds apart and beamed a shaft of golden light right on the façade of the cathedral. The sharp contrast between the purple-gray of the sky and the tessellated gold of the masonry strikes me now as a reflection of my own life.

Dark and light. Down and up. Agony and ecstasy. Despair and elation. Discouragement and inspiration.

Always extremes, always pairs of opposites.

I've become weary of bouncing between them. It's time to hold the middle path.

The church steeples shoot up, tall, elegant, pencil-like. Their spires, like perfectly sharpened points, poke the clouds. They seem to speak to me; speak of purpose, patience, strength … victory.

"Good job, this afternoon." I hear Dwight's voice, then feel his hands on my shoulders. I turn my face halfway toward him, and he plants a gentle kiss on my cheek. He embraces me from behind and holds me in his arms. We stand embraced for a good while, watching the cathedral shrouded in golden light.

"I don't want to go to that dark hole," Dwight protests the next morning when I suggest having breakfast at a café across from the cathedral.

Last night we explored the neighborhood and I noticed a café facing the southern portal. Though it was quite gloomy, a few steps below ground level and with a dark-wood interior, it was also ideally positioned to sip coffee and gaze at the cathedral.

"Trust me," I repeat, "having breakfast there will tune us in for the visit. We'll be in the energy field of the church."

Dwight grumbles and points to another café that's right on our way, but that one doesn't pass our requirements either. "All right," he sighs. "We'll go where you want."

Wet from the rain that's been seeping the whole morning, we walk down a few stairs into the *pénombre* of the empty café. "Humpf," grunts Dwight, scanning the shadowy room. But there is a side room that looks onto the church, and I head right there. Only one patron is sitting at the table in a corner—a bespectacled man in his fifties—and he is just finishing his breakfast. I choose a table by the window and deposit all our books on the table, to review the material before our visit. While waiting for our breakfast, I leaf through the books, reading important paragraphs to Dwight.

"So, looks like we won't be able to walk the labyrinth," I say. "It's been covered by a new altar."

"Well, just what you'd expect from the Catholic authorities," smirks Dwight.

After a few moments, I hear a cough from the corner. "Excuse my interruption," comes a polite voice in English, "but the labyrinth is in the middle of the nave. True, you can't walk it, but you can see it; it's covered only by chairs."

Both Dwight and I turn, surprised, toward the guest sitting in the corner. The man goes on with a slight, sharp accent that betrays his German origins, "But allow me to introduce myself. My name is Wolfgang, and I serve as a guide for the church and the crypt. I am also a scholar in residence."

"How fortuitous," Dwight replies promptly, his face suddenly enlivened. "We were just planning our visit. Why don't you join us?" And he scoops our books from the table, making room for our new acquaintance.

We soon learn that the German researcher has been working here for the past thirty years—his whole life devoted to the Chartres Cathedral. He's very gentle and very, very polite. When he disagrees with something we read in a book, he brings it up with embarrassment, as if he's really sorry that he has to correct our erroneous information. As I'm listening to the German, I still can't believe our incredible luck … or synchronicity—bumping into a scholar in residence of Chartres!

"So, what would you say is the most important thing about the cathedral?" Dwight asks.

Wolfgang takes his time thinking, then begins unhurriedly: "There are many, many facets that comprise the mystery of Chartres. But the point with which I always begin is the energy of the place. Telluric forces or *Wouivre*, as they were called by the Celts, are particularly strong here, amplified by underground water veins. Unlike most churches that are oriented east-west, this cathedral exhibits an aberration—it is positioned northeast-southwest. This was a deliberate design in order to follow the path of the *Wouivre*. Everything about the church is done with one purpose in mind: to augment the energetic properties of the site through the use of harmonies, proportions, and light. And this, in turn, facilitates the expansion of consciousness."

"How exactly was the light used?" I ask.

"With stained glass windows," the German answers, then pauses looking up at the rain-washed windows of the café. He turns to me and continues with deliberation: "You see, the colors that were used were special; they were the product of alchemical science. As light passes through them, it is transformed. Not only does the light bathe the interior in special frequencies, but it also filters out harmful frequencies of the sunlight, frequencies that are not beneficial to the religious experience. Transmutation of matter into spirit, to use alchemical terminology, cannot be attempted in the daylight. It has to occur under the protection of semi-darkness, or in the crypt. You could say—underground."

"Ah!" I can't suppress a squeal of a sudden insight, a fleeting memory.

But Dwight immediately asks, "So that's what the crypt was used for—initiation?"

Wolfgang doesn't answer right away. He tilts his head, then says, "I prefer to refer to the crypt as a lower church. Because that's what it really was. The early upper church, built in the first half of the twelfth century, followed exactly the plan of the lower church. They were like carbon copies—pardon my old-fashioned analogy," he says with a smile, "one above, the other below." Then he adds as an afterthought:

"The sacredness of this mound was such that Chartres is the *only* church in France where no burial was permitted, no king or bishop interred."

Dwight nods approvingly. "That would preserve the energy for sure."

"And what about the Black Madonna?" I ask.

"Oh, the Lady of the Underground," Wolfgang says with a slight, almost mysterious smile. "That too is another aspect of Chartres' dual function, above and below. The Virgin Mary is worshipped in the upper church, the Black Madonna in the lower church. One could look at them as the White and the Black Madonna. The latter was also renowned for effectuating healing. Chartres was not only a cathedral, but also a major healing center. Naturally, because of the particularly strong telluric forces." Wolfgang pauses for a moment, looks at Dwight then at me, and says:

"If you are so interested in the crypt, would you care to join the special group I'm going to be guiding at noon?"

"You bet!" Dwight and I exclaim.

"Very well then. I will see you at the entrance to the crypt by the southern portal. I should be going now." Wolfgang glances through the window and adds, "It is raining heavily. Best to be inside."

"I can't believe it's raining like this in June," I remark, looking through the window too.

Our German acquaintance flashes a quick smile at me. "But you know, it is a good omen," he says in his measured voice. "Chartres is all about water, both underground and above the ground. In the remote past, this used to be an island surrounded by water. And water is a symbol of creation." He collects his raincoat and umbrella, then concludes:

"The cathedral is truly a place of birth ... and rebirth."

And with that, Wolfgang gets up, slightly bows to us in farewell, and departs.

CHAPTER 36

CHARTRES CATHEDRAL:

LOCKED IN THE CRYPT

As soon as the door closes behind Wolfgang, I turn gleefully to Dwight. "All right, all right," he laughs before I have time to gloat in my triumph. "I shouldn't let my food preferences get in the way of your intuition."

"No, you shouldn't. Maybe this will finally teach you." I cross my arms victoriously and flash at Dwight my ultimate I-told-you-so look. Then I pack all our books and glance at my watch. We have over two hours before we meet with Wolfgang and his group. Leisurely, we walk across the square to the cathedral.

After everything Wolfgang has told us about the proportions and harmonies of the church, I'm expecting to have a mind-altering experience when we walk inside. But instead I'm only surprised—the interior is so dark. In this *pénombre*, I feel a bit disoriented. I'm definitely not inspired, elated, or transported to any heights, as I was in Bourges, for example. I'm in awe. This is, beyond doubt, a Mother Goddess place, dark and womb-like. I walk to the middle of the transept, from where I can see all three rose windows, stunning in their beauty. The colors and shapes form such intricate geometrical patterns that I almost expect them to start whirling like kaleidoscopes. Staring at these rose windows, I'm beginning to understand what Plato meant when he said, "God geometrizes."

I move to one of the original twelfth-century stained glass window, called Notre Dame de la Belle Vérrière or just simply the Blue Virgin. I gaze, transfixed, at the renowned "Chartres blue" color that hasn't been reproduced since the thirteenth century. I've never seen a shade of blue like this: it's a nuance between lapis blue and purple, but it has a tint of another tone that gives it a unique, luminous hue. As Wolfgang told us, the original alchemical formulae for making these colors had been lost long ago. With all our modern technology, no one has been able to reproduce this particular shade of blue.

I continue along the southern aisle to the Mary Magdalene window, close to the main entrance. In three large circles placed vertically is depicted the story of Mary Magdalene landing on the French coast—the earliest record of this "legend" in France. The colors, again, are other-worldly in their effulgence.

I join Dwight, who is sitting on a chair nearest to the center of the labyrinth. The center marks the node where many currents of Earth energies—or *Wouivre*—cross. We sit and meditate for a good while. But I feel nothing. Maybe that's because the labyrinth was designed to be walked, not sat upon.

I hear the little coughing noises that Dwight makes when he wants to say something important, so I open my eyes and turn to him. "Yes?"

"Well, I've been thinking…" he begins, "this is not really a true labyrinth."

"What do you mean?"

"You see, the way it's supposed to be walked is fixed. There is only one way to the center, and you just follow the outlined path; you don't make any choices where to turn, as you would in a regular labyrinth."

Dwight strokes his chin, his gaze cast down at the labyrinth. "So all the currents come together at this very spot where the labyrinth ends. It's like a vortex of energy right there. And, as Wolfgang said, those currents are more active at certain times of the year—precisely when pilgrimages were undertaken in the past centuries.

"So, think about it," Dwight continues in a voice that is becoming more animated. "In the past, people would make a pilgrimage to Chartres at the time when the *Wouivre* was particularly active and pulsating through the church. After weeks of journeying on foot—and in those times traveling was hard and dangerous—they would arrive in the right frame of mind, open and receptive. They would attend the service in the upper church, follow the procession to the crypt, bow to the Black Madonna. Then they'd come up here again and walk the labyrinth very slowly, meditating, praying, but always following the outlined path—left, right, right, left—making certain geometric patterns while walking. They often walked barefoot, and we know from our experience in Brittany that stone accumulates Earth energy.

"And—let me finish—" Dwight makes a gesture to silence my attempt to ask a question, "we know that seventy percent of the body and ninety percent of the brain is made up of water. We also know that molecules of water are altered when different frequencies pass through the water. So put all these facts together and what do you think happens here?"

"Consciousness gets altered?"

"Exactly. Your body is immersed in a very strong electromagnetic field right here. By walking the labyrinth slowly, you stay in the field for a long time and you follow a precise pattern of movement. Your father has probably taught you that bodies in movement through an electromagnetic field acquire certain properties. That's how electricity is made."

I shake my head vaguely. Maybe he did try to teach me something about electricity, but I certainly don't remember much.

"So of course your consciousness is going to be altered!" Dwight concludes, beaming with a puzzle-solved expression on his face.

"But not now, when we're just sitting here," I say somewhat sadly.

"No, not now. But, then again, you never know. Because it's not only the labyrinth. This whole church is designed like a huge chamber for raising the frequency of human consciousness."

I look at my watch and realize it's time to meet the German guide and his group. I sweep one last glance at the huge, shadowy interior, perhaps a bit disappointed that I haven't experienced any transformation. Of course, being me, I was hoping for such an experience.

Five minutes before noon we present ourselves at the southern entrance to the crypt and immediately spot Wolfgang. He looks a bit disoriented.

"There was a misunderstanding," he shoots out as soon as he sees us, "the group is waiting for me at the hotel."

"Oh!" Dwight and I both look at him from under the umbrella, not knowing how this twist would affect our visit.

"I have to go and get them, but the shuttle will not arrive for another ten minutes. So we'd better go inside rather than stand in this rain," Wolfgang says and leads the way down into the crypt.

He closes the heavy wooden door after we walk in, then changes his mind and leaves the door ajar. We descend into the darkness, slowly, reverently. We are in the true womb of the Mother Goddess, the place of worship of the Black Madonna, the place of healing, the old Druidic sanctuary. The energy is so thick you can feel it on your skin.

Wolfgang flips several light switches, then walks to the panel showing the map of the crypt. "I can give you a short introduction while we're waiting. The crypt follows the shape of a horseshoe—" he begins, but his words are interrupted with a bang, a thud, and the sound of a key turning in a lock.

"Oh, no!" Wolfgang bellows and dashes up the stairs. We follow.

"The guard has locked us in!" he exclaims, shaking the heavy door.

"Why would he do that?" asks Dwight.

"He was doing his security rounds and saw the door open." Wolfgang answers, fumbling through the pockets of his jacket. "He must have thought that no one was in here." The German is now checking his pants pockets, then his shoulder bag. Finally, he heaves a sigh, opening his arms helplessly: "And I don't have the key!"

"Oh, no!" I sigh in return.

"So what are we going to do? Can you call someone?" Dwight asks calmly.

"I don't have my cell phone with me." Wolfgang's voice sounds embarrassed now.

"Ah, but we do!" Dwight turns to me with an outstretched hand. "Svetlana, give your cell phone to Wolfgang so he can make a call."

"I can't," I squeal. "My card ran out of minutes yesterday. And they didn't have one in that tobacco shop where I stopped this morning."

"*What?*" Dwight stares at me.

"I didn't tell you because I thought we wouldn't need the phone this morning. I was planning to replace the card after our visit."

"So, we can't call for help...." Dwight now says in a grave tone.

We look at our guide, and he looks back at us.

"So what are we going to do?"

"Well," Wolfgang says after a few moments, his voice composed again, "there are chairs in the northern aisle where the services are held. And there is another door on that side. I'm sure somebody will hear if we bang chairs and shout loudly."

"Let's do it." Dwight nods and follows our guide. I follow too, but now that my initial shock has worn off, I'm actually reconsidering our situation. I fall behind the two men and look around the cavernous rooms, lit sparsely and dimly. What an amazing situation ... it's actually exciting, to be locked in the crypt of Chartres Cathedral. I mean, what are the odds of that happening? With unusual certainty, I feel that this has been orchestrated ... from above. Just like the power outage in the Great Pyramid, so that we could be alone in the King's Chamber.

Already I hear the bangs of chairs hitting the wooden door on the other side of the crypt, then Wolfgang's shouts. I take my time. I amble along the curved part, called the ambulatory, of the horseshoe-shaped crypt. I count seven chapels that open from it, some dimly lit and some pitch black. On the other side of the wall of the ambulatory is the heart of the crypt, the original dolmen-cave from Neolithic times that, much later, was appropriated by the Druids. I feel slight shivers rising in my body. I am at the ancient center of the Druids, their holy of holies; this is where they gathered yearly to discuss matters of importance, this is where they taught their magical lore to neophytes.

Wolfgang comes running, carrying a chair. He zips by me, then Dwight emerges from the darkness.

"What's happening?"

"Oh, he decided to try the other door. I better go and help him."

I stay.

The difference in the energy between the upper and the lower church is so pronounced that I feel as though I'm in some other place, in a different church. The energy is thickening as I'm progressing further along the ambulatory and closer to the northern aisle. A narrow passage on the left leads to the original dolmenic grotto. I'm just about to walk to it when Wolfgang runs by me again. Then Dwight appears. From a distance, Wolfgang's shouts resonate through the crypt again.

"Still nothing?"

Dwight shakes his head. "Someone will hear ... eventually. Or they'll call from the hotel to see where he is. Don't worry."

"Oh, I'm not worried at all. I'm actually enjoying it."

Wolfgang has stopped shouting and banging. There is a moment of deep silence, then we hear his voice again, but this time it sounds as if he's talking to somebody. After a few minutes he appears, a big smile on his face that glistens with beads of perspiration.

"Somebody finally heard me. They went to call the guard." He takes out a handkerchief from his pocket—a real cotton handkerchief, the kind my father used to use—then wipes off his forehead. "So, we'll be free in a few minutes."

We start walking back to the southern door.

"It's wonderful they heard us, but ... er," I venture, "I wouldn't have minded more time alone, actually."

"Oh?" Wolfgang tilts his head and looks at me for a few moments. "Well, then," he says, as if making up his mind, "you stay here while I go to fetch my group."

"Really?" I can hardly suppress a shriek. "That's wonderful, Wolfgang!" I start skipping and clasping my hands, thrilled.

Dwight turns to our guide and says, "Thank you, Wolfgang. This is a rare opportunity."

Just as we arrive at the door, the guard appears and apologizes profusely to the German, who dashes off to find the shuttle bus. The heavy wooden door is locked again.

"Wow!" I turn to Dwight, chills of excitement running up my spine.

He shakes his head in disbelief. "You *are* given an opportunity for something. This is not just a coincidence. So what do you want to do?"

"I think I want to be in the chapel with the Black Madonna ... or the Lady of the Underground, as Wolfgang called her."

So we retrace our steps through the southern aisle and along the ambulatory to the northern aisle, passing by the old sacred well that the Druids used in their rituals. All their sacred places were located near a body of water, either a spring or a well. This well here is deeper than the water table and it was thought to exercise magical powers. I glance at it, but decide not to linger. I'm drawn to the black bride with a child, even though I know that the original statue was destroyed during the French Revolution.

But Dwight motions to the well and stops. "Wolfgang was talking about the healing properties of the water in this well. The crypt used to be packed with the sick, paralytics, blind, you name it ... a major healing center. Come to think of it—just like Epidauros."

I turn and stare at Dwight. "Epidauros, you said?"

"Well, not exactly, but in general—"

"Wait a second ... the incubation process that took place in the sleeping ward at Epidauros.... There, just like here, the underground, chthonic powers helped the healing process. The dark forces of the Mother Goddess ... the black bride!" I almost shout the last words. "Remember, at Epidauros the sick would lie swaddled like *babies* in womb-like cavities. All creation comes out of the black virgin, that's where everything is born. And from blackness, of course, you move to whiteness—

"Dwight," I scream, "it just occurred to me!" I dig my fingers into his jacket sleeves and shake him in excitement. "Anubis!"

"What about Anubis?"

"I know what that dog in Epidauros symbolized! It just hit me." I let go of Dwight's arms and speak, as if in a trance: "That dog lay on the wall in the same posture as Anubis is represented, right? Anubis—the Guide to the Underworld. And *that* was the message. The appearance of the dog announced that I was going to make a voyage into the underworld, descend into the darkness … which is actually my own subconscious, the dark place where memories of past lives are stored. And there I had to overcome my fears and work out all the karmic stuff. Undergo a process of shedding the old—"

"That's when you nearly died in Antibes," Dwight adds.

I feel thoughts colliding in my head. Insights are emerging faster than I can express them. "But I had to come *here*, to this underground crypt, to figure out the message of Anubis."

"That's because you had to understand it with your conscious mind before you could emerge from the underworld. Which, symbolically, is also the womb. After all, this church is the place of rebirth, as Wolfgang said."

Even in the darkness, I can see that Dwight is beaming. "So, you were brought here to finish your journey through the underworld, and…" he sweeps his arm at the darkness, "you are certainly given the opportunity."

"Let's go." I tug on his sleeve.

It's really dark in the chapel with the Black Madonna, the only dim light squinting further down at the end of the northern aisle. This chapel feels different from the rest of the crypt. There is a definite power here, a power that feels alive, throbbing, heaving, shape-shifting its invisible outline. The energy is so heavy, I can hardly breathe. Or maybe it's my excitement.

"Right here," Dwight calls me. He's checking the energy in front of the altar where the original statue used to stand. "Many strands of energy come together right here." He puts away the pendulum and opens his arms for me. "This is the spot," he whispers, sweeping me into his embrace.

"For the new beginning," he says solemnly.

"For the new beginning," I repeat, curling my arms around his waist and placing my head on his shoulder. I hold him tightly, very tightly, as if something might crawl out of the darkness and snatch my beloved away from me. Just like Orpheus lost his Eurydice on their way out of Hades.

After several minutes Dwight says, "Now I'll leave you alone. You'll know what to do."

I watch him disappear into the darkness that closes upon me, heavy and throbbing. I'm a teensy bit nervous, now that I'm all alone at this very spot. As soon as I direct my attention to the dark space around me, I feel waves of energy running through my body, just as happened in the *tholos* of Epidauros. A flutter of apprehension in my heart dissolves, and I close my eyes.

Images begin to flash on the screen of my mind, images from times past,

like movie trailers. Tribes sitting in a circle on the ground with lowered heads
… solitary figures making a bonfire … young men walking in a procession,
filled with awe…. A priestess standing at the spot where Earth energies gush
out, opening her arms, then fainting to the ground. Around her cloaked figures,
standing and chanting in low voices. It's a symbolic death, the sacrifice of the
old so that the new can be born. A part of the initiation ritual…. The scenes
continue, one changing into another. All the past seems to be present simultaneously in this energy field where the Earth currents converge with the force
of spring floods.

After a while the images disappear, and I'm back in the present moment,
aware of *this* darkness. My body begins to turn in the four directions, although I
can no longer tell where north is. I'm perfectly calm, all the anguish gone, even
the usual fervor and zeal with which I always invoke my Soul. Calmly, I affirm:
I offer this body and mind to helping the Higher Plan. Purge me. Let me serve You.
Just show me what You want me to do.

My body is throbbing with energy. Waves are passing through, my head
tingling as though topped with a crown through which run electrical currents.
At the same time I feel calm, ever so calm, as if I had been given a shot of
sedative. *Just show me … what I should do … to serve.*

Feeble voices filter through the silence. Wolfgang must be back with his
group. My attention drops from whatever heights I was in to that man, gentle
and polite, who has given me these moments alone in the crypt. I'm overwhelmed with gratitude. I think of my journey, Dwight, my entire life. Always,
I was given so much. I have to give that much more in return. I bow my head,
waves of gratitude surging from my heart.

In that state of deep gratitude I become aware of a shimmering white that
slowly fills my head: the all-knowing, infinitely sweet, shimmering white light—
my Soul. But unlike at the *tholos* in Epidauros when the sensations were above
my head, *outside* myself, now the shimmering white is *inside* my head. My sense
of self merges, naturally and effortlessly, with this other identity, my Soul-self.
This fusing is not unsettling, as it was that one time in Tuscany when I first
experienced it. Now I feel stronger and fuller and better than when I'm just *me*.
Now I know that this overlapping of selves is the true Me.

From this merging, a knowing slowly takes shape—a knowing of myself in
my totality.

I'm the little girl with her face glued to the window, dreading the punishment
for a broken vase. I'm the pubescent girl lying in bed, encased in a clammy

plaster cast, desperately wanting to be out of that prison. I'm the teenage girl looking through the window of her room, wondering about the meaning of life and death. I'm the young woman struggling to escape from under the drunken body of her short-time lover on a deserted beach in Mexico. I'm the journalist who has just interviewed the Dalai Lama. I'm the woman in love, having found the man of her dreams, her teacher, her beloved. I'm the seeker, meditating in a cave in India. I'm the adventurer, lying in the sarcophagus in the pitch black of the Great Pyramid. I'm the emaciated body, riddled with parasites and Candida in Cyprus. I'm the insecure, doubting aspirant, searching for her path in Italy. I'm the strong woman nurturing her beloved in France.

All these facets of me from the past make me who I have become. But the facets of me from the future, they too, make me who I am now. Because I'm also the attentive daughter taking care of her ill parents in Belgrade. I'm the enthusiastic teacher of self-introspection in New Zealand. I'm the disconsolate widow, not wanting to wake up in the morning. I'm the teacher at Continuing Education, teaching English and citizenship to immigrants. I'm the writer, reading from her just-published book. I'm the artist, creating new forms of artistic expression. I'm the wise spiritual being at the end of life's trajectory, looking to the other side of the veil, the transition into the formless realm.

I am all of these facets that shine like a diamond in this dark place underground.

But I am also much more.

I'm the Egyptian priestess, honoring her mistress Hathor on the roof of the temple in Dendera. I'm the Druidic neophyte, apprenticing with the wise but elusive Mage, then betraying the secrets to another tribe. I'm the Cathar holy woman, preaching the religion of Love by a village well. I'm the Renaissance Lady, adoring her regal and kind Lord, then dying in childbirth. I'm the servant, and the courtesan, and the warrior, and the aristocrat, and the ballerina....

The diamond continues to rotate. All these facets shine, too, in this dark place underground.

But I am even more than that.

I'm the neuroscientist, mapping out the uncharted territory of the brain. I'm the singer, transporting the audience into an altered state with her singing. I'm the interstellar space researcher, exploring previously unknown forms of life.

As the diamond continues to spin, it dispels, little by little, the darkness of the underground. I see now all of its facets.

Slowly the diamond stops turning. It begins to glow with the light of all its sides together.

Then I see how much more I still am. Much, much more.

Ultimately, I *am* this sweet, shimmering white light, all-knowing, all-good. I am the being of joy and beauty, infinitely loving, infinitely giving.

And this shimmering white light now begins to speak in my head. I recognize, without surprise, the Voice from my childhood:

"Now you know yourself in all your stages, past, present, and future. Now you know yourself in all the roles you have played and will continue to play. Create a pathway to bridge them so that all of them will know each other, so that your future selves will re-experience the richness of your past selves, and your past selves will learn from the wisdom of your future selves. Because time is one, and we are all together, always. You are me, and ... if only you could know how much I am you."

Yes, I know you now—I know myself. I smile gratefully. *You were always with me, ever since I can remember. But—why did you change? Why did you stop talking to me?*

"I did not. I merely changed the frequency of communication. I dispensed with the language so that you could develop your intuition." The shimmering white flickers and all of a sudden a feeling of just-rightness, a compelling urge swoops down, and I'm filled with utmost inner certainty. A sense of inevitability.

The Guidance, I scream silently, *that was you, all along!*

The shimmering white quivers a little, like the gauziest veil in the breeze. "All the same, but on different levels ... ever higher frequencies."

I stand, unmoving, and gaze inward. All the same, all along, merely different frequencies....

But wait—why are you using words now, if I was supposed to learn to recognize you non-verbally?

"The need of the moment."

Ah, so you switch between guidance and direct communication and dreams and intuition—

"Depending on your progress, circumstances, and the need of the moment, yes."

But it's always you!

"It is me ... and it is you. Because we are one. You only perceive me as separate—your *brain* perceives me so."

Somehow I always knew that, but not like *this*. Before, it was an idea that felt right; now I'm beginning to experience it in my body, in my emotions and thoughts. But my old, burning question, the question that set me off on this journey, is still unanswered.

I get the point. But still, I have to ask you: what do you want me to do in life? What is my mission? Because I'm here to do your will. Just show me....

A little smile appears in this shimmering white field. "Ah, you thought I was going to tell you what to do? Or show you in your meditations? You are expecting me to take you by the hand like a little child and point—'Here, this is your calling, this is your service, this is what I want you to do?' Tsk-tsk." The field is now actually gently flickering, as if laughing.

"Those, my dear, are the ways of the past. You, on the other hand, have to forge new ways. It is *you* who has to find your purpose. It is *you* who has to discover what your calling is, how you can be of help to others. I can give you but one hint: do not wait for anything to come to you. Do not sit back and wait for things to happen to you. You reach out and happen to things.

"And you have to start from who you are and what you already have."

I hear the voices from the other side of the crypt getting louder. Wolfgang's group is coming closer to the chapel. The shimmering white begins to fade.

Wait! Don't go yet! Will I be able to communicate with you when I leave the crypt? Will you help me?

The field is weakening, dissipating. Just barely I make out the whisper:

"Never doubt. As you work your purpose you will draw to yourself what you need."

As the last spark vanishes, a thought materializes without words:

Never fear. I'm always with you.

I'm surrounded again by darkness, throbbing and alive. But now, this darkness feels like an accomplice, almost a friend. I'm very grateful to this darkness. Wolfgang's group is quite close to the chapel. From just the other side, I make out his voice:

"In the past, people went on a pilgrimage to find what they couldn't have, had they stayed at home."

I smile. I'm going back now to the place that used to be my home, the place from which I started this long journey six years ago. And I'm going back with the knowledge of Myself, even if I don't know my mission—which I trust I'll find once I start shaping the idea that has been waiting for me all this time to give it life.

A gentle touch on my shoulder interrupts my thinking. "Svetlana, Wolfgang is here with his group. You'd better finish what you're doing," I hear Dwight's whisper.

I turn to see his eyes, glowing with understanding and deep love. I stare into Dwight's eyes, standing on my toes and leaning closer until our noses touch. His eyes have now become two deep pools reflecting images of many adventures, trials, learning, and suffering I've experienced over the past six years. People, temples, ruins, churches, *piazzas*, cappuccinos, meadows, mountains, all reflected in Dwight's eyes. Then their surface ripples and I see a shimmering white light, infinitely sweet and infinitely loving. I have a deep sense of having found my home.

At that moment, in that dark place underground, I understood with full clarity the feeling of inevitability; I *had* to take this journey.

It was as simple as that. And as complex.

GRATEFUL...

As I look back to the past five years of birthing this book, I'm struck by how much help it took to reach the end of the creative journey. One book, but many people contributed to its making; many other books provided inspiration for my own. In the end, *Meet Me in the Underworld* is a product of many experiences, meetings, conversations, and written words. I was but a bee, collecting honey from all these sources.

First and foremost, my profound gratitude goes to the spirit of Dwight Johnson, who believed in me when I didn't, and who provided continuous support both on this plane of existence and from the other side. I could never express in words everything I owe to you, Dwight. Therefore, let me convey it non-verbally, through my heart.

Paying respects to those who have departed, I'm grateful to Nevill Cramer, my friend and first editor who taught me the nuances of English language while cracking jokes. And very grateful to his widow, Pat Cramer, my friend, surrogate mother, and photo mentor who has continued to provide valuable guidance, help, and advice about every visual aspect of the book.

It took four editors to shape and polish my rough manuscript—and it so happened they are also good friends. Grateful to Nancy Marriott for the initial coaching and editing, as well as the final input; to Ilene Segalove for structural editing and looking at the big picture; to Barbara Ann Maré for line editing and feedback; and to John Enrico Douglas for the last round of edits and for proofing the galley. I learned so much from all of you!

Much gratefulness goes to my friend Steven Redden, who has helped me generously at every step of the road, from editing and playfully keeping score of my mistaken use of articles (there are no articles in Serbian!), to spiritual and technical matters. I have extensively drawn on his lucid formulation of the principles of the Ageless Wisdom.

Four graphic designers contributed to the final look of the book. Thank you so much Barbara Cooper, Adina Cucicov, Steven Catizone, and Vesna

Petrovic! I very much appreciate your patience with the many changes and versions I requested until we arrived at what I had envisioned. Grateful to my media consultant Ray Estrada for going the extra mile; and to Noel Solomon, my talented and very competent book production assistant, who appeared at the very moment I needed help.

For opening their house to me after Dwight's transition and offering me a taste of home and family which I had lost, I'm ever so grateful to my friends Tara Blasco and Lyn Hebenstreit in Ojai. A good portion of this book was written in the peace and inspiring energy of their Wisdom Center. And to Lyn's daughter Monica Marshall, for playful, giggly hours while creating my website.

Grateful to my present teacher, Georgia Lambert, for providing a continual spiritual grounding, words of wisdom and inspiration that were embedded in the fabric of this book.

To my friends: Nancy Farrand for sticking to the end of a long first draft, and to Ljiljana Coklin for her incisive feedback and inspiring words. To Pico Iyer for providing literary guidance at the beginning of my creative journey. Grateful to Jonathan Young who showed me that I had no choice but to write this book, and who so generously provided introduction at the book launch.

Of course, grateful for everything I learned from many friends I made during our travels: to Kyriacos, whose books provided the inspiration for this journey, and to his equally inspirational wife Emily; to Stalo, my soul-sister in Cyprus, for understanding me; to Aldo in Rome, for healing me; to Noemi and Gianni in Umbria for opening their homes to us; to Pierre in France for being an embodiment of the Hippocratic physician. And to Shree and Davina who have helped me through the darkest moments with their wise words and loving hearts.

My parents would have been very proud to see this book, but it was not meant to be. Nevertheless, without their unconditional support I would not have made the first step—coming to California.

And last but not least, very grateful to John Enrico Douglas who came into my life like a gift and helped me in so many ways in the last stages of the book production. Thank you for the unrelenting attention to every detail in the manuscript.

For all the help I've received, my heart is full to the brim. My greatest desire is that this book may help others to take their own journeys into the unnervingly unknown but infinitely rewarding realms of the spirit.

In fact, we have no choice but to make that journey—sooner or later.

MORE ABOUT...

Aldous Huxley (1894-1963): British novelist, essayist, philosopher, poet, screenwriter, and esotericist. Best known for his dystopian novel *Brave New World*, and *The Doors of Perception*, a personal account of psychedelic experience with mescaline (this book would inspire Jim Morrison to call his band "The Doors"). Closely associated with the Theosophical movement, Huxley developed the concept of "Perennial Philosophy"—the term first coined by German philosopher G.W. Leibniz—a universal philosophy which postulates that all major world religions and spiritual traditions share a universal truth and the same foundation of spiritual principles. I interviewed Huxley's late widow, Laura, in their home in the Hollywood Hills, which gave me a rare insight into his life and beliefs.

Barbara Brennan: As a physicist for NASA, Barbara Brenna discovered that she had psychic and healing gifts, which she later developed into a system of energy healing, described in her two books: *Hands of Light*, and *Light Emerging*. She established a Barbara Brennan School of Healing, the first alternative medicine school in the United States. Thousands of energy healers from around the world were trained there.

Cairn (see **Megalithic Architecture**)

Carl Gustav Jung (1875-1961): Swiss psychiatrist and a prolific writer, one of the most influential psychotherapists of the 20th century. He founded analytical psychology and was renowned for dream analysis. In his early career he collaborated with Freud, who considered Jung his successor. After six years he parted with Freud due to differences in their view of the nature and role of the subconscious. Jung left us the legacy of some of the best known psychological concepts such as: archetypes, collective unconscious, shadow, individuation, synchronicity, extroversion and introversion, as well as a system of psychological types that later became known as Myer-Briggs Type Indicator (MBTI). Jung's work was one of the main influences in the formation of Depth psychology and in particular on **James Hillman**'s Archetypal psychology.

Cenotaph (Greek *kenotaphion, "empty tomb"*): a monument erected in honor of a person whose remains are elsewhere.

Ceramics (vs. pottery, porcelain, and majolica): Ceramics is the most general term that includes both pottery and porcelain. The word comes from the Greek *keras* ("horn") and refers to the working of clay—*Keramica*. When clay is mixed water and left to harden under the hot sun, the result is pottery, albeit a primitive one. The difference between pottery and porcelain is that porcelain has a hard finish and is translucent to some degree, while pottery is porous and doesn't hold water unless it's glazed and fired in a kiln. In the sixth century AD Arab potters discovered a sophisticated glazing technique by using certain mineral oxides. Italians thought that these glazed objects originated in Majorca, an island south of Spain, and called them Majolica. Porcelain, on the other hand, was an invention of the East. Only Chinese and Persians made porcelain in ancient times—and they jealously guarded the secret. It wasn't until the eighteenth century that the key ingredient for firing porcelain, kaolin, was discovered in Germany.

Commedia dell' Arte: a dramatic genre that developed in 1500s' Italy and was characterized by the use of masks to convey stereotypical character types (i.e. a Captain, a Doctor, a Lover). The plots were usually based on love intrigues and included mime, farce, buffoonery, and music.

Cyclopean architecture: ancient structures made of huge, irregular slabs of stone fitted tightly without mortar. The term usually refers to the Mycenaean culture of ancient Greece (1500 BC), but examples of Cyclopean masonry can be found all over the world, from Mexico, Bolivia, and Peru, to Egypt and Malta. The term "cyclopean" is attributed to Aristotle who, Pliny the Elder reports, believed that only the mythical race of giant Cyclopes could have moved and built with such huge and heavy boulders.

Dionysian Mysteries: an ancient Greek, female-dominated cult that first appeared between 3000 and 1000 B.C., and was best known for using wine and drugs to liberate primal natures of the participants through trance-like dancing. In its later phase the cult changed its emphasis from a chthonic (underworld) orientation to a transcendental, mystical one. By its nature, a mystery religion was reserved for the initiated, hence the knowledge of those practices was lost (*mysteria*, Greek for "secrets," implies that religious rites were kept secret from the outside world). Other mystery cults were the **Eleusinian Mysteries** and **Mithraic Mysteries.** Eleusinian Mysteries, which began during the Mycenaean period around 1500 BC and later spread to Rome, were considered the most important. The Mithraic cult was particularly popular among Roman soldiers. The rituals were practiced in the dark, with the representation of Mithra (the Zoroastrian divinity) slaying a sacred bull.

Doric, Ionian, Corinthian: the three orders in classical Greek architecture, most easily differentiated by the capitals of columns. The Doric order appeared first during the Archaic period (750—480 BC) on mainland Greece, then spread to Italy. The Ionic order co-existed with the Doric, predominantly in Asia Minor and the Aegean Islands. The Corinthian style grew out of the Ionic in the Late Classical period (5ᵗʰ century BC). It was a highly decorative variant later popularized by the Romans.

EMF: abbreviation for low frequency electromagnetic fields. EMFs are artificial energies generated by electrical devices and appliances—TV's, computers, microwave ovens, and the worst of all, cell phones—which adversely affect human health.

Geopathic Stress: Earth-generated harmful energies that comprise a wide variety of energies arising from the earth in one form or another. The most common originates from underground water, especially where two underground streams cross. The Chinese make a distinction between *ch'i* or good energy, life-giving and life-supporting, and *sha* or bad energy that is life-threatening. Among professional dowsers, the *sha* is called "black streams." Researchers in a 1930 study conducted in a town that had the highest mortality rate from cancer in Germany at that time, showed a correlation between cancer and black streams. When a map of houses where someone had died of cancer was compared with a map of black streams made by local dowsers, the two maps matched exactly.

Green Man: god of vegetation and plant life, found in many ancient cultures. It is usually represented as a face surrounded by or made from leaves, and symbolizes rebirth or cycle of growth.

Golden Mean: also known as **Golden Ratio** and **Golden Section**, describes aesthetically pleasing proportions in art and architecture. This effect is created by the ratio—1: φ (*phi*), which has the numeric equivalent of 1.618.... There is now scientific evidence that our brains are hard-wired to recognize this pattern: the relation of small elements to larger elements is the same as the relation of larger elements to the whole: $\frac{a}{b} = \frac{a+b}{a} = 1.618...$

Intuition (vs. instinct): In esoteric literature, intuition is defined as the purest form of Soul communication, not to be confused with *instinct* or "gut feeling," which is psychic sensitivity registered in the solar plexus.

Jiddu Krishnamurti (1895-1986): Indian-born philosopher, spiritual teacher, and reformist. As a teenager, he was groomed to become the spiritual leader of the Theosophical movement that regarded him as a new World Teacher. Krishnamurti eventually rejected the title and broke free from the movement. The fundamental principle of his teachings and his life mission was to set people unconditionally free. He encouraged the development of critical thinking and denounced all organized belief, including the guru-disciple relationship. He resided in Ojai, California for much of his life.

Kirlian Photography: Semyon Kirlian was a Russian scientist who photographed the energy grid (etheric field) around objects by placing them on a photographic plate and connecting them to a high-voltage source. Kirlian described the photograms of leaves and fingers as "corona discharges." In contemporary science, this grid is referred to as a "bio-electric energy field."

Megalithic architecture (elements): menhir—Breton for an upright, large stone, a megalith; **alignment**—a row of menhirs; **tumulus**—a mound of earth and stones (also known as **barrow**) raised over a grave; **cairn**—a tumulus composed entirely of dry stones instead of earth; **dolmen**—("stone table" in Breton), two vertical megaliths topped by a horizontal one, sometimes many tables lined up to form a corridor that ends in a semi-circular chamber.

Philosopher King: an ideal which Plato developed in his dialogue *The Republic*. According to this idea, the best rulers are philosophers, defined as lovers of wisdom and seekers of Truth. The ideal of "philosopher king" is based on the philosophy of service and duty.

Romanesque: an architectural style that dominated Western Europe in the 11th and 12th centuries. The term—coined in the 19th century and meaning "from Rome"—reflects the fact that Romanesque buildings, like those of the ancient Roman Empire, are solid and robust, display a strong sense of proportion and order, and feature rounded arches and vaults. However, despite its name, the inspiration behind Romanesque architecture was not Rome, but the architecture of the Byzantine Empire.

Sacred Geometry: a blueprint of geometrical shapes found at the root of all creation in nature. It reflects the metaphysical postulate "as above so below," which means that geometric order on earth is a reflection of the celestial geometry. Sacred geometry uses particular proportions, as well as specific shapes— circles, squares, pentagrams, octagons—to achieve a desired effect on human consciousness.

Stendhal (Marie-Henri Beyle; 1783-1842): 19th-century French writer, exponent of the realism, best known for his novels *The Red and the Black*, and *The Charterhouse of Parma*.

Tau Cross: named after the Greek letter T, the Cross of Tau represents a crucifix from antiquity. Saint Francis of Assisi adopted it as his personal coat of arms. Today it is used as a symbol of the Franciscan Order.

Tetractys: a mystical symbol of the Pythagorean School by which the Pythagoreans swore. It is formed by ten points in the shape of a triangle, arranged in four rows. This was a representation of a triangular number 10 ($1+2+3+4=10$), the symbol of perfection.

Tumulus (see **Megalithic Architecture**)

ABOUT THE AUTHOR

Svetlana Meritt was a journalist and a foreign correspondent for *Illustrated Politics*, a popular Serbian magazine, before she went on a ten-year long journey of self-discovery. She is currently a writer, teacher, and professional photographer in Santa Barbara, California.

HYPATIA HOUSE

HYPATIA
HOUSE
Feminine Wisdom in Action

Hypatia House is dedicated to honoring female wisdom, suppressed and crushed throughout the ages by male ignorance and religious fanaticism.

Hypatia of Alexandria (born c. 370; died 415) was a Greek philosopher of the Neoplatonist school, scientist, astronomer, and inventor (the plane astrolabe and hydroscope were attributed to her). Known for her wisdom and grace, she was the head of the Plato Academy in Alexandria. Men from all over the Hellenistic world flocked to sit at her feet and listen to her lectures. Hypatia was brutally murdered by a fanatical Christian mob (illiterate monks, according to one source) that stripped the flesh from her bones with oyster shells, tore her body to pieces, then scattered them through the streets and burned the remains.

CPSIA information can be obtained at www.ICGtesting.com
Printed in the USA
LVOW06s2311200115

423623LV00006BA/9/P